FIFTH EDITION

Literature
for
Children

A Short Introduction

DAVID L. RUSSELL
FERRIS STATE UNIVERSITY

PEARSON

Boston • New York • San Francisco
Mexico City • Montreal • Toronto • London • Madrid • Munich • Paris
Hong Kong • Singapore • Tokyo • Cape Town • Sydney

To my grandchildren, Mason, Mariya, and Emily

Series Editor: Aurora Martínez-Ramos
Editorial Assistant: Erin Beatty
Senior Marketing Manager: Elizabeth Fogarty
Manufacturing Buyer: Andrew Turso
Cover Designer: Linda Knowles
Production Coordinator: Pat Torelli Publishing Services
Editorial/Production Services: Stratford Publishing Services
Electronic Composition: Stratford Publishing Services

For related titles and support materials, visit our online catalog at www.ablongman.com.

Library of Congress Cataloging-in-Publication Data

Russell, David L.
    Literature for children : a short introduction / David L. Russell.–5th ed.
      p. cm.
    Includes bibliographical references and index.
    ISBN 0-205-41033-2
    1. Children's literature–History and criticism.   2. Children–Books and reading.   I. Title.

PN1009.A1R87 2004
028.5–dc22   2004044484

Printed in the United States of America

10 9 8 7 6 5 4 3 2 1   08 07 06 05 04

Contents

PART II

THE KINDS OF CHILDREN'S LITERATURE   97

Preface to the Fifth Edition

It is indeed an honor to be able to provide yet another edition of *Literature for Children*—and it gives me yet another opportunity to remedy past faults, to bring the book up to date, and to accommodate philosophical and pedagogical shifts in my own thinking.

The only reorganization I have undertaken is to move the chapter on Social and Cultural Diversity to the end of Part I, providing a better segue into Part II and the discussion of the various types of literature. I am not convinced that one perfect way of organizing the chapters exists; therefore, my advice to instructors is to use the chapters in an order that makes sense in the context of their own courses. Certainly, an understanding of the material presented in Part I might be helpful before embarking on discussions of the literature in Part II, but the chapters are not written in a cumulative fashion such as a history or mathematics textbook might be.

My emphasis is still on children's literature as literature, rather than creating a book of instructional exercises or teaching aids. The best tools any teacher can have for presenting literature to students are a love of books, a sense of the beauty of language, and a joy in the magic of story. Only then can the literature be shared effectively with children—no amount of classroom wizardry or pedagogical gimmickry will ever take the place of a love for, and understanding of, good literature.

In my own courses, I place the emphasis on the primary works—the picture books, folktales, poetry, fantasies, realistic novels, and information books. This text is intended as a supplement, to provide background about the literature that might help my students become more perceptive and more sensitive readers. This is why I have tried to keep the text short—I want it to be inviting, not forbidding. I have tried to keep the writing crisp and focused and the examples cogent. Some readers of past editions have lamented the absence of full-color illustrations, and this has been purely an economic consideration, for that would dramatically increase the cost of the book. (My solution is to make sure my students see plenty of examples of good picture books in class, and I require them to find many more on their own.)

Ultimately, our purpose is to send our students out into the world with a love of books and a desire to share that love with their own students and children. For it is truly as the writer of *Ecclesiasticus* wrote, so many centuries ago:

If thou has gathered nothing in thy youth, how canst thou find anything in thine age?

ACKNOWLEDGMENTS

I would like to thank the reviewers of the Fifth Edition for their helpful comments: Mike Cadden, Missouri Western State College; Charles Davis, Barton County Community College; Nancy Hurd, Cuesta College; Dottie Kulesza, University of Nevada, Las Vegas; and Patricia Leek, University of Texas, Dallas.

PART I

THE CONTEXTS OF CHILDREN'S LITERATURE

CHAPTER

I

The History of Children's Literature

Surveying the landscape of the past may not necessarily provide us with an accurate map for the future, but it will make us more astute observers of the present. Although a true literature written explicitly for children has come about only in the past two or three hundred years, its roots are very deep indeed.

THE CLASSICAL WORLD

All literature began with the ancient art of storytelling. Our ancestors told stories to entertain each other, to comfort each other, to instruct the young in the lessons of living, to pass on their religious and cultural heritage. Storytelling is an integral part of every world culture. In early times, people did not distinguish between adult and children's literature. Children heard and, presumably, enjoyed the same stories as their parents, whether they were the adventurous tales of cultural heroes–as retold by Homer in *The Iliad* and *The Odyssey*–or the wondrous tales of gods and demons and magic spells and talking animals–as are found throughout the world.

Western civilization has its roots in the cultures of ancient Greece and Rome, which flourished between about 500 BCE and 400 CE, now known as the Classical period. Greece in the fifth century BCE is in many ways the birthplace of Western culture and so that is where our story begins. In this cradle of democracy and individualism, children grew up with the stories of the Trojan War (from Homer's *Iliad*) and of the travels of Odysseus (from Homer's *Odyssey*) and the stories of Jason and the Golden Fleece and the adventures of

Hercules. They also knew of the now-famous fables attributed to the slave Aesop, believed to be a teacher, writing to instruct his students in cultural and personal values.

With the decline of Greek civilization, the Roman Empire rose to power, but the Romans remained under the long shadow of Greeks, whom they greatly admired. The children of Rome in the first century CE undoubtedly knew not only Homer's tales, but also Virgil's *Aeneid,* which recounted the stories of Aeneas, the Trojan hero who was credited with founding the Roman race. They also knew the wildly imaginative tales of Ovid's *Metamorphoses,* the tales of the gods, goddesses, heroes, and heroines of the classical world. The power of these ancient stories remains with us, and modern writers and illustrators frequently turn to the Greek and Roman myths for inspiration and retelling.

Our culture is filled with references to these Classical stories—we speak of Achilles' heels, Herculean tasks, the Midas touch, Pandora's box, and sour grapes (a reference to one of Aesop's fables). Planets, galaxies and star clusters, days of the week, months of the year, automobile tires, and tennis shoes—all bear names of classical gods and heroes. These stories are both exciting and an important part of our cultural heritage—they should not be missed. A great many of these stories live today and children continue to find them fascinating. The retellings by the poet Padraic Colum (*The Children's Homer* and *The Golden Fleece*) are excellent sources for children. Most recently, Jeanne Steig's *A Gift from Zeus: Sixteen Favorite Myths* is a lively—sometimes racy—version for modern middle and high school audiences, and it is illustrated by William Steig's earthy, even ribald, drawings. It is just the kind of rendition to bring the stories to life for older readers. These myths are an essential part of culture and indispensable to any well-rounded education.

THE MIDDLE AGES

Following the fall of the Roman Empire in 476 CE, European civilization entered a period of decline. Much of the knowledge of the Classical world was lost during the early chaotic period historians once referred to as the Dark Ages. We now call the period between the fall of Rome and the rise of the Renaissance (in about the fourteenth century) the Middle Ages—literally because they fell between the Classical and Renaissance periods. During the Middle Ages the Roman Catholic Church dominated the social and political scene and was responsible for what education there was. Throughout the Middle Ages, poverty was widespread and life for the average person was very difficult—much harsher than it had been in the ancient Greek and Roman worlds. Education was a luxury, and few people could read or write. Books were extremely rare and expensive, for they had to be hand copied on costly parchment. A single bible could take as long as three years to produce, and in many medieval libraries the books were chained to the desks to discourage theft. As it was in the Classical world, the oral tradition was the principal entertainment for most people. Local storytellers and professional bards (the famous wandering minstrels) recited stories and poems for eager audiences.

What stories did they recite? Biblical stories were among the most popular—both Old and New Testament—and so were the stories of the lives of saints of the church. The lives of saints were used to set examples for young people. In addition to religious tales, nonreligious—secular—stories were also popular. The romantic tales of the legendary King Arthur and the Knights of the Round Table or of the great heroes Roland (from France) or the Cid (from Spain) or even Beowulf (from the Norse) surely thrilled many children—and adults, for, as in the Classical period, children and adults shared a common literature. The exciting battle scenes, powerful heroes, and wondrous enchantments of these romances made them very popular—and many remain so today.

Children's versions of these tales are easy to find. Rosemary Sutcliff's *Dragon Slayer* (1976) is a retelling of the old English epic, *Beowulf*, and she has also retold the legends of King Arthur and his knights in *The Light Beyond the Forest* (1979), *The Sword and the Circle* (1981), and *The Road to Camlann* (1981). Some of the Arthurian stories have been transformed into modern picture books, as in Selma Hastings's *Sir Gawain and the Green Knight* (1981). Barbara Cooney's picture book, *Chanticleer and the Fox* (1958), adapted from Chaucer, is a retelling of a favorite medieval trickster tale about Reynard the Fox. Many of the stories from this period are exciting narratives that have become an indelible part of our society. Our entire reading experience is enriched if we know the stories of Adam and Eve, Cain and Abel, Noah and the flood, Jonah and the whale, and the tower of Babel—side by side with those of King Arthur and Sir Launcelot and Queen Guinevere.

THE RENAISSANCE WORLD

Around 1400, a new era began in Europe. It was called the Renaissance, a term meaning "rebirth," because people saw it as a rebirth of the ideals of ancient Greece and Rome—their art, literature, philosophy, and especially their respect for learning. Of course, the changes did not happen overnight, but the changes did come. The Crusades of the eleventh and twelfth centuries had opened up trading routes to the Far East, which brought both wealth and new ideas to Europe. Strong rulers rose up and established stable kingdoms with written laws. Trade, industry, and learning advanced. In 1492, Columbus's voyage to the Americas resulted in the founding of overseas empires, which brought great wealth to many European kingdoms (sadly, at great expense to the native peoples). However, one development would overshadow all others.

Around 1450, a German named Johannes Gutenberg invented the movable-type printing press—said by many to be the most significant invention of the last thousand years. (Actually the Chinese originally developed the technology, but the Europeans put it to practical use.) It is difficult to exaggerate the importance of this event. The printing press made it possible to make multiple copies of books in a fraction of the time it took to hand copy them. In just a few decades, books became plentiful. Now it was possible to spread information quickly, and this opened the door to mass education.

During the early Renaissance, most books specifically for children were textbooks or educational books. Sir Thomas Elyot's *The Book Named the Governor* (1531) and Roger Ascham's *The Scholemaster* (1570) are two examples of "books of courtesy," giving lessons in proper behavior for young gentlemen. (Women did not yet merit their own books.) The

Renaissance, like the Middle Ages, was a religious period and during this time the hatred between the Roman Catholics and the Protestants resulted in much bloodshed. John Foxe's *Book of Martyrs* (1563), an anti-Catholic work filled with grisly scenes of violent deaths for religion's sake, was one of the most popular books among England's schoolchildren. On a cheerier note, about one hundred years later, John Comenius's *Orbis Sensualium Pictus* (1658) appeared. It is generally regarded as the first children's picture book and was intended as a textbook for the teaching of Latin through pictures (see Figure 1.1).

Ludi Pueriles,

Boyes-Sport

Boys used to play either with *Bowling-stones* 1. or throwing a *Bowl*, 2. at *Nine-pins*, 3. or striking a *Ball*, through a *Ring*, 5. with a *Bandy*, 4. or scourging a *Top*, 6. with a *Whip*, 7. or shooting with a *Trunk*, 8. and a *Bow*, 9. or going upon *Stilts*, 10. or tossing and swinging themselves upon a *Merry-totter*, 11.

Pueri solent ludere vel *Globis fictilibus*, 1. vel jactantes *Globum*, 2. ad *Conas*, 3. vel *mittentes* Sphærulam per *Annulum*, 5. *Clava*, 4. versantes *Turbinem*, 6. *Flagello*, 7. vel jaculantes *Sclopo*, 8. & *Arcu*, 9. vel incidentes *Grallis*, 10. vel super *Petaurum*, 11. se agitantes & oscillantes.

FIGURE 1.1 John Comenius's *Orbis Sensualium Pictus* is often considered the first children's picture book. It first appeared in 1658 as a German/Latin textbook and was an immediate success. It revolutionized Latin instruction, a necessity in a society in which Latin was still the language of scholarship. The English/Latin version, from which this illustration is taken, appeared in 1659. Although the woodcut illustrations appear crude, they provide a wealth of information about seventeenth-century European life.

Puritanism

At least two specific influences of the seventeenth century heightened society's awareness of the special needs of the child: the rise of Puritanism and the philosophy of John Locke. The Puritans were a very strict religious sect who believed that everyone was responsible for his or her own salvation and that success in life was a sign of God's favor. They placed a high value on reading, because they believed the Bible should be accessible to everyone, and on education in general, since it helped ensure material success. Persecuted in England, many came to North America, where they soon established Harvard College (1636), emphasizing their commitment to education. If they did little to foster fine literature (they disapproved, in fact, of most literature as frivolous and ungodly), the Puritans are credited with encouraging literacy among the middle classes.

Schooling was an important part of a Puritan child's upbringing, and Puritan children used a variety of schoolbooks. *Hornbooks* consisted of simple wooden slabs, usually with a handle (many looked like paddles). Parchment containing rudimentary language lessons (the alphabet, numbers, and so on) was fastened to the wood and was then covered with transparent horn (from cattle, sheep, goats), a primitive form of lamination that made these books very durable. *Battledores*, cheap books made of folded cardboard and usually containing educational material, were widely used into the nineteenth century. The most famous of early schoolbooks was the *New England Primer*, which first appeared sometime around 1690 and continued in print in some form or another until 1886. It introduced young Puritan children to the alphabet through rhymes ("In Adam's fall/We Sinned all" for the letter A) and then to increasingly sophisticated reading material–all with a religious intent (see Figure 1.2). *Chapbooks*, small and cheaply made books containing fairy tales and other secular works, were also widespread during the period, but the Puritans frowned on these forerunners of the dime novel.

John Locke and Educational Philosophy

The second great influence on children's literature during this period was the English philosopher John Locke (1632–1704), who in 1693 wrote a famous essay, *Thoughts Concerning Education*. In this work, he formulated his notion that the minds of young children were similar to blank slates (he called them *tabula rasa*) waiting to be filled up. All children had equal capabilities to learn and adults had the responsibility to provide the proper learning environment. For Locke, heredity was unimportant, since everyone, he believed, began life pretty much the same. Thus began the perennial argument over the relative influence of heredity and the environment (or nature and nurture).

Bunyan, Defoe, and Swift

English children also continued to adopt certain adult works of literature. They were especially drawn to the fanciful allegory of John Bunyan's *A Pilgrim's Progress* (1678), the story of a man's journey to Heaven; children were undoubtedly delighted by the horrific monsters

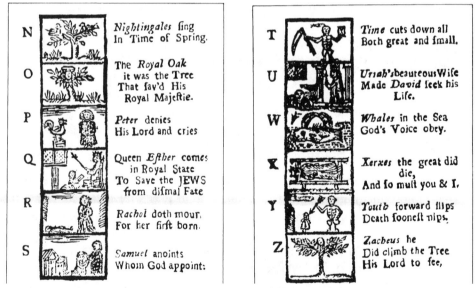

FIGURE 1.2 The *New England Primer* was one of the longest-lived school texts in American history, flourishing from approximately 1690 to 1830. The earliest surviving copy is from 1727, from which these illustrations are taken. Intended to teach the children of the early Puritans how to live a godly life, the book is unabashedly didactic, which is evident even in its rhyming alphabet, recalling a time when church and state were not so completely separate as they are now.

that plagued him on the trip to the religious ecstasy of his safe arrival in Heaven. Two other works, both originally for adults, were exceedingly popular with children in the early eighteenth century. The first was Daniel Defoe's *Robinson Crusoe* (1719), a shipwreck adventure tale that is the ancestor of numerous survival stories still relished by children to this day. The second was Jonathan Swift's *Gulliver's Travels* (1726), a satirical travel fantasy that is still retold from time to time for children and has been the subject of several movies for young people. The moral and ethical messages of these works did not concern the youthful readers, who were simply after a good tale.

THE EIGHTEENTH AND EARLY NINETEENTH CENTURIES

John Newbery and Children's Book Publishing

By the mid-eighteenth century the serious publishing of children's books began, notably by John Newbery (1713–1778), a clever English bookseller. It was Newbery who first successfully promoted children's literature. His books were largely collections of stories and poems by various (usually anonymous) writers (including himself). His publication *A Little Pretty Pocket Book* (1744) is one of the first published children's books designed to entertain children as well as to teach them. Newbery's contribution to children's literature was recognized in 1922 when Frederic Melcher established the annual Newbery Medal, awarded in the United States for the most distinguished book written for children.

Rousseau and the Moral Tale

The French philosopher Jean Jacques Rousseau (1712–1778) added yet another point of view to the concept of children's reading. His ideas about education were expressed in a book called *Emile* (1762), in which he emphasized the importance of *moral* development (the Puritans' concern had been spiritual; Locke's had been intellectual). For Rousseau, proper moral development could be best accomplished through living a simple life (even 200 years ago people were becoming distressed with the pace of civilization). Rousseau's followers wrote didactic and moralistic books to teach children how to be good and proper human beings. (Newbery also contributed his fair share of moralistic tales, *Little Goody Two Shoes* being the most famous.) A great many writers, most of them women (men still looked on writing for children as an inferior occupation), emulated Rousseau and churned out a great number of moralistic tales through the remainder of the eighteenth and well into the nineteenth centuries.

Among the best known of these writers is Maria Edgeworth (1744–1817), whose most famous works for children are her short story "The Purple Jar" (1796) and her book *Simple Susan* (1796), about a country girl whose goodness helps her to triumph over an ill-intentioned city lawyer. Sarah Trimmer (1741–1810) wrote the *History of the Robins* (1786), an animal story that was unusual in a time that frowned on tales of talking animals (the eighteenth-century rationalists thought it was illogical and religious zealots thought it unholy). One of the first reviewers of children's books, Mrs. Trimmer believed that literature must preach Christian morality above all, and she condemned fairy stories for children because they were sacrilegious and lacked moral purpose. Mrs. Anna Laetitia Barbauld (1743–1825) wrote in a similar vein; her most famous works were *Lessons for Children* (1778) and *Hymns in Prose for Children* (1781). Hannah More (1745–1833) and Mrs. Sherwood (1775–1851) were also part of this moralizing company, and Mrs. Sherwood's *History of the Fairchild Family* (1818) includes frighteningly vivid stories about the souls of impious children moldering in the cold grave or being consigned to the fires of hell.

The Rise of the Folktales

The didactic element in children's books persisted through the early nineteenth century. But alongside the moralistic tales came the revival of the old folktales from the quickly fading oral tradition. Actually, folktales were printed in England as early as 1729, when *Tales of Mother Goose,* originally retold by the Frenchman Charles Perrault (1628–1703), was first translated and published in English. These retellings of old stories, including "Cinderella," "Little Red Riding Hood," and "Sleeping Beauty in the Wood," soon became staples in English nurseries. In the middle of the eighteenth century, a Frenchwoman, Mme. de Beaumont, retold numerous fairy stories, including "Beauty and the Beast" and "The Three Wishes," usually with a moral purpose. John Newbery's successor, Elizabeth Newbery, published the first children's edition of the Middle Eastern *Tales from the Arabian Nights,* featuring Sinbad the Sailor, Aladdin and his lamp, and others, in about 1791.

At the beginning of the nineteenth century, two German brothers, Jacob (1785–1863) and Wilhelm (1786–1859) Grimm, collected a great number of folktales and published them (once again not expressly for children), and the Grimms' tales are still the most famous of all collections. The Grimms also inspired a flurry of folktale collecting throughout Europe, including Hans Christian Andersen in Denmark and Asbjörnsen and Moe in Norway. Folk rhyme collections were equally popular (see Figure 1.3) By the end of the nineteenth century, the collectors Joseph Jacobs (*English Fairy Tales*) and Andrew Lang (*The Blue Fairy Book, The Red Fairy Book,* and so on) were delighting children and adults alike.

THE VICTORIANS: THE GOLDEN AGE

Before children's literature could fully mature, it had to abandon the shackles of moral didacticism that was more interested in the message than literary quality. These books tended to offer up what adults believed was good for children, not necessarily what children themselves enjoyed. It was not until the later nineteenth century that talented writers who were committed to writing entertaining stories for children—as opposed to morality tales—began to emerge. This phenomenon has been attributed to several developments:

9

The man in the moon came down too soon
To inquire the way to Norridge;
The man in the south, he burnt his mouth
With eating cold plum-porridge.

FIGURE 1.3 Abel Bowen's woodcut illustration of "The Man in the Moon," from *Mother Goose's Melodies*, dramatically depicts the contrast between the ridiculous and the sublime that underlies much of children's literature. On the left-hand side, with grace and elegance, a youth descends from the crescent moon; on the right-hand side, a buffoonish character is engaged in a nonsensical act. Dating from 1833, it is among the earliest American children's books designed purely for the pleasure of young readers.

- the strengthening of the family unit (brought about in part by a lowered infant mortality rate that helped to stabilize the family)
- rapidly developing technology that made possible still cheaper books along with high-quality full-color printing
- the slow, but inexorable, rise of the status of women (who have dominated children's writing from the end of the eighteenth century)
- the growth of widespread educational opportunities, including mandatory education legislation in both the United States and Great Britain, creating more readers
- the continued growth of the middle class, which further broadened the reading audience (most writers must necessarily seek a broad appeal if they are to earn a living, and writing for children was not a truly profitable enterprise until the second half of the nineteenth century)

The confluence of these forces made possible the first "Golden Age" of children's books during the reign of Britain's Queen Victoria—hence the Victorian Period.

British Children's Literature

ADVENTURE OR BOYS' STORIES In the second half of the nineteenth century, British children's literature was dominated by the *adventure* or *boys' stories* (including the so-called *school story*) and by *fantasy stories*. The far-flung British empire may have encouraged an internationalism in British adventure stories, but it also resulted in a fair amount of jingoism—or chauvinistic nationalism that depicted British culture as superior to that of the colonies (and everyone else's, for that matter).

British superiority is either implied or directly stated, for example, in the works of Captain Marryat, R. M. Ballantyne, and G. A. Henty, among others. Marryat, who was a seaman, was the first to write historical adventures for children, most notably *Mr. Midshipman Easy* (1836) and *Children of the New Forest* (1847). R. M. Ballantyne wrote *The Coral Island* (1857), a Robinsonnade or survival story inspired by Defoe's *Robinson Crusoe* and the inspiration for William Golding's *Lord of the Flies* (1954). G. A. Henty, a war correspondent who traveled widely throughout the British Empire, wrote historical adventure books about the places he visited, among which is *With Clive in India* (1884).

Robert Louis Stevenson is remembered for *Treasure Island* (serialized in 1881, published in book form in 1883), which has become the quintessential pirate story, swashbuckling and melodramatic, but not without its tantalizing ambiguity that keeps adults returning to it as well as children. (Stevenson also wrote *A Child's Garden of Verses* [1885], a vision of childhood as seen through an adult's eyes. Although it has always been immensely popular, Stevenson himself had little regard for his poetry, which some critics believe is chiefly responsible for perpetuating triteness and sentimentality in children's verse.)

FANTASY STORIES The glory of this first "Golden Age" is its fantasy, and at the top of the list must naturally be Lewis Carroll (the pseudonym for Charles Dodgson, a mathematics professor at Oxford), whose *Alice's Adventures in Wonderland* (1865) abandoned all the rules of writing for children. An extraordinary fantasy filled with a delightful mixture of satire and nonsense and almost devoid of instructional moralizing, it is usually considered the first important work for children that completely broke the bonds of didacticism. Alice, the March Hare, the Mad Hatter, the Cheshire Cat, and the Red Queen have all become a part of childhood mythology, familiar to children who have never read the original. This book and its sequel, *Through the Looking-Glass* (1871/2), along with Sir John Tenniel's black-and-white illustrations, are justly celebrated.

George MacDonald is regarded as one of the outstanding Victorian fantasists. *The Princess and the Goblin* (1872; originally serialized) is a literary fairy tale with Princess Irene as the heroine. Its sequel, *The Princess and the Curdie* (1883; also serialized earlier), is noteworthy for its rather bitter ending, indicative, some say, of MacDonald's general attitude toward humanity. But the fantasy world he created has kept his works popular to this day.

Two minor fantasies deserve mention. Juliana Horatia Ewing's *The Brownies and Other Tales* (1870) is a collection that recalls the moralizing of the eighteenth century. The title story, about dutiful and helpful children, remains part of our culture for it gave its name to the junior Girl Guides (Girl Scouts in the United States). Charles Kingsley's *Water Babies* (1863) is a rambling morality story describing the adventures of a chimney sweep in an enchanted underwater world. Despite the heavy-handed didacticism, the fantasy world is imaginative.

One of fantasy's earliest writer–illustrators is Beatrix Potter, whose talking animal tales, beginning with *The Tale of Peter Rabbit* (1901), have set a high standard for children's illustrated books. Potter refuses to talk down to her child audience, but rather treats them as confidants and equals. Her language is sophisticated and her stories often contain gentle irony. And Potter probably gave the best advice on writing for children that has ever been penned: "I think the great point in writing for children is to have something to say and to say it in simple, direct language" (quoted in Hunt, *An Introduction to Children's Literature*, 88).

J. M. Barrie wrote *Peter Pan* (1904), originally a play and eventually a prose story entitled *Peter and Wendy* (1911). Despite the criticism that the hero, the boy who would not grow up, is at best enigmatic and at worst self-centered and cruel, the story has enjoyed immense popularity, undoubtedly through the imaginative power of its characters. (Barrie is credited also with inventing the feminine personal name, Wendy.)

Kenneth Grahame is remembered for *The Wind in the Willows* (1908), one of the most enduring of animal fantasies. The work is a paean to an idyllic and masculine world, the quintessence of Edwardian England. It is an episodic work filled with affable characters–Rat, Mole, Badger, and, of course, Mr. Toad–engaged in a variety of adventures. As with much great fantasy, this is a sophisticated work with a fair share of commentary about the adult world.

REALISTIC STORIES Few British writers of the Victorian period excelled in realistic stories; perhaps they too closely associated them with the moralistic tales of the past. Two British writers did earn fine reputations as writers of both fantasy and realism, and a third writer of realistic stories is British by birth, but American by adoption. Edith Nesbit excelled not only in fantasies (*Five Children and It*, 1902, and *The Phoenix and the Carpet*, 1903), but in the *family adventure story*, most notably the stories of the Bastable children (*The Story of the Treasure Seekers*, 1899, and others). Her work looks backward to earlier Victorian literature in its sometimes condescending portrayal of children, but her best books contain interesting and strongly drawn characters engaged in compelling plots.

Rudyard Kipling experimented with a wide variety of genres for children. In 1894 he published *The Jungle Book*, a collection of fantasy tales set in India, featuring Mowgli, a boy who enjoys a special relationship with jungle creatures. Kipling turned to realism in *Stalky & Co.* (1899), an almost brutally frank school story. (The school story was a subgenre for Victorian boys focusing on the antics of boys at private boarding schools—called public schools in Britain. The best known of this variety is Thomas Hughes's *Tom Brown's School Days* [1857].) Kipling's novel *Kim* (1901) is the story of a boy of mixed heritage growing up in British India; a coming-of-age tale, it is generally regarded as his finest work.

Frances Hodgson Burnett is a bridge between Great Britain, where she was born, and the United States, where she eventually settled. She gained a lasting reputation with her modernized Cinderella stories, *Little Lord Fauntleroy* (1886), about an American youth who inherits an English noble title; *A Little Princess* (1905), about a girl who must overcome adversity through her essential goodness of heart; and her most celebrated work, *The Secret Garden* (1911), the story of Mary Lennox's redemption in the bleak English moors. *The Secret Garden* is a deliciously romantic work, with Gothic atmosphere, mysterious characters, and rich symbolism.

The United States

ADVENTURE OR BOYS' STORIES   Like British boys, American boys of the nineteenth century enjoyed adventure stories, but the Americans preferred stories set in their own country. Perhaps it was the isolationist tendencies that have never been far from the American consciousness, perhaps it was the fact that the American frontier was still a reality, but until the late nineteenth century most Americans felt no need to go looking for adventure abroad. Very popular among nineteenth-century boys (and girls as well if my own great-grandmother is any indication) were the stories of Oliver Optic (pseudonym of William Taylor Adams), who wrote *Outward Bound; or, Young America Afloat* (1867), and Horatio Alger, Jr., whose works included *Ragged Dick; or, Street Life in New York* (1867). Alger's name became almost a household word, and his heroes became beacons for the poor. These heroes were always downtrodden boys who struggled for financial security and respectability, both of which they ultimately gained through a combination of moral uprightness and hard work.

However, clearly the best of writers of boys' stories in America was Samuel L. Clemens, better known as Mark Twain. *The Adventures of Tom Sawyer* (1876), loosely based on Twain's own boyhood experiences in Hannibal, Missouri, seems very clearly suited to children, with its mystery, adventure, and comedy. *The Adventures of Huckleberry Finn* (1884), one of the greatest American novels ever written, is a more sophisticated book filled with biting satire and, underlying the sometimes rollicking humor, a serious tone. Twain never really saw himself as a writer of children's literature and would probably be surprised to find his name mentioned so prominently in a text on the subject.

DOMESTIC OR GIRLS' STORIES Although the British writer Charlotte Yonge wrote one of the earliest domestic stories (also called girls' or family stories), *The Daisy Chain* (1856), it was in the United States that domestic novels were most favorably received. In these stories virtuous heroines, often coming from dire circumstances, achieve good fortune and ultimate happiness, typically in the arms of a handsome young man. (If the themes of both the Alger stories and the domestic stories sound vaguely familiar, they should—they are essentially updated versions of the old folktales, in which persons of humble origins rise to wealth, fame, and happiness, primarily because they are good individuals.) The American Susan Warner, writing under the name of Elizabeth Wetherall, wrote one of the earliest American domestic novels, *The Wide, Wide World* (1850). This enormously popular work was both highly sentimental and religious.

The most famous of the domestic novelists was Louisa May Alcott, whose masterpiece, *Little Women* (1868), is still popular today. It is a thinly disguised history of Alcott's own family, and the work rose above most domestic stories of its day through its strong characters and lack of didacticism or sentimentality.

Susan Coolidge (pseudonym for Sarah Chauncy Woolsey) is best known for *What Katy Did* (1872), a sentimental story of the unruly Katy who, through experiencing a spinal injury that impairs her walking, learns kindness and responsibility. The book remains in print today, which some skeptics attribute to its catchy title.

Other popular writers of these "girls'" stories include Margaret Sidney (pseudonym for Harriet Lothrop), whose *Five Little Peppers and How They Grew* (1880) and its sequels recount the adventures of a fatherless, poor, but happy family. Kate Douglas Wiggins's *Rebecca of Sunnybrook Farm* (1903) was given a new lease on life in the 1930s by a Shirley Temple film. And Eleanor Porter's *Pollyanna* (1913), about the irrepressibly cheerful Pollyanna Whittier who brings sweetness and light to a dour New England town, has been kept alive by the media. It was first filmed in 1920 and starred Mary Pickford. The most famous version was Walt Disney's 1960 production, starring Hayley Mills. In 1989 came "Polly," a musical remake featuring an African-American cast in a made-for-television film. These works, all sentimental in tone, contain their share of moralizing.

FANTASY STORIES Fantasy has never been as appealing to Americans as to the British— perhaps it has something to do with the Puritan, no-nonsense, work ethic that has imbued the American culture and made fantasy suspect. However, one American fantasy from this early period bears notice and that is L. Frank Baum's *The Wonderful Wizard of Oz* (1900), now much better known in its film version than in its book form. Baum blatantly attempted to give the fairy tale a distinctly American dress in this story—and famously succeeded. Its powerful visual imagery and strong characters lent themselves well to the wide screen, and many believe the film to be superior to the book's rambling structure and stilted style. The story is, nevertheless, an American institution. Baum wrote numerous, largely mediocre, sequels on the demand of his youthful readers.

Children's Book Illustration in the Golden Age

Children's books of the eighteenth century and earlier either lacked illustrations altogether or contained crude wood-block illustrations such as those in the *Orbis Pictus*. Serious artists could not be enticed to draw for children's books. But the growth of children's book publishing and the development of printing technology that allowed for full-color printing attracted many talented artists to the field by the end of the nineteenth century. The earliest great illustrator of English children's books was George Cruikshank, who in 1823 illustrated the first English translation of Grimms' fairy tales, and he was also the first illustrator for Charles Dickens's works, most notably for *Oliver Twist* (1838). Walter Crane produced lavish illustrations for many children's books, including *The Baby's Opera* (1877), a collection of nursery rhymes complete with music. Randolph Caldecott illustrated *John Gilpin's Ride* (1878) and numerous other poems and nursery rhymes in a stunning series for children (see Figure 1.4). Caldecott, for whom the American Library Association's Caldecott Medal is named, is credited with bringing liveliness and humor to children's book illustration. Kate Greenaway illustrated Browning's *The Pied Piper of Hamelin* (1888) and other works, including some of her own poetry (see Figure 6.5). Greenaway, for whom the British Library Association's Greenaway Medal is named, had her own delicate and distinctive style, which became so popular that it actually influenced children's clothing styles at the end of the nineteenth century. L. Leslie Brooke's *Johnny Crow's Garden* (1903) is notable for the wry humor of its illustrations and its delightful characters. Arthur Rackham (see Figure 6.6) was an artist of great originality and versatility. Particularly good with line, he was one of the few early illustrators who dared to experiment with the new impressionistic style in children's illustrations. Rackham illustrated a vast number of children's books, including *Fairy Tales of the Brothers Grimm* (1900), *Alice's Adventures in Wonderland* (1907), *Aesop* (1912), *Mother Goose* (1913), and Grahame's *The Wind in the Willows* (published posthumously, 1940).

Popular Literature—Great Britain and America

Undoubtedly, most child readers spent much of their time reading not the celebrated classics, but the popular press, just as they do now. This included comic strips (which first cropped up in the Victorian era) and the so-called penny dreadfuls, which were cheap, sensationalized periodical publications (originally costing one penny) with no pretensions to literary quality. In the United States, the dime novels hit the market about 1860. These books, early paperbacks wrapped in yellow (hence they were also called "yellow-backs" or "yellow-back literature"), sold for ten cents, and consisted largely of imitations of Gothic novels or Charles Dickens or Sir Walter Scott. A later favorite was detective fiction, most popularly the stories of Deadwood Dick. These were often the work of hack writers, and they became the progenitors of the series book. The recent "Babysitters' Club" and R. L. Stine's "Goosebump" books are examples of this continuing tradition in popular literature.

FIGURE 1.4   Randolph Caldecott, the great nineteenth-century English illustrator, was one of the pioneers of children's book illustration. His art is characterized by an economy of line and a playfulness of manner that make his work appealing today, more than a century after his death. The American Library Association annually awards the Caldecott Medal, named in his honor, to what it judges the most distinguished picture book published in the United States. This illustration from *The Frog He Would A-Wooing Go* (1883) depicts Caldecott's lively sense of humor.

The nineteenth century also saw the rise of children's magazines. Generally, a publication was aimed at one sex or the other; hence the popular *Aunt Judy's Magazine* in Britain appealed largely to girls, whereas *Union Jack* and *Pluck* were quite clearly for boys. One of the first and longest lived of the American periodicals was *Youth's Companion*, which was published from 1827 to 1929. The venerable *St. Nicholas*, published in the United States from 1873 until 1940, had as its first and most famous editor Mary Mapes Dodge, author of the beloved children's novel *Hans Brinker; or, The Silver Skates* (1865). Both of these magazines could boast a high quality of writing, but most periodicals were the products of hack writers producing ephemeral writing intended for the moment only.

BETWEEN THE WARS: 1920–1940

The period between the two world wars saw the emergence of some of the most notable fantasy figures in children's literature, which may reflect the need for escape felt by the adult writers in the wake of the devastation of the First World War. Most of the great fantasies of this period were British.

Hugh Lofting's *The Story of Doctor Dolittle* (1920), about a physician who talks with animals, was the first in a series. The Doctor Dolittle stories are highly imaginative, and the later books in the series seem to improve over the earlier—something almost unheard of in series writing. Although the earlier books have been cited for racial insensitivity, Lofting's works generally promote admirable ideals, including pacifism, love for animals, and general tolerance.

A. A. Milne's *Winnie-the-Pooh* (1926) has become a cultural phenomenon with its appealing cast of anthropomorphic toy animals engaging in adventures under the watchful eye of the young Christopher Robin (Milne's own son). The work seems intended for the very young, although much of the humor in this book and its sequel, *The House at Pooh Corner* (1928), speaks as readily to adults as to children, which may account for its lasting appeal and for the keen interest shown by literary critics.

A work of some controversy was P. L. Travers's *Mary Poppins* (1934), a collection of wildly fanciful stories about an eccentric nanny. The acerbic character of the outrageous nursemaid has raised many an adult eyebrow, and, indeed, her nature was dramatically altered in the 1964 Disney movie—which, as with *The Wizard of Oz*, some consider an improvement over the book. In fact, the film and the book are two quite different creations.

J. R. R. Tolkien's *The Hobbit; or, There and Back Again* (1937) is the prequel to his great trilogy, *The Lord of the Rings*, a fantasy for adults. But *The Hobbit* is quite suitable for children with its lovable, self-deprecating hero, Bilbo Baggins. The story is high fantasy, featuring dramatic battles, fanciful creatures, very real dangers, and just a touch of humor. Tolkien's work achieved cult status in the 1970s and certainly must be accounted one of the great fantasy works. The recent filming of the trilogy has ensured fans for another generation.

In the realm of British realism, the most notable figure between the wars was Arthur Ransome, whose *Swallows and Amazons* (1930) and eleven sequels through 1947 recount the adventures of the Walker children and their friends on their summer holidays, engaged in a variety of outdoor activities. Despite Ransome's attention to realistic detail, his books are quite escapist in temperament.

One British writer who must be mentioned if only because of her phenomenal output and enormous popularity is Enid Blyton, who wrote over 600 books (37 in the year 1951 alone!). Her popularity was worldwide, and her books were translated into several languages. One of her best-known works was *The Magic Faraway Tree* (1943). Blyton's works have been criticized by adults for their farfetched plots, their simplistic and stereotyped vocabulary, and their conventional attitudes. On the other hand, it was precisely her formulaic writing that made her popular (in very much the same way that Danielle Steele is popular among adults today).

Perhaps the best-known American writer between the wars was Laura Ingalls Wilder, whose *Little House in the Big Woods* (1932) began a series of nine books based on her childhood and young adult experiences on the American frontier in the later years of the nineteenth century. This combination of domestic story with frontier adventure proved the perfect formula for one of the most successful publishing ventures of the era. Carol Ryrie Brink's *Caddie Woodlawn* (1935) is, in the Wilder vein, also a frontier/family story. And Eleanor Estes's *The Moffats* (1941), the first of a series, was a family tale set at the time of the First World War. In all cases, the family is viewed as an anchor and source of strength, a perspective that would change by the end of the century.

Also during this period, the United States excelled in the publication of picture books, beginning with Wanda Gág's acclaimed *Millions of Cats* (1928), a charming, yet earthy work with folktale qualities that is still in print. Other luminaries included Marjorie Flack (*The Story About Ping*, 1933), Munro Leaf (illustrating Richard Lawson's *The Story of Ferdinand*, 1936, among others), Ludwig Bemelmans (*Madeline*, 1939), and Dr. Seuss (*And to Think That I Saw It on Mulberry Street*, 1937, and a host of rollicking books spanning five decades).

FROM WORLD WAR II TO THE PRESENT

A dramatic change in the attitude toward children occurred shortly after the Second World War. The collapse of totalitarian regimes at the end of the war also spelled the end of the old class systems—socialism was on the rise and education was seen as the means of overcoming the ignorance and prejudice that had contributed to the war. Studies in child psychology, especially those by Jean Piaget, and advances in early childhood education, such as those made by Maria Montessori (whose work actually began in the early 1900s), helped to refocus concerns on the development of the child as an individual. Then, in 1946, Dr. Benjamin Spock published *The Common Sense Book of Baby and Child Care*, which revolutionized how society as a whole looked at children. Spock's influence was widespread and he used it to advocate for the personal needs of the child over the requirements of society, which in turn nurtured such movements as the empowerment of children in the classroom, the advocacy of children's rights in the legal system, indeed, the entire "youth culture" that has dominated Western society for the last half century.

In this atmosphere, children's literature began to flourish on a variety of fronts. The theme running through all the literature of this period is the focus on children themselves—their likes, dislikes, triumphs, and tragedies. The didactic, adult tone of so much of earlier children's literature no longer succeeded in this new child-centered environment—and, indeed, adults are often depicted in an unflattering light in these new books, for they are portrayed as children often see them (and undoubtedly as they sometimes are). Today's world of children's literature has proven to be rich and exciting.

In fantasy, a number of series have appeared in the past fifty years that have remained favorites of children. These include the controversial works of Christian allegory, C. S. Lewis's Narnia chronicles (*The Lion, the Witch and the Wardrobe*, 1950, and sequels); Mary Norton's *The Borrowers* (1952) and sequels; Lucy Boston's Green Knowe series (*The Children of Green Knowe*, 1954), and sequels; Lloyd Alexander's Prydain chronicles (*The Book of Three*, 1965, and sequels); and Ursula Le Guin's Earthsea cycle (beginning with *A Wizard of*

Earthsea, 1967). We would be remiss not to mention E. B. White's *Charlotte's Web* (1952), Philippa Pearce's *Tom's Midnight Garden* (1956), and Natalie Babbitt's *Tuck Everlasting* (1975), all of which have been accorded status as modern fantasy classics. Most famous of all is, of course, J. K. Rowling, whose Harry Potter series (beginning with *Harry Potter and the Sorcerer's Stone,* 1998) has been nothing short of a publishing phenomenon in the wild enthusiasm it has spawned. And Lois Lowry's *The Giver* (1993) reveals just how penetrating–and chilling–children's fantasy can be. The salient feature of children's fantasy since World War II is its focus on real children (animal and toy characters, although still found, especially in books for the very young, are relatively rare). Modern fantasy does not have the romantic and escapist quality found in much of the fantasy written between the two world wars.

Similarly, in realistic fiction, the trend has been toward greater realism in children's books. The family story has been perpetuated by such writers as Beverly Cleary (her Ramona books have been immensely popular), but for the most part it has given way to a less romanticized vision of the family. And writers such as Judy Blume helped to introduce the so-called *problem novel,* which focuses on some crisis of childhood or adolescence. The other notable trend in modern realism is what has come to be known as the *new realism,* characterized by a franker and more open approach to subjects once thought taboo in children's books: sexuality, violence, drugs, war, and so on. It was perhaps J. D. Salinger's *Catcher in the Rye* (1951), a book for adolescents rather than children, that signaled the trend toward greater realism, harsher language, and a willingness to face head-on the problems of growing up. African-American writers such as Virginia Hamilton, Mildred Taylor, and Walter Dean Myers have sought to correct the cultural disparity that once prevailed in children's literature–through the 1950s it was virtually impossible to find a children's book that included any but very white children. The disparity is still apparent, but at least it is now possible to find books about African Americans, Hispanic Americans, Native Americans, and a wide variety of world cultures–all written for children.

Finally, in children's illustration, the postwar era has seen some stunning work. Consummate artists Maurice Sendak, David Macauley, Barbara Cooney, Chris Van Allsburg, Margot Zemach, John Burningham, and John Steptoe, to name just a few, have given children some of the most imaginative and beautiful picture books that have ever been created.

CHILDREN'S LITERATURE FROM AROUND THE WORLD

The field of children's literature has grown worldwide. We have room to mention only some of the most famous and influential works of the past two centuries.

As early as 1812–1813, Swiss author Johann David Wyss wrote a story that would appeal to children around the world: *Swiss Family Robinson,* inspired by Defoe's work. As with so many other classics, Walt Disney has helped to keep this work in the public eye. Another Swiss writer, Johanna Spyri, achieved fame with her story of an orphaned girl, *Heidi* (1881), popularized by the 1937 film starring Shirley Temple.

Carlo Collodi's *The Adventures of Pinocchio* (1883) is the world's most famous puppet story and Italy's most famous children's story. Its theme is familiar, that of a toy wishing to be alive. The work contains some memorable scenes (and occasionally frightening ones) and intriguing symbolism.

Among the most notable French contributions is Antoine de Saint-Exupéry's *The Little Prince* (1943), an enchanting fantasy about a stranded aviator who encounters the little prince, an observant child living alone on an asteroid. It is doubtful that this was ever considered a child's book, for it is a highly allegorical exploration of the human condition, but its popularity among all ages is undisputed. France also has given us Jean de Brunhoff, the creator of *The Story of Babar, the Little Elephant* (1931), the first of a series of picture books (seven in all) about a little elephant who becomes a wise and benevolent ruler. The books are characterized by charming illustrations, hand-lettered texts, and a subtle wit. The series was continued by de Brunhoff's son, Laurent.

Germany, in addition to the Brothers Grimm, can also boast Heinrich Hoffmann who wrote *Struwwelpeter* (1848), a collection of cautionary tales that some view as hilarious and others as horrifying. It was nevertheless tremendously successful and influential. Felix Salten's *Bambi* (1923) and Erich Kästen's *Emil and the Detectives* (1929) are two modern German works that have become minor classics.

Sweden has produced two children's writers this century who have achieved international stature. Selma Lagerlöf, who won the Nobel Prize for Literature in 1909, wrote *The Wonderful Adventures of Nils* (in two volumes, 1906–1907), a highly imaginative work of fantasy. In 1945 Astrid Lindgren published *Pippi Longstocking*, the fanciful story of a remarkable girl with superhuman strength, unconventional values, and complete independence—in other words, every child's hero.

The Finnish writer Tove Jansson has created the Moomin family in a popular series of books beginning with *Comet in Moominland* (1946). These books about the gentle Moomins and their eccentric friends contain a healthy dose of philosophy as their adventures and misadventures unfold in a delightfully amorphous way.

Australia, Canada, and New Zealand have all made significant contributions to children's literature, particularly in the twentieth century. Kate Langloh Parker's *Australian Legendary Tales* (1896) was among the first to explore aboriginal legends. The first Australian classic was Ethel Turner's *Seven Little Australians* (1894), a domestic tale of middle-class Australian values. Dorothy Wall's *Blinky Bill* (1933) was the first of a series about (of course) a koala, the most popular talking animal in Australia. Among the best-known modern Australians are Patricia Wrightson, much of whose work is based on aboriginal traditions (*The Ice Is Coming*, 1977), and Ivan Southall, a writer of vivid survival stories, often with bleak endings (*Ash Road*, 1965).

Among the early Canadian writers are the naturalists Ernest Thompson Seton (*Wild Animals I Have Known*, 1898) and Charles G. D. Roberts (*Red Fox*, 1905), who are usually credited with inventing the realistic animal story. Survival themes were popular in early Canadian literature, although perhaps the most famous Canadian writer, Lucy Maud Montgomery (*Anne of Green Gables*, 1908), wrote domestic stories about life on Prince Edward

Island. Modern trends include literature by and about the native peoples of Canada (Basil Johnston's *Tales the Elders Told: Ojibway Legends,* 1981).

The literature of New Zealand contains two principal themes: the Maori culture and the natural landscape of the islands. Among the first early successes was Edith Howes, remembered for her adventure story *Silver Island* (1928). But the best-known New Zealand children's writer is probably Margaret Mahy, much of whose work was originally published in Britain. *The Haunting* (1981) and *The Changeover* (1983) both won the Carnegie Medal, given to the most distinguished children's book published in the United Kingdom.

Summary

It has been a long journey from the days when children's literature consisted merely of those snippets children gleaned from the oral stories their elders told to the twenty-first century when thousands of new children's books appear on the market each year. Now children's literature has gained a stature of its own and has even become politicized. The past fifty years have seen important changes in the field, perhaps none more important than the emphasis on cultural and social diversity (which will be discussed more fully in Chapter 5). The Civil Rights Movement in America ultimately influenced children's books, which had, until the 1960s, focused mainly on white children. By the end of the century, the heroes of children's books came in all colors.

The heroes also came in both genders—for the feminist movement had an impact as well. Children's books began to examine the roles of females and to give us heroines with forceful and imaginative personalities, in marked contrast to the delicate, retiring female characters of earlier generations.

Another change is a move toward "Political Correctness" (PC), the idea that as a society we should eliminate all language and practices that might be politically offensive—usually related to racial, gender, ethnic, or religious matters. An unfortunate by-product of this well-intentioned movement is the belief that all ideas are equally valid, that the contributions of all cultures are equally important, that one person's opinion is just as good as another's. Some critics today are challenging these beliefs (see especially Ravitch) and arguing that Political Correctness, if taken to its logical conclusion, will deprive us of all cultural values—in other words, some choices are, indeed, better than others.

On a different, and more positive note, children's literature has benefited from society's growing interest in the child. As a result of this keen interest in children, more and more talented writers and illustrators have chosen to do their best work for children. The number of children's book publishers has exploded in the past twenty-five years, and, although much mediocre work is still being published, many stunning picture books for younger children and many powerful novels for older children have appeared.

A clear example of this growing interest in children's literature is the emergence of hundreds of awards for children's books. This began in 1922 when the American Library Association instituted the Newbery Medal, awarded to the author of the book judged to be the best children's book published in the United States. This was followed in 1938 by the Caldecott Medal, presented annually in the United States to a children's illustrator. Great Britain, in turn, awards the Carnegie Medal (for distinguished writing) and the Greenaway Medal (for distinguished illustrating). Around the world hundreds of annual awards are given—perhaps thousands. Two of the most important of these are the Hans Christian Andersen Award, given every two years to an author and an illustrator for the body of their work, and the Astrid Lindgren Memorial Award, established in 2003 by the government of Sweden and given annually in honor of the beloved author of *Pippi Longstocking*. The Lindgren Award is given to an individual or individuals (as many as two a year may be selected) whose life's work has promoted children's reading. It will undoubtedly become the most coveted of children's awards, the first two recipients having each received over a half million U.S. dollars.

The study of children's literature began in earnest in the last quarter of the twentieth century—some colleges even offer degrees in the field. Professional organizations, such as the Children's Literature Association, have emerged to promote the study of literature and every year numerous conferences are held throughout the world. Several great library collections of children's literature have been formed, including the Kerlan Collection at the University of Minnesota, the de Grummond Collection at the University of Southern Mississippi, the Baldwin Collection at the University of Florida, and the collections at the Toronto Public Library. All this attention has, at the very least, made the publishing world a far more friendly—and profitable—place for children's writers. Indeed, some see the last half of the twentieth century as a "Second Golden Age" of children's writing, with some justification.

All this attention is fitting, for reading is the great indispensable tool of our culture. Without reading, civilization as we know it would disappear in one generation; the ideas of the past would be lost forever and we would be forced naked into the world. And so, perhaps the greatest purpose of the study of children's literature is to make readers of our children and give them the tools they will need to build a better world than their parents have known.

RECOMMENDED READINGS

Aries, Philippe. *Centuries of Childhood: A Social History of Family Life.* New York: Knopf, 1962.

Avery, Gillian. *Behold the Child: American Children and Their Books, 1621–1922.* Baltimore: Johns Hopkins University Press, 1994.

Avery, Gillian, and Julia Briggs. *Children and Their Books.* Oxford: Oxford University Press, 1989.

Bator, Robert, comp. *Signposts to Criticism of Children's Literature.* Chicago: ALA, 1983.

Butts, Dennis, ed. *Stories and Society: Children's Literature in Its Social Context.* London: Macmillan, 1992.

Carpenter, Humphrey. *Secret Gardens: A Study of the Golden Age of Children's Literature.* Boston: Houghton Mifflin, 1985.

Carpenter, Humphrey, and Mari Prichard. *The Oxford Companion to Children's Literature.* Oxford: Oxford University Press, 1984.

Chevalier, Tracy, ed. *Twentieth-Century Children's Writers,* 3rd ed. Chicago: St. James Press, 1989.

Coody, Betty. *Using Literature with Young Children,* 2nd ed. Dubuque, Iowa: Wm. C. Brown, 1979.

Cott, Jonathan. *Pipers at the Gates of Dawn: The Wisdom of Children's Literature*. New York: Random House, 1981.

Coveney, Peter. *The Image of Childhood*. London: Harmondsworth, 1967.

Cullinan, Bernice, and Diane G. Person, eds. *The Continuum Encyclopedia of Children's Literature*. New York: Continuum, 2001.

Cunningham, Hugh. *Children and Childhood in Western Society since 1500*. New York: Longman, 1995.

Darton, F. J. Harvey. *Children's Books in England, Five Centuries of Social Life*. Cambridge: Cambridge University Press, 1982.

Demers, Patricia. *Heaven Upon Earth: The Form of Moral and Religious Children's Literature, to 1850*. Knoxville: University of Tennessee Press, 1993.

Demers, Patricia, and Gordon Moyles, eds. *From Instruction to Delight*. Toronto: Oxford University Press, 1982.

Egoff, Sheila A. *Only Connect: Readings on Children's Literature*. 2nd ed. Toronto: Oxford University Press, 1980.

——. *Thursday's Child: Trends and Patterns in Contemporary Children's Literature*. Chicago: ALA, 1981.

Egoff, Sheila A., and Judith Saltman. *The New Republic of Childhood: A Critical Guide to Canadian Children's Literature in English*. Toronto: Oxford University Press, 1990.

Fraser, James H., ed. *Society and Children's Literature*. Boston: Godine, 1978.

Harrison, Barbara, and Gregory Maguire, comps. and eds. *Innocence & Experience: Essays & Conversations on Children's Literature*. New York: Lothrop, Lee & Shepard, 1987.

Haviland, Virginia, ed. *Children and Literature: Views and Reviews*. Glenview, IL: Scott, Foresman, 1973.

Hazard, Paul. *Books, Children, and Men*. Boston: The Horn Book, 1983.

Hunt, Peter, ed. *Children's Literature: An Illustrated History*. Oxford: Oxford University Press, 1995.

——. *An Introduction to Children's Literature*. Oxford: Oxford University Press, 1994.

Hunter, Mollie. *Talent Is Not Enough*. New York: Harper & Row, 1976.

Inglis, Fred. *The Promise of Happiness: Meaning and Value in Children's Fiction*. Cambridge: Cambridge University Press, 1981.

Jackson, Mary V. *Engines of Instruction, Mischief, and Magic: Children's Literature in England from Its Beginnings to 1839*. Omaha: University of Nebraska, 1990.

Lystad, Mary. *From Dr. Mather to Dr. Seuss: 200 Years of American Books for Children*. Cambridge: Harvard UP, 1980.

MacDonald, Ruth. *Literature for Children in England and America from 1646 to 1774*. Troy, NY: Whitston, 1982.

Manlove, Colin. *From Alice to Harry Potter: Children's Fantasy in England*. Christchurch, New Zealand: Cybereditions, 2003.

McLeod, Anne Scott. *A Moral Tale: Children's Fiction and American Culture, 1820–1860*. Hamden: Archon, 1975.

Meek, Margaret, Aidan Warlow, and Griselda Barton. *The Cool Web: The Patterns of Children's Reading*. New York: Atheneum, 1978.

Meigs, Cornelia, Elizabeth Nesbitt, Anne Thaxter Eaton, and Ruth Hill. *A Critical History of Children's Literature: A Survey of Children's Books in English*. New York: Macmillan, 1969.

Nelson, Claudia, and Lynne Valone, eds. *The Girls' Own: Cultural Histories of the Anglo-American Girl, 1830–1915*. Athens: University of Georgia Press, 1994.

Nikolajeva, Maria, ed. *Aspects and Issues in the History of Children's Literature*. Contributions to the Study of World Literature, 60. Westport, CT: Greenwood 1995.

Pickering, Samuel F., Jr. *John Locke and Children's Books in Eighteenth-Century England*. Knoxville: University of Tennessee Press, 1981.

——. *Moral Instruction and Fiction for Children, 1749–1820*. Athens: University of Georgia Press, 1993.

Pollack, Linda. *Forgotten Children: Parent-Child Relations from 1500 to 1900*. Cambridge: Cambridge University Press, 1983.

Ravitch, Diane. *The Language Police: How Pressure Groups Restrict What Students Learn*. New York: Knopf, 2003.

Sadker, Myra Pollack, and David Miller Sadker. *Now Upon a Time: A Contemporary View of Children's Literature*. New York: Harper & Row, 1977.

Schorcsh, Anita. *Images of Childhood: An Illustrated Social History*. New York: Mayflower, 1979.

Summerfield, Geoffrey. *Fantasy and Reason: Children's Literature in the Eighteenth Century*. Athens: University of Georgia Press, 1983.

Summerville, C. John. *The Discovery of Childhood in Puritan England*. Athens: University of Georgia Press, 1992.

Thwaite, Mary F. *From Primer to Pleasure in Reading: An Introduction to the History of Children's Books in England*. Boston: The Horn Book, 1972.

Townsend, John Rowe. *Trade and Plumb-Cake for Ever, Huzza! The Life and Work of John Newbery, 1713–1769*. Cambridge, U.K.: Colt, 1994.

——. *Written for Children: An Outline of English-Language Children's Literature*. 5th rev. ed. London: Kestrel, 1990.

Tucker, Nicholas. *The Child and the Book: A Psychological and Literary Exploration*. Cambridge: Cambridge University Press, 1981.

Wall, Barbara. *The Narrator's Voice: The Dilemma of Children's Fiction*. London: Macmillan, 1991.

Watson, Victor, ed. *The Cambridge Guide to Children's Books in English*. Cambridge: Cambridge University Press, 2001.

Wooden, Warren W. *Children's Literature of the English Renaissance*. Lexington: University of Kentucky Press, 1986.

2

The Study of Childhood

THE DISCOVERY OF CHILDHOOD

The concept of childhood as we know it today—a stage of life separate from that of adulthood—is a fairly recent phenomenon, arising in about the seventeenth century. Prior to that, widespread infant mortality, brief life spans, and a general naiveté about human development all conspired to keep children in social obscurity. Children were regarded as miniature adults, and their chief responsibility was to grow up as fast as possible. By the seventeenth century, a combination of religious, economic, and educational reforms helped to change the general attitude. Increased wealth, better education, and a greater emphasis on the importance of the individual all helped to elevate the status of the child in both the family and society.

In Chapter 1 we noted John Locke's contribution to the study of childhood—and his widespread influence. Locke argued against another famous philosopher, Thomas Hobbes, who believed that most human traits were inherited—or innate. John Locke developed his concept of the *tabula rasa,* or the blank slate, which he believed to be the state of the mind at birth. All knowledge, all ideas, then were imprinted on that blank slate by experience. This means that all human beings are quite equal at birth, with the same capabilities to learn and succeed. It also suggests that education is crucial, since it forms an important part of one's experience. This is a very appealing concept, because it gives humans a sense of control.

Today, Locke's concept is being challenged by new ideas about human development, especially by those coming out of the recent scientific research into the DNA code. Simply put, we are not all born with equal ability or equal potential. It now appears that Hobbes's theories of heredity were more accurate than we supposed. I know, for example, that singing lessons from Luciano Pavarotti himself could not get me a starring role at the Metropolitan

Opera. No amount of basketball practice will ever get me a contract with the Boston Celtics. Some things we are just born with. In fact, our brains are quite thoroughly wired at birth, and experts believe that close to fifty percent of who and what we are is already determined by the time we see the first light of day (see especially Steven Pinker, *The Blank Slate*). We should not despair, however, for that still leaves another fifty percent to work with after we are born—our environment, our education, our experiences, our family, and our friends do make a difference. In other words, there is still much we can learn. It bears mentioning that, just because we do not all enjoy equal talents, does not mean that we do not all deserve equal rights and equal respect.

LANGUAGE ACQUISITION

Language acquisition is one human feature that depends on the combination of heredity and environment. How humans acquire language seems nothing short of miraculous. How do toddlers, in a few short years and without formal training, master the abstract concept of attaching meaning to sounds and constructing intelligible sentences? Indeed, by the time most children are four or five, they have a working knowledge of most grammatical rules. (Steven Pinker, in *The Language Instinct*, argues that language is, in fact, innate.) Of course, young children can't explain those rules or use the terminology, but they can use them to express almost anything that is on their minds—from then on it's just adding new words and polishing the fine points.

Children's ability to grasp new ideas quickly can be seen by how rapidly they pick up new vocabulary and how new and unusual sounds fascinate them. Despite the popular notion that pronunciation is difficult for children, they actually have a much easier time making sounds than do adults—children are great at imitating. The sounds peculiar to a specific language are learned. So, for example, a Japanese baby born in the United States and surrounded by English-speaking adults will be much more at ease making English sounds than Japanese sounds. We are not predisposed to a particular language at birth—we are simply born with the capacity to make the abstract connections between sound and sense.

For this same reason, young children, because they do find it easier to make new and unusual sounds and are not thoroughly ingrained in the grammar of one language, can pick up other languages surprisingly quickly. Hispanic children in the American Southwest are frequently bilingual from their preschool years. Our schools make an unfortunate mistake in not offering foreign language training to elementary school students for they are the ones who can pick up new languages with the least effort. High school is too late for many.

What we need to do as adults is to build on our children's language abilities and their natural curiosity about sounds and language. And we cannot begin too early—mothers and fathers are now even reading to the baby in the womb, which, even if it does little for the baby, gives the parents a head start at what should be one of their most important tasks, introducing the world of books to their children.

Books can help satisfy children's insatiable desire to experiment with sounds and to expand their vocabulary. Even the simplest Mother Goose rhymes offer exciting and challenging vocabulary, with their nonsense words and archaisms. Take, for example, Old Mother Hubbard who successively went to the "joiner's," the "fishmonger's," the "cobbler's," and the "hosier's," or the crooked man who "found a crooked sixpence against a crooked stile." Early on children discover the joy of tongue twisters—"Peter Piper picked a peck of pickled peppers" or "Billy Button bought a buttered biscuit." Through books we can nurture children's curiosity about language, expose them to new words, and invite them to try new sounds. And as children grow and their skills and tastes become more sophisticated, they can move on to the complexities of story plots. Folktales are so popular among young children because they are plot centered with simple and clearly defined characters—and, of course, they are wildly imaginative. Books provide children with vivid models of language (imagine how limited the vocabularies of children would be if the only words they knew were those they heard from their parents and siblings). Just as important, books offer stimulation for the imagination, inviting children to explore creative worlds of their own and to reach beyond the confines of their daily existence. Reading a book can be like throwing open a window.

MODERN THEORIES OF CHILD DEVELOPMENT

Children develop quite rapidly during their first few years—they quickly outgrow their clothes, their beds, their toys, and their books. The books that fascinated two-year-olds are likely to bore five-year-olds (they will get interested in them again when they are twenty or thirty years old). Parents, teachers, librarians, and other adults who work with children need to be aware of the basic developmental changes children experience in order to see how the changes affect children's reading habits and preferences.

We will look at three of the more prominent theories of child development, all of which complement each other (see Table 2.1). Jean Piaget was concerned with intellectual or cognitive development, Erik Erikson with social development, and Lawrence Kohlberg with the development of moral judgment. All three viewed human development as occurring in a series of stages through which children pass as they progress toward maturity. Progressing up these stages is like climbing a slippery slope: if we don't have sure footing or a firm grasp, we will slip back down the mountain. Also, the movement between stages is gradual and almost imperceptible, and all individuals develop at different rates. Consequently, the age spans mentioned here can be only approximations.

We should note that Piaget and Kohlberg have been criticized for ignoring female development, which, some argue, is not the same as male development. Males generally value competition, self-assertiveness, individual rights, and social rules. Females, on the other hand, value human relationships, responsibilities to others, cooperation, community values, and tolerance for opposing viewpoints. Additionally, some argue that females reach

TABLE 2.1 Comparative chart of developmental stages identified by Piaget, Erikson, and Kohlberg

Piaget	Erikson	Kohlberg
Sensorimotor Period (0–2 years)	Trust vs. Mistrust (0–18 months)	Preconventional Level (0–7 years) *Stage 1 Punishment/Obedience Orientation*
Preoperational Period (2–7 years)	Autonomy vs. Doubt (18 months–3 years)	*Stage 2 Instrumental/Relativist Orientation*
Preconceptual Stage (2–4 years) Intuitive Stage (4–7 years)	Initiative vs. Guilt (3–7 years)	
Period of Concrete Operations (7–11 years)	Industry vs. Inferiority (7–11 years)	Conventional Level (7–11 years) *Stage 1 Interpersonal Concordance Orientation*
		Stage 2 "Law and Order" Orientation
Period of Formal Operations (11–15 years)	Identity vs. Role Confusion (11–15 years)	Postconventional Level (Adolescence/Adulthood) *Stage 1 Contractual/Legalistic Orientation* *Stage 2 Universal/Ethical/Principle Orientation*

these developmental stages more quickly than males do. The psychological development of members of minority groups, who tend to reflect different values from those of the majority, have also been neglected. These theories, like all others, are not infallible and are offered here only as a general guide.

Piaget's Cognitive Theory of Development

The *Cognitive Theory of Development,* devised by the Swiss psychologist Jean Piaget, is the earliest and perhaps the most famous of the theories. Piaget outlined four major periods of intellectual development, some of which he subdivided into stages.

SENSORIMOTOR PERIOD The first period Piaget identified is the *Sensorimotor Period,* which he estimated as lasting from birth to about two years of age, during the early stages of which the child is incapable of establishing *object permanence*–the child does not realize that objects continue to exist even if they are out of sight. The infant's world is entirely egocentric, and the only things that matter to the child are what she sees, feels, hears, tastes, and smells. It is also during this period that the infant is concerned with the development of coordination, figuring out how to use the hands and arms and legs.

What impact does this early period of cognitive development have on reading? It is most important in these early years that we plant the seeds of reading, encourage the physical handling of books, and establish habitual story times. The stories themselves are not so important as is a happy experience during the story time. Durable cardboard and cloth books are helpful in providing infants and toddlers with a sense of the book's physical characteristics. Tactile books, such as Dorothy Kunhardt's *Pat the Bunny* in which the young child can touch the cottony fur of the bunny or feel the sandpaper roughness of daddy's facial stubble, can provide considerable entertainment. For the very young, nursery rhymes have appeal with their lilting rhythms and curious sounds (for example, "Higglety, pigglety, my black hen," or "Hickory, dickory dock"). The infant does not care so much for the meaning as for the engaging sounds of the language.

PREOPERATIONAL PERIOD The second of Piaget's periods—the *Preoperational Period*—occurs between the ages of two and seven. During the first two or three years of this period, children are in what Piaget termed the *Preconceptual Stage,* characterized by a very subjective logic. For example, they cannot make generalizations about the physical world, such as reversibility (the notion that some things can be undone), assimilation (using past knowledge to explain new information), or accommodation (revising past knowledge in light of new information). Children can, however, at a very young age, grasp certain rudimentary concepts, such as colors, shapes, and sizes; children respond well to *concept books* that present these ideas. Children at this stage cannot grasp abstractions and tend to classify objects according to variable criteria. For instance, they might describe anything that moves in human terms (including animals and machines). This may explain their fondness for books about talking animals and animated machines—for example, Hardy Gramatky's *Little Toot,* the story of a tugboat, and Virginia Burton's *Mike Mulligan and His Steam Shovel.*

The second stage of this *Preoperational Period* is what Piaget termed the *Intuitive Stage,* which occurs typically between the ages of four and seven. Children at this stage use, for lack of a better term, "intuition" or their feelings to help them make judgments about their world. They are developing language skills and are becoming less egocentric. Now stories about human relationships carry new meaning, as do stories that explore inner emotions. Although fantasies remain popular with these children, realism often becomes more meaningful as they grow curious about other people and their own relationships with others. A realistic story such as Robert McCloskey's *One Morning in Maine,* a picture book describing the simple pleasures of family life, will hold appeal for children in this age group. This is a time of experimentation when children often discover hidden interests. Reading a wide variety of books on many different topics can help them in this discovery process.

PERIOD OF CONCRETE OPERATIONS The third period—the *Period of Concrete Operations*—occurs roughly between the ages of seven and eleven. This is when children begin to use rudimentary logic and problem solving. They begin to understand time and spacial relationships. At this stage young readers begin to read longer books that are divided into chapters, and they can comfortably pause between chapters and pick up the story at a later time. Historical fiction (such as Laura Ingalls Wilder's Little House books) becomes more meaningful, since the children now have a grasp of the passage of time. Because children at this stage are more aware of people around them and of their own role in society, they may turn to novels such as Judy Blume's *Blubber* and *Tales of a Fourth Grade Nothing* or Lois Lowry's Anastasia books.

PERIOD OF FORMAL OPERATIONS Finally, the *Period of Formal Operations* occurs from about the age of eleven through about the age of fifteen (when full cognitive maturity, according to Piaget, is established). During this period young people become capable of using formal logic, engaging in a true exchange of ideas, comprehending the viewpoints of others, and understanding the world as a social phenomenon requiring human interaction. Most readers at this stage of development have already entered adolescence or young adulthood. Examples of topics found in books for this age group include inner-city gang wars (S. E. Hinton's *The Outsiders*), homosexuality (John Donovan's *I'll Get There. It Better Be Worth the Trip*, Sandra Scoppettone's *Trying Hard to Hear You*, and M. E. Kerr's *Deliver Us from Evie*), racial prejudice (Mildred Taylor's *Roll of Thunder, Hear My Cry*), premarital sex (Judy Blume's *Then Again, Maybe I Won't*), just to name a few. The controversial works of Robert Cormier (*I Am the Cheese, The Bumblebee Flies Anyway,* and others) treat such subjects as social and government corruption and have overall negative tones. They remain popular because they address head-on some of the doubts, fears, and anxieties that active young minds naturally experience.

Erikson's Psychosocial Development Theory

In addition to developing intellectually, individuals develop in their social interaction. Erik Erikson's psychosocial development theory classifies the maturation process into a series of psychosocial conflicts, each of which must be resolved before one can move on to the next, in much the same way that Piaget sees successive levels in cognitive development. Erikson's theory includes five principal stages of development throughout childhood.

TRUST VERSUS MISTRUST *Trust Versus Mistrust,* from birth to roughly eighteen months, occurs when children have little option but to trust those who are their caregivers, but at the same time they must overcome such fears as abandonment when they are put to sleep in their own beds. Books at this stage can provide both security and reassurance. Margaret Wise Brown's classic, *Goodnight Moon,* has long been popular as a story for early childhood. It exudes warmth and coziness as we observe a little bunny saying good night to all his favorite possessions in his womblike bedroom. The repetitive pattern in both text and illustration is comfortably reassuring. Children at this stage also like hearing familiar books read night after night and these books become like old, reliable friends, providing stability and a sense of security.

AUTONOMY VERSUS DOUBT *Autonomy Versus Doubt,* from eighteen months to about three years, results when children begin to exercise their first impulses toward autonomy or independence. At the same time, however, they must overcome doubts about whether they can do what they attempt. Consequently, this is a period of exploration, which can be exasperating for parents who have labeled this time "the terrible twos." Crockett Johnson's imaginative story *Harold and the Purple Crayon,* about a boy who creates his own world with a magical crayon, charmingly portrays an autonomous child who proves capable of handling his new-found independence—and extricating himself from some interesting dilemmas.

INITIATIVE VERSUS GUILT The third stage, *Initiative Versus Guilt,* occurring between the ages of three and six, is when children begin to realize their own responsibilities and to understand the conflicts that arise between people. Children want to take the initiative, not only to do things on their own but also to decide what to do and when to do it. They must also struggle with guilt when they make the wrong choices. In Ezra Jack Keats' *Peter's Chair,* young Peter exhibits hostility when his parents decide to paint all his baby furniture pink for his new sister. Peter decides to run away but eventually comes to regret his selfishness in refusing to share his things, and he finally offers them to his sister of his own free will. Peter has arrived at a higher stage of social development, which is shown by his willingness to change his attitude and behavior.

INDUSTRY VERSUS INFERIORITY The fourth stage, *Industry Versus Inferiority,* which takes place between the ages of seven and eleven, is characterized by a determination to achieve success, often working in concert with others. At the same time, however, children have a tendency to measure themselves against their peers and find themselves wanting; hence, feelings of inferiority may develop. Beverly Cleary's Ramona books effectively demonstrate these feelings; young readers view Ramona with a sympathetic eye as she strives for acceptance among her peers. On the other hand, Louise Fitzhugh's *Harriet the Spy* humorously deals with the experiences of a young girl who suffers the wrath of her friends when they read her brutally frank journal. Whereas Harriet once felt superior to her friends, she comes to realize how much their acceptance means to her.

IDENTITY VERSUS ROLE CONFUSION The fifth stage, *Identity Versus Role Confusion,* is achieved at adolescence. Perhaps the great crisis of adolescence is the discovery of identity (not only personal identity, but cultural and social identity as well). Young adults struggle with what their roles in life are to be, what society expects of them, and what they expect of themselves. Individuals at this stage often appear to be fickle and in a state of almost constant flux, as they are torn between the familiar security of childhood and the temptation of the exciting possibilities of adult independence. Add to all this their emerging sexuality and we can easily understand the turmoil of adolescence. Readers at this stage crave openness and honesty, and most prefer stories about others like themselves. Still, such varied works as Virginia Hamilton's *M.C. Higgins, the Great,* about an African-American boy on an impoverished mountain farm, Katherine Paterson's *The Great Gilly Hopkins,* about a difficult foster child, and Sharon Creech's *Walk Two Moons,* about a Native American family enduring losses, all portray the individual's search for identity.

Kohlberg's Theory of the Development of Moral Judgment

Lawrence Kohlberg's theory examines the development of moral reasoning and moral judgment—that is, how individuals determine what is right and wrong. Like Piaget, he sees development occurring in a series of stages through which an individual passes to moral maturity. Kohlberg identifies three different levels of development, each divided into two stages.

PRECONVENTIONAL LEVEL The *Preconventional Level* is when children respond only to the immediate consequences of an action—as to a reward or punishment or to the threat of punishment. At this level, children move through two stages. The first, termed the *Punishment/Obedience Orientation,* is when a child obeys rules and authority to avoid punishment or unpleasant physical consequence. In Beatrix Potter's *The Tale of Peter Rabbit,* we see the moral dilemma that faces children in this stage, for Peter must decide whether to obey his mother or follow his desires and risk punishment. Peter disobeys and is nearly killed, loses his coat, and catches cold. Children, thus, are likely to judge Peter's actions as bad because they have unfortunate results. The second stage, the *Instrumental/Relativist Orientation,* is when a child conforms to group behavior in return for rewards or favors. Templeton the rat in E.B. White's *Charlotte's Web* is persuaded to do good deeds only by the promise of food. He is otherwise a thoroughly self-centered creature.

CONVENTIONAL LEVEL The second level, the *Conventional Level,* roughly corresponding with Piaget's Period of Concrete Operations (ages seven to eleven), is when children begin to value the family, group, and community. Conformity and loyalty to societal conventions or norms become important. The first stage in this level is the *Interpersonal Concordance* (or *"Good Boy/Nice Girl"*) *Orientation* in which a child conforms to group behavior to please or have the approval of others and to avoid rejection by peers. This is when peer pressure begins to exert tremendous influence. Children now want to wear clothes like their friends wear, eat foods like their friends eat, and, perhaps most important, they just want to have friends. Patricia MacLachlan's *Cassie Binegar* is the story of a girl embarrassed by her unconventional family; "Why can't we be like everyone else?" Cassie laments. Her cry echoes the sentiments of every child going through this stage of life, yearning for acceptance.

The second stage in this level, the *"Law and Order" Orientation,* occurs when individuals conform to group behavior to avoid disrupting the social order, incurring the censure of authority and suffering the guilt that comes from such transgressions. Eleanor Estes's classic family story, *The Moffats,* depicts Janey Moffat, although typically respectful of her elders, one day mimicking the peculiar walk of the superintendent. She is discovered and then becomes convinced that the chief of police is out to arrest her for her "crime." She escapes by jumping into a large wooden breadbox at the grocer's to hide from him. It is a comical, but quite understandable, reaction.

POSTCONVENTIONAL LEVEL The final level is the *Postconventional,* which occurs when the individual begins making rational, independent judgments on the basis of some external standard outside purely personal considerations. This begins to take us outside the limits of this book, since it is a phenomenon usually not realized until adolescence. The first stage in this level is the *Contractual/Legalistic Orientation* in which individuals recognize the value of social contracts and rules to preserve and protect the common good. Books on social problems, such as S. E. Hinton's study of gang violence, *The Outsiders*, and Robert Cormier's unsettling tale of corruption, *The Chocolate War*, address readers at this stage, revealing the potential catastrophes that can occur when certain societal rules and obligations are subverted.

The second stage is the *Universal/Ethical/Principle Orientation*, in which an individual lives by chosen ethical principles and is willing to defy established laws if they are perceived as doing more harm than good. The nineteenth-century writer Henry David Thoreau chose to go to prison rather than pay taxes to support a war he found unconscionable. Acting according to the Golden Rule or some other abstract principle is an example of this type of moral reasoning. But it should be pointed out that psychologists disagree as to whether such a stage actually exists—or rather whether human beings are actually capable of attaining this stage. (Perhaps prophets and saints come close, but few ordinary individuals do.)

CHILDREN'S LITERATURE AND DEVELOPMENTAL ISSUES

Most psychologists agree that human beings develop in stages, that the lengths of these stages vary with each individual, that there is much overlap in these stages, and that there may be occasional regression or a temporary going backward as children develop. Healthy individuals progress successfully through these stages, generally moving from a state of complete egocentricism to one of relative maturity and concern for others. Although they may not always be able to identify developmental stages by name or recite psychological theory, the best writers are fully cognizant of human behavior. They are keenly aware of the problems, fears, hopes, and dreams of children as they move through childhood. In their first seven years, children go through more developmental changes more rapidly than they will throughout the rest of their lives. Consequently, it is important to keep in mind the cognitive abilities and social and moral development of children when we help them choose their books. The one-year-old enjoys simple cloth wordless books, but by the age of seven many children are ready for chapter books. Of course, children develop at differing rates, and we, as adults, are challenged to tune in to each child's needs and abilities. And fortunately today, we can find children's books to meet virtually every requirement and satisfy every desire.

Adults are frequently guilty of underestimating children and their emotional and intellectual development. Many adults refuse to share books about such difficult subjects as illness, old age, death, war, violence, or sex with children. This is probably a mistake. Sheltering young children from life's unpleasantness will not protect them from it. Remember, children may encounter death (the death of a pet or grandparent or anyone else) at any time. Preschoolers notice the physical difference between the sexes. And, regrettably, some very young children know all too well the reality of domestic violence. On a larger human scale, children were victims of Hitler's death camps and of the bomb at Hiroshima–these tragedies are the subject of children's picture books (Roberto Innocenti's *Rose Blanche* and Toshi Maruki's *Hiroshima No Pika*), as well as books for older readers (such as David A. Adler's *We Remember the Holocaust* or Inge Auebacher's *I Am a Star: Child of the Holocaust*).

The portrayal of death in children's literature is nothing new. In the eighteenth century, children frequently read stories with vivid descriptions of death and dying–usually with some moral significance. Death was seen as either punishment for wicked ways or as the gateway to Heaven, a reward for a life of piety. Today we see a marked tendency to shelter children from the realities of death–many people cannot even bring themselves to say the word, preferring to use euphemisms such as "passed away" or "gone asleep" (which is cruelly misleading). Yes, it is difficult to discuss, but death is a natural part of life and denying it or disguising it will not make it go away or lessen the pain. Children are stronger and wiser than we think, and Margaret Wise Brown knew this well. Her picture book, *The Dead Bird*, is a wonderfully simple story of some children who find a dead bird. They interrupt their play and give the bird a proper funeral and burial, after which they return to their normal activities. This skillful portrayal of death as one part of the natural cycle of life removes the aspect of fear, replacing it with acceptance. This is one of many children's books that explore the many facets of death and dying–terminal illness, accidental death, suicide, funeral customs, the stages of grief (including denial, guilt, bargaining, anger, and acceptance)–all aimed at helping young readers come to terms with the great final mystery.

Finally, one last note on child psychology. The philosopher Gareth Matthews takes issue with some of the fundamental arguments of developmental psychology particularly as espoused by Piaget and Kohlberg–because he believes these theories imply that "maturation" is "improvement," that it is somehow better to be mature than childlike. Matthews points to many examples of very young children exhibiting profound philosophical observations and keen moral judgments, perhaps because their perceptions have not yet been stifled by the norm of maturity or their imaginations deadened by the trappings of adult responsibility. He notes particularly that long before they are aware of moral conflicts, children "can have a strong empathetic response to the victims of suffering, or injustice, and a working understanding of central paradigms for terms of moral assessment" (65). Matthews argues for a rejection of the "maturity assumption," and for an opening of our minds to the spiritual and intellectual contributions that children have to offer. Children's literature need not shy away from the hard issues; children, in fact, demand them. It may be only the adults who fear the philosophical questions.

Society has achieved a new and more sophisticated level of appreciation for children's literature–and we are all the richer for it. C. S. Lewis, the author of the beloved children's classics, the Narnia Chronicles, wrote "When I was ten, I read fairy tales in secret and would have been ashamed if I had been found doing so. Now that I am fifty I read them openly. When I became a man I put away childish things, including the fear of childishness and the desire to be very grownup" (210). He further reminds us that growing up consists not of putting away old pleasures, but adding new ones:

I now enjoy Tolstoy and Jane Austen and Trollope as well as fairy tales and I call that growth; if I had had to lose the fairy tales in order to acquire the novelists, I would not say that I had grown but only that I had changed. A tree grows because it adds rings; a train doesn't grow by leaving one station behind and puffing on to the next. (211)

Works Cited

Lewis, C. S. "On Three Ways of Writing for Children." In *Only Connect,* 2nd ed., edited by Sheila Egoff, 207–220. New York: Oxford University Press, 1980.

Matthews, Gareth B. *The Philosophy of Childhood.* Cambridge, MA: Harvard University Press, 1994.

Recommended Readings

Brainerd, Charles J. *Recent Advances in Cognitive Developmental Research.* New York: Springer-Verlag, 1983.

Brief, Jean-Claude. *Beyond Piaget: A Philosophical Psychology.* New York: Teachers College Press, 1983.

Celebration staff and Kenneth L. Donelson. *Literature for Today's Young Adults,* 6th ed. New York: Longman, 1997.

Cullinan, Bernice. *Literature and the Child.* 5th ed. San Diego, CA: Harcourt, 2001.

Erikson, Erik. *Childhood and Society.* New York: Norton, 1950.

Fields, M. V., K. Spangler, and D. M. Lee. *Let's Begin Reading Right.* 2nd ed. Columbus, OH: Merrill, 1991.

Gilligan, Carol. *In a Different Voice: Psychological Theory and Women's Development.* Cambridge: Harvard University Press, 1982.

Greven, Philip. *Spare the Child: The Religious Roots of Punishment and the Psychological Impact of Physical Abuse.* New York: Alfred A. Knopf, 1990.

Huck, Charlotte S., Susan Hepler, and Janet Hickman. *Children's Literature in the Elementary School,* 8th ed. New York: McGraw-Hill, 2003.

Hyde, Janet Shibley. *Half the Human Experience: The Psychology of Women.* Lexington, MA: D. C. Heath, 1985.

Kaestle, Carl F. *Literacy in the United States: Readers and Reading Since 1880.* New Haven: Yale University Press, 1991.

Kohlberg, Lawrence. *The Philosophy of Moral Development.* San Francisco: Harper & Row, 1981.

——. *Essays on Moral Development. Vol. II: The Psychology of Moral Development, the Nature and Validity of Moral Stages.* San Francisco: Harper & Row, 1985.

Lindfors, J. W. *Children's Language and Learning,* 2nd ed. Englewood Cliffs, NJ: Prentice Hall, 1987.

Neubauer, John. *The Fin-De-Siecle Culture of Adolescence.* New Haven: Yale University Press, 1992.

Piaget, Jean. *The Language and Thought of the Child.* New York: Harcourt, Brace, 1926.

——. "Piaget's Theory." In *Handbook of Child Psychology*. P. H. Mussen, ed. 4th ed. W. Kessen, ed. *Vol. 1: History, Theory, and Methods*. New York: John Wiley & Sons, 1983.

Pinker, Steven. *The Blank Slate: The Modern Denial of Human Nature*. New York: Viking, 2002.

——. *How the Mind Works*. New York: Norton, 1998.

——. *The Language Instinct*. New York: Harper-Collins, 2000.

Sugarman, Susan. *Piaget's Construction of the Child's Reality*. Cambridge: Cambridge University Press, 1987.

Vidal, Fernando. *Piaget before Piaget*. Cambridge, MA: Harvard University Press, 1994.

Walsh, Mary Roth, ed. *The Psychology of Women: Ongoing Debates*. New Haven: Yale University Press, 1987.

CHAPTER

3

The Study of Literature

One literary critic describes children's literature this way:

> Children's literature will often have less complexity of plot, less profundity of psychological analysis, and more simple pleasures and pains than are found in adult writing; and it will, usually, have the security of the happy ending; yet in its creations of new worlds, its explorations of alien points of view, its subtle investigations of language and metaphysics, and its continual spiritual penetration, it gives us a creative country as 'mature' as the adult's. (Manlove 9)

The capable critic approaches children's literature with this respectful attitude. Of course, we might very well ask why we need literary criticism in the first place. It is because literature is filled with ideas that need to be explored. Literature helps us to see our world in new ways. It brings us to a deeper understanding of life. Literature, therefore, invites discussion and encourages debate. And that is what literary criticism is—a discussion of ideas. The critic Peter Hunt writes: "Literary criticism . . . provide[s] ways of talking about texts, and without some vocabulary, there is considerable danger that those who want to talk about children's books will not understand each other—or not seem worthy of anyone else's attention" (19).

THE ELEMENTS OF LITERATURE

This chapter presents a vocabulary with which we can discuss literature and offers some suggestions for judging literature. What we say here about the elements of literature applies chiefly to fiction, including fantasy and realism. Poetry and nonfiction require different criteria, which will be treated in Chapters 9 and 12 respectively.

Characters

At the heart of every good story are believable and memorable characters. The principal characters of a story include *protagonist,* the central figure with whom we usually sympathize or identify, and the *antagonist,* the figure who opposes the protagonist and creates the conflict. We sometimes call these characters the hero and villain. Typically several supporting characters are included as well. Readers prefer characters to be properly motivated. That is, characters ought to have good reasons for behaving as they do. This is called *character motivation* and derives from the belief that human beings are in some way responsible for their own acts.

Characters may also be identified by their depth. *Flat characters* have no depth—we see but one side or aspect of them. Frequently they are *stock characters* or *stereotypes* used primarily to advance the plot, such as a helpful police officer, a kindly store clerk, a strict teacher, and so on. As readers, however, we are mainly interested in the *round characters,* who have more fully developed personalities. We expect the protagonists and antagonists to be rounded individuals who express a range of emotion—joy, sorrow, confidence, fear, remorse, pity. In most children's stories, the protagonist is a *dynamic* character, that is, one who changes throughout the narrative, usually toward greater maturity. In *Charlotte's Web,* Wilbur the pig grows from an immature, self-centered, and insecure character into a mature, caring, and confident creature. On the other hand, most supporting characters are *static;* that is, they do not change significantly. Templeton, the self-centered rat in *Charlotte's Web,* is a static character; he is virtually the same at the book's close as he was at its beginning. Templeton is also an example of a *foil character,* one whose personality traits are the opposite of another character's, often the main character. Foil is a jeweler's term for a gem setting, which makes a stone appear larger and more brilliant. Likewise, a character can be made to shine when compared with another who has undesirable traits. Templeton's selfishness makes Charlotte's ultimate sacrifice that much more impressive.

An author uses several techniques for revealing a character to us:

1. *What the narrator says about the character*—this usually is the least memorable way (this is like getting our information about someone from a lecture).

2. *What the other characters say about the character*—this evidence is only as reliable as the speaker; we must be wary of hidden motives or prejudices.

3. *What the character says about him- or herself*—this is usually quite reliable, but we should remember that people do not always mean what they say.

4. *What the character actually does*—actions, we all know, speak louder than words, and it is through actions that some of the most convincing evidence about character is revealed.

Setting

The setting refers to the time, the geographical location, and the general environment and circumstances that prevail in a narrative. The setting can help establish the mood of a story. In Laura Ingalls Wilder's *Little House on the Prairie,* the setting is on the Great Plains in the latter half of the nineteenth century. But the setting goes beyond simply establishing the time and place. It includes descriptions of the daily occupations of the Ingalls family, poor settlers eking out a living in a fairly inhospitable environment, where wells have to be dug by hand, the nearest neighbor is miles away, and a family must huddle in a log cabin behind a blanket for a door while wolves lurk perilously close outside. Writers of historical fiction, gothic romance, and fantasy often devote a great deal of time to describing the setting, since it is likely to be unfamiliar to the reader.

Following is the opening paragraph of Natalie Babbitt's *Tuck Everlasting.* Notice the sensory imagery that leaves us with a foreboding of things to come:

> The first week of August hangs at the very top of summer, the top of the live-long year, like the highest seat of a Ferris wheel when it pauses in its turning. The weeks that come before are only a climb from a balmy spring, and those that follow a drop to the chill of autumn, but the first week of August is motionless, and hot. It is curiously silent, too, with blank white dawns and glaring noons, and sunsets smeared with too much color. Often at night there is lightning, but it quivers all alone. There is no thunder, no relieving rain. These are strange and breathless days, the dog days, when people are led to do things they are sure to be sorry for after. (3)

The references to motionlessness, blank dawns, glaring noons, lightning quivering "all alone," and breathless days all suggest an unworldliness as well as a sense of loneliness, two themes that pervade the story of a family who is immortal, having drunk by chance from a magic spring. But their immortality is a bane, for, realizing the disastrous consequences should everyone learn of the spring, they live in self-imposed isolation, without the joy of human love or the stimulating challenge offered by mortal life.

Narrative point of view

The narrator is simply the storyteller, or, more accurately, the *persona* of the storyteller, as created by the author. Never assume the author to be the narrator. Stories are related to us through one of three types of narrators.

INTERNAL NARRATOR An internal narrator is one who is also a character in the story—often, but not necessarily, the protagonist. The use of the internal narrator is quickly identified by the narrator's use of the first-person pronoun—"I"—when referring to him- or herself. This narrative point of view allows for a very personal touch in the storytelling and it is usually very easy for readers to identify with this type of narrator. Richard Peck opens his Newbery-Honor book, *A Long Way from Chicago,* this way: "It was always August when we spent a week with our grandma. I was Joey then, not Joe: Joey Dowdel, and my sister was Mary Alice. In our first visits we were still just kids, so we could hardly see her town because of Grandma. She was so big, and the town was so small" (1). From this beginning, we know that the narrator is one of characters in the story, that the events happened some time in the past, and, we can reasonably guess, Grandma is going to be a major character. A good opening paragraph can tell us a lot.

EXTERNAL OMNISCIENT NARRATOR   The other two types of narrators are both outside (or external) storytellers—not characters in the story itself. The omniscient narrator is, as the term implies, "all-knowing." In an almost godlike fashion, the omniscient narrator can show us the thoughts and experiences of any character in the story. This technique is used effectively in C. S. Lewis's Narnia chronicles, and Lewis's narrator (who occasionally refers to himself as "I" but is clearly not a character in the story) is able to show us in one instance what our heroes are doing, and in another instance what the villains are up to. (We are reminded of that well-worn expression from old Westerns, "Meanwhile, back at the ranch." Only an omniscient narrator can shift perspectives like that.) It is sometimes difficult to determine whether an omniscient narrator is being used until we have read several chapters. E. B. White's *Charlotte's Web* opens with the exclamation of the young girl, Fern, "Where's Papa going with that axe?" We might suspect that this story is being told from Fern's point of view. But in the second chapter the focus shifts to the little pig, Wilbur. Later on, we see things through the eyes of the farmer and hired hand and then through Fern's parents' eyes. This use of multiple points of view is typical of the external omniscient narrator and it permits the writer the broadest scope. Of course, if we are to care about the story, ultimately one character or group of characters (such as Wilbur and the spider Charlotte) will win our sympathies.

EXTERNAL SUBJECTIVE NARRATOR   Similar to the omniscient narrator, the subjective narrator is not a character in the story. But in this case, the narrator only looks at things through the eyes of a single character. In the first chapter of *Little House in the Big Woods,* Laura Ingalls Wilder introduces her characters thus:

> So far as the little girl could see, there was only the one little house where she lived with her Father and Mother, her sister Mary and baby sister Carrie. A wagon track ran before the house, turning and twisting out of sight in the woods where the wild animals lived, but the little girl did not know where it went, nor what might be at the end of it.
>
> The little girl was named Laura and she called her father, Pa, and her mother, Ma. In those days and in that place, children did not say Father and Mother, nor Mamma and Papa, as they do now. (2–3)

Clearly we are looking at things through the eyes of Laura and we will not learn where the wagon track goes and ends up until she does. The narrator, however, is not Laura, but confines the narrative comments to Laura's subjective–her highly personal–point of view. This restrictive point of view is peculiar to the external subjective narrator. This type of narrative permits the narrator to quickly build a close bond between the protagonist and the reader, without being confined by the protagonist's educational or language restrictions. (In other words, even though Laura is only five, the subjective narrator is not bound to use a five-year-old's vocabulary.)

Plot

The plot of a story is more than just a series of events–it is a series of interconnected events. The kindergartner may describe a day at school like this: "We sang a song and we painted a picture and we took a nap and we ate a snack and we played outside and the teacher read us a book." That is a series of events, and in life, this is how things happen–the phone may ring, a visitor may come to the door, we receive a letter in the mail, and none of these events is related to the others. But in literature, we usually expect every occurrence to have a specific purpose–and this is what makes a plot. The ringing telephone is *not* a wrong number or a telemarketer, the visitor is *not* merely collecting for charity, and the letter is *not* without consequence. A plot is all about establishing connections, suggesting causes, and showing relationships. In a good plot, events hint at, or *foreshadow,* coming events, characters' words and actions all serve some purpose, and loose ends are tied up at the last. The good writer chooses plot elements carefully. As perceptive readers, we are always asking ourselves, now why did that happen? how will that affect what happens next?

The plot structure may follow one of three general patterns. A *dramatic plot* first establishes the setting and conflict, then follows the *rising action* through to a *climax* (the peak of the action and turning point), and concludes with a *dénouement* (a wrapping up of loose ends). This structure, with its chronological arrangement, is probably the most familiar; it is the structure of most folktales, and *Charlotte's Web* is a good example in fiction.

The second type of plot structure is the *episodic plot* consisting of a series of loosely related incidents, usually of chapter length, tied together by a common theme and/or characters. Wilder's *Little House* books are organized episodically. Each chapter is capable of standing on its own much like a short story or individual episodes of a television situation comedy. But taken together the episodes give us a complex picture of the family relationships and other issues important to the story. Unity is provided by the predominant theme of love and family togetherness overcoming hardship. Episodic plots work best when the writer wishes to explore the personalities of the characters, the nature of their existence, and the flavor of an era.

It is possible for an author to weave two dramatic plots in a single book, creating what we call a *parallel plot* structure. The two plots are usually linked by a common character and a similar theme. Sharon Creech's *Walk Two Moons* consists of a story within a story, both told by the protagonist, Sal, and both about self discovery.

Conflict

What makes a plot gripping is the *conflict*. Conflicts are often depicted in terms of good versus evil or right versus wrong. In most cases, a goal is to be accomplished and something is at stake. It is to see the resolution of the conflict that most readers continue reading until the end of the story. Conflicts come in many varieties, the most common being the following:

1. *The Protagonist Against Another* occurs when two persons are at odds over the same goal, or perhaps one person is determined to prevent another from achieving a goal. A folktale such as "Little Red Riding Hood" pointedly demonstrates this type of conflict.

2. *The Protagonist Against Society* occurs when the protagonist (and sometimes the protagonist's family or close associates) is pitted against mainstream society and its values and mores. This struggle is evident in many stories of racial prejudice, such as Mildred Taylor's *Roll of Thunder, Hear My Cry*.

3. *The Protagonist Against Nature* occurs when the protagonist is engaged in a struggle for survival, usually alone in some natural wilderness or unfamiliar place, as in Scott O'Dell's *Island of the Blue Dolphins*.

4. *The Protagonist Against Self* occurs when the conflict is an emotional or intellectual struggle within the protagonist him- or herself. Sendak's *Where the Wild Things Are* is an interesting example of a picture book rendition of this sort of conflict, where Max is torn by the conflicting desires to do exactly as he pleases or to obey his mother.

A single story may contain more than one type of conflict, although one often predominates. The conflict provides the excitement and makes possible the growth and development of the protagonist's character.

Theme

If the plot tells us what happens in a story, the theme tells us why it happens. The theme is the main, underlying idea of a piece of literature. Most writers have specific ideas they wish to share about people, society, and life in general. Stories and poems are written to illustrate the writer's ideas. However, most readers prefer to have the themes woven subtly into the fabric of the story or poem rather than having the author lecture or preach to them. Literature for young readers offers many important themes (and a single book often includes several minor themes in addition to the major one). Among the frequently found thematic issues in children's literature are the problems of growing up and maturing, including the individual's adjustment to society, the importance of love and friendship, the acceptance of a stepparent, achieving one's identity, and finding one's place in the world.

Style

It is not enough that a writer has a good story to tell; the story should be told well—with the right words in the right order.

WORDS In children's stories, word choice is particularly important because of the child's naturally limited vocabulary. Consequently, we would not expect to find abstract terminology in a work intended for preschoolers. On the other hand, if the vocabulary is too simple, the child will never grow as a reader. Beatrix Potter does not hesitate to use such words as "exert," "fortnight," and "chamomile tea." She has faith that young children will either pick up the meanings from the context or, if it is very important, they will ask somebody. Concrete terms are usually easily explained, and it is good if a text introduces a manageable number of new words to a young reader.

SENTENCES Sentences, both by their length and their construction, can increase or diminish our enjoyment of a work. Short sentences best convey suspense, tension, and swift action. Longer sentences work best when explanations and descriptions are needed. A well-written long sentence can be just as easy to understand as a short sentence. Notice how E. B. White, in the following paragraph from *Charlotte's Web*, effectively combines short and long sentences as he moves from describing action to thought and back to action:

> Wilbur looked everywhere. He searched his pen thoroughly. He examined the window ledge, stared up at the ceiling. But he saw nothing new. Finally he decided he would have to speak up. He hated to break the lovely stillness of dawn by using his voice, but he couldn't think of any other way to locate the mysterious new friend who was nowhere to be seen. So Wilbur cleared his throat. (34)

Prose has rhythm just as poetry does. The best writers can make a prose paragraph read as beautifully as a well-crafted poem. The juxtaposition of sounds, the use of repetition with a slight variation of patterns, the simple nature images so well suited to a story of pioneer life, all work together to create a lyrical passage in the conclusion to Patricia MacLachlan's *Sarah, Plain and Tall*:

> Autumn will come, then winter, cold with a wind that blows like a wind off the sea in Maine. There will be nests of curls to look for, and dried flowers all winter long. When there are storms, Papa will stretch a rope from the door to the barn so we will not be lost when we feed the sheep and the cows and Jack and Old Bess. And Sarah's chickens, if they aren't living in the house. There will be Sarah's sea, blue and gray and green, hanging on the wall. And songs, old ones and new. And Seal with yellow eyes. And there will be Sarah, plain and tall. (58)

EXPOSITION *Exposition* refers to the narrator's passages that are required to provide background information to help us understand the events of a story. Exposition may be used to introduce a character: "Dorothy lived in the midst of the great Kansas prairies, with Uncle Henry, who was a farmer, and Aunt Em, who was the farmer's wife" (Baum, *The Wonderful Wizard of Oz*, 7). Sometimes exposition is used to move the action along:

> When Laura and Mary had said their prayers and were tucked snugly under the trundle bed's covers, Pa was sitting in the firelight with the fiddle. Ma had blown out the lamp because she did not need its light. On the other side of the hearth she was swaying gently in her rocking chair and her knitting needles flashed in and out above the sock she was knitting. (Wilder, *Little House in the Big Woods*, 236)

If exposition is not handled efficiently and in a lively manner, it can slow down a story. Children prefer a balance between exposition and dialogue.

DIALOGUE *Dialogue* refers to the words spoken by the characters, usually to each other, as opposed to exposition, the words of the narrator to the reader. Most works of fiction rely on both dialogue and exposition. Young readers especially enjoy dialogue as a realistic and convincing way of defining character. Dialogue allows the author to convey individual peculiarities, such as the goose's quirky speech in *Charlotte's Web* when she replies to Wibur's inquiry about the time: "Probably-obably-obably about half-past eleven . . . Why aren't you asleep, Wilbur?" (33). Charlotte's intellectual superiority over the other barnyard animals is clearly demonstrated by her greeting to Wilbur: "'Salutations!' said [Charlotte]. Wilbur jumped to his feet. 'Salu-*what*?' he cried" (35). Believable dialogue is written to fit the speaker's character; otherwise it appears stilted and unnatural.

Tone

Tone refers to the author's mood and manner of expression in a work of literature. For example, the tone may be serious, humorous, satirical, passionate, sensitive, zealous, caustic, indifferent, poignant, warm, agitated, and so on. The tone of a story is revealed through the author's words—and sometimes through what the author does not say. (For example, Beatrix Potter avoids a didactic tone in *The Tale of Peter Rabbit* by *not* having Mrs. Rabbit scold her wayward son or telling him "I told you so.")

HUMOR IN LITERATURE Rare is the child who does not like a funny story—quite often, it is our sense of humor that makes it possible for us to survive in this world. Most scholars agree that incongruity is the foundation of humor—we laugh at the tension resulting from something out of the ordinary. But humor is also elusive; a joke told by one person can be a hoot, but told by someone else can be a complete dud. And humor tends to be age specific; what is funny when we are three is seldom funny when we are twenty-one. Since humor is so pervasive in children's books, it is helpful to look at what children find funny. Katharine Kappas identifies the following ten types of humor most common in books for children from preschool through early adolescence:

1. *Exaggeration*—outlandish overstatement or understatement, a favorite type of American humor as in the tall tales of Sid Fleischman or the Paul Bunyan stories.

2. *Incongruity*—a seeming incompatibility or lack of harmony, such as the pairing of the lean Jack Sprat and his portly wife in the nursery rhyme; one form of incongruity is *irony*, when things are different from what they appear to be. In the tale of "Jack and the Beanstalk," Jack appears to be foolish when he trades his cow for a handful of beans, but his foolishness proves to be wisdom when the magical beans provide him the way to his fortune.

3. *Surprise*—the unexpected, such as the sudden popping of a balloon; the resulting laughter may be a release of tension, like a sigh of relief.

4. *Slapstick*—farcical physical activity or horseplay, such as that found in many children's animated cartoons.

5. *Absurdity*—the absence of reason, which results in a world turned upside down, such as the nonsense of Edward Lear or Lewis Carroll's "Jabberwocky."

6. *Situational Humor*—predicaments in which a character looks foolish or suffers misfortune or discomfort, usually resulting in a feeling of superiority or inferiority, such as Milne's *Winnie-the-Pooh,* where the child reader is obviously intended to feel superior to the rather silly, if lovable, bear and his companions.

7. *Ridicule*—teasing or mocking others for their human weaknesses or differences; *satire* is a sophisticated form of ridicule.

8. *Defiance*—the violation of social conventions or the expression of the forbidden, such as the use of profanity, or Max's retort to his mother, "I'll eat you up," in Sendak's *Where the Wild Things Are.*

9. *Violence*—an action of physical extremes, such as that portrayed in Roald Dahl's controversial works (*Charlie and the Chocolate Factory* and others).

10. *Verbal Humor*—including word play, name-calling, jokes and puns, malapropisms (the unintentional misuse of language), or the misinterpretation of language, such as that in Peggy Parish's books about the silly maid, Amelia Bedelia, who thinks that "drawing the curtains" involves using a pencil and paper. (Kappas, passim.)

Humor can be either sympathetic, as when we laugh with others and not at them, or negative, as when we release hostile emotions. Roald Dahl's books remain controversial largely because his humor results from ridicule, defiance, or violence. However, laughter can be a healthy means of releasing social tension and a way of coping with uncomfortable, out-of-the-ordinary situations. Through laughter we learn to survive. Take, for example, a familiar comic situation: a man steps on a banana peel, his heels go straight up in the air, and he lands on his behind. People laugh at this for several reasons. The movement is incongruous and unexpected, and it contains a touch of slapstick. It also makes the observers feel superior (they weren't the ones who fell), and they are relieved the man was not hurt. One of the important prerequisites for laughter provoked by someone else's misfortune is that the victim must seem to deserve the fate or the harm must not be critical. (The banana peel mishap is funnier if the victim is a pompous bore, but it is not funny if the victim is killed.)

Because it puts everyone on the same human level, laughter becomes the salve of the oppressed, the balm of the weak and vulnerable. And who in our society feels weaker and more vulnerable than the child? It is little wonder children find humor so indispensable to their well-being.

PARODY A parody is a literary imitation of another piece of literature, usually for comic effect. Parody is to literature what cartoon caricature is to art—both exaggerate in order to ridicule. Parody also implies a degree of sophistication; after all, if we are not familiar with the original work, we will not get the joke. Once rare in children's literature, parodies are becoming especially popular in children's picture books. Jon Scieszka's *The True Story of the Three Little Pigs* is a popular retelling of the familiar tale from the Wolf's point of view (he was framed!). Another reversal is found in Eugene Trivizas's *The Three Little Wolves and the Big Bad Pig*, which has a heavy-handed, but very funny, message of nonviolence. And David Wiesner's *The Three Little Pigs* is a sophisticated tale that cleverly deconstructs the story and depicts the characters forming alliances with characters from other nursery stories. Parodies can demonstrate the vitality of literature and can suggest to children new ways of interpreting old tales.

CONDESCENDING TONES Most critics and children would agree that some literary tones are inappropriate for children's stories, and these are the ones that condescend or talk down to young children, placing the adult narrator in a superior position. A *moralizing* or *didactic* tone may be fine for a Sunday morning sermon, but it seldom works in literature for enjoyment. Too often, when an author tries to teach a moral lesson, the other literary features suffer, such as plot credibility or character development. A *sentimental tone* suggests an overindulgence in emotion, often arising from a writer's exaggerated sense of the goodness of human nature. Sentimentalism can lead to condescension in children's books when the author talks down to children as if they were inferior beings. Most children can readily sense this lack of respect. We find sentimentalism in the overly cute portrayals of children in picture books or in the syrupy sweetness of pious children in many eighteenth- and nineteenth-century children's stories. Its opposite is *cynicism,* the notion that human nature is fundamentally corrupt and the world a rotten place to be. In general, the extremes of attitude and behavior are best avoided.

★ LITERARY CRITICISM

Literary criticism is the discussion of literature undertaken in order to interpret its meaning and to evaluate its quality. The purpose of criticism is to promote high standards in literature and to encourage a general appreciation of literature among readers. Literary criticism can focus on the literature as a work of art, on the literature as a personal or social message, on the writer, or on the reader. Here we will look briefly at five common approaches used in children's literature.

Formal Criticism

Formal criticism assumes that the important thing is the text—and the text alone. The formalist critic looks at the literary work itself—its forms, designs, or patterns—and assesses how the work functions as a harmonious whole. Formal criticism makes considerable use of the terminology we have just examined, and formal criticism prefers to categorize literature into kinds or genres—much like this book does.

Let us briefly consider a formal approach to "Hansel and Gretel," the story of the brother and sister abandoned in the woods by their wicked stepmother and wimpy father because they could no longer feed them. Formal criticism would look for the essential unity of the text, perhaps focusing on the rising and falling dramatic action and the building of suspense in the children's overhearing their parents' plotting. The conflict is between the children and the stepmother/witch, who, if they are not the same person, represent the same perverted values and must be defeated in order to resolve the tension. The witch is foreshadowed in the person of the children's stepmother, and we note the sharp contrasts between the two houses—the woodcutter's barren cottage and the witch's delicious home made of gingerbread. All contribute to the unity of the plot.

The formalist might also examine the language, paying special attention to its figurative meaning as it contributes to the artistic whole. In one version of the tale, for example, Gretel, on seeing the witch's gingerbread cottage, says, "It looks good enough to eat," an ironical statement when we consider the witch's intentions.

The strength of formal criticism is that it causes us to read the literature carefully and thoughtfully, and it provides, as suggested above, a common vocabulary for the discussion of literature. But formal criticism generally ignores the interconnectedness of literature, the influence of society on literature, and the importance of the author's individualism. Nor does its rigidity allow for the impact of the reader's personal experiences. For those, we look to other critical approaches.

Archetypal Criticism

The psychologist and physician Carl Gustav Jung (1875–1961) believed in a collective unconscious that lay deep within all of us and contained the "cumulative knowledge, experiences, and images of the entire human race" (Bressler 92). Jung argued that this explains why people the world over respond to the same myths and stories (why we find, for instance, the Cinderella story everywhere from Vietnam to Egypt to northern Europe). Jung identified certain archetypes, which are simply repeated patterns and images of human experience—the changing seasons; the cycle of birth, death, rebirth; the hero and the heroic quest; the beautiful temptress, and so on. Archetypal criticism therefore depends heavily on symbols and patterns operating on a universal scale. Joseph Campbell explores these patterns in his book, *The Hero with a Thousand Faces,* about the nature of the universal hero appearing in cultures around the world.

Some readers, for example, have interpreted the tale of "Little Red Riding Hood" as an *archetypal* narrative of the sun's daily progress across the sky to its final envelopment in the bowels of night. The girl in her red cloak becomes symbolic of the sun and the wolf who devours her as the night. Jungians would argue that this interpretation is valid since these images are part of our collective unconscious and that the stories' creators themselves would not have been fully aware of the symbolic implications of their tales.

The basis of archetypal criticism—whose great champion was Northrop Frye—is that all literature consists of variations on a great mythic cycle within the following pattern:

1. The hero begins life in a paradise (such as a garden)
2. The hero is displaced from paradise (alienation)
3. The hero endures time of trial and tribulation, usually a wandering (a journey)
4. The hero achieves self-discovery as a result of the struggles on that journey
5. The hero returns to paradise (either the original or a new and improved one)

The journey motif is very common in children's stories and usually takes one of two forms: the *linear journey,* where the hero moves away from home, encounters adventures, and eventually finds a new home better than the first, and the *circular journey,* where the hero moves away from home, encounters adventures, and returns home a better person. An example of the linear journey is Cynthia Voigt's *The Homecoming,* about four children seeking their grandmother after being abandoned by their mother. Linear journeys are usually found in books for older readers. More common in children's literature is the circular journey, such as the journey of Potter's Peter Rabbit and of Sendak's Max in *Where the Wild Things Are.* Sometimes the journey is a dream taking place in the psyche of the hero—for Max's journey is a dream, of course. He departs a little monster and returns a little boy, which, we are to understand, is an improvement. The circular journey pattern in "Hansel and Gretel" is obvious, and we see two confident and presumably self-sufficient children returning home.

Archetypal criticism allows us to see the larger patterns of literature, although it tends to ignore the individual contributions of the author and the specific cultural and societal influences.

Historical Criticism

Historical criticism examines the culture and the society from which a literary work came and how these influences affect the literature. Historical criticism asks such questions as these:

1. Who is the author, where did he or she come from, and what was his or her object in writing the work?

2. How did the political events of the time influence what the writer wrote?

3. How did the predominant social customs of the time influence the writer's outlook?

4. What is the predominant philosophy that influenced the work?

5. Were there any special circumstances under which the work was written?

One of the troubling aspects of "Hansel and Gretel" is how parents can be so callous as to abandon their children. We may also want to know the significance of the gingerbread house or why the witch dies in the oven. Because this tale in its present form is of Western European origin, some of these questions can be answered by examining the historical context out of which the tale grew.

In medieval Europe, which is the approximate setting of the tale, numerous factors contributed to widespread famine, and peasants lived on the verge of starvation. The historian Barbara Tuchman writes that during the fourteenth century "reports spread of people eating their own children, of the poor in Poland feeding on hanged bodies taken down from the gibbet" (24). In light of this ghastly information, the tale of "Hansel and Gretel" seems tame indeed. The abandonment of children might not have been so unusual a thing in a society that still did not necessarily condemn infanticide (particularly if the infant was a female). The overwhelming emphasis on food—the children drop breadcrumbs, they are enticed by a gingerbread house from which they eat delicious candies, the witch is killed in her own oven where she had planned to bake Hansel—can be viewed as the product of an age when providing food occupied much of the average person's daily activities.

A knowledge of the historical times in which a piece was written can enrich our understanding of the literature. However, the historical approach often overlooks the literary elements and structure as well as the author's individual contributions.

Psychoanalytical Criticism

A psychoanalytical reading of a text attempts to "offer maps to the unconscious stages of psychic development" (McGillis 77). Based on the work of Sigmund Freud in the early twentieth century, psychoanalytical criticism attempts to explain the reasons for human actions. Freud believed that the motivations for much of our behavior—our fears, our desires, our ambitions—lay hidden in our unconscious. Freud explained in great detail how he believed certain personality types developed—almost always as a result of some childhood experience, good or bad. He further believed that most artists were neurotics who used their art to vent their unconscious anxieties.

The psychoanalytical critic sees a work of literature as the outward expression of an author's unconscious mind, and it becomes the reader's or critic's task to discover the author's hidden fears, desires, and motivations. This type of criticism can coexist comfortably with other types, since it does not bother with either formalist or historical elements.

To examine a work psychoanalytically is to probe the unconscious of the characters, to determine what their actions really reveal about them. The most famous modern example in children's literature of psychoanalytical reading is Bruno Bettelheim's study of folktales, *The Uses of Enchantment* (1976). Here is a brief summary of Bettelheim's psychoanalytical interpretation of "Hansel and Gretel." He interprets the story as a symbolic representation of the child emerging from the developmental stage of oral fixation, and for his support he points to the importance of food in the tale–the children must be abandoned because of lack of food, the children find a gingerbread house that they begin to eat, the house is inhabited by a cannibal witch. Bettelheim sees in Hansel's initial efforts to find his way back home "the debilitating consequences of trying to deal with life's problems by means of regression and denial, which reduce one's ability to solve problems" (160). The return home is seen as denial and regression–literally Hansel's denying that the parents do not want him and his desire to return to the tenuous security of home, and symbolically Hansel's own resistance to moving beyond the oral stage. The gingerbread house, Bettelheim contends, "stands for oral greediness and how attractive it is to give in to it" (161). He goes yet a step further in suggesting that the house is also a symbol of the body, "usually the mother's," and that the children's devouring of the house symbolically represents their nursing. The witch personifies "the destructive aspects of orality" and also represents the threatening mother. On the other hand, the witch has jewels that the children inherit, but only when they have reached a higher stage of development, represented by the wisdom they use in deceiving the witch (by substituting a bone for their own fingers and tricking her into the oven). Bettelheim concludes:

> This suggests that as the children transcend their oral anxiety, and free themselves of relying on oral satisfaction for security, they can also free themselves of the image of the threatening mother–the witch–and rediscover the good parents, whose greater wisdom–the shared jewels–then benefit all. (162)

Bettelheim's analysis is a great deal more complex than this, but such a summary does reveal some of the basic tenets of psychoanalytical criticism.

The most evident danger in all psychoanalytical criticism is in overreading, in seeing a symbol in every object, in seeing unconscious desires and fears lurking in every utterance.

Feminist Criticism

Feminist criticism, an offspring of the feminist movement of the mid-twentieth century, actually combines other critical methods while placing its focus on the questions of how gender affects a literary work, writer, or reader. The feminist approach might ask such questions as these:

1. How are women portrayed in the work? As stereotypes? As individuals?
2. How is the woman's point of view considered?
3. Is male superiority implied in the text?
4. In what way is the work affected because it was written by a woman? or a man?

A major concern of feminist criticism is the masculine bias in literature. Historically, most works (including those written by women) were written from a masculine point of view and for male audiences. Literature has traditionally celebrated the masculine traits and cast aspersion on the feminine. Among the first works to come under attack were the folktales with their stereotypically beautiful, helpless princesses who needed only a good man to set their lives aright and enable them to live happily ever after. The feminist critic looks for the presence of female stereotypes, for example, the woman as the dark-haired, sensuous, submissive *femme fatale*, or as the fair-haired, virginal, plaster saint. If we look again at "Hansel and Gretel," we can see that the feminist critic might object to the portrayal of the woman as either selfish wife or cannibalistic witch. The mother/wife is, on the other hand, simply taking a desperate situation in hand, assuming authority where her ineffectual husband will not. Hansel, the boy, proves equally ineffectual, marking the path with breadcrumbs that are quickly eaten by the birds and then finding himself imprisoned by the witch. It is Gretel who must take the decisive action and rescue them by cleverly deceiving the witch and then killing her. Gretel is, of course, an exception to the rule and refuses to fit into the traditional feminine mold. But the feminist critic looks for societal misconceptions that treat the masculine viewpoint as the norm and the feminine viewpoint as a deviation.

The point here is we need to challenge the way we have traditionally read literature—and that is from the point of view of a male-dominated society. The feminist critic believes that, in the words of Simone de Beauvoir, "One is not born, but rather becomes, a woman." Or, as another critic says, "Feminists do not deny that women exhibit group characteristics. However, they do not accept the thesis that similarities in female behavior are biologically determined" (Register 13). Looking at a literary text from a feminist point of view can enrich a reading, making us aware of the complexity of human interaction. To read a text as a woman, according to some theorists, is to read it with "the skeptical purity of an outcast from culture" (Auerbach 156). To read a text as a woman "means questioning its underlying assumptions about differences between men and women that usually posit women as inferior" (Waxman 150). Feminist criticism therefore ultimately becomes cultural criticism.

Literary criticism is an old preoccupation, going back as far as Aristotle in the fourth century BCE. And ever since Aristotle, it has been the critic's task to study the art of literature, to explore the ways that poems, plays, stories, and novels affect us emotionally, intellectually, and aesthetically. So long as thinking people read, there will be fresh and inventive ways of looking at literature. And all of us become critical readers when we think about and react to what we read. When we begin to analyze the reasons for our responses, when we try to discover why we feel the way we do, when we search for relationships between the works we read, when we draw connections between our reading and our life experiences, then we are responding as informed critics. The results will be reading experiences that bring us both deeper understanding and greater pleasure.

WORKS CITED

Auerbach, Nina. "Engorging the Patriarchy." In *Feminist Issues in Literary Scholarship*. Ed. Shari Benstock. Bloomington: Indiana University Press, 1987: 150–160.

Babbitt, Natalie. *Tuck Everlasting*. New York: Farrar, Straus & Giroux, 1975.

Baum, L. Frank. *The Wizard of Oz*. 1900. Ed. Michael Patrick Hearn. Illus. W. W. Denslow. New York: Schocken, 1983.

Bettelheim, Bruno. *The Uses of Enchantment: The Meaning and Importance of Fairy Tales*. New York: Knopf, 1976.

Bressler, Charles E. *Literary Criticism: An Introduction to Theory and Practice*. Englewood Cliffs, NJ: Prentice-Hall, 1994.

Forster, E. M. *Aspects of the Novel*. New York: Harcourt, Brace, 1954.

Hunt, Peter. *An Introduction to Children's Literature*. Oxford: Oxford University Press, 1994.

Kappas, Katherine H. "A Developmental Analysis of Children's Response to Humor." *The Library Quarterly* 37 (January 1967): 67–77.

MacLachlan, Patricia. *Sarah, Plain and Tall*. New York: Harper & Row, 1985.

Manlove, Colin. *From Alice to Harry Potter: Children's Fantasy in England*. Christchurch, New Zealand: Cybereditions, 2003.

McGillis, Roderick. *The Nimble Reader: Literary Theory and Children's Literature*. New York: Twayne, 1996.

Peck, Richard. *A Long Way from Chicago*. New York: Dial, 1998.

Register, Cheri. "American Feminist Literary Criticism: A Bibliographic Introduction." In *Feminist Literary Criticism: Explorations in Theory*. Ed. Josephine Donovan. Lexington: University of Kentucky Press, 1975: 1–28.

Tuchman, Barbara. *A Distant Mirror: The Calamitous 14th Century*. New York: Knopf, 1978.

Waxman, Barbara Frey. "Feminist Theory, Literary Canons, and the Construction of Textual Meanings." In *Practicing Theory in Introductory College Literature Courses*. Ed. James M. Calahan and David B. Downing. Urbana, IL: National Council of Teachers of English, 1991: 149–160.

White, E. B. *Charlotte's Web*. New York: Harper, 1952.

Wilder, Laura Ingalls. *Little House in the Big Woods*. Illus. Garth Williams. New York: Harper & Row, 1953.

RECOMMENDED READINGS

Campbell, Joseph. *The Hero with a Thousand Faces*. Princeton, NJ: Princeton University Press, 1949.

Cameron, Eleanor. *The Green and Burning Tree*. Boston: Little, Brown, 1969.

——. *The Seed and the Vision: On the Writing and Appreciation of Children's Books*. New York: Dutton, 1993.

Carlson, Ruth Kearney. *Emerging Humanity: Multi-Ethnic Literature for Children and Adolescents*. Dubuque, IA: Wm. C. Brown, 1972.

Cart, Michael. *What's So Funny?: Wit and Humor in American Children's Literature*. New York: HarperCollins, 1995.

Cullinan, Bernice, and Carolyn Carmichael, eds. *Literature and Young Children*. Urbana, IL: National Council of Teachers of English, 1977.

Frye, Northrop. *Anatomy of Criticism*. Princeton: Princeton University Press, 1957.

Hearne, Betsy, and Roger Sutton, eds. *Evaluating Children's Books: A Critical Look.* Urbana: University of Illinois Press, 1993.

Hilkick, Wallace. *Children and Fiction.* Cleveland: World, 1971.

Lukens, Rebecca J. *A Critical Handbook of Children's Literature,* 5th ed. Glenview, IL: Scott, Foresman, 1995.

May, Jill P. *Children's Literature and Critical Theory.* New York: Oxford University Press, 1995.

Nodelman, Perry. *The Pleasures of Children's Literature,* 2nd ed. New York: Longman, 1995.

Otten, Charlotte F., and Gary D. Schmidt, eds. *The Voice of the Narrator in Children's Literature: Insights from Writers and Critics.* New York: Greenwood, 1989.

Purves, Alan C., and Dianne L. Monson. *Experiencing Children's Literature.* Glenview, IL: Scott, Foresman, 1984.

Purves, Alan, et al. *How Porcupines Make Love: Teaching a Response-Centered Literature Curriculum.* White Plains, NY: Longman, 1990.

Rosenblatt, Louise. *The Reader, the Text, and the Poem.* Carbondale: University of Southern Illinois Press, 1978.

Sale, Roger. *Fairy Tales and After: From Snow White to E. B. White.* Cambridge, MA: Harvard University Press, 1978.

Shapiro, Jon, ed. *Using Literature & Poetry Effectively.* Chicago: International Reading Association, 1979.

Shavit, Zohar. *The Poetics of Children's Literature.* Athens: University of Georgia Press, 1986.

Smith, James Steel. *A Critical Approach to Children's Literature.* New York: McGraw-Hill, 1967.

Smith, Lillian. *The Unreluctant Years.* Chicago: American Library Association, 1953 (rpt. Viking, 1967).

Stewig, John Warren, and Sam L. Sebesta, eds. *Using Literature in the Elementary Classroom.* Urbana, IL: National Council of Teachers of English, 1978.

Wolfenstein, Martha A. *Children's Humor: A Psychological Analysis.* Bloomington: Indiana University Press, 1978.

CHAPTER

4

The Literature Experience

The great seventeenth-century philosopher Sir Francis Bacon wrote, "Some books are to be tasted, others to be swallowed, and some few to be chewed and digested." This chapter will suggest ways we as parents and educators can help children taste, swallow, and, in some cases, chew and digest the books they read. And our goal in all this is to help children realize the rich feast awaiting them between the covers of a book.

One of the greatest gifts a parent or teacher can give to a child is a love for reading. This love is usually developed early in life. However, a college student once described to me the summer of his eighteenth year, which he spent in a cabin in the wilderness without electricity or running water. Until that time he had not been a keen reader, but lacking television or video games to entertain him, he turned to books. Since that time, he confessed, "Now I can't read enough." So it's never too late to acquire a love for reading, but we cannot count on young people isolating themselves in the north woods to accomplish this. As adults, we have a responsibility to do whatever we can to encourage reading and instill a passion for books. As with most lessons of life, example is the best teacher. Children are more likely to read if they see the adults around them reading and if books are readily available. Also, there are many exciting ways to promote good reading experiences for children, both at home and in the classroom. This chapter will describe some of those methods, with particular emphasis on the classroom.

LITERATURE-BASED LEARNING

Books should be an integral part of every good preschool and elementary school classroom. The best classrooms are those saturated with books–books on shelves and tables, bulletin-board displays of literature, book-club opportunities by which children can purchase their own books. The entire curriculum can be literature based, with good books integrated into all studies from reading to mathematics to science and social studies. In such a curriculum the practice of reading, both silently and aloud, is part of the daily activities. Additionally, children are given the opportunity to respond to their reading through discussion, writing, drama, arts and crafts, and other means. Simply put, books become an inseparable part of education and an invaluable part of life.

The Reader-Centered Approach to Literature

One of the most popular approaches to using books in the classroom emphasizes the individual as a reader-responder. This approach is based on reader-response criticism, which argues that reading a literary text is part of a complex process that includes a collaboration between the writer (who has a message), the text (consisting of the symbols the writer uses to convey the message), and the reader (who receives the message and embellishes it with his or her own experiences, thoughts, and beliefs). Consequently, a text is re-created every time someone new reads it, and it becomes, in the process, increasingly richer.

The text is no longer an object whose meanings we are supposed to unlock. Rather, the text is a stimulus that elicits responses from us based on our past experiences, our previous reading, our thoughts, and our feelings. Furthermore, each time we reread a text we may feel differently about it than we did before, since the circumstances surrounding the reading are different each time. So the text acts on the reader and the reader interacts with the text (some call this *transaction*, and hence this method is often referred to as *transactional analysis*).

The familiar folktale "Rumpelstilskin" provides an interesting opportunity for a response activity. "Rumpelstilskin," you will remember, is the story of a miller who lied to the king about his daughter's ability to spin straw into gold, the greedy king who promised to marry the daughter if she would spin a roomful of straw into gold each night for a year, and a mysterious dwarfish stranger, Rumpelstilskin, who demands the girl's firstborn child in return for his help. Students could examine their own ethical attitudes by rank-ordering the characters—Rumpelstilskin, the miller, the daughter, the king—according to their ethical behavior. A comparison of student responses often reveals a wide range of attitudes and little general agreement. Each of the characters is likely to be ranked first by some of the respondents and last by others. Often, no agreement can be reached on just who is the hero and who the villain. What explains this discrepancy?

The answer lies in the varying attitudes and value systems the readers bring to the text—attitudes and value systems formulated over a lifetime of experiences, readings, thoughts, and feelings. Some readers, very sensitive to the issue of child abuse, are likely to be horrified at the thought of the daughter bargaining with the life of her own child (and these readers likewise find some sympathy for Rumpelstilskin, whom they believe to be genuinely lonely and in need of human companionship). Others react very negatively toward the miller for his basic dishonesty and the careless way in which he puts his daughter's life in jeopardy, whereas still others say he was simply trying to give his daughter a break in life by arranging for her marriage to the king. Many people regard the king as merely greedy, but some see him as a victim, deceived by the miller and his daughter, and the only character who remains true to his bargain. This exercise causes the readers to evaluate their own ethical beliefs, to prioritize their own values. And as readers share their ideas, they soon discover how difficult it is to establish absolutes—and reader-response critical theory teaches us that there are no absolutes. Such an exercise points out the complexity of human behavior and motivation, the difficulty in ascertaining right and wrong, and the interdependencies involved in any social construct.

Reader-response approaches have proved very popular in the elementary classroom (and they are enormously successful with older readers as well). In *How Porcupines Make Love: Teaching a Response-Centered Literature Curriculum*, Purves, Rogers, and Soter (47) identify four objectives of the reader-centered approach:

1. To encourage individual readers to feel comfortable with their own responses to a literary work
2. To encourage the readers to seek out the reasons for their responses and thereby come to understand themselves better
3. To encourage the readers to recognize, in the responses of others, the differences among people and to respect those differences
4. To encourage readers to recognize, in the responses of others, the similarities among people

Such an approach is not so much an attempt to "teach" literature as it is an effort to bring children and literature together.

In a response-centered approach, we, as adults interested in the interaction of children with books, do a variety of things. Again, Purves, Rogers, and Soter (56) have suggested specific actions that define the role of adults in effecting a successful reading experience in young people. The adult's responsibilities are to:

1. Bring children and books together
2. Give them as many different types of literature as possible
3. Encourage honest and open responses
4. Challenge them to explore those responses and learn something about themselves
5. Provide them with the critical language that they might clearly express their responses
6. Encourage toleration
7. Encourage mutual understanding

The following activities are possible ways for bringing about a connection between children and the books they read. This list is meant to be suggestive, not exhaustive.

READING ALOUD From the parent's gentle singing of a lullaby while rocking an infant to sleep to the reading of such childhood classics as *Alice's Adventures in Wonderland* or *Pinocchio,* sharing literature orally with children can be one of the most fulfilling of human experiences. The relaxing moments of storytime with young children are among the most cherished memories of parenthood. And the times are equally magical when young children want to read the stories to us. Effective reading aloud can be modeled by observing a few guidelines.

1. Read stories you enjoy (unless you are a very good actor and can pretend to like the story). Your own enthusiasm will rub off.

2. Choose stories that are suitable to the children's emotional and social developmental levels. Don't be afraid if the text includes a few challenging words—that never bothers children.

3. Be sure the illustrations in a picture book can be seen easily by everyone. This is easy when you're reading to a single child, but trickier when reading to a class of 25. Breaking a large class into smaller groups can be a help. However, it is most effective if your audience can see the pictures as you are reading—not before or afterwards.

4. Keep the reading experience an interactive one. Depart from the text when it seems necessary. Allow for questions and comments as you read—and you should feel free to ask questions as well.

5. Be sure to pronounce the words correctly. Rehearse your reading and be sure to use the proper inflections, the right tone (some books call for a soothing voice, others require a livelier delivery). If there is dialogue, assume different voices. Children love this.

The reward for you is a grateful and delighted audience—and that is well worth the effort you put into this exercise.

STORYTELLING Storytelling, the art of narrating a tale from memory rather than reading it, is one of the oldest of all art forms, reaching back to prehistoric times. Through storytellers, virtually all the traditional folktales were preserved for centuries, most having been committed to paper only in the past two or three centuries. Storytelling involves two elements—selection and delivery. First, a successful storyteller chooses good stories; most prepare a repertoire of stories, often specializing in certain types of stories such as tall tales, tales of a specific culture or region, and so on. Second, a successful storyteller is also a performer, for the delivery is crucial and requires both preparation and rehearsal.

Folktales are natural sources for storytellers. They include easily memorized patterns and ample dialogue to enliven the story, and they are brief enough to be relayed in a single sitting. Also, they lend themselves well to adaptation, so the storyteller can adjust the tale to the audience. Some storytellers like to create their own tales, sometimes from their own experiences, or they may adapt stories. Regardless of their source, stories work best when they gradually build to a climax and quickly end while the audience's interest is still at a peak.

Of course, a rich, mellifluous voice is an asset to any would-be storyteller. If you don't have such a voice, develop some other assets—effective body movement, facial expressions, eye contact, clear enunciation, meaningful inflection, and appropriate pauses. And, with practice, you can develop a greater vocal range and a voice that will project. Much of the storyteller's skill derives from knowing how to pace the telling, when to slow down, when to speed up, when to talk in near whispers, when to shout, and so on. For the storyteller, movement on a staging area can be significant. Natural body gestures (and at times even exaggerated ones, depending on the nature of the story) and direct eye contact help to engage the audience totally. Finally, don't be afraid to ham it up. This is no time to be shy.

BOOK DISCUSSIONS One of the most common classroom approaches to literature is the book discussion, which, if successful, will go beyond a simple series of questions from the teacher and the expected "correct" answers from the students. A good book discussion requires serious preparation (see Figure 4.1). Also, a good book discussion evolves and metamorphoses as it proceeds. Be sure that you are well prepared before beginning the book discussion. This means not only reading the book carefully, but also finding out what other readers (including critics) have said. Prepare visual stimulants, such as photographs of the author, a story map of the plot (see the section on webbing and mapping), a time line (if it seems appropriate), charts, posters, Powerpoint presentations, and anything else that might give young readers some useful insight. Integral to most book discussions are the questions posed by the leader, and questions can be posed to elicit varying levels of responses. The following levels of questions progress from least to most sophisticated.

Memory Questions. At the first level, *memory* or *factual questions* ask the audience to recall facts from the story or poem: plot incidents, character identifications, details of the setting, and so on. It is good to begin a discussion with memory questions because they can help determine if the readers understand the basic elements of the work.

An example of a good memory question might be, "In Beatrix Potter's *The Tale of Peter Rabbit,* what happened to Peter's father?" The answer to this question has a direct bearing on the theme of the story, since it shows that Peter was aware of the dangers of entering Mr. McGregor's garden. In a discussion of E. B. White's *Charlotte's Web,* for example, we may begin with memory questions such as these: "Why was Wilbur's life in danger?" "How did Fern save Wilbur?" "How did Charlotte save Wilbur?" and "How did Wilbur repay Charlotte?" All these questions can be answered from a reading of the book, and all have some thematic significance. It would be unproductive to ask such questions as "How large was Wilbur?" or "What was Charlotte's oldest child's name?" These details have little bearing on the story, and there is no reason to expect a reader to recall trivia. Memory questions designed to trick the careful reader serve no purpose.

FIGURE 4.1   Sample Outline For Leading a Classroom Book Discussion

---

Preparation (before the Discussion)

Leader(s) should read the book, gather background materials, and plan:

- Read book reviews, critical studies, or other information relating to the book.
- Research the author's background (consult *Something About the Author, The Dictionary of Literary Biography*, a biography, etc.).
- Peruse other works by the same author, other literary works with similar themes, and nonfiction works on the same general subject.
- Plan the exploration (from the suggestions below, from other ideas in this chapter, and/or from Figure 4.4–*Twenty-Five Things to Do with a Book*).

Exploration (during the Discussion)

Leader(s) may select from the following options:

- Share a story map, a time line, or other visual aids to illustrate the plot and/or the theme.
- Pose interpretation, application, and critical evaluation questions to the entire class or to small groups, and explore the responses in depth (small groups may be used to encourage broader participation, and the small groups can report to the class as a whole).
- Share significant book passages to focus on the setting, characters, theme, and so on.
- Present a dramatic interpretation (readers' theater, story theater, etc.) of an important scene and discuss its meaning.
- Share a web that illustrates the growth of the main character.

Application (after the Discussion)

Leader(s) may offer selections from the following options:

- Create an artistic response to the book (diorama, mobile, map, collage, etc.).
- Compose a written response to the story (a new ending, a news article, a review, a radio promotion, etc.).
- View a film version (if available) or a film about a related theme.

Interpretation Questions. The second level of questioning consists of interpretation questions, which require the readers to make inferences and draw conclusions from the facts of the story or poem. These questions may require analysis (lifting individual facts from the story and examining them carefully) or synthesis (putting together disparate facts in a new way). "Why does Peter's mother not punish him for his disobedience?" might be a good interpretation question, for it will lead into a discussion of one of the major ideas of the story. For *Charlotte's Web*, we might ask such questions as these: "How does the relationship between Fern and Wilbur change over the course of the book?" and "How does Wilbur's character change from the beginning to the end of the book?" In any case, it is important that readers understand that any conclusions they draw be based soundly on the evidence found in the work itself. Personal opinions should be supported by specific details from the text.

Application Questions. The third level of questioning is that of application. These questions ask the readers to consider the work in a larger context, and they tend to focus on further extensions of the theme as well as on matters of style, imagery, symbolism, and so on. Application refers to the transfer of information acquired from the literary work to another experience (one's own life, for example, or another literary work). After hearing the story of *The Tale of Peter Rabbit,* children might be asked to discuss a time when they were in a situation similar to Peter's. While discussing *Charlotte's Web,* students might be asked, "In what ways do Templeton, Charlotte, and Wilbur remind you of people you know?" Application questions should ultimately help us to see the relationships between literature and life and should, when possible, ask us to draw on our own experiences. Here is where the personal response to literature comes into play. These questions can result in some of the more meaningful and exciting discussions.

Evaluation Questions. Ultimately, we may bring readers to the fourth level of questioning, which involves critical evaluation, but these must be reserved for older, more experienced readers. It is not realistic to expect the very young to read on this level, but with older children we might ask, "Compare *Charlotte's Web* with Kenneth Grahame's *The Wind in the Willows* or with Robert Lawson's *Rabbit Hill.*" "How are they alike?" "How are they different?" "Which most believable and why?" "Compare *Charlotte's Web* with another of E. B. White's fantasies–*Stuart Little* or *Trumpet of the Swan.*" "What similarities do you see?" "What differences?" "If you prefer one over another, why?" Asking young readers which of two books they prefer is useful only if we can get them to articulate their reasons and thereby help them to understand their own tastes a little better. This is also the beginning of the acquisition of critical taste and judgment. It is good to remember that with most interpretation and evaluation questions, there are no clear wrong or right answers, only answers that are more convincingly supported than others.

Writing Experiences

As early as second grade, most children are capable of responding to literature through writing, and certainly by the time they reach the middle elementary grades, children should be writing as a regular part of their total curriculum. Several possibilities are available at all grade levels.

WEBBING AND MAPPING Webbing is a visual means of demonstrating relationships between story elements or concepts. A *web* consists of a figure (the simplest resembles a spider's web, which is where the term comes from) on which labels are placed showing the connections between aspects of a literary work. For example, the web in Figure 4.2 illustrates the ways in which the principal characters in the folktale *Cinderella* are opposites. Any visual

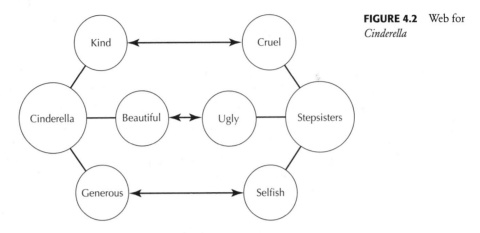

FIGURE 4.2 Web for *Cinderella*

representation is a potential tool for webbing or mapping a story. The petals of a flower, the steps of a stairway, the points of a star, the branches of a tree are just some of the images that can be used to demonstrate the connections in a work of literature. And if the web is truly successful, the image itself makes a statement. For example, we might label the petals of a flower with a character's personality traits to show how the individual grows (or "blossoms") throughout the course of a story. Since many people are visual learners and grasp ideas more quickly if they can see them illustrated, webbing is an effective tool for examining relationships in a poem, story, or play. Virtually any aspect of literature can be applied to a web—character development, symbols, imagery, themes. Very similar to a web, a *story map* charts the progress of the plot in a visual manner. Figure 4.3 is a very simple story map illustrating the circular journey of Hansel and Gretel from their home to the witch's cottage and back. The

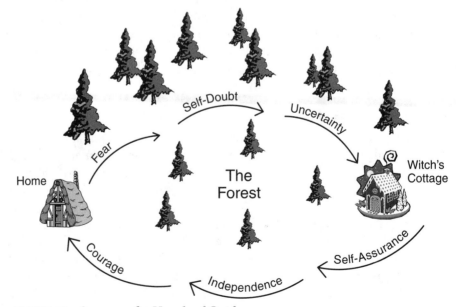

FIGURE 4.3 Story map for *Hansel and Gretel*

labels suggest possible character development that might occur in the children along the way. In addition to being a useful instructional tool, a webbing exercise can be fun for children to create.

RESPONSE JOURNALS When we have to commit our ideas to writing, we are compelled to think them through more thoroughly. A response journal, in which young readers can freely record their feelings, is an easy way to add this written dimension to their reading experience.

Sharing journals can also be a rewarding experience. Students can share journal entries with others, who can then write back to them their own responses. One way to do this is to draw a line down the middle of the page, with the original writer using the left-hand side and the respondent using the right-hand side. It can also be done by using facing pages in a spiral-ring notebook. Teachers (and parents or other adults) can also be respondents. Of course, writers should be told at the outset if they will be asked to share their journals, for journal writing can be a very private affair. Journal writing is most effective when it is habitual and when the individual entries are long enough to explore ideas and feelings.

BOOK REPORTS: VARIATIONS ON AN OLD THEME Many exciting projects can replace the old "book report," which was often a dull exercise in which the reader summarized the plot of the book (see Figure 4.4). Children may enjoy making up their own endings to stories, for example, or writing new episodes with their favorite characters: Peggy Parrish's Amelia Bedelia series or Beverly Cleary's Ramona books can provide starting points for younger readers. Newspaper stories based on events in books can also be fun to write: Roald Dahl's *James and the Giant Peach* and *Charlie and the Chocolate Factory* offer some interesting possibilities here. Some children may enjoy reading and writing about the life of a favorite author. Some may wish to write open letters to authors, living or dead, to share their own attitudes and opinions about a book. The letters do not need to be mailed. Beverly Cleary's *Dear Mr. Henshaw* describes the therapeutic value of letter writing, even though the letters are not mailed. Writing the imaginary diary of a fictional character can help children understand the concept of point of view. Children might create a story from their own life experiences, which can help them gain firsthand knowledge of plot. Script-writing, in which children must devise dialogue for characters, can enrich their understanding of language differences, characterization, and setting.

One final word on the book report. Sometimes it is very useful to give children the opportunity to be book reviewers for the class—some may be familiar with film reviews on television. The opinions of their peers tend to carry far more weight with children than the opinions of adults. The success of the Harry Potter books had as much to do with the enthusiastic word of mouth from child to child as it did with clever marketing by adults.

CREATING BOOKS Making their own books is a rewarding activity for children of all ages. Very young children can create alphabet, counting, or concept books, or do take-offs on favorite nursery rhymes or poems. Older children may want to experiment with ghost stories, adventure stories, family stories, or poetry. Of course, much of the fun lies in illustrating

FIGURE 4.4   Twenty-five Things to Do with a Book

1. Create a story map for the book.

2. Prepare a two-minute radio spot promoting the book.

3. Write a biographical sketch of the author.

4. Turn one chapter into a child's picture book.

5. Create a collage or montage emphasizing the plot or theme.

6. Write a three- or four-paragraph book review for the local newspaper.

7. Create a dust jacket for the book.

8. Make a list of your ten favorite things about the book.

9. Create a poster advertising the book.

10. Write a defense for the villain's actions.

11. Pick a favorite scene or chapter and prepare a dramatic reading.

12. Create a diorama of your favorite scene.

13. Create a mobile or stabile representing the theme or a character.

14. Make a cast list of well-known actors for a film of the book.

15. Create a geographical map of the setting based on evidence from the book.

16. Prepare a time line for events in the story.

17. Write a news article reporting on an event in the story, as if it just happened.

18. Write a new episode for the book using the same characters.

19. Create a bulletin board display to entice others to read the book.

20. Rewrite an episode from a different point of view.

21. Write a poem about the book.

22. Create a web illustrating the interactions of the main characters.

23. Rewrite a scene to include yourself as a new character.

24. Write a fictional biographical sketch of your favorite character.

25. Rewrite one chapter as a one-act play.

the books, and a variety of media can be used—crayon, watercolor, collage, montage, pencil, and so on. Individuals can write their own books, or, if the budget permits, an anthology of stories, poems, or illustrations created by the children can be assembled and duplicated for everyone.

Binding the books can be as simple as fastening them in a loose-leaf folder or as elaborate as sewing the leaves and making cloth-covered cardboard covers. Not only does this project give children firsthand experiences in designing books and laying out pages, it can also result in an attractive finished product that is fit for a gift or a keepsake. Such a project is a rewarding way of bringing a writing exercise to a satisfying climax.

Dramatic Responses to Literature

Dramatic responses to literature offer opportunities for individual creativity and cooperative achievement. It is often difficult to find suitable plays for elementary children, but most of the following dramatic exercises can be adapted to folktales or to chapters from favorite books.

ORAL INTERPRETATION Oral interpretation usually consists of a single individual presenting a poem or brief prose passage—usually memorized—in a dramatic way, with voice modulations and meaningful gestures. This can be a bit sophisticated for elementary children, but certainly by the middle or upper elementary grades, children can be asked to recite humorous poems (and later, serious poems or passages). Memorization has been given, unjustly, a bad name—probably by well-meaning teachers who forced their students to memorize the teacher's favorite poem. Children have no trouble memorizing things that interest them. Allow them to choose their favorite poems or stories and reserve some time for sharing these—to break the ice, you might begin with your own favorites. If possible, move everyone into a circle to make it seem less like a classroom and more like an intimate gathering around a campfire. Keep it purely voluntary. Make this a regular feature in the classroom. In time, most children will participate and many will look forward to their moment in the limelight. This can be a very pleasant way to nurture a love of the spoken word and the rhythms of language.

STORY THEATER Story theater is a pantomime accompanied by a narrator who reads or tells the story while others act out the plot. Since even inanimate objects (such as a tree) might be portrayed by an actor, story theater allows for a very flexible number of performers (some children may enjoy the idea of portraying objects like the moon, for example). The performance can be as simple or elaborate as the means dictate. Pantomime, because it does not require line memorizing, is one of the least threatening dramatic forms for children. It does require one good reader, however, and some uninhibited actors. Since the youngest children tend to be the least inhibited, story theater is a good exercise to begin in the early elementary years. The best tales for a story theater presentation are those with plenty of action; otherwise the pantomimists would be little more than furniture. Many folktales are good sources for story theater, particularly the farcical tales, such as "Clever Gretel," where action rather than dialogue dominates. Story theater is a great way to introduce play production with costumes, scenery, and props.

READER'S THEATER Reader's theater, as the name implies, involves the reading of a script as opposed to acting it out. The participants assume various speaking roles in a story–usually one reader for each speaking character and one narrator to read the exposition. True reader's theater is traditionally performed without any action whatever, with the readers sitting on chairs and using only their voices to convey meaning. The old-time radio dramas were, in essence, reader's theater. All the audience's attention is directed to the language, so the readers must be expressive and read with clarity and precision. To avoid distraction from the reading, performers in most reader's theater wear nondescript but uniform clothing–usually in black or black and white. Since no memorization, physical movement, scenery, or properties are involved, reader's theater provides a convenient and affordable outlet for self-expression. The best reader's theater stories are those with several speaking parts, ample dialogue, a fairly easy vocabulary but with expressive language, and, finally, a good conflict. "Hansel and Gretel" might be adapted easily for reader's theater, since it includes several engaging parts.

CREATIVE DRAMATICS Creative dramatics is the dramatization of a story with improvised dialogue. This allows children to perform their own versions of stories without strict adherence to a script–although in creative dramatics, the actors are expected to remain faithful to the story line. This activity requires considerable preparation and may be as elaborate in setting, properties, and theatrical accoutrements as the director desires. Creative dramatics can be less threatening than a more traditional play, since no one has to memorize lines. It also allows for improvisation. One of the great advantages of creative dramatics is that many folktales and other short stories or even chapters from favorite books (e.g., *Winnie-the-Pooh* or *The Wind in the Willows*) can be readily adapted to its form.

ROLE-PLAYING Role-playing is similar to creative dramatics, but it removes us one step further from the literary source. The actors assume specific character roles and are expected to invent not only the dialogue but the action as they proceed. Typically, individuals are assigned character roles, a problem is posed, and, through improvised dialogue and action, the role players arrive at a solution. The experience requires an examination of the issues from varying points of view. Role-playing is a way to extend literature and to explore personal and social values. Children, for example, could be assigned the roles of various fictional characters (such as those from Cleary's Ramona books), and they could then be presented with a dilemma to solve. It is important that each assigned role is a distinct personality type who will respond appropriately as the personality suggests. This exercise requires deductive reasoning and, as with many of the dramatic responses we have discussed, works best with children in the middle or upper elementary grades.

PUPPET THEATER Combining both dramatic and artistic responses to literature, puppet theater is a favorite medium of children. Puppet making is an elaborate and time-honored art form, and one in which children of most ages can readily participate. Puppets can be made from old socks, paper bags, construction paper and sticks, cardboard cylinders, vegetables (they make wonderful puppets, but don't wait too long to do the show), or, for the truly creative, string-operated marionettes with movable hands, feet, eyes, and mouths. The puppet theater itself can be as simple as a table draped with a sheet to hide the puppeteers. Large appliance boxes open up many possibilities. Once the puppet is made, the dramatic part of the experience begins. Stories with ample dialogue and action work best. And, since lines need not be memorized and the puppeteers are hidden from the audience's view, puppet theater can be an ideal form for beginning thespians. It is also perfect for shy children who, behind the mask of the puppet, may find an exhilarating outlet for their deepest feelings.

Artistic Responses to Literature

Another popular means of extending literature is through art. As soon as they can handle a crayon or pencil, even the youngest children can be asked to draw pictures in response to a story. Art can enrich the literary experience in many ways. A few of the more widely used methods will be discussed briefly here.

THE GRAPHIC ARTS Children love working with paints, watercolors, crayons, and pencils. Drawings and paintings require the simplest of art supplies and minimal initial instruction, yet they allow for a great deal of originality. Having children draw pictures suggested by picture storybooks can be a means of getting them to explore different artistic styles, such as Maurice Sendak's impressionism in Charlotte Zolotow's *Mr. Rabbit and the Lovely Present,* Beatrix Potter's delicate representational style in *The Tale of Peter Rabbit,* or Ludwig Bemelmans's expressionism in *Madeline.* Encouraging children to draw pictures after hearing stories read to them can result in some of the most highly individualistic creations, for they do not have another artist's work to imitate.

For those who have limited graphic skills, a collage or montage is a viable alternative. A *collage* is a picture created from nonpainterly materials (cloth, wood, cotton, leaves, rocks, and so on), which are typically fixed to a posterboard to make a unified work. Quite similar is the *montage,* which is composed entirely of pictures (cut from magazines, newspapers, and so on). Creating a collage or a montage about a favorite story can be both enjoyable and enlightening, since it requires a certain amount of synthesis and analysis. Posters can be made to represent a theme, a character, plot details, or even mood, using the collage or montage method.

THE PLASTIC ARTS The plastic arts include the three-dimensional, nonpainterly works, such as sculpture and pottery. Figures made from clay or from paper cutouts or wood can represent story characters or objects. *Mobiles* are free forms usually cut from paper or cardboard and interconnected and suspended by string or wire so that when hung they turn freely in the breeze. A mobile can demonstrate ingeniously the relationships between plot elements or characters of a story. One popular art form used widely in the classroom is the *diorama,* a three-dimensional scene often created from a shoe box or other carton (an unused fish aquarium, with its glass sides, provides some interesting opportunities as well) and decorated with cardboard cutouts, plastic figures, or other suitable objects. By a further extension of the diorama, children can create miniature stages and puppet figures with which to re-enact a story, thus combining an artistic and a dramatic response to literature. A natural development of the miniature stage is for the children to create stories of their own to dramatize. The diorama requires attention to detail, which is why this form is used so frequently for social studies projects, asking students to create a diorama of the Ice Age or of Colonial America and so on.

Regardless of the art project, it is important to remember that the art is an extension of the literature and not an end in itself. In other words, we are not reading *Pinocchio* for the purpose of making our own puppet when we are finished. And the art should not be simply gratuitous—"Now that we have read *Pinocchio,* let's all draw a picture of his nose." The art project should become a meaningful part of the study of the literature, helping children to understand and appreciate the literature.

CHILDREN'S LITERATURE AND FILM

In our media-driven age, classroom teachers are often seduced into using film adaptations of books, sometimes in lieu of spirited book discussions. Showing a film is, after all, an easy way out, and many educators find it difficult to compete with the glitzy performances children see every day on television and videos.

Film adaptations of literary sources have been standard since the beginning of the cinema, and inevitable comparisons between the film and the book are made. But these are two distinctly different art forms, and the techniques of one do not always translate satisfactorily to the other. It is possible to be charmed by the visual splendor and music of Walt Disney's *Snow White and the Seven Dwarfs* (1937) and fully recognize that Disney has not been very faithful to the folktale. One critic said of Disney, "[he persevered] in his belief that a children's amusement was an endlessly adaptable form that was fully capable of encompassing whatever the human mind could imagine" (Giannetti and Eyman 231). Nevertheless, many critics lament the saccharine sentimentalism that too often creeps into films for children, including many of the animated films of Disney (see Sayers and Weisenberg). Equally sentimental are the popular films from the 1930s of Shirley Temple, who starred in numerous cinematic versions of classic children's stories, including Laura Richards's *Captain January,* Kate Douglas Wiggins's *Rebecca of Sunnybrook Farm,* Frances Hodgson Burnett's *The Little Princess,* and Johanna Spyri's *Heidi.*

Readers often lament a book's translation into film, for usually the plot must be telescoped and characters and scenes omitted in order to fit the tale into an appropriate cinematic time frame. In many cases, the spirit of the original literature is sacrificed when adapted to film, and the story becomes something else. However, the result is not always detrimental. One film that is often considered an improvement over the book is MGM's 1939 version of *The Wizard of Oz.* The film script is markedly different from L. Frank Baum's

The Wonderful Wizard of Oz, which tends to ramble, lacks fundamental coherence, and is at times tedious. The film, by contrast, is quite unified, particularly in its use of the dream device wherein the characters in Kansas become characters in Dorothy's dream of Oz. Some would argue that making the story a dream—which Baum did not do—cheats young audiences out of the chance to believe in the magic. (Even as adults, we may feel cheated if we learn that the story and the characters in which we have invested so much time are nothing but a dream.) But the cinematic version, with its endearing characters, clearly focused plot, and memorable music, remains among the best loved films of all time.

A modern film surely destined to become a classic is *Babe* (Universal Studios), based on Dick King-Smith's *Babe, the Gallant Pig.* This live-action film uses both live animals and extraordinarily lifelike puppets, along with human characters. The story itself is a talking animal fantasy about a pig raised by a sheep dog. The original book is a slender volume, and in this case the film actually adds characters and scenes—most notable is the addition of a neurotic duck who creates havoc for Babe. Several of the books of Patricia MacLachlan have been transformed into made-for-television movies, the best-known being *Sarah* (Hallmark Hall of Fame), based on her Newbery Award-winning *Sarah, Plain and Tall.* As with *Babe,* the story had to be fleshed out for the film. Characters and episodes were added, but perhaps the most important change was a shift from the first-person narrator of the book to an omniscient narrator in the film. Whereas the book is clearly intended for an audience of fourth or fifth graders, the film aims at a broader television audience, one including adults as well as children. The film adaptations of J. K. Rowling's Harry Potter books have proved quite faithful to the original stories, largely because the books themselves have been so widely read and loved that audiences would doubtless have rebelled if they had been altered drastically.

In all film adaptations, one element that is usually sacrificed is much of the original language. Filmmakers often use a book's dialogue—sometimes word-for-word—but the exposition must be accomplished through visual imagery, through a narrator's voice-over, or through further dialogue. What we lose, then, are the author's original words, which are, or ought to be, the strength of the book in the first place. The point is that film is an entirely different medium from literature, neither better nor worse. It is sometimes useful to compare the film adaptation with the book, but the purpose should be to show varying points of view or different artistic techniques, not to show which is superior. Books can be fairly compared only to other books, films only to other films.

Perhaps our greatest concern should be whether cinema and television are substituting for reading. That is almost certainly the case. That children are not reading as much as they should presents some danger. Vast numbers of Americans are functionally illiterate and cannot read even supermarket labels. We have all heard stories such as a man mistakenly purchasing a can of vegetable shortening thinking it contained the cookies pictured on the label. We are becoming a world dependent on visual images and sound bites. Television with its rapid-fire commercial messages interrupting equally fast-paced programs every seven to ten minutes seems to have created a society that is both restless and easily bored. The pleasures of curling up with a good book and spending an evening of leisurely reading are lost to so many.

Before we leave this subject, one final distinction should be made between the cinema and literature. Film controls our imaginations: it shows what the characters look like (which may not be as we had pictured them), it tells what parts of the story the director thought important (they may not have been our favorite parts). Books allow us to exercise much more imaginative freedom. A book requires that we think, and that is the great advantage to reading.

CHILDREN'S BOOKS AND CENSORSHIP

Censorship is the act of regulating art or literature judged to be too sensitive or harmful—usually on political, social, religious, or moral grounds. The censor believes that art and literature possess the power to corrupt. The censor further believes that he or she is qualified to make judgments on behalf of society.

Censorship has been practiced since the earliest civilizations and it has been a tool used widely by despots in an attempt to stamp out any ideas that they perceive as threatening to their existence. The censor acts out of ignorance, insecurity, and fear. It should not be surprising to discover that many of those who seek to ban a particular book have never actually read it and those who wish to ban certain films or artworks do not understand them. If we are comfortable in our own beliefs, we generally need not feel threatened by contradictory beliefs. For example, anti-gay and anti-lesbian protestors are sometimes people who are insecure about their own sexuality.

What is disturbing in our own society—a society that never tires of touting its belief in freedom—is that it is quite often too eager to embrace censorship. Too many of our citizens find literature threatening because it dares to suggest new ideas, fresh points of view, and opposing opinions. (It is no coincidence that most dictators are famous book burners—they don't want their people exposed to new or contradictory ideas.) It is sadly ironic that many of those who are passionately patriotic are also the very ones who threaten our freedom of speech as guaranteed by the U.S. Constitution's First Amendment.

Censorship has been particularly pervasive in children's literature, which may be the result of the natural inclination to protect childhood innocence. In the United States, censorship has been widespread and, sometimes, rather indiscriminate. We have seen folktales tidied up and rid of anything that adults find unpleasant, and the result has been boring stories. We have also seen the banning of such books as E. B. White's *Charlotte's Web* (certain fundamental religious groups object to stories with talking animals because they are contrary to God's creation), William Steig's *Sylvester and the Magic Pebble* (Steig portrayed the police as pigs in this animal fantasy—an innocent choice, but unfortunate during the radical turmoil of the 1970s), Robert Cormier's *I Am the Cheese* (too negative), and J. D. Salinger's *The Catcher in the Rye* (too many four-letter words). And the list goes on.

Those who think that removing offensive books from the shelves will preserve their children's youthful innocence are kidding themselves. Children are going to grow up—with or without help from adults. Regulating children's reading throughout censorship will not protect them from the seamier side of life. In fact, censoring books almost always backfires. The quickest way to make a book popular is to ban it. Of course, I am not suggesting that as teachers it is our duty to expose young children to stories of pornography, unrestrained violence, or seditious ideas. Most intelligent people agree that some subjects and approaches require mental and emotional maturity. It would be foolish to share a story about a teenage girl's first menstrual cycle with a preschooler. On the other hand, many preschoolers have had to deal with deaths in the family, child abuse, divorce, and other traumas. So it is not unreasonable to think that many of them have some experience in these areas and they may benefit from well-written books on these subjects. Common sense is every educator's best asset.

Unfortunately, common sense is not always enough to avoid trouble. In 1998, a young, well-meaning elementary teacher was forced from her job because she shared Carolivia Herron's *Nappy Hair,* a picture book containing the rollicking story of an African-American girl with "the kinkiest, that nappiest, the fuzziest, the most screwed up, squeezed up, knotted up, tangled up, twisted up" hair (see Clemetson and Martin). The teacher found herself in the midst of a whirlwind of irate parents who mistakenly thought the book was racially insensitive, making fun of African Americans. Of course, none of the complaining parents had actually read the book and none knew that the author herself was a distinguished African-American professor. Nor did they know the book had been on recommended reading lists throughout the country. Nor did it matter that few of the complaining parents actually had children in the teacher's classroom. Nor did it seem to matter that the children in the class—most of whom were African American or Hispanic—loved the book. As so often happens in such cases, the school administration buckled under public pressure and fired the teacher. When all the evidence finally came out, the school attempted to bring back the teacher, who had been very popular with the students—but she wisely declined their invitation.

The pattern is all too familiar. A small, but very vocal minority—often ill informed and poorly educated themselves—manage to impose their will on feckless school administrators. Censors are dangerous because they threaten our intellectual freedom and jeopardize the fundamental tenets of a democratic society. The writers of the Declaration of Independence and of the Constitution of the United States would be horrified at the thought of these attempts to suppress ideas and points of view.

One of the subtler, but no less egregious, forms of censorship in America today is the censorship of school textbooks. In many states, committees of people—usually not educators—exert tremendous influence on the choice of textbooks and are able to further self-serving agendas, usually political or religious. (See Ravitch's *The Language Police*.)

Teachers are, in many ways, the guardians of our intellectual freedom, and this charge must be taken seriously and not tainted by poor judgment or foolhardiness. (See Figure 4.5 for a guide to combating censorship and preserving intellectual freedom in our schools.) One place to turn for help is the National Coalition Against Censorship, an organization dedicated to protecting free speech, particularly in the classroom. The Coalition's Web site is a good place to go to keep abreast of current censorship issues.

As teachers or parents we should never compromise our standards and surrender to fear and ignorance. Books can stimulate thinking, suggest new possibilities, and challenge old attitudes—and these are the very things that some people find threatening. Interestingly, most people who favor censorship do so on the premise that they are protecting established

FIGURE 4.5   A Brief Guide to Preserving Intellectual Freedom in the Classroom

1. **Know your rationale for using a book in the classroom. Answer these questions:**
   - Is the book appropriate for this age level?
   - Does the book meet your objectives in the class, and how?
   - Does the book appear on recommended lists, and what have been the reactions of critics?
   - What possible objections could be raised to the book—language, tone, theme, subject matter—and how can you best address these objections?
   - As a last resort, what alternative readings can you offer in place of this book?

2. **Have guidelines for handling community and parental objections. Carefully organized procedures can do much to stem the tide of emotionalism. Include the following:**
   - A complaint form on which specific objections are to be recorded
   - A clearly designated procedure for dealing with the complaint
   - A broad-based committee of teachers, administrators, and community representatives for hearing the complaints
   - A clear philosophical statement articulating the school's educational principles

3. **Join with other teachers and the administration to protect students' right to read (and the teachers' right to teach).**

4. **Actively support other teachers when they encounter censorship challenges.**

5. **Educate the community about the importance of intellectual freedom.**
   - Write letters or articles for the local newspaper.
   - Lobby the school board members and other community leaders.
   - Conduct or sponsor community workshops on censorship

6. **Keep informed about censorship issues through professional journals, reports, association meetings, and new media.**

values. But without the kind of challenges offered through books, society's values begin to stagnate and weaken. If we never question our values and our way of life, we will eventually lose sight of what is really important. We should never be afraid of challenges to our thoughts and values—those challenges will only make us stronger.

WORKS CITED

Clemetson, Lynette. "Caught in the Cross-Fire." *Newsweek* 14 December 1998: 38–39.

Giannetti, Louis, and Scott Eyman. *Flashback: A Brief History of Film.* Englewood Cliffs, NJ: Prentice-Hall, 1986.

Martin, Michelle H. "Never Too Nappy." *The Horn Book Magazine* April/May 1999: 283–288.

Purves, Alan, et al. *How Porcupines Make Love: Teaching a Response-Centered Literature Curriculum.* White Plains, NY: Longman, 1990.

Sayers, Frances Clarke, and Charles M. Weisenberg. "Walt Disney Accused." *Horn Book Magazine* 40 (December 1965): 602–611.

RECOMMENDED READINGS

Aquino, John. *Fantasy in Literature.* Washington, DC: National Education Association, 1977.

Barton, Bob, and David Booth. *Stories in the Classroom.* Portsmouth, NH: Heinemann, 1991.

Bauer, Caroline Feller. *This Way to Books.* Bronx, NY: Wilson, 1982.

Blatt, Gloria T., ed. *Once Upon a Folktale: Capturing the Folklore Process with Children.* New York: Teachers College Press, 1993.

Bosma, Betty. *Fairy Tales, Fables, Legends, and Myths: Using Folk Literature in Your Classroom.* 2nd ed. New York: Teachers College Press, 1996.

Bromley, Karen D'Angelo. *Webbing with Literature: Creating Story Maps with Children's Books.* 2nd ed. New York: Simon & Schuster, 1995.

Bruno, Janet, and Peggy Dakan. *Cooking in the Classroom.* Belmont, CA: Fearon Pitman, 1974.

Chambers, Aidan. *Introducing Books to Children.* 2nd ed. Boston: Horn Book, 1983.

Cioni, Alfred J., ed. *Motivating Reluctant Readers.* Newark, DE: International Reading Association, 1981.

Coody, Betty. *Using Literature with Young Children,* 5th ed. Dubuque, IA: Brown and Benchmark, 1996.

Currell, David. *The Complete Book of Puppetry.* Boston: Plays, 1975.

Hanford, Robert Ten Eyck. *Puppets and Puppeteering.* New York: Sterling, 1981.

Leonard, Charlotte. *Tied Together: Topics and Thoughts for Introducing Children's Books.* Metuchen, NJ: Scarecrow, 1980.

MacDonald, M. R. *The Storyteller's Sourcebook: A Subject, Title and Motif Index to Folklore Collections for Children.* Detroit, MI: Heal-Schuman, 1982.

McCaslin, N. *Creative Drama in the Classroom.* 7th ed. New York: Pearson, 1999.

National Coalition Against Censorship, 275 Seventh Avenue, New York, NY 10001. http://www.ncac.org.

Pellowski, Ann. *The Storytelling Handbook: A Young People's Collection of Unusual Tales and Helpful Hints on How to Tell Them.* New York: Simon & Schuster, 1995.

Raines, Shirley, and Rebecca Isbell. *Tell It Again: Easy-to-Tell Stories with Activities for Young Children.* Beltsville, MD: Gryphon House, 2000.

Ravitch, Diane. *The Language Police: How Pressure Groups Restrict What Students Learn.* New York: Knopf, 2003.

Rothlein, Liz, and Anita Meyer Menibach. *Legacies: Using Children's Literature in the Classroom.* New York: HarperCollins, 1997.

Routman, Regie. *Transitions: From Literature to Literacy.* Portsmouth, NH: Heinemann, 1990.

Rudman, Masha, ed. *Children's Literature: Resource for the Classroom.* 2nd ed. Norwood, MA: Christopher-Gordon, 1993.

Sawyer, Ruth. *The Way of the Storyteller*. New York: Penguin, 1942.

Schickedanz, J. A. *More Than the ABCs: The Early Stages of Reading and Writing*. Washington, DC: National Association for the Education of Young Children, 1999.

Shapiro, Jon E., ed. *Using Literature & Poetry Effectively*. Newark, DE: International Reading Association, 1971.

Shedlock, Marie. *The Art of the Storyteller*. 1915. New York: Dover, 1951.

Sloan, Glenna Davis. *The Child as Critic: Developing Literacy through Literature, K–8*. 4th ed. New York: Teachers College Press, 2003.

Strickland, D. S., and L. M. Morrow, eds. *Emerging Literacy: Young Children Learn to Read and Write*. Newark, DE: International Reading Association, 1989.

Trelease, Jim. *The Read-Aloud Handbook*. 5th ed. New York: Penguin, 2001.

Troeger, Virginia Bergen. "Student Storytelling." *Teaching K–8* March 1990: 41–43.

Watson, Dorothy J., ed. *Ideas and Insights: Language Arts in the Elementary School*. Urbana, IL: National Council of Teachers of English, 1987.

Yopp, Ruth Helen, and Hallie Kay Yopp. *Literature-Based Reading Activities*, 3rd ed. New York: Pearson, 2003.

CHAPTER

5

Cultural and Social Diversity

In an ideal world, a chapter on cultural and social diversity would be unnecessary, for we would ignore the petty distinctions of outward appearance and accept all peoples, in the words of Dr. Martin Luther King, Jr., "on the content of their character." In an ideal world, people would not only accept individual differences, but would celebrate them, for our individual differences have enabled the human race to survive. If all human beings were identical, we certainly would have become extinct eons ago. As the celebrated sociobiologist Edward O. Wilson puts it, "diversity is the way a parent hedges its bets against an unpredictably changing environment" (122). Diversity helps to make us adaptable, and in our adaptability lies our success as a species. So you see, being diverse is our greatest strength.

At the same time, our quest for survival also leads to fear, mistrust, hatred, and bigotry. We want to protect ourselves, our families, and our communities from outside threats. Indeed, the aggressive tendencies in human beings may derive from the biological need to respond to these outside threats—and not infrequently these threats are posed by other human beings (see Wilson 99–120). As a culture and a species, we need diversity to survive; yet as individuals we must be alert to threats posed by outsiders. These two impulses frequently work at cross-purposes. Fortunately, human beings are also blessed with considerable intelligence, and we can come to appreciate diversity and usually recognize when it is and is not a threat to our existence. In other words, bigotry, hatred, and unfounded fears can best be combatted with knowledge.

Literature has the power to shape our thinking, to broaden our horizons, to deepen our understanding. It can, in fact, increase our sensitivity by showing us the feelings, beliefs, and attitudes of people the world over. What we finally learn is that we all belong to the same great community and share the same fundamental humanity.

CULTURAL DIVERSITY

Culturally diverse literature in the United States is usually defined as stories about people outside the Anglo American ethnic group. The appearance of heroes from minority cultural groups has been a belated one in children's literature. Given the increasing cultural diversity of our society, it is important that children's reading reflect the influence of African Americans, Native Americans, Hispanic Americans, Asian Americans, and the myriad other ethnic groups that contribute to the splendid array of peoples in the United States.

Rudine Sims Bishop has very clearly identified the necessity for culturally diverse literature, as well as the dangers for not having it:

> If literature is a mirror that reflects human life, then all children who read or are read to need to see themselves reflected as part of humanity. If they are not, or if their reflections are distorted and ridiculous, there is the danger that they will absorb negative messages about themselves and people like them. Those who see only themselves or who are exposed to errors and misrepresentations are miseducated into a false sense of superiority, and the harm is doubly done (quoted in Harris 43).

So, culturally diverse literature enriches everyone. First, it provides the minority cultures with positive role models and bolsters cultural pride and individual dignity. Second, it provides the majority culture with exposure to the various minority cultures and thus helps to break down old prejudices and dispel misunderstandings. However, multicultural literature should also be good literature with well-written stories, compelling characters, stimulating language, and well-paced action.

One of the significant controversies surrounding culturally diverse literature is whether an author outside a specific cultural or social group can write authentically about that group. August Wilson, an African-American playwright, says that "Someone who does not share the specifics of a culture remains outside, no matter how astute a student or well-meaning the intentions" (quoted in Harris 42). In other words, Wilson insists that only African Americans should write about African Americans, only Native Americans about Native Americans, and so on. However, another African American, the critic Henry Louis Gates, Jr., disagrees: "No human culture is so inaccessible to someone who makes the effort to understand, to learn, to inhabit another world" (Gates 30). Gates believes that true empathy is possible between individuals from different cultures, that cultural differences can be bridged, that human beings have the capacity to embrace other traditions and other peoples. In other words, a writer does not have to be Chinese to write about the Chinese, but she does have to know a lot about them and she does have to be able to empathize with them, to put herself in their shoes. Let us hope that Gates is correct, for therein lies the promise of a better world.

The best works of multicultural literature demonstrate a knowledge of and sensitivity to the cultural groups involved. Following are some guidelines we may use in evaluating a literary work for its attention to cultural consciousness:

1. The characters are portrayed as individuals, with genuine feelings, thoughts, and beliefs, and not as types representing a specific cultural group.

2. The author (or illustrator) has avoided cultural stereotyping that suggests all members of a specific cultural group share the same socioeconomic status, similar occupations, tastes, and so on.

3. The culture is accurately portrayed without exaggeration or romanticism.

4. Any problems facing the group are dealt with seriously, faithfully, and honestly, and without oversimplification.

5. All factual details are accurate, and there are no omissions or distortions that may cast an unfair light on the picture.

Let us take a closer look at the literature of some of the more common cultural groups in the United States.

African Americans

African Americans were seldom portrayed in children's books prior to the 1940s, and then usually as servants or other menials and almost always as comical characters. Indeed, it is virtually impossible to find a picture book about an African American child published before the 1960s. All the widely used elementary basal school readers of the first half of the twentieth century depicted European American families, and never hinted that the society included any people of color.

Contemporary picture storybooks with African-American characters began in earnest with Ezra Jack Keats's *The Snowy Day* (1962) and its sequels, with a young, inner-city African American as a protagonist. Keats's critics point out that his books lack "cultural specificity"– that is, nothing except Peter's skin color identifies him as an African American, but they remain important groundbreakers and are enjoyed by children yet today. (It is possible that some of the criticism stems from the fact that Keats himself was white.) Lucille Clifton's picture books about Everett Anderson (*Some of the Days of Everett Anderson* and its sequels) trace the joys and heartaches of a young African-American boy who experiences the separation of his parents, the remarriage of his mother, the birth of a new half-sister, and the death of his father. By not romanticizing life, these books honestly represent current social realities.

Always the least controversial of multicultural books are folktales. Gail E. Haley and Verna Aardema, both of European American heritage, have gained reputations for their retellings of African folktales (including Haley's *A Story–A Story: An African Tale* and Aardema's *Why Mosquitoes Buzz in People's Ears*, illustrated by Leo and Diane Dillon, both of which won the Caldecott Medal). Virginia Hamilton, one of the most celebrated of African-American authors, collected and retold numerous African folktales. Her collection, *The People Could Fly*, is beautifully illustrated by Leo and Diane Dillon.

Novels for older readers featuring African American protagonists can be traced back to 1945 when Jesse Jackson (not the minister/politician/activist) wrote what was considered a groundbreaking book, *Call Me Charley*. It is the story of a young African-American boy attempting to assimilate into the white, middle-class neighborhood to which his parents have moved. Jackson deals frankly with racial conflict, and his main character, Charley, sets the tone when he retorts to a boy who refers to him as "Sambo": "My name is Charles . . . Sometimes I'm called Charley. Nobody calls me Sambo and gets away with it" (8). The story seems dated now. Charley and his family possess white, middle-class values, which seems to be why he is finally accepted as an equal in the white community. Later, African Americans would decry the necessity for Charley to abandon his identity and his cultural roots to gain entry into the white world. But Charley was only operating in accordance with the widely accepted practices of the day, when everyone believed the ideal society to be that of the melting pot in which all distinguishing cultural features were abandoned in favor of those of the dominant white culture. It was not until the 1970s, in the aftermath of the Civil Rights revolution, that books appeared extolling African-American values and cultural identity. Virginia Hamilton's *M. C. Higgins, the Great* (1974) and Mildred Taylor's *Roll of Thunder, Hear My Cry* (1976)–both Newbery Medal winners–are just two notable works that paved the way for writers such as Eloise Greenfield, Rosa Guy, Sharon Bell Mathis, and Walter Dean Myers. These writers all aim to capture the vitality of the African-American culture, dispelling stereotypes and portraying genuine, flesh-and-blood characters engaged in the business of living. The establishment of the Coretta Scott King Award in 1970, honoring African-American contributions to children's literature, has helped to encourage continued high quality in the field of African-American literature.

Native Americans

Native Americans have been the subject of a mythology that continues to cloud the general public's perception. Too often we lump together all Native Americans (some Native Americans prefer the term *American Indian* and still others prefer *Amerind*) into one vision of a beaded, feathered, and moccasined warrior. For a long time, children's picture books either ignored the Native American altogether or fell back on the stereotypes. Native Americans argue that even the modern picture books rely on the old images and fail to portray the modern American Indian realistically. Indeed, by and large, picture books on Native Americans still tend to focus on the traditional images—feathered headdresses, teepees, tomahawks, and papooses—and ignore the fact that today about two million Native Americans live in America without these trappings.

Several types of literature by and about Native Americans exist. Most very young children are exposed first to the Native American folktales. Some of these have resulted in handsomely illustrated books (those by Paul Goble, such as *Iktomi and the Berries,* 1989, have been among the most admired for their faithfulness to the oral character of the tales and his sensitive use of form and color to capture the Native American spirit). Because many Native American tales are still essentially within the oral tradition and remain a significant aspect of the culture, it is important that the sources of these tales be respected. Many children's versions of these folktales are now identifying not only the specific Native American society where the tales originated (that is, Iroquois, Sioux, Ojibway, etc.), but the Native tellers themselves. Richard Erdoes's *The Sound of Flutes and Other Indian Legends* (1976) specifically names the storytellers, for example, as does Joseph Bruchac's *Flying with the Eagle, Racing the Great Bear* (1993).

Two important and popular types of Native American literature are historical fiction and nonfiction. Since about 1970, the predominant theme of this literature is a correcting of old misconceptions (about the relationships between whites and Indians, for example). Dee Brown's famous adult book, *Bury My Heart at Wounded Knee* (1970), erased forever our romanticized vision of the Old West by revealing the American government's disreputable treatment of the Indian population, which was nothing short of genocide. Scott O'Dell was one of the earliest children's writers to attempt to set the record straight. His *Sing Down the Moon* (1970) is a fictionalized account of the forced relocation of the Navajo in the nineteenth century. He writes frankly about the brutal treatment of the Navajo at the hands of the American soldiers. True stories are every bit as compelling as fiction. Ignatia Broker's *Night Flying Woman: An Ojibway Narrative* (1983) describes the life of the author's great-great-grandmother and the uprooting of her people by nineteenth-century whites. Another nonfictional work, Russell Freedman's *Indian Chiefs* (1987) counters myths and misconceptions about famous tribal leaders—who were decidedly not bloodthirsty savages roaming the plains in search of white men's scalps.

Perhaps the rarest type of Native American book is the contemporary novel—that is, a story about Native Americans in modern society. Many modern American Indians see themselves as trapped between two cultures—the traditional culture of their parents and the overpowering culture of modern America. Once again, Scott O'Dell ventured into this region with his book *Black Star, Bright Dawn* (1988), which describes an Inuit girl's amazing feat during the famed Iditarod dogsled race in Alaska. The book has been criticized because the heroine eventually rejects her traditional religion along with many of her native customs. On the other hand, O'Dell is recognizing the virtually unavoidable clash of cultures that young Native Americans face. In fact, the book has proved popular among Native American children in Alaska, suggesting that O'Dell, despite being a white writer from southern California, was able to write sympathetically about another culture (see Russell). Similarly, Jean Craighead George's popular survival story, *Julie of the Wolves* (1972), describes a modern Eskimo girl torn between the values of her family and the enticements of modern society. The choice is never an easy one.

Many recent picture books by and about contemporary Native Americans have been published, some of the best of these coming out of Canada, such as *Byron through the Seasons: A Dene-English Story Book,* by the children of La Loche and Friends, the text of which is in both English and Chipewyan. The themes of most of the books on contemporary Native

Americans include the need to preserve cultural identity and of the importance of the extended family. For older readers, A. E. Cannon's *The Shadow Brothers* (1990) and Sharon Creech's Newbery-Award-winning *Walk Two Moons* (1994) have won acclaim. Creech's book is an intricately woven tale complete with a mystery and filled with the warmth of familial love in the face of adversity (see Stewart).

Culturally conscious books include portraits of Native Americans as individuals, sensitive descriptions of Native American cultural traditions, and an awareness that each Native American society is a distinctive cultural entity—that there are Ojibway, Iroquois, Sioux, and so on. These books reject demeaning vocabulary, artificial dialogue, and cruel and insensitive Indian stereotypes. Donnarae MacCann puts it simply: ". . . is there anything in the book that would make a Native American child feel embarrassed or hurt to be what he or she is? Can the child look at the book and recognize and feel good about what he or she sees?" (quoted in Harris 161).

Hispanic Americans

The largest commonly recognized minority group in the United States consists of the Hispanic Americans, a variously described group of Latin American descent, sometimes combining a Native American and Spanish/Portuguese heritage. In the Southwestern states, Hispanic Americans are becoming the dominant cultural group. Literature, however, has not yet reflected that influence. Until very recently, few good books on Hispanic Americans have been available. Many of the books present an inaccurate picture of the culture and perpetuate stereotypes. For example, despite the fact that most Hispanic Americans live in cities, they are often depicted in children's books as rural people or migrant workers, and usually living in poverty (see Wagoner). The earliest works depicting Hispanic Americans were pieces of historical fiction or stories that focused exclusively on the Hispanic American culture in isolation. Joseph Krumgold's . . . *and now Miguel* (1953), a Newbery-Award winner from the early 1950s, is the story of the coming of age of a Hispanic American boy from a family of sheepherders in northern New Mexico. Although a sensitive and well-told narrative, the book unfortunately contributes to the stereotype of the rural, poor Hispanic, uneducated and out of the mainstream. Among the early picture books featuring Hispanic Americans are several award winners, including Leo Politi's *Pedro, The Angel of Olvera Street* (Caldecott Honor Book in 1947) and *Song of the Swallows* (Caldecott Medalist in 1950), both set in California, and Marie Hall Ets's *Nine Days to Christmas,* winner of the 1960 Caldecott Medal. A popular trend in modern picture books is the dual-language book, such as Carmen Lomas Garza's *Family Picture/Cuadros de Familia.* Attention to the Spanish language is an important feature of books dealing with Hispanic American culture.

Novels for older readers can be traced to Hila Colman's *The Girl from Puerto Rico* (1961) and Frank Bonham's *Viva Chicano* (1970), both pioneering examples of works depicting the urbanized Hispanic American in the modern world. Theodore Taylor's *The Maldonado Miracle* has been praised as a work by an "outsider" that captures the spirit of the Mexican American experience, although this is a rare accomplishment. By the 1990s, a growing number of Hispanic American writers began to appear. Gary Soto's prose works include *Baseball in April* and *Buried Onions,* and his poetry includes *A Fire in My Hands* and *Canto Familiar.* Pat Mora writes poetry (*Borders, Chants,* and *Communion*) and family stories for children (*A Birthday Basket for Tia*). Sandra Cisneros's *The House on Mango Street* is not to be missed.

Asian Americans

The group usually referred to as Asian Americans might be more accurately described as Asian Pacific Americans, since the terms generally include those whose ancestry derives from Asian countries bordering on the Pacific Ocean. They are a diverse collection of people, many of whom have little in common. To lump people of Chinese, Japanese, Korean, and Vietnamese descent all together as if they were a single national/ethnic group is both inaccurate and insensitive. Literature can and should reflect these differences and celebrate their distinctions.

Picture books depicting Asian American culture are not especially common. Among the earliest was Claire Huchet Bishop's 1938 retelling of an old Chinese folktale, *The Five Chinese Brothers,* a story celebrating the individual strengths of each brother. However, the illustrations by Kurt Weise, an award-winning illustrator, fall into old stereotypes, making the brothers little more than caricatures lacking all individuality. The tale was retold in 1990 by Margaret Mahy and entitled *The Seven Chinese Brothers.* The renderings for this version by Jean and Mou-Sien Tseng are more faithful to the tale's cultural roots. Ed Young's illustrations for Ai-Ling Louie's retelling of *Yeh-Shen: A Cinderella Story from China* evoke the traditional culture, and his *Lon-Po-Po: A Little Red-Riding Hood Story from China* won the 1990 Caldecott Medal. Picture books with realistic stories appeared fairly early, with Thomas Handforth's *Mei Lei,* a story of China, winning the Caldecott Medal in 1939. Taro and Mitsu Yashima's *Umbrella,* one of the first books to depict a Japanese American living in modern America, was a Caldecott Honor book in 1959. Allen Say's beautifully illustrated books such as *Grandfather's Journey* (the 1994 Caldecott medalist), which tells the story of Japanese American immigrants, are fine examples of culturally sensitive narratives.

Novels for older children with Asian American protagonists began appearing as early as the 1930s, with *Young Fu of the Upper Yangtze,* by Elizabeth Foreman Lewis, winning the Newbery Medal. But Asian American writers did not enter the picture until some time later. J. S. Wong's *Fifth Chinese Daughter,* which appeared in 1950, is among the earliest books to portray Chinese Americans with realism; it is the story of a girl growing up in San Francisco and her desire to become an artist. Among the most talented of modern writers in this vein is Laurence Yep. Yep's *Dragonwings,* which provides us with a view of San Francisco's Chinatown in the early 1900s, is just one of his many books about Chinese Americans adapting to a new culture. In *Coolies,* Rosanna Yin describes the experiences of the earliest Chinese immigrants, the workers who helped lay the transcontinental railroad in the nineteenth century. An Na's *Step from Heaven* beautifully describes the experiences of Korean Americans.

The harrowing story of the Japanese American internment during World War II has given rise to several moving books, both fictional and historical. One of the first and most famous is the autobiographical *Farewell to Manzanar* by Jeanne Wakatsuki and James D. Houston. Yoshiko Uchida's *Journey to Topaz* is a book on the same theme, also drawn from personal experience. Finally, we should mention books of poetry, which have been less common. Janet S. Wong's *A Suitcase of Seaweed and Other Poems,* including Korean, Chinese, and American poetry, suggests the great possibilities in this genre.

Worldwide Cultures

The nature of the modern world demands that we all become more aware of and sensitive to the diverse cultures found, not only in our own nation, but in the world at large. One of the most important cultural groups that transcends national boundaries is formed by the Jewish people. An important development is the increasing number of books describing the devastating experiences of the Holocaust. Of course, the parent of all these is Anne Frank's moving *The Diary of a Young Girl,* first published in 1947, but recently released in a much more complete edition, which recounts the horrors of Nazi occupation in The Netherlands. It is now even possible to find picture books on the subject (see Roberto Innocenti and Christophe Gallaz's *Rose Blanche*). Aranka Siegal's *Upon the Head of a Goat: A Childhood in Hungary, 1939–1944* describes the Nazi atrocities against the Jews from the perspective of yet another nation. Chaim Potok's *My Name Is Asher Lev,* Yuri Suhl's *The Merrymaker,* and the wonderful works of Isaac Bashevis Singer, including the autobiographical stories of *In My Father's Court*, his popular *Yentl the Yeshiva Boy,* and *The Death of Methuselah* are all lovely expressions of the Jewish culture.

Books are now available on a wide variety of cultures around the globe, from the Cholistan Desert tribes in Pakistan in Suzanne Fisher Staples' *Shabanu: Daughter of the Wind* to the Australian outback in Mavis Thorpe Clark's *The Min-Min* to modern-day Africa in Bess Clayton's *Story for a Black Night.* Persecution knows no cultural bounds, as demonstrated in David Kherdian's *The Road from Home: The Story of an Armenian Girl.* This is a biographical account of the author's mother's experiences during the massacre of Armenian Christians in Turkey just after World War I, bringing to light one of the lesser-known, but no less horrifying, crimes against humanity. This cataloguing sounds like a grim list indeed, but it is important that neither we nor our children ever forget these deplorable chapters in the world's history. The ultimate purpose of exposing children to a rich variety of cultures is to enable them to live and thrive in this wonderful diversity.

Rosa Guy, a distinguished writer of books for young adults (*The Friends, Ruby,* and others) and a native of the former British colony of Trinidad, has issued this call to arms for all cultural groups:

> I reject the young of each succeeding generation who dare to say: "I don't understand *you* people . . ." "I can't stand *those people* . . ." or, "Do you see the way *they* act . . . ?" They are us! Created by us for a society which suits our ignorance.
>
> I insist that Everychild understand this. I insist that Everychild go out into the world with this knowledge: there are no good guys. There are no bad guys. We are all good guys. We are all bad guys. And we are all responsible for each other. (34)

SOCIAL DIVERSITY

Social diversity crosses cultural boundaries and affects people regardless of their ethnic, racial, or religious background. Social diversity includes such issues as gender, sexual preference, and physical, emotional, and intellectual differences. Again, our biases generally stem from ignorance, and books can be a bridge to greater human understanding.

Gender Awareness

For thousands of years, most of human society has been patriarchal, dominated by the male. Our patriarchal culture has effectively relegated the woman's position to one of subservience and has caused us to see feminine traits as inferior to masculine traits. Society has come to value physical strength, assertiveness, independence, power, aggressiveness, ambition—all of which we tend to see as masculine features. Conversely, we denigrate passivity, docility, emotionalism, physical weakness, dependence, resignation—all of which we tend to see as feminine features. These values have been so ingrained in our culture that we generally accept them unquestioningly. For a woman to be taken seriously, she must perform like a man, and such behavior is just as likely to win her ridicule from both sexes. In recent years significant strides have been taken to eliminate this male bias in Western culture.

In literature, as we might expect, the bias is reflected in several ways, most notably in the prevalence of male protagonists over female, the celebration of the typically male traits of physical strength and aggression, and the perpetuation of the image of the female as weak and ineffectual. Children's books have not escaped this stereotyping, and they reflect in their own way society's subtle antifeminine bias. There are three principal ways literature conveys this negative message.

GENDER-BIASED LANGUAGE Language can perpetuate gender bias, and English is particularly notable for this transgression. The use of the masculine pronoun "he" to refer to everyone, for example, effectively eliminates at least half the human race. Compound words such as "chairman," "mailman," "policeman," and "businessman" indicate the historical dominance of the male. We use "sissy" as a disparaging term, but it's seen as good for someone to "stand up and take it like a man."

GENDER ROLES Society has traditionally assigned certain roles to men—breadwinners, leaders, and defenders—and other roles to women—nurturers, caregivers, and supporters. In the past, children's books have portrayed doctors, airline pilots, school principals, and corporate executives as male, whereas nurses, stewardesses, teachers, and secretaries have been depicted as female. This is, of course, little different from cultural bias in which, for example, whites are depicted in leadership positions and people of color in subservient roles. Additionally, the tasks performed by women have been typically undervalued—ask those in the nursing profession or in secretarial positions, for example, two areas still dominated by underpaid women.

GENDER BEHAVIOR In addition to casting men and women in predetermined roles, society has traditionally differentiated between what it perceives to be male and female behavior or standards of conduct. Women have been cast as the fairer and weaker sex, weaker physically, emotionally, and intellectually. The male child is expected to be physically active, even mischievous. The female child who shows such traits may be labeled a "tomboy," another disparaging term. Tears are expected of a female and condemned in a male. Males are expected to be clever and inventive, but similar traits in females are often acknowledged with surprise.

It is important to find books that give children positive images of women and that avoid stereotyping of roles and behavior. These might include Louise Fitzhugh's *Harriet the Spy*, the story of a clever and independent young girl who decides she wants to be a spy, or Mildred Taylor's *Roll of Thunder, Hear My Cry*, about a young African-American girl facing prejudice during the Great Depression. Books that provide positive adult role models are equally important, such as Peggy Mann's *Amelia Earhart, First Lady of Flight*, one of the many biographies of this pioneer pilot, or Patricia MacLachlan's *Cassie Binegar*, with its portrait of a remarkable grandmother. Nor should we forget books that depict males in other than stereotypical roles. John Steptoe's *My Daddy Is a Monster . . . Sometimes* depicts a nurturing father as seen through the eyes of children. And Mark Wandro and Joanie Blank's *My Daddy Is a Nurse* describes ten fathers in professions traditionally associated with women. Books in which males are depicted as sensitive, artistic, or anything other than macho sports fanatics are also helpful. Patricia MacLachlan's *Arthur, for the Very First Time* and Katherine Paterson's *Bridge to Terabithia* are two notable examples.

Gender bias in children's books does not create the problem, but it may reinforce it. A steady diet of books in which females are depicted in submissive roles, or as weak, deferential, and reliant on males for success will ultimately influence a child's attitude. On the other hand, much foolishness has been perpetrated in the name of "political correctness." It seems foolish, for example, to deprive children of some of the classics of literature simply because they were written in an era that did not observe the gender decorum we prefer today. We can't expect Mark Twain, having lived in the nineteenth century, to share our twenty-first-century values on womanhood, but his writings are wise and entertaining nevertheless. Or, to quote a well-worn saw, let's not toss the baby out with the bathwater.

Following are some guidelines we may use when evaluating a literary work for gender awareness:

1. The author uses inclusive language, avoiding the universal "he" and gender-specific words like "mailman" and "chairman." (Of course, we may not fault

earlier writers for not observing this practice, for only since the 1980s has inclusive language become the norm.)

2. The author avoids stereotyping roles according to gender—men as breadwinners, women as housewives; men as doctors, women as nurses; and so on.

3. The author avoids stereotyping certain behaviors and personality traits as "feminine"—especially those suggesting weakness, docility, and passivity.

4. The author avoids stereotyping certain behaviors and personality traits as "masculine"—especially those suggesting toughness, insensitivity, and aggressiveness.

Alternative Families and Lifestyles and Family Problems

Few children grow up in homes in the suburbs with two parents, a sibling, and a dog. No longer do most mothers don their aprons in the morning and spend their days cleaning and cooking for their families. Single-parent homes are commonplace, and the vast majority of women now work outside the home. Modern children's books are at last coming to reflect this reality. Children who have step-parents, step-siblings, and half-siblings may find comfort in books depicting other families like theirs. Books that were once controversial, such as Norma Klein's *Mom, the Wolfman, and Me* (1972), which deals with an unmarried mother, her boyfriend, and her daughter, are now familiar. Katherine Paterson's *The Great Gilly Hopkins* (1978), about an unruly child in foster care, and Cynthia Voigt's *Homecoming*, about four children abandoned by their mother in a parking lot, are tragically realistic in their portrayal of modern dysfunctional families.

Today, few subjects for children at puberty are so delicate as homosexuality. Virtually ignored—even taboo—in children's literature until the 1980s, sexual preference is now being recognized by many writers as an important social issue about which children need sensitive education. Pioneering works in this field include John Donovan's *I'll Get There. It Better Be Worth the Trip* and Isabelle Holland's *The Man Without a Face*. Other treatments of the subject include Marion Dane Bauer's *Am I Blue?: Coming Out from the Silence* (a selection of short stories by various writers), M. E. Kerr's *Deliver Us from Evie* (about a teenage lesbian), and Paula Fox's *The Eagle Kite*. Michael Willhoite's *Daddy's Roommate* is a picture book describing the weekends a young boy spends with his father and his father's male companion. The ultimate theme of all these works is that of understanding and acceptance of an individual's sexual orientation. This is just one more hurdle of bigotry and prejudice that we must help our children overcome.

The subject of child abuse—physical, emotional, and sexual—has come late to children's books, despite the fact that it is one that concerns children deeply. Among the recent offerings on the subject are Chris Crutcher's *Staying Fat for Sarah Byrnes*, James Howe's *The Watcher*, and Mirjam Pressler's *Halinka*. This subject, like so many delicate issues, has been swept under society's carpet of respectability for too long. We do young people no service by ignoring the problem, and, in the hands of a capable writer, much good can come of sharing both facts and feelings.

The Physically, Emotionally, and Intellectually Challenged

Another change taking place in our society is a more receptive attitude toward individuals with special needs. These individuals were once virtually ignored in children's books, undoubtedly a holdover from the time when people with physical, emotional, or intellectual differences were largely hidden away from society—either institutionalized or secluded at home. Society is now more sensitive to the needs of this group. Our laws now recognize the existence of physically challenged individuals, and our schools seek to accommodate the intellectually challenged. Among the children's books dealing with this issue are Taro Yashima's *Crow Boy,* about a Japanese boy suffering from shyness, Lucille Clifton's *My Friend Jacob,* describing the relationship between a young black boy and his older white friend who is intellectually disabled, and Virginia Hamilton's *Sweet Whispers, Brother Rush,* about a family coping with an inherited mental disorder. Physical disabilities are featured in such books as Carolyn Meyer's *Killing the Kudu,* which attacks stereotypes about people in wheelchairs.

In our effort to find children's books that treat all people with fairness and sensitivity, we can observe a few general guidelines:

1. The author treats the subject with intelligence—no sloppy or incorrect facts.
2. The author treats the subject with sensitivity—no prejudice or callousness.
3. The characters are portrayed without sentimentality—pity is not the answer.
4. The characters are portrayed with realism—pain, doubt, fear, even death are all a part of this realism (otherwise it's a fantasy).
5. The solutions—when solutions are offered—seem to grow naturally from the characters and situations—no magic pills, no silver bullets, no fairy godmothers.
6. The author does not let a didactic message get in the way of a good story—for then it would be a sermon. Most readers will forgive an author anything but boredom.

Our goal as individuals and as a society should be to become more sensitive to the needs of every person, to acknowledge, as the *Universal Declaration of Human Rights* proclaims, that "All human beings are born free and equal in dignity and rights." It is an ignorant or foolish writer who belittles others because they happen to be of a certain gender, race, religion, or ethnic origin, or because nature or society has dealt them a rough hand. Such a writer cannot have anything important to tell us.

Works Cited

Gates, Henry Louis, Jr. "'Authenticity,' or The Lesson of Little Tree." *The New York Times* 24 November 1991: 1, 26–30.

Guy, Rosa. "Innocence, Betrayal, and History." *School Library Journal* November 1985: 33–34.

Harris, Violet, ed. *Teaching Multicultural Literature in Grades K–8*. Norwood, MA: Christopher-Gordon, 1993.

Russell, David L. *Scott O'Dell*. New York: Twayne, 1999.

Stewart, Michelle Pagni. "Judging Authors by the Color of Their Skin? Quality Native American Children's Literature." *MELUS* 27.2 (Summer 2002): 179–196.

Wagoner, Shirley A. "Mexican-Americans in Children's Literature Since 1970." *The Reading Teacher* December 1982: 274–279.

Wilson, Edward O. *On Human Nature*. Cambridge, MA: Harvard University Press, 1978.

Recommended Readings

Belensky, Mary Field, and others. *Women's Ways of Knowing*. New York: Harper, 1986.

Broderick, Dorothy M. *Image of the Black in Children's Fiction*. New York: Bowker, 1973.

Brown, Dee. *Bury My Heart at Wounded Knee*. New York: Holt, 1970.

Carlson, Ruth Kearney. *Emerging Humanity: Multi-Ethnic Literature for Children and Adolescents*. Dubuque, IA: Wm. C. Brown, 1972.

Frye, Northrop. *The Educated Imagination*. Bloomington: Indiana University Press, 1969.

Gilligan, Carol. *In a Different Voice*. Cambridge, MA: Harvard University Press, 1982.

Gilliland, Hap. *Indian Children's Books*. Billings: Montana Council for Indian Education, 1980.

Harris, Violet J. "Continuing Dilemmas, Debates, and Delights in Multicultural Literature." *The New Advocate* 9.2 (Spring 1996): 107–122.

Giorgis, Cyndi, and Janelle Mathis. "Visions and Voices of American Indians in Children's Literature." *The New Advocate* 8.2 (Spring 1995): 125–142.

John, L., and S. Smith. *Dealing with Diversity Through Multicultural Fictions: Library-Classroom Partnerships*. Chicago: ALA, 1993.

LeBeau, Patrick R. *The Codical Warrior: The Codification of American Indian Warrior Experience in American Culture*. Unpublished Dissertation, University of Michigan, 1993.

Lindgren, Merri V. *The Multicultural Mirror: Cultural Substance in Literature for Children and Young Adults*. Fort Atkinson, WI: Highsmith Press, 1991.

Lo, Suzanne, and Ginny Lee. "Asian Images in Children's Books: What Stories Do We Tell Our Children?" *Emergency Librarian* 20.5 (May-June 1993): 14–18.

Luecke, Fritz J., comp. *Children's Books: Views and Values*. Middletown, CT: Xerox Education Publications, 1973.

Manna, Anthony L., and Carolyn S. Brodie, eds. *Many Faces, Many Voices: Multicultural Literary Experiences for Youth*. Fort Atkinson, WI: Highsmith, 1992.

McCann, Donnarae, and Gloria Woodard. *The Black American in Books for Children: Readings in Racism*. Metuchen, NJ: Scarecrow, 1985.

——. *Cultural Conformity in Books for Children*. Metuchen, NJ: Scarecrow, 1977.

McIntosh, Peggy. "White Privilege: Unpacking the Invisible Knapsack." *Peace and Freedom* July/August 1989: 10–12.

Miller-Lachman, L., ed. *Our Family, Our Friends, Our World: An Annotated Guide to Significant Multicultural Books for Children and Teenagers.* New Providence, NJ: R. R. Bowker, 1992.

Pratt, Linda, and Janice J. Beaty. *Transcultural Children's Literature.* Upper Saddle River, NJ: Merrill/Prentice Hall, 1999.

Rochman, Hazel. *Against Borders: Promoting Books for a Multicultural World.* Chicago: American Library Association, 1993.

Rudman, Masha K. *Children's Literature: An Issues Approach*, 3rd ed. New York: Longman, 1995.

Sims, Rudine. *Shadow & Substance: Afro-American Experience in Contemporary Children's Fiction.* Urbana, IL: NCTE, 1982.

——. "Walk Tall in the World: African-American for Today's Children." *Journal of Negro Education* 1990: 58, 556–565.

CULTURAL DIVERSITY IN CHILDREN'S LITERATURE: A SELECTED BIBLIOGRAPHY

(The following list contains books about diverse cultural groups. Books on social issues have been excluded since many of those are included in the bibliographies following Chapters 7 and 11, and to list them here would be redundant. The suggested reading levels are only approximations.)

AFRICAN AMERICAN

Books for Younger Readers (Grades K–4)

Bryan, Ashley. *All Night, All Day: A Child's First Book of African-American Spirituals.* New York: Atheneum, 1991.

——. *Beat the Story Drum, Pum-pum.* New York: Atheneum, 1980.

——. *The Dancing Granny.* New York: Atheneum, 1977.

Caines, Jeanette. *Abby.* New York: Harper, 1973.

——. *Daddy.* New York: Harper, 1977.

——. *I Need a Lunchbox.* New York: Harper, 1988.

——. *Just Us Women.* New York: Harper, 1982.

Clifton, Lucille. *All Us Come Cross the Water.* New York: Holt, 1973.

——. *My Friend Jacob.* New York: Dutton, 1980.

——. *Some of the Days of Everett Anderson.* New York: Holt, 1970.

——. *Sonora Beautiful.* New York: Dutton, 1981.

Dunbar, Paul. *Little Brown Baby.* 1895. New York: Dodd, Mead & Co., 1968.

Feelings, Tom. *Soul Looks Back in Wonder.* New York: Dial, 1993. (A collection of poems for all ages)

Greenfield, Eloise. *Big Friend, Little Friend.* New York: Black Butterfly Children's Books, 1991.

——. *Grandpa's Face.* New York: Philomel, 1988.

——. *Honey, I Love.* New York: Harper, 1973.

——. *Night on Neighborhood Street.* New York: Black Butterfly Children's Books, 1991.

——. *Under the Sunday Tree.* New York: Harper, 1988.

Herron, Carolivia. *Nappy Hair.* Illus. Joe Cepeda. New York: Knopf, 1997.

Hoffman, Mary. *Amazing Grace.* Illus. Caroline Binch. New York: Dial, 1991.

Howard, Elizabeth. *Aunt Flossie's Hats.* New York: Clarion, 1991.

——. *Chita's Christmas Tree.* New York: Bradbury, 1989.

——. *The Train to Lulu's.* New York: Bradbury, 1988.

Johnson, Angela. *Do Like Kyla.* New York: Orchard, 1990.

——. *One of Three.* New York: Orchard, 1991.

——. *The Rolling Store*. New York: Orchard, 1997.

——. *Tell Me a Story, Mama*. New York: Orchard, 1989.

——. *When I Am Old with You*. New York: Orchard, 1990.

Jordan, June. *His Own Where*. New York: Crowell, 1971.

Lowry, Lois. *Anastasia's Chosen Career*. Boston: Houghton Mifflin, 1987.

McKissack, Patricia C. *Goin' Someplace Special*. Illus. Jerry Pinkney. New York: Atheneum, 2001.

Nolen, Jerdine. *Big Jabe*. Illus. Kadir Nelson. New York: Lothrop, 2000.

Steptoe, John. *Baby Says*. New York: Harper, 1988.

——. *Daddy Is a Monster . . . Sometimes*. New York: Viking, 1980.

——. *Mufaro's Beautiful Daughters*. New York: Lothrop, 1947.

——. *Stevie*. New York: Harper, 1969.

——. *Uptown*. New York: Harper, 1970.

Stuve-Bodeen, Stephanie. *Mama Elizabeti*. Illus. Christy Hale. New York: Lee & Low, 2000.

Woodson, Jacqueline. *Visiting Day*. Illus. James E Ransome. New York: Scholastic, 2002.

Books for Older Readers (Grades 5 and Up)

Brooks, Bruce. *Everywhere*. New York: Harper, 1990.

Burch, Robert. *Queenie Peavy*. New York: Viking, 1966.

Cameron, Eleanor. *To the Green Mountains*. New York: Dutton, 1975.

Childress, Alice. *A Hero Ain't Nothin' But a Sandwich*. New York: Coward, 1973.

Colman, Hila. *Classmates by Request*. New York: Morrow, 1964.

Curry, Barbara K., and James Michael Brodie. *Sweet Words So Brave: The Story of African American Literature*. Middleton, WI: Zino, 1996.

Fair, R. L. *Cornbread, Earl, and Me*. New York: Bantam, 1975.

Feelings, Tom. *The Middle Passage: White Ships/Black Cargo*. New York: Dial, 1995.

Fox, Paula. *The Slave Dancer*. New York: Bradbury, 1973.

Giovanni, Nikki. *Spin a Soft, Black Song*. New York: Farrar, Straus & Giroux, 1987.

Graham, Lorenz. *North Town*. New York: Thomas Crowell, 1965.

——. *South Town*. New York: Thomas Crowell, 1958.

Greene, Bette. *Get on Out of Here, Philip Hall*. New York: Dial, 1981.

——. *Philip Hall Likes Me, I Reckon Maybe*. New York: Dial, 1974.

Guy, Rosa. *The Disappearance*. New York: Delacorte, 1979.

——. *The Friends*. New York: Holt, 1973.

——. *Ruby*. New York: Viking, 1976.

——. *The Ups and Downs of Carl Davis*. New York: Delacorte, 1989.

Hamilton, Virginia. *Anthony Burns*. New York: Knopf, 1988.

——. *The House of Dies Drear*. New York: Macmillan, 1968.

——. *The Magical Adventures of Pretty Pearl*. New York: Harper, 1983.

——. *M. C. Higgins, the Great*. New York: Macmillan, 1974.

——. *The People Could Fly*. New York: Knopf, 1985.

——. *The Planet of Junior Brown*. New York: Macmillan, 1971.

——. *Sweet Whispers, Brother Rush*. New York: Philomel, 1981.

——. *Zeely*. New York: Macmillan, 1967.

Hentoff, Nat. *Jazz Country*. New York: Harper, 1965.

Hunter, Kristin. *Guests in the Promised Land*. New York: Scribner's, 1973.

——. *The Soul Brothers and Sister Lou*. New York: Scribner's, 1968.

Jackson, Jesse. *Call Me Charley*. New York: Dell, 1945.

Johnson, Angela. *Toning the Sweep*. New York: Orchard, 1993.

Langstaff, J. *What a Morning! The Christmas Story in Black Spirituals*. New York: Margaret K. McElderry, 1987.

Lester, Julius. *To Be a Slave*. New York: Dial, 1966.

Mathis, Sharon Bell. *Listen for the Fig Tree*. New York: Viking, 1974.

——. *Teacup Full of Roses*. New York: Viking, 1972.

McKissack, Patricia. *Mirandy and Brother Wind*. New York: Knopf, 1988.

——. *Nettie Jo's Friends*. New York: Knopf, 1989.

McKissack, Patricia, and Frederick McKissack. *The Long Hard Journey*. New York: Knopf, 1989.

Myers, Walter Dean. *Fallen Angels*. New York: Scholastic, 1988.

——. *Dream Bearer*. New York: HarperCollins, 2003.

——. *Me, Mop, and the Moondance Kid*. New York: Dell, 1988.

——. *Monster*. New York: HarperCollins, 1999.

——. *The Mouse Rap*. New York: Harper, 1990.

——. *Now Is Your Time!* New York: HarperCollins, 1991.

——. *Scorpions*. New York: Harper, 1988.

Neufeld, John. *Edgar Allan*. Chatham, NY: Phillips, 1968.

Ringgold, Faith. *Tar Beach*. New York: Crown, 1991.

Robinet, Harriette. *Twelve Travelers, Twenty Horses*. New York: Atheneum, 2003.

Sebestian, Ouida. *Words by Heart*. Boston: Little, Brown, 1979.

Tate, Eleanora E. *Blessing in Disguise*. New York: Dell, 1996.

Taylor, Mildred. *Let the Circle Be Unbroken*. New York: Dial, 1981.

——. *Mississippi Bridge*. New York: Dial, 1990.

——. *The Road to Memphis*. New York: Dial, 1990.

——. *Roll of Thunder, Hear My Cry*. New York: Dial, 1976.

Yates, Elizabeth. *Amos Fortune, Free Man*. New York: Dutton, 1967.

Wilkinson, Brenda. *Ludell*. New York: Harper, 1975.

——. *Ludell and Willie*. New York: Harper, 1977.

Wyeth, Sharon Dennis. *Message in the Sky: Corey's Underground Railroad Diary*. New York: Scholastic, 2003.

NATIVE AMERICAN

Books for Younger Readers (Grades K–4)

Andrews, Jan. *Very Last First Time*. Illus. Ian Wallace. Vancouver, BC: Douglas & McIntyre, 2002.

Bruchac, Joseph. *Crazy Horse's Vision*. Illus. S. D. Nelson. New York: Lee & Low, 2000.

——. *Fox Song*. Illus. Paul Morin. New York: Philomel, 1993.

——. *Iroquois Stories: Heroes and Heroines, Monsters and Magic*. Freedom, CA: The Crossing Press, 1985.

——. *Flying with the Eagle, Racing the Great Bear: Stories from Native North America*. Mahwah, NJ: Troll, 1993.

The Children of La Loche and Friends. *Byron through the Seasons: A Dene-English Story Book*. Calgary, AB: Fifth House, 1990.

Dorris, Michael. *Guests*. New York: Hyperion/Disney, 1994.

——. *Morning Girl*. New York: Hyperion/Disney, 1992.

Keeshig-Tobias, Lenore. *Bird Talk*. Illus. Polly Keeshig-Tobias. Toronto: Sister Vision: Black Women and Women of Color Press, 1991.

——. *Emma and the Trees*. Illus. Polly Keeshig-Tobias. Ojibway tr. Rose Nadjiwon. Toronto: Sister Vision: Black Women and Women of Color Press, 1996.

Lacapa, Kathleen, and Michael Lacapa. *Less than Half, More than Whole*. Illus. Michael Lacapa. Menomonie, WI: Northland, 1994.

Lacapa, Michael. *The Flute Player*. Menomonie, WI: Northland, 1990.

Manitonquat (Medicine Story), reteller. *The Children of the Morning Light: Wampanoag Tales*. New York: Macmillan, 1994.

McDonald, Megan. *Tundra Mouse: A Storyknife Tale*. Illus. S. D. Schindler. New York: Orchard, 1997.

Sanderson, Esther. *Two Pairs of Shoes*. Illus. David Beyer. Saint Paul, MN: Pemmican Publications, 1990.

Savageau, Cheryl. *Muskrat Will Be Swimming.* Illus. Robert Hynes. Menomonie, WI: Northland, 1996.

Sneve, Virginia Driving Hawk. *Dancing Teepees: Poems of American Indian Youth.* Illus. Stephen Gammell. New York: Holiday House, 1989.

——. *High Elk's Treasure.* New York: Holiday, 1972.

Strete, Craig Kee. *Big Thunder Magic.* Illus. Craig Brown. New York: Greenwillow, 1990.

——. *The Bleeding Man and Other Science Fiction Stories.* New York: Greenwillow, 1977.

——. *When Grandfather Journeys into Winter.* Illus. Hall Frenck. New York: Greenwillow, 1979.

Waboose, Jan Bourdeau. *Morning on the Lake.* Illus. Karen Reczuch. Toronto: Kids Can Press, 1998.

Wheeler, Bernelda. *Where Did You Get Your Moccasins?* Illus. Herman Bekkering. Grand Forks, ND: Peguis Publications, 1992.

——. *I Can't Have Bannock, But the Beaver Has a Dam.* Illus. Herman Bekkering. Grand Forks, ND: Peguis Publications, 1993.

Yellow Robe, Rosebud. *Tonweya and the Eagles and Other Lakota Stories.* Illus. Jerry Pinkney. New York: Dial, 1979.

Books for Older Readers (Grades 5 and Up)

Armer, Laura Adams. *Waterless Mountain.* New York: McKay, 1931.

Brooke, Lauren. *Every New Day.* New York: Scholastic, 2002.

Brown, D. *Creek Mary's Blood.* New York: Franklin Library, 1980.

Cannon, A. E. *The Shadow Brothers.* New York: Delacorte, 1990.

Clark, Ann Nolan. *Medicine Man's Daughter.* New York: Farrar, 1963.

Craven, Margaret. *I Heard the Owl Call My Name.* New York: Bantam, 1973.

Embry, Margaret. *Shadi.* New York: Holiday, 1971.

Fuller, Iola. *The Loon Feather.* New York: Harcourt, 1940.

George, Jean Craighead. *Julie of the Wolves.* New York: Harper, 1972.

——. *The Talking Earth.* New York: Harper, 1983.

——. *Water Sky.* New York: Harper, 1987.

Highwater, Jamake. *Anpao: An American Indian Odyssey.* New York: Harper, 1977.

Hill, Kirkpatrick. *Minuk: Ashes in the Pathway.* Middleton, WI: Pleasant Company, 2002.

Hirschfelder, Arlene. *Rising Voices: Writings of Young Native Americans.* New York: Random House, 1993.

Houston, John. *Ghost Fox.* New York: Harcourt, 1977.

Hudson, Jan. *Sweetgrass.* New York: Philomel, 1989. (Tree Frog, 1984)

Katz, Jane B. *This Song Remembers: Self-Portraits of Native Americans in the Arts.* Boston: Houghton Mifflin, 1980.

Katz, William Loren. *Black Indians: A Hidden Heritage.* New York: Atheneum, 1986.

LaFarge, Oliver. *Laughing Boy.* Boston: Houghton Mifflin, 1929.

Lauritzen, Jonreed. *The Ordeal of the Young Hunter.* Boston: Little, Brown, 1954.

Lampman, Evelyn Sibley. *The Potlatch Family.* New York: Crowell, 1953.

Means, Florence Crannell. *Our Cup Is Broken.* Boston: Houghton Mifflin, 1969.

Mikaelsen, Ben. *Touching Spirit Bear.* New York: HarperCollins, 2002.

O'Dell, Scott. *Black Star, Bright Dawn.* Boston: Houghton Mifflin, 1988.

——. *Island of the Blue Dolphins.* Boston: Houghton Mifflin, 1960.

——. *Sing Down the Moon.* Boston: Houghton Mifflin, 1970.

Richter, Conrad. *Light in the Forest.* New York: Knopf, 1953.

Shaw, Janet Beeler. *Kaya: An American Girl.* Middleton, WI: Pleasant Company, 2002

Speare, Elizabeth George. *The Sign of the Beaver.* Boston: Houghton Mifflin, 1983.

HISPANIC AMERICAN

Books for Younger Readers (Grades K–4)

Anaya, Rudolfo. *Maya's Children: The Story of La Llorona*. Illus. Maria Baca. New York: Hyperion, 1997.

Brown, Tricia. *Hello, Amigos!* New York: Holt, 1986.

Cisneros, Sandra. *Hairs/Pelitos*. Illus. Terry Ybánez. New York: Knopf, 1994.

Dorros, Arthur. *Abuela*. New York: Dutton, 1991.

Garcia, Maria. *The Adventures of Connie and Diego/Las adventuras de Connie y Diego*. San Francisco: Children's Book Press, 1978.

Garza, Carmen Lomas. *Family Picture/Cuadros de Familia*. San Francisco: Children's Book Press, 1990.

Griego, M. C., and others. *Tortillitas para Mama and Other Nursery Rhymes, Spanish and English*. New York: Holt, n.d.

Hewett, Joan. *Hector Lives in the United States Now: The Story of a Mexican-American Child*. New York: Lippincott, 1990.

Krumgold, Joseph. *. . . and now Miguel*. New York: Crowell, 1953.

Mora, Pat. *Borders*. Houston, TX: Arte Público Press, 1985.

——. *Chants*. Houston, TX: Arte Público Press, 1984.

——. *Communion*. Houston, TX: Arte Público Press, 1991.

——. *Pablo's Tree*. New York: Macmillan, 1993.

——. *Tomás and the Library Lady*. New York: Knopf, 1993.

Soto, Gary. *The Cat's Meow*. San Francisco: Strawberry Hill, 1987.

——. *Snapshots from the Wedding*. Illus. Stephanie Garcia. New York: Putnam, 1997.

Tafolla, Carmen. *Patchwork Colcha: A Children's Collection*. Flagstaff, AZ: Creative Educational Enterprises, 1987.

Torres, Leyla. *Subway Sparrow/Gorrión del Metro*. New York: Farrar, Straus & Giroux, 1993.

Ulibarrí, Sabine. *Pupurupú: Cuentos de Ninos/Children's Stories*. Mexico, D. F.: Sainz Luiselli Editores, 1987.

Viramontes, Helena Maria. *The Moths and Other Stories*. Houston, TX: Arte Público Press, 1985.

Books for Older Readers (Grades 5 and Up)

Anaya, Rodolfo. *Bless Me, Ultima*. Berkeley, CA: Tonatiuh International, 1972.

——. *The Farolitos of Christmas: A New Mexico Christmas Story*. Santa Fe: New Mexico Magazine, 1987.

Bonham, Frank. *Viva Chicano*. New York: Dutton, 1970.

Buss, Fran Leeper, and Daisy Cubias. *Journey of the Sparrows*. New York: Lodestar, 1991.

Chavez, Denise. *The Last of the Menu Girls*. Houston, TX: Arte Público Press, 1988.

Cisneros, Sandra. *The House on Mango Street*. New York: Random House, 1984.

Colman, Hila. *The Girl from Puerto Rico*. New York: Morrow, 1961.

Foresman, Bettie. *From Lupita's Hill*. New York: Atheneum, 1973.

Galarza, Ernesto. *Barrio Boy*. Notre Dame, IN: University of Notre Dame Press, 1971.

Martinez, Victor. *Parrot in the Oven: Mi Valda*. New York: HarperCollins, 1996.

Means, Florence Crannell. *Us Malthbys*. Boston: Houghton Mifflin, 1966.

Meltzer, Milton. *The Hispanic Americans*. New York: Crowell, 1982.

Mohr, Nicholasa. *El Bronx Remembered: A Novella and Stories*. New York: Harper, 1975.

——. *Nilda*. New York: Harper, 1973.

O'Dell, Scott. *The Black Pearl*. Boston: Houghton Mifflin, 1967.

Pinchot, Jane. *The Mexicans in America*. Minneapolis, MN: Lerner, 1989.

Rice, David. *Crazy Loco*. New York: Dial, 2001.

Soto, Gary. *Baseball in April*. San Diego: Harcourt, 1990.

——. *Buried Onions*. San Diego: Harcourt, 1997.

——. *A Fire in My Hands: A Book of Poems*. New York: Scholastic, 1990.

Taylor, Theodore. *The Maldonado Miracle*. New York: Avon, 1986.

ASIAN AMERICAN (INCLUDING ASIAN HERITAGE)

Books for Younger Readers (Grades K–4)

Bang, Molly. *The Paper Crane*. New York: Greenwillow, 1985. (Japanese)

Coutant, Helen, and Vo-Dinh Coutant. *First Snow*. New York: Knopf, 1974. (Vietnamese)

Lord, Bette Bao. *In the Year of the Boar and Jackie Robinson*. New York: Harper, 1984. (Chinese)

Louie, Ai-Ling. *Yeh-Shen: A Cinderella Story from China*. Illus. Ed Young. New York: Philomel, 1982.

Mahy, Margaret. *The Seven Chinese Brothers*. Illus. Jean and Mou-Sein Tseng. New York: Scholastic, 1990.

Say, Allen. *The Bicycle Man*. New York: Parnassus, 1982. (Japanese)

——. *El Chino*. Boston: Houghton Mifflin, 1990. (Chinese)

——. *Grandfather's Journey*. Boston: Houghton Mifflin, 1994. (Japanese)

Wang, Rosalind C. *The Fourth Question*. Illus. Ju-Hong Chen. New York: Holiday House, 1991. (Chinese)

Wong, Janet S. *Buzz*. Illus. Margaret Chodos-Irvine. San Diego: Harcourt, 2000. (Chinese)

Yacowitz, Caryn. *The Jade Stone*. Illus. Ju-Hong Chen. New York: Holiday House, 1992. (Chinese)

Yagawa, Sumiko. *The Crane Wife*. Tr. Katherine Paterson. Illus. Suekichi Akaba. New York: Mulberry, 1987. (Japanese)

Yashima, Taro, and Mitsu Yashima. *Umbrella*. New York: Viking, 1958. (Japanese)

Yep, Laurence. *Dragon Prince: A Chinese Beauty and the Beast Tale*. Illus. Kam Mak. New York: HarperCollins, 1997.

Young, Ed. *Lon Po Po: A Red-Riding Hood Story*. New York: Philomel, 1990.

Books for Older Readers (Grades 5 and Up)

Crew, Linda. *Children of the River*. New York: Bantam, 1989. (Cambodian)

Degens, T. *On the Third Ward*. New York: Harper, 1990. (Chinese)

DeJong, Meindert. *The House of Sixty Fathers*. New York: Harper, 1956. (Chinese)

Fritz, Jean. *Homesick: My Own Story*. New York: Putnam, 1982. (Chinese)

Ho, Minfong. *Rice without Rain*. New York: Lothrop, 1990. (Thai)

——. *The Clay Marble*. New York: Farrar, 1991. (Cambodian)

Houston, Jeanne Wakatsuki, and James D. Houston. *Farewell to Manzanar*. New York: Bantam, 1973. (Japanese)

Kim, Helen. *The Long Season of Rain*. New York: Holt, 1996. (Korean)

Lewis, Elizabeth Foreman. *Young Fu of the Upper Yangtze*. New York: Holt, 1932. (Chinese)

Na, An. *A Step from Heaven*. Asheville, NC: Front Street, 2001. (Korean)

Takashima, Shizue. *A Child in Prison Camp*. New York: Morrow, 1971. (Japanese)

Uchida, Yoshiko. *The Best Bad Thing*. New York: Atheneum, 1985. (Japanese)

——. *A Jar of Dreams*. New York: Atheneum, 1991. (Japanese)

——. *Journey to Topaz*. New York: Scribner's, 1971. (Japanese)

——. *The Promised Year*. New York: Harcourt, 1959. (Japanese)

Wong, Janet S. *Fifth Chinese Daughter*. New York: Harper, 1950.

——. *A Suitcase of Seaweed and Other Poems*. New York: Simon & Schuster, 1996.

Yee, Paul. *Tales from Gold Mountain: Stories of the Chinese in the New World*. New York: Macmillan, 1990.

Yep, Laurence. *Child of the Owl*. New York: Harper, 1977. (Chinese)

——. *Angelfish*. New York: Putnam, 2001. (Chinese)

——. *Dragonwings*. New York: Harper, 1975. (Chinese)

——. *The Rainbow People*. New York: Harper, 1989. (Chinese)

Yin, Rosanna Yin Lau. *Coolies*. New York: Penguin, 2001. (Chinese)

JEWISH

Books for Younger Readers (Grades K–4)

Blanc, Esther Silverstein. *Berchick*. Illus. Tennessee Dixon. Volcano, CA: Volcano, 1989.

Bresnick-Perry, Roslyn. *Leaving for America*. Illus. Mira Reisberg. Danbury, CT: Children's, 1992.

Chaikin, Miriam. *I Should Worry, I Should Care*. Illus. by Richard Egielski. New York: Harper, 1979.

Cohen, Barbara. *Molly's Pilgrim*. Illus. by M. J. Deraney. New York: Lothrop, Lee, and Shepard, 1983.

Geras, Adele. *My Grandmother's Stories*. New York: Knopf, 1990.

Innocenti, Roberto, and Christophe Gallaz. *Rose Blanche*. New York: Creative Education, 1985.

Polacco, Patricia. *The Keeping Quilt*. New York: Simon and Schuster, 1988.

Sussman, Susan. *Hanukkah: Eight Lights Around the World*. Illus. Judith Friedman. Chicago: Whitman, 1988.

Books for Older Readers (Grades 5 and Up)

Frank, Anne. *The Diary of a Young Girl: The Definitive Edition*. New York: Doubleday, 1995. (Dutch)

Heyman, Anna. *Exit from Home*. New York: Crown, 1977. (Russian)

Hurwitz, Johanna. *Once I Was a Plum Tree*. New York: Morrow, 1980.

——. *The Rabbi's Girls*. New York: Morrow, 1982.

Lasky, Kathryn. *The Night Journey*. New York: Warne, 1981. (Russian)

Oriev, Uri. *The Man from the Other Side*. Boston: Houghton Mifflin, 1991. (Eastern European)

Potok, Chaim. *My Name Is Asher Lev*. New York: Knopf, 1972.

Schmidt, Gary. *Mara's Stories: Glimmers in the Darkness*. New York: Holt, 2001.

Singer, Isaac Bashevis. *The Death of Methuselah and Other Stories*. New York: Farrar, Straus & Giroux, 1971.

——. *Stories for Children*. New York: Farrar, Straus & Giroux, 1984.

——. *Yentl, The Yeshiva Boy*. (1962) Illus. Antonio Frasconi. New York: Farrar, Straus & Giroux, 1983.

Suhl, Yuri. *The Merrymaker*. New York: Four Winds, 1975.

Taylor, Sydney. *All-of-a-Kind Family*. Chicago: Follett, 1951. (Includes several sequels)

OTHER CULTURES

Primarily for Older Readers (Grades 5 and Up)

Beskow, Elsa. *Pelle's New Suit*. New York: Harper, 1929. (Swedish)

Boissard, J. A. *A Matter of Feeling*. Boston: Little, Brown, 1981. (French)

Case, Dianne. *Love, David*. New York: Dutton, 1991. (South African)

Clark, Ann Nolan. *Secret of the Andes*. New York: Viking, 1952. (Peruvian Indian)

Clark, M. T. *The Min-min*. New York: Macmillan, 1978. (Australian)

Cunningham, Julia. *The Silent Voice*. New York: Dutton, 1981. (French)

DeJong, Meindert. *Journey from Peppermint Street*. New York: Harper, 1968. (Dutch)

Hall, Lynn. *Danza!* New York: Scribner's, 1981. (Puerto Rican)

Joseph, Lynn. *The Color of My Words*. New York: HarperCollins, 2000. (Dominican Republic)

Kherdian, David. *The Road from Home: The Story of an Armenian Girlhood*. New York: Greenwillow, 1979. (Armenian)

Lingard, Joan. *Tug of War*. New York: Lodestar, 1990. (Latvian)

Mitchell, Barbara. *Down Buttermilk Lane*. Illus. John Sandford. New York: Lothrop, Lee and Shepard, 1993. (Amish)

Moeri, Louise. *The Forty-third War*. Boston: Houghton Mifflin, 1989. (Central American)

Naidoo, Beverley. *Chain of Fire*. New York: Lippincott, 1990. (South African)

——. *No Turning Back: A Novel of South Africa*. New York: HarperCollins, 1997.

——. *The Other Side of Truth*. New York: HarperCollins, 2001. (Nigeria)

Newth, Mette. *The Abduction*. New York: Farrar, Straus & Giroux, 1989. (Norwegian)

O'Dell, Scott. *My Name Is Not Angelica*. Boston: Houghton Mifflin, 1989. (African, Caribbean Islanders)

Rubinstein, Gillian. *Beyond the Labyrinth*. New York: Watts, 1990. (Australian)

Ryan, Pam Muñoz. *Esperanza Rising*. New York: Scholastic, 2000. (Mexico)

Siegal, Aranka. *Upon the Head of the Goat: A Childhood in Hungary, 1939–1944*. New York: Farrar, Straus & Giroux, 1981. (Hungarian)

Staples, Suzanne Fisher. *Shabanu: Daughter of the Wind*. New York: Knopf, 1989. (Pakistani)

Wojciechowska, Maia. *Shadow of a Bull*. New York: Atheneum, 1964. (Spanish)

PART 2

THE KINDS
OF CHILDREN'S
LITERATURE

CHAPTER

6

Books of Early Childhood

Few things in life are more rewarding than sharing a good picture book with an eager young child. The picture book—a collaboration of the talents of the writer and the artist—has the power to shape a child's lifelong tastes and attitudes toward reading. This and the next chapter will explore the many facets of the picture book. The focus of this chapter will be books of early childhood—Mother Goose books, wordless books, toy books, and alphabet, counting, concept, and easy-to-read books. Chapter 7 will examine the picture books for older readers (approximately five years old and older) and the art of picture-book illustration.

MOTHER GOOSE BOOKS

Mother Goose rhymes (in England they are called "nursery rhymes") are typically a child's first introduction to literature, beginning with the parents' singing of lullabies, such as "Rock-a-bye, Baby," or counting out tiny toes with "This little pig went to market." Many of these rhymes are indelibly impressed on our culture and find their way into a multitude of references in our daily lives. Mother Goose rhymes share the characteristics of two types of literature. First, they are folk literature—songs that were passed on by word of mouth long before they were written down. Second, they are a form of poetry, with rhyme and rhythm being a large part of their charm.

A great deal of time has been devoted to speculations on the origin of the term "Mother Goose." The seventeenth-century French reteller of folktales, Charles Perrault, named his book *Tales from Mother Goose,* and by the end of the eighteenth century "Mother Goose" was clearly associated with a mythical teller of nursery rhymes for young children—at least in the

United States. No one is sure where Perrault found the name. It may have been the appella-tion given to the woman who, in earlier times, kept the village geese and who was the tradi-tional community storyteller.

Nursery rhymes are derived from a number of sources: war songs, romantic lyrics, proverbs, riddles, political jingles and lampoons, and street cries (the early counterparts of today's television commercials). But one thing can be said for certain: Few of these rhymes were initially intended for children. Whereas some nursery rhymes are exceedingly old (the counting-out rhyme "Eena, meena, mona, my" and its variations may recall ancient names for the numbers), most date from the sixteenth, seventeenth, and eighteenth centuries. "The Three Blind Mice" was set to music as early as 1609; "Jack Sprat" may have ridiculed a cer-tain Archdeacon Spratt in the mid-seventeenth century, and some identify "Jack Horner" with Thomas Horner of Mells whose "plum" was much valuable land he acquired through Henry VIII's dissolution of the monasteries in 1536. The heroes of nursery rhymes typically come from the lower walks of life: Simple Simon, Tom the Piper's Son, Mother Hubbard, the Old Woman in the Shoe, and so on. Those that do include kings and queens ("Sing a Song of Six Pence" or "Old King Cole," for example) are often comical and irreverent. Scarcely hidden beneath the surface of these rhymes and jingles are the jibe and the barb.

It has often been pointed out that nursery rhymes contain their share of violence, some of which could be shocking if we take it literally: babes dropping from treetops, cradle and all; a farmer's wife cutting off the tails (some say "heads") of three blind mice; a beleaguered old woman giving her children broth without bread and soundly whipping them; a man imprisoning his troublesome wife in a pumpkin shell. One assiduous critic, Geoffrey Handley-Taylor, discovered, in a collection of 200 familiar nursery rhymes, at least 100 rhymes with "unsavoury elements," including eight allusions to murder, two cases of chok-ing to death, one case of decapitation, seven cases of severing of limbs, one case of body snatching, four cases of breaking of limbs, and the list goes on (Baring-Gould 20).

Even considering that these verses come from less squeamish days, the "violence" in them is not sensationalized, we find no grisly elements, and the context of the violence is not only fictional but absurd. (Who puts wives in pumpkin shells? Who really lives in a shoe?) It can also be argued that this verbal expression of aggressive behavior may help chil-dren to vent natural hostilities and pent-up anxieties. This may be the secret to the success of Eve Merriam's *The Inner City Mother Goose*, for older readers, consisting of modern-day parodies of popular nursery rhymes peppered with the sometimes jarring reality of contem-porary society. Merriam boldly includes among her subjects senseless street killings, home-lessness, hunger, and nuclear waste, all reminding us of the adaptability of the nursery rhyme. We may suspect, in fact, that exposure to such literature works a cathartic effect on children, relieving them of the need to engage in physical violence. Finally, it is safe to say that no child has ever been transformed into a brute from the influence of nursery rhymes.

Perhaps the only defense that Mother Goose rhymes need is that they are pure fun; their delightful nonsense and eccentric characters remain with us long beyond childhood. We should never underrate the sheer pleasure that literature can offer, but these rhymes, in fact, provide much more than an enjoyable pastime. Mother Goose rhymes may actually contribute significantly to a child's development in a surprising variety of ways.

Cognitive Development

With such rhymes as "One, two, buckle your shoe/Three, four, shut the door," and "One, two, three, four, five/Once I caught a fish alive," young children begin to learn numbers and counting. The letters of the alphabet are subjects of such rhymes as "A–apple pie." Nursery rhymes—perhaps because many of them were originally intended for adults—often include challenging words. "Mary, Mary, quite *contrary*," "Jack be *nimble*," and "Peter Piper picked a *peck of pickled peppers*," all help young children expand their vocabularies. Big words in children's books are good so long as the words can easily be explained and do not involve abstract thinking beyond the children's capacity. It is also good to remember that, because nursery rhymes are easily memorized, young children frequently are able to "pretend" to read them, and in time they begin to recognize the words. In this way, Mother Goose rhymes encourage reading.

Finally, the appreciation of nonsense, such as that in most nursery rhymes, requires a firm grasp of reality. Nonsense is only amusing if we recognize its absurdity when placed next to what we know to be real. Therefore, it might be argued that Mother Goose rhymes help children to develop a sense of humor and that the rhymes force intellectual comparisons between fantasy and reality.

Aesthetic Development

Aesthetic development is the forming of an appreciation for beautiful things; in literature, this means a love of the sounds and rhythms of language. Mother Goose rhymes, with their lively meter, appeal to a child's natural sense of rhythm, perhaps hearkening back to the womb and the rhythmical beat of the mother's heart. The repeated refrains provide children with the pleasures of anticipating something familiar. The playful sounds of nonsense words ("Hickory, dickory dock," "Diddle, diddle dumpling, my son John," "Higgledy, piggledy, my black hen") appeal to the natural delight most children find in language. The rhymes encourage very young children to experiment in creating sounds, a necessary developmental process toward learning to speak.

In addition to providing children with an introduction to linguistic sounds, the nature of rhyming, and the joy of rhythm, nursery rhymes also develop a child's sensitivity to pattern. The idea of pattern forms the basis of much art, for pattern results in order, and beauty. "A little girl was sitting on the ground eating and was scared away by a spider" describes an event in life. But notice how much more memorable the scene is when we impose a pattern of rhyme and rhythm:

Little Miss Muffet sat on a tuffet
Eating her curds and whey;
Along came a spider
And sat down beside her
And frightened Miss Muffet away.

Mother Goose rhymes can nurture the love of language that is needed so that, with maturity, readers come to appreciate more sophisticated poetry. (Notice also that the unfamiliar terms "tuffet," "curds," and "whey," do not diminish our enjoyment, but expand our vocabulary.)

Social and Physical Development

Many nursery rhymes are based on cooperative play. "Pat-a-cake, pat-a-cake" calls for physical coordination and interpersonal contact; "Ring-a-ring o' roses" and "London Bridge Is Falling Down" call for the exercise of large motor skills as well as social interaction. Jump-rope rhymes are simply nursery rhymes gone to the playground, and they appear to be an almost worldwide childhood pastime (see Butler, *Skipping Around the World*). Some also exhibit a considerable amount of aggression and even hostility. Take, for example, this popular jump-rope jingle:

> Fudge, fudge, tell the judge
> Mother has a newborn baby;
> It isn't a girl and it isn't a boy;
> It's just a fair young lady.
> Wrap it up in tissue paper
> And send it up the elevator:
> First floor, miss;
> Second floor, miss;
> Third floor, miss;
> Fourth floor,
> Kick it out the elevator door.

In one playful action, the skipping children are developing large motor coordination skills, engaging in a cooperative social activity, and harmlessly verbalizing the hostility that is an inevitable part of every sibling relationship. It is more socially acceptable than punching out one's kid brother—and almost as efficacious. (Incidentally, the reference to an "elevator" shows that this rhyme is a relatively new adaptation.)

Choosing Mother Goose Books

A good Mother Goose book should be a staple in every child's home. Below are some points to consider when choosing from the many collections available:

1. Does the book present an overall attractive appearance? This is likely to be one of our most widely used books; it ought to be a book we enjoy looking at.

2. Is there a balance between the familiar rhymes and those that are less often anthologized? We want the old standbys, but it's good to have some fresh verses as well.

3. Are the illustrations examples of good illustrative art, both imaginative and well executed? It is usually best for each rhyme to have its own illustration, although if the collection is very large some illustrations are often sacrificed.

4. Are the pages uncluttered in appearance and are the rhymes juxtaposed with the proper pictures? The format should be clear enough for the child to follow.

5. Are rhymes from other cultures included—African, Asian, Native American, for example? Since multiculturalism is a relatively recent development in children's literature, we may find this diversity only in newer anthologies. It would be a mistake to reject such classic collections as Blanche Fisher Wright's *The Real Mother Goose* or Marguerite de Angeli's *Book of Nursery and Mother Goose Rhymes* or Raymond Briggs's *The Mother Goose Treasury* because they are not sufficiently multicultural. But we may wish to supplement them with nursery rhyme collections from other lands and cultures.

6. Are there enough rhymes to justify the cost of the book? Of course, if we have unlimited resources, this is not a concern. But if we can afford only one Mother Goose book, we probably want an ample one.

7. Is there an index so specific rhymes can be easily located? This is more for the adult reader than for the child audience, but an index is very helpful when we're trying to fill special requests.

Illustrators of Mother Goose

Mother Goose rhymes are widely illustrated and have attracted some of the best children's artists. On the following pages are comparative examples of illustrations of two favorite rhymes—"Jack Sprat" and "Little Miss Muffet" (see Figures 6.1–6.7).

"Jack Sprat" has been especially popular among illustrators of Mother Goose rhymes and has inspired a wide variety of individual interpretations, probably because of the opportunity afforded by its two distinctive characters, each with a clearly defined personality trait.

"Little Miss Muffet" is a wonderfully constructed rhyme, a complete story with setting, characters, conflict, climax, and resolution. It has been among the most popular of all Mother Goose verses, and most illustrators choose to depict the moment just prior to or at the point of the climax since it provides the most drama and the greatest possibilities for interpretation.

FIGURE 6.1   This rather crude wood engraving from one of the earliest American editions of Mother Goose depicts the Sprats licking the platter clean. The illustration lacks the comic touch of Raymond Briggs (see Figure 6.2) and the result is nearly grotesque.

Source: From *Mother Goose's Melodies*, Munroe & Francis, Boston, 1833.

FIGURE 6.2   Raymond Briggs captures the Sprats in their most bizarre behavior—that of licking the platter clean. Appropriate to the subject, Briggs's style is cartoon, which heightens the effect of the absurd.

Source: Illustration by Raymond Briggs. Reprinted by permission of Coward, McCann & Geoghegan from *The Mother Goose Treasury* by Raymond Briggs, Copyright © 1966 by Raymond Briggs.

JACK SPRAT could eat no fat,
His wife could eat no lean:

And so, betwixt them both, you see,
They lick'd the platter clean.

FIGURE 6.3 L. Leslie Brooke depicts a decidedly older couple and from an earlier
time—the costumes are Renaissance. As always with Brooke, a close examination
of his illustration reveals his wry humor: notice the bovine fattened for market
prominently displayed on the Sprats's coat-of-arms. Like many Victorian
children's artists, Brooke imbued his representational drawings with rich, subtle
details.

Source: From *The Nursery Rhyme Book* by Andrew Lang. Illustrated by L. Leslie Brooke. Copyright
© 1972 by Dover Publications, Inc. Reprinted by permission.

FIGURE 6.4 Blanche Fisher Wright depicts an eighteenth-century husband and his solicitous mate. Typical of her illustrations for the popular collection, *The Real Mother Goose*, the lines are clean and sharp and her characters well-defined.

Source: From *The Real Mother Goose* illustrated by Blanche Fisher Wright. Copyright © 1916, 1944 Checkerboard Press, a division of Macmillan, Inc. All rights reserved. Used by permission.

Little Miss Muffet,
Sat on a tuffet,
Eating some curds and whey;
There came a great spider,
And sat down beside her,
And frightened Miss Muffet away.

FIGURE 6.5 Kate Greenaway could not bring herself to include unsavory elements in her illustrations; consequently she detracts from the drama by focusing all attention on the prim and proper Miss Muffet. The spider is barely noticeable off to the left. The colors are subdued and contribute to the air of quietness belying the circumstances.

Source: Kate Greenaway, *Mother Goose Nursery Rhymes*, London: Frederick Warne & Co., Ltd.

FIGURE 6.6 Arthur Rackham, in contrast to Greenaway, portrays a truly monstrous-looking, but not ungentlemanly, spider. The spider's appearance completely overwhelms the picture, and there is a wonderful contrast between the sedate Miss Muffet (somewhat more mature than Greenaway's), her lip daintily pursed, and the grotesque creature about to interrupt her. Rackham's surrealistic, frequently nightmarish quality is tempered here by a bit of wry humor as the spider gallantly doffs his hat.

Source: Little Miss Muffet by Arthur Rackham, reproduced with the kind permission of his family./Bridgeman Art Library.

LITTLE MISS MUFFET

Little Miss Muffet
Sat on a tuffet,
Eating her curds and whey;
There came a big spider,
Who sat down beside her
And frightened Miss Muffet away.

FIGURE 6.7   Raymond Briggs portrays a looming creature, but his Miss Muffet looks more like a nineteenth-century school marm. The fact that Briggs's spider does not have the anatomically correct number of legs need not bother us, since the illustration is in a cartoon style, and exaggerations and distortions are to be expected.

Source: Illustrated by Raymond Briggs. Reprinted by permission of Coward, McCann & Geoghegan from *The Mother Goose Treasury* by Raymond Briggs, Copyright © 1966 by Raymond Briggs.

WORDLESS PICTURE BOOKS

A *wordless picture book* contains only pictures and little or no text. (For example, Nancy Tafuri's *Have You Seen My Duckling?* contains that sentence alone.) Because these books contain no language, they have been the subject of much controversy over whether they actually constitute "literature." They surely cannot be evaluated according to the same criteria as a book with a written text. On the other hand, many wordless picture books contain familiar literary elements, including plot, point of view, theme, character, setting, and tone. Thus they can help children develop linguistic and storytelling skills. Also, because wordless picture books seem to demand an oral response from the "reader," they play an important role in the development of positive reading habits and attitudes among children. (See the essays by Cianciolo [1984] and Groff [1984] for two different viewpoints on the value of wordless picture books.)

Although the wordless picture book would seem to be aimed at the very youngest of audiences, many are in fact quite elaborate and over the heads of most preschoolers. Mitsumasa Anno's *Anno's Journey,* Lynd Ward's *The Silver Pony,* and Raymond Briggs's *The Snowman,* for example, all contain complex plot structures, subtle imagery, and sophisticated tone. In *Anno's Journey* a lone traveler makes his way through Europe on horseback; moving from countryside to village to city, he travels across time as well. If we look closely we will see, among other things, Little Red Riding Hood and the wolf, the Emperor in his "new suit," Don Quixote tilting at a windmill, Big Bird and Kermit the Frog from "Sesame Street," a developing romance, an escaping prisoner, children at play, and parodies of famous paintings, including Seurat's "Sunday Afternoon on the Island of Grand Jatte" and Millet's "The Gleaners." And all through it we are invited to locate the traveler in each picture. It is a feast of Western culture, which is both fun and challenging for children and adults alike.

TOY BOOKS

The so-called *toy books*—cardboard books, cloth books, pop-up books—include some gimmick in addition to (or in place of) a story. Toy books have to be judged differently from the typical picture storybooks or concept book. (In a toy book, for example, we might be concerned with the very practical question of how well the pop-up mechanism operates.) Usually these books are intended for the very youngest children, even babes in arms. Cardboard and cloth books are durable, can be easily washed, and will withstand rough treatment. They work well for instructing children on the proper handling of books, but they do not substitute for books. Scratch-and-sniff books are temporary objects indeed, seldom serving more than a few readings. But some very imaginative toy books have become classics. Dorothy Kundhardt's *Pat the Bunny* contains textured surfaces (cotton to suggest the bunny's fur and sandpaper to represent Daddy's scratchy beard) and movable parts. With such a book, reading is necessarily an interactive process.

Pop-up or mechanical books, a Victorian invention, can be extraordinarily intricate with dramatic three-dimensional scenes and several moving parts. (Robert Sabuda's lavish pop-up book of L. Frank Baum's *The Wonderful Wizard of Oz* contains several moving parts on each page, and the mechanisms make the book more than an inch and a half thick.) Almost always in a toy book, however, the text is relegated to second place as the visual medium takes over. Pop-up or mechanical books must necessarily contain fewer pages (otherwise they would be so thick we couldn't open them), so the story must be fairly simple. When a folk-tale is transformed into a toy book, plot details and interesting language are usually replaced by moving figures and three-dimensional castles and forests. Pop-up books remain, therefore, essentially visual art and not literature.

ALPHABET BOOKS

Most, but not all, alphabet books are designed to teach children to recognize the letters and sounds of the alphabet. All good alphabet books have some unifying element that helps to make them a satisfying artistic whole. Occasionally, an author will attempt to illustrate the letters through a story, as in Wanda Gág's *ABC Bunny,* which describes a bunny's adventures and at the same time presents the alphabet.

Far more common are those books that are unified by some thematic or artistic concept. Margaret Musgrove's *Ashanti to Zulu: African Traditions* is a rather sophisticated alphabet book for older children that presents the alphabet through descriptions of traditional African cultures. In a similar vein, Alice and Martin Provensen use American Shaker traditions in their alphabet book, *A Peaceable Kingdom.* Jan Garten's *The Alphabet Tale* uses wild animals to represent the letters and Rachel Isadora's *City Seen from A to Z* discovers the letters in the everyday sights of the city. *Dr. Seuss's ABC* uses rollicking nonsense verse and comical cartoon figures, and in Chris Van Allsburg's *Z Was Zapped,* we witness a series of alphabetical disasters befalling each letter in turn. The possibilities are endless, which is why the alphabet book has remained so popular with illustrators.

Content of Alphabet Books

Perhaps the most important aspect of an alphabet book is that it be clear; otherwise, the purpose of teaching children the sounds of letters is defeated. *Dr. Seuss's ABC* comically reinforces the phonetic associations with such lines as "Big A, little a, what begins with A? Aunt Annie's Alligator–A–A–A" or "Y–A yawning, yellow yak and young Yolanda Yorgenson is yelling on his back." Three- or four-year-olds may not initially know what an alligator or a yak is, but the illustrations will quickly teach them. Bert Kitchen's dramatic alphabet book, *Animal Alphabet,* includes stunning paintings of such creatures as an "umbrella bird" and an "ibex"–unfamiliar animals to be sure, but children (and adults) can readily understand what they are by looking at the pictures. After all, how are they to learn new concepts and facts if their reading never introduces them? On the other hand, Joan Walsh Anglund's *A Is for Always* uses such concepts as "C [for] Courteous"; "D [for] Determined"; "E [for] Exuberant"–abstract words that will have little meaning for the preschoolers for whom the book is presumably written.

Additionally, we are usually dealing with phonetic sounds when teaching the alphabet. In other words, the alphabet book's purpose is to help the child associate the shape of a letter with the sound it customarily makes. This is not as simple as it sounds. Vowels, for instance, make several sounds, from long to short to everything in between. So the letter "A" can be accurately represented by an "apple" or by an "ape" or by an "auto." Some alphabet books (such as Gyo Fujikawa's *A to Z Picture Book*) take care of this problem by offering several illustrations on the same page to represent the letter. *Dr. Seuss's ABC* demonstrates the various sounds in the text: "Oscar's only ostrich oiled an orange owl today" describes the several ways to say "O."

Consonants can also present problems. Two consonants–"C" and "G"–can be hard or soft. So "G" may be represented by a giraffe or a gorilla, for example. And then there is the troublesome "X." When in an initial position, "X" sounds like "Z"–as in "xylophone." In another position in a word, "X" sounds like "ks"–as in "extra." In this respect, "X" is akin to "C" (which is pronounced like either "S" or "K") in not having a unique sound. We should also remember that a difference exists between phonics—the sounds of letters—and the spelling of words. An alphabet book that uses "Knife" to represent "K" or "Gnat" to represent "G" may be teaching the reader something about quirky English spellings, but very little about the sound of either "K" or "G."

Design of Alphabet Books

The design and the illustrations of an alphabet book require attention to detail. If the letters are drawn too fancifully (𝔄, 𝔅, ℭ, for example), children may have a difficult time recognizing them in other contexts. It is helpful if both upper- and lower-case letters are illustrated since children will need to know both in order to read. Children also need to know the differences between the way some letters are printed in texts and the way we normally write them by hand (*a* and *a* or *g* and *g*, for instance). Eventually children will have to learn all forms of the letter, and no single picture book can be expected to provide all this information.

Most alphabet books juxtapose the letters and the pictures that represent them; that is, they are side by side on the same page or facing pages. However, talented artists often make their own rule. Judith Viorst's *The Alphabet from Z to A (With Much Confusion on the Way)* even casts aside the traditional order of the letters.

It is important to realize that not all alphabet books have a didactic purpose. Books by artists such as Van Allsburg, Graeme Base (*Animalia*), and Mitsumasa Anno (*Anno's Alphabet*) are not intended to teach the alphabet, but are more sophisticated explorations of the artistic possibilities of alphabet books. *Anno's Alphabet* contains stunning, detailed illustrations, each letter drawn as a wood carving with photographic realism in a style known as *trompe l'oeil;* however, if we look closely at the illustrations, we see that they depict visual tricks creating objects that could not exist in reality. Graeme Base's *Animalia* is also a richly detailed book, using, as the title suggests, animals to introduce the letters of the alphabet. The full-color pictures abound with objects that help to reinforce the letter sounds, and throughout are hidden pictures of the artist as a child. The result is a visual feast that accompanies an imaginative, tongue-twisting text—a treat for adults as well as for children.

It is unlikely that a single alphabet book will accommodate all the eccentricities of the English language. On the bright side, this simply gives us an excuse to read several different alphabet books to our children.

COUNTING BOOKS

Counting books are similar to alphabet books in their purpose and requirements. Most are designed to teach children the concept of counting and recognizing numbers—although, as with alphabet books, some artists have developed quite sophisticated and very beautiful counting books that might prove quite difficult for children just learning to count. (*Anno's Counting Book* by Mitsumasa Anno is a good example.)

Content of Counting Books

Sometimes, as with simple alphabet books, counting books contain virtually no text, just the numbers and the objects to be counted. As adults we take counting for granted, but it is an extremely abstract concept. We assign both names (*one, two, three*) and symbols (1, 2, 3 or I, II, III, and so on) to numbers, and these numbers in turn identify quantities, so we are dealing with more than one level of abstraction. Because of this complexity, perhaps the most important aspect of the content of a counting book is that the countable objects be clearly identifiable. It usually makes the most sense to count similar objects—how many cows? how many apples?

On the other hand, counting books need not be totally simplistic. Only a writer's or illustrator's imagination need restrict the possibilities. Molly Bang's award-winning *Ten, Nine, Eight* is an example of an effective counting book that counts backwards. Children can benefit from this kind of number play once they have mastered the fundamental elements of enumeration. Pat Hutchins's *The Doorbell Rang* includes the concepts of division and addition. Tom and Muriel Feelings's very beautiful counting book, *Moja Means One: A Swahili Counting Book*, introduces cultural information along with counting concepts. Such books go far beyond teaching numbers and letters and suggest that we do not necessarily outgrow alphabet and counting books. For the more sophisticated reader, there are Russell Hoban's *Ten What? A Mystery Counting Book* and Arthur Geisert's *Pigs from 1 to 10*, which play games with the reader. The familiar counting rhymes, such as "Over in the Meadow," have inspired counting books by such noted illustrators as Feodor Rojankovsky and Ezra Jack Keats. The beautiful counting rhyme by S. T. Garne, *One White Sail*, takes the reader to the magic of the Caribbean with such evocative lines as "Five blue doors / in the baking hot sun / Six wooden windows / let the cool wind run."

Design of Counting Books

As with alphabet books, the simplest design in a counting book is best for beginners, especially if the object is to teach numbers and the concept of counting. The juxtaposition of text and pictures is an important feature in the design of counting books. Naturally, we expect to see the Arabic numerals depicted (1, 2, 3), but even some very simple counting books include the spelling of the number words (*one, two, three*). Since most counting books go only up to ten, they are often shorter than other books and make use of full-page spreads. Or, they may depict the number on one page with the illustration on the facing page. When a multitude of items appears on a single page, the artist can avoid a cluttered appearance by grouping the objects. Today, counting books have joined the ranks of the many very handsome picture books being produced for young children, and we no longer have to settle for the ordinary and humdrum.

CONCEPT BOOKS

The purpose of a concept book is not to tell a story, but to present factual material through illustrations and accompanying text. Alphabet and counting books are concept books in that their purpose is to present cognitive concepts to young children. But concept books go far beyond teaching letters and numbers. In fact, concept books can deal with almost any subject. Some of the concepts they present are opposites (Bernice Kohn's *How High Is Up?*), colors (E. L. Konigsburg's *Samuel Todd's Book of Great Colors*), spatial relationships (Shirley Hughes's *All Shapes and Sizes* or Tana Hoban's *Is It Larger, Is It Smaller?*) or sounds (Margaret Wise Brown's *The Indoor Noisy Book*).

Concept books are clearly didactic books—in the good sense of the term. They educate but do not preach. A good concept book will convey its information in a clear and entertaining way. The material is accurately presented, although for the very young it is greatly simplified. No subject seems to be taboo any longer. A series of books that has proven very popular—and controversial—deals frankly with bodily functions. Taro Gomi's *Everyone Poops* and Shinta Cho's *The Gas We Pass: The Story of Farts,* are designed to help young children understand how their bodies work. Some adults may think the subject or the approach a bit too indelicate, but sometimes an open discussion can serve to remove the feelings of shame or indecency and might even subvert "bathroom" humor so appealing to children.

Somewhere in between the concept book and the picture storybook are those books intended to teach some concept—often a social concept—through a fictional setting and with fictional characters. Michael Wilhoite's *Daddy's Roommate*, mentioned in Chapter 5, is a narrative of story vignettes designed to educate young children on the social acceptance of homosexuality, but without relating any factual information on sexuality or sexual preference. Leslea Newman's *Heather Has Two Mommies* treats a similar subject, this time with lesbianism. If at first it seems startling to find books on these issues for young children, we need to remind ourselves that, in fact, many young children are growing up, quite healthily, in these situations, and that it might be comforting for them (and their friends) to have books that share their experiences.

SHARING BOOKS WITH THE VERY YOUNG

Naturally, the attention spans of one-to-two-year-olds are limited. But these children are not too young to have books of their own and many will pore over the pictures for long periods of time—albeit, often to forestall bedtime. By the time they are three, however, most children are able to sit through simple picture storybooks, alphabet books, counting books, and Mother Goose books. Finding a quiet time to read in the afternoon or at bedtime establishes a pleasant routine that children will come to anticipate. Soon we discover that they are outgrowing these books and ready for more complex stories, more challenging illustrations.

This development does not happen magically, however. It is the result of loving patience on the part of adults—adults who see to it that books are a staple in the home and readily available to all children, regardless of their age.

WORKS CITED

Baring-Gould, William S., and Ceil Baring-Gould. *The Annotated Mother Goose*. New York: Potter, 1962.

Butler, Francelia. *Skipping Around the World: The Ritual Nature of Folk Rhymes*. New York: Ballantine, 1989.

RECOMMENDED READINGS

Bodger, Joan. "Mother Goose: Is the Old Girl Relevant?" *Wilson Library Bulletin* December 1969: 402–408.

Bodmer, George R. "The Post-Modern Alphabet: Extending the Limits of the Contemporary Alphabet Book, from Seuss to Gorey." *Children's Literature Association Quarterly* Fall 1989: 115–117.

Bremmer, Moyra. "The World According to Mother Goose." *Parents Magazine* December 1983: 61–67.

Butler, Francelia. "Skip-Rope Rhymes as a Reflection of American Culture." In *Sharing Literature with Children*. ed. Francelia Butler. New York: Longman, 1977: 8–14.

Chaney, Jeanne H. "Alphabet Books: Resources for Learning." *The Reading Teacher* 47.2 (October 1993): 96–104.

Chisolm, Margaret. "Mother Goose—Elucidated." *Elementary School English* December 1972: 1141–1144.

Cianciolo, Patricia. "Use Wordless Picture Books to Teach Reading, Visual Literacy, and to Study Literature." In *Jump Over the Moon*. Ed. Pamela Barron and Jennifer Q. Burley. New York: Holt, 1984. 139–144.

Debes, John L., and Clarence M. Williams. "The Power of Visuals." *Instructor* December 1974: 32–39.

Eckenstein, Lina. *Comparative Studies in Nursery Rhymes*. 1906. Detroit: Singing Tree, 1968.

Freeman, Evelyn B., and Diane Goetz Person, eds. *Using Nonfiction Trade Books in the Elementary Classrooms: From Ants to Zeppelins*. Urbana, IL: National Council of Teachers of English, 1992.

Green, Percy B. *A History of Nursery Rhymes*. Detroit: Singing Tree, 1968.

Groff, Patrick. "Children's Literature Versus Wordless Books?" In *Jump Over the Moon*. Ed. Pamela Petrick Barron and Jennifer Q. Burley. New York: Holt, 1984: 145–154.

Hall, Mary Anne, and Jane Mantango. "Children's Literature: A Source for Concept Enrichment." *Elementary English* April 1975: 487–494.

Hopkins, Lee Bennett. "Pop Go the Books." *CLA Bulletin* 16 (Fall 1990): 10–12.

Kiefer, Barbara. "Critically Speaking: Literature for Children." *The Reading Teacher* January 1985: 458–463.

Lindauer, Shelley L. Knudson. "Wordless Books: An Approach to Visual Literacy." *Children's Literature in Education* (1988) 19.3: 136–142.

MacCann, Donnarae, and Olga Richard. *The Child's First Books*. New York: Wilson, 1973.

Nadasan, Ardell. "Mother Goose Sexist?" *Elementary School English* March 1974: 375–378.

Opie, Iona, and Peter Opie. *The Oxford Dictionary of Nursery Rhymes*. Oxford: Oxford University Press (Clarendon Press), 1951.

Pritchard, David. "'Daddy, Talk!' Thoughts on Reading Early Picture Books." *The Lion and the Unicorn* 7/8 (1983/84): 64–69.

Rollins, Lucy. *Cradle and All: A Cultural and Psychological Study of Nursery Rhymes*. Jackson: University Press of Mississippi, 1992.

Schoenfield, Madalynne. "Alphabet and Counting Books." *Day Care and Early Education* 10 (Winter 1982): 44.

Stewig, John Warren. "Alphabet Books: A Neglected Genre." In *Jump Over the Moon*. Ed. Pamela Barron and Jennifer Q. Burley. New York: Holt, 1984: 115–120.

Thomas, Della. "Count Down on the 1-2-3's." *School Library Journal* 15 March 1971: 95–102.

Thomas, Katherine Lewis. *The Real Personages of Mother Goose*. New York: Lothrop, 1930.

SELECTED BIBLIOGRAPHY OF BOOKS FOR THE VERY YOUNG

(The following books are organized according to types described in this chapter. This is only a representative selection of the many fine picture books available to young readers, and an effort has been made to balance the enduring classics with the more recent fare. Unless otherwise indicated, the author is also the illustrator.)

MOTHER GOOSE BOOKS

Alderson, Brian, comp. *The Helen Oxenbury Nursery Rhyme Book*. Illus. by Helen Oxenbury. New York: Morrow, 1986.

Baring-Gould, William S., and Ceil Baring-Gould, eds. *The Annotated Mother Goose*. New York: New American Library, 1967.

Briggs, Raymond, illus. *The Mother Goose Treasury*. New York: Coward, McCann & Geoghegan, 1966.

de Angeli, Marguerite, illus. *Book of Nursery and Mother Goose Rhymes*. Garden City, NY: Doubleday, 1953.

Glazer, Tom. *The Mother Goose Songbook*. Illus. David McPhail. New York: Doubleday, 1990.

Goldstein, Bobbie, ed. *Mother Goose on the Loose*. New York: Abrams, 2003.

Hader, Berta, and Elmer Hader. *Picture Book of Mother Goose*. 1930. New York: Crown, 1987.

Lang, Andrew, ed. *The Nursery Rhyme Book*. Illus. by L. Leslie Brooke. New York: Dover, 1972.

Lines, Kathleen, ed. *Lavender's Blue*. Illus. by Harold Jones. New York: Watts, 1973.

Lobel, Arnold, illus. *The Random House Book of Mother Goose*. New York: Random House, 1986.

Marcus, Leonard S., and Amy Schwartz, selectors. *Mother Goose's Little Misfortunes*. Illus. by Amy Schwartz. New York: Bradbury, 1990.

Merriam, Eve. *The Inner City Mother Goose*. (1969) Illus. David Diaz. New York: Simon & Schuster, 1996.

Opie, Iona, ed. *Tail Feathers from Mother Goose: The Opie Rhyme Book*. Boston: Little, Brown, 1988.

Opie, Iona, and Peter Opie, eds. *I Saw Esau*. Illus. Maurice Sendak. New York: Candlewick, 1992.

——. *The Oxford Nursery Rhyme Book*. New York: Oxford University Press (Clarendon Press), 1955.

Petersham, Maud, and Miska Petersham, illus. *The Rooster Crows: A Book of American Rhymes and Jingles*. New York: Macmillan, 1945.

Polacco, Patricia. *Babushka's Mother Goose*. New York: Philomel, 1995.

Provensen, Alice, and Martin Provensen, illus. *The Mother Goose Book*. New York: Random House, 1976.

Rackham, Arthur, illus. *Mother Goose*. 1913. New York: Marathon, 1978.

Reed, Philip, illus. *Mother Goose and Nursery Rhymes*. New York: Atheneum, 1963.

Scarry, Richard, illus. *Richard Scarry's Mother Goose*. New York: Western, 1983.

Smith, Jessie Willcox, illus. *The Jessie Willcox Smith Mother Goose*. New York: Derrydale, 1986.

Sutherland, Zena, comp. *The Orchard Book of Nursery Rhymes*. Illus. Faith Jaques. New York: Orchard, 1990.

Tripp, Wallace, illus. *Granfa' Grig Had a Pig and Other Rhymes Without Reason from Mother Goose*. Boston: Little, Brown, 1976.

Tudor, Tasha, illus. *Mother Goose: Seventy-Seven Verses with Picture by Tasha Tudor*. New York: Oxford University Press, 1944.

Watson, Clyde. *Father Fox's Pennyrhymes*. Illus. Wendy Watson. New York: HarperCollins, 2001.

Wildsmith, Brian, illus. *Brian Wildsmith's Mother Goose*. New York: Watts, 1965.

Withers, Carl, collector. *A Rocket in My Pocket: The Rhymes and Chants of Young America*. Illus. Susane Suba. New York: Holt, 1946.

Wright, Blanche Fisher, illus. *The Real Mother Goose*. New York: Rand McNally, 1916.

WORDLESS PICTURE BOOKS

Alexander, Martha. *Bobo's Dream*. New York: Dial, 1970.

Aliki. *Tabby*. New York: HarperCollins, 1995.

Anno, Mitsumasa. *Anno's Britain*. New York: Philomel, 1982.

——. *Anno's Journey*. New York: Philomel, 1978.

——. *Anno's U.S.A.* New York: Philomel, 1983.

Banyai, Istvan. *Zoom*. New York: Viking, 1995.

Briggs, Raymond. *Father Christmas*. New York: Puffin, 1973.

——. *The Snowman*. New York: Random House, 1978.

Carle, Eric. *Do You Want to Be My Friend?* New York: Crowell, 1971.

de Paola, Tomie. *The Hunter and the Animals: A Wordless Picture Book*. New York: Holiday House, 1981.

Drescher, Henrik. *The Yellow Umbrella*. New York: Bradbury, 1987.

Geisert, Arthur. *Oink*. Boston: Houghton Mifflin, 1991.

Goodall, John S. *The Adventures of Paddy Pork*. New York: Harcourt, 1968.

——. *An Edwardian Summer*. New York: Atheneum, 1976.

——. *The Story of an English Village*. New York: Atheneum, 1979.

——. *The Story of Main Street*. New York: Macmillan, 1987.

Hutchins, Pat. *Changes, Changes*. New York: Macmillan, 1971.

Jenkins, Steve. *Looking Down*. Boston: Houghton Mifflin, 2003.

Louchard, Antonin. *Little Star*. New York: Hyperion, 2003.

Mayer, Mercer. *Oops!* New York: Dial, 1977.

McCully, Emily Arnold. *New Baby*. New York: Harper, 1988.

——. *School*. New York: Harper, 1987.

Rohmann, Eric. *Time Flies*. New York: Crown, 1994.

Spier, Peter. *Noah's Ark*. New York: Doubleday, 1977.

——. *Peter Spier's Rain*. New York: Doubleday, 1982.

Tafuri, Nancy. *Have You Seen My Duckling?* New York: Greenwillow, 1984.

——. *Junglewalk*. New York: Greenwillow, 1988.

Vincent, Gabrielle. *Ernest and Celestine's Patchwork Quilt*. New York: Greenwillow, 1985.

Ward, Lynn. *The Silver Pony*. Boston: Houghton Mifflin, 1973.

Weisner, David. *Free Fall*. New York: Lothrop, 1988.

——. *Sector 7*. New York: Clarion, 1999.

——. *Tuesday*. New York: Clarion, 1991.

Winter, Paula. *Sir Andrew*. New York: Crown, 1980.

Young, Ed. *The Other Bone*. New York: Harper, 1984.

TOY BOOKS

Baum, L. Frank. *The Wonderful Wizard of Oz*. Illus. Robert Sabuda. New York: Little Simon, 2000.

Brown, Margaret Wise. *The Goodnight Moon Room: A Pop-Up Book*. Illus. Clement Hurd. New York: Harper & Row, 1984. (A variation on the 1947 classic)

Carle, Eric. *The Very Hungry Caterpillar*. Cleveland: World, 1968.

Kundhardt, Dorothy. *Pat the Bunny*. Racine, WI: Golden, 1962.

Hoban, Tana. *Look! Look! Look!* New York: Greenwillow, 1988.

Pienkowaki, Jan. *Haunted House*. New York: Dutton, 1979.

Scarry, Richard. *Is This the House of Mistress Mouse?* New York: Golden, 1968.

ALPHABET BOOKS

Anno, Mitsumasa. *Anno's Alphabet*. New York: Harper, 1975.

Base, Graeme. *Animalia*. New York: Abrams, 1987.

Bourke, Linda. *Eye Spy: A Mysterious Alphabet*. New York: Chronicle, 1991.

Brown, Marcia. *Peter Piper's Alphabet*. New York: Scribner's, 1959.

Burningham, John. *John Burningham's ABC's*. New York: Crown, 1985.

Chandra, Deborah. *A Is for Amos*. Illus. Keiko Narahashi. New York: Farrar, Straus & Giroux, 1999.

Duvoisin, Roger. *A for the Ark*. New York: Lee & Shepard, 1952.

Feelings, Muriel. *Jambo Means Hello: A Swahili Alphabet Book*. Illus. Tom Feelings. New York: Dial, 1974.

Fujikawa, Gyo. *A to Z Picture Book*. New York: Grosset & Dunlap, 1974.

Gag, Wanda. *The ABC Bunny*. New York: Coward-McCann, 1933.

Garten, Jan. *The Alphabet Tale*. New York: Random House, 1964.

Grover, Max. *The Accidental Zucchini: An Unexpected Alphabet*. New York: Harcourt, 1993.

Hoban, Tana. *A, B, See*. New York: Greenwillow, 1982.

Isadora, Rachel. *City Seen from A to Z*. New York: Greenwillow, 1983.

Kitamura, Satoshi. *From Acorn to Zoo: And Everything in Between in Alphabetical Order*. New York: Farrar, 1992.

Kitchen, Bert. *Animal Alphabet*. New York: Dial, 1984.

Lester, Alison. *Alice and Aldo*. Boston: Houghton Mifflin, 1998.

Lionni, Leo. *The Alphabet Tree*. New York: Pantheon, 1968.

MacDonald, Suse. *Alphabatics*. New York: Bradbury, 1986.

Martin, Bill, Jr., and John Archambault. *Chicka Chicka Boom Boom*. Illus. Lois Ehlert. New York: Simon & Schuster, 1989.

Merriam, Eve. *Where Is Everybody? An Animal Alphabet*. New York: Simon & Schuster, 1989.

Miles, Miska. *Apricot ABC*. Illus. Peter Parnall. Boston: Little, Brown, 1969.

Mullins, Patricia. *V for Vanishing: An Alphabet of Endangered Animals*. New York: HarperCollins, 1994.

Munari, Bruno. *Bruno Munari's ABC*. New York: Philomel, 1960.

Musgrove, Margaret. *Ashanti to Zulu: African Traditions*. Illus. Leo and Diane Dillon. New York: Dial, 1976.

Napier, Matt. *Z Is for Zamboni: A Hockey Alphabet*. Illus. Melanie Rose. Chelsea, MI: Sleeping Bear, 2002.

Oxenbury, Helen. *Helen Oxenbury's ABC*. New York: Delacorte, 1983.

Pack, Linda Hager. *A Is for Appalachia*. Louisville: Harmony House, 2002.

Poulin, Stephane. *Ah! Belle Cité!/A Beautiful City ABC*. Montreal: Tundra, 1985.

Rankin, Laura. *The Handmade Alphabet*. New York: Dial, 1991.

Seuss, Dr. (pseud. of Theodore Geisel). *Dr. Seuss's ABC*. New York: Random, 1988.

Tudor, Tasha. *A Is for Annabelle*. New York: Walck, 1954.

Van Allsburg, Chris. *Z Was Zapped*. Boston: Houghton Mifflin, 1987.

Viorst, Judith. *The Alphabet from Z to A (With Much Confusion on the Way)*. New York: Atheneum, 1994.

Wilbur, Richard. *The Disappearing Alphabet*. Illus. David Diaz. Orlando: Harcourt, 1998.

Wildsmith, Brian. *Brian Wildsmith's ABC*. New York: Watts, 1962.

COUNTING BOOKS

Anno, Mitsumasa. *Anno's Counting Book*. New York: Crowell, 1977.

——. *Anno's Magic Seeds*. New York: Philomel, 1995.

Bang, Molly. *Ten, Nine, Eight*. New York: Greenwillow, 1983.

Burningham, John. *John Burningham's 1,2,3's*. New York: Crown, 1985.

Carle, Eric. *1, 2, 3 to the Zoo*. Cleveland: World, 1968.

——. *The Very Hungry Caterpillar*. Cleveland: World, 1970.

Cousins, Lucy. *Count with Maisy*. New York: Candlewick, 1997.

Feelings, Muriel. *Moja Means One: A Swahili Counting Book*. Illus. Tom Feelings. New York: Dutton, 1971.

Garne, S. T. *One White Sail*. San Marcos, CA: Green Tiger, 1992.

Geisert, Arthur. *Pigs from 1 to 10*. Boston: Houghton, 1992.

Hoban, Russell. *Ten What? A Mystery Counting Book*. New York: Scribner's, 1974.

Hoban, Tana. *Count and See*. New York: Macmillan, 1972.

——. *26 Letters and 99 Cents*. New York: Greenwillow, 1987.

Hutchins, Pat. *The Doorbell Rang*. New York: Greenwillow, 1986.

Keats, Ezra Jack. *Over in the Meadow*. New York: Scholastic, 1971.

Kitchen, Bert. *Animal Numbers*. New York: Dial, 1987.

Langstaff, John. *Over in the Meadow*. Illus. Feodor Rojankovsky. New York: Harbrace, 1973.

McMillan, Bruce. *Eating Fractions*. New York: Scholastic, 1991.

——. *Here a Chick, There a Chick*. New York: Lothrop, 1983.

Merriam, Eve. *Twelve Ways to Get to Eleven*. Illus. Bernie Karlin. New York: Simon & Schuster, 1993.

O'Keefe, Susan Heyboer. *One Hungry Monster: A Counting Book in Rhyme*. Boston: Little, Brown, 1989.

Oxenbury, Helen. *Numbers of Things*. New York: Watts, 1968.

Rankin, Laura. *The Handmade Counting Book*. New York: Dial, 1998.

Reiss, John. *Numbers*. New York: Bradbury, 1971.

Scott, Ann Herbert. *One Good Horse: A Cowpuncher's Counting Book*. Illus. Lynn Sweat. New York: Greenwillow, 1990.

Sis, Peter. *Waving*. New York: Greenwillow, 1989.

Wadsworth, Olivia. *Over in the Meadow*. Illus. Anna Vojtech. New York: North South Books, 2002.

Wildsmith, Brian. *Brian Wildsmith's 1,2,3's*. New York: Watts, 1965.

CONCEPT BOOKS

Cognitive Development

Anno, Mitsumasa. *Anno's Sundial*. New York: Philomel, 1987.

Brown, Marcia. *Listen to a Shape*. New York: Watts, 1979.

Brown, Margaret Wise. *The Indoor Noisy Book*. Illus. Leonard Weisgard. New York: Harper, 1942.

Burningham, John. *John Burningham's Opposites*. New York: Crown, 1986.

Charles, N. N. *What Am I? Looking Through Shapes at Apples and Grapes*. New York: Scholastic, 1994.

Cho, Shinta. *The Gas We Pass: The Story of Farts*. Tr. Amanda Mayer Stinchecum. La Jolla, CA: Kane/Miller, 1994.

Clouse, Nancy L. *Puzzle Maps U.S.A*. New York: Holt, 1990.

Cole, Joanna. *Evolution*. New York: Crowell, 1987.

Crews, Donald. *Freight Train*. New York: Greenwillow, 1978.

——. *Truck*. New York: Greenwillow, 1980.

Ehlert, Lois. *Color Farm*. New York: Lippincott, 1990.

——. *Color Zoo*. New York: Lippincott, 1989.

Emberley, Rebecca. *City Sounds*. Boston: Little, Brown, 1989.

——. *Jungle Sounds*. Boston: Little, Brown, 1989.

Fisher, Leonard Everett. *Look Around! A Book about Shapes*. New York: Viking, 1987.

Floca, Brian. *Five Trucks*. New York: DK Ink, 1999.

Gillham, Bill, and Susan Hulme. *Let's Look for Opposites*. Photographs by Jan Siegieda. New York: Coward, 1984.

Gomi, Taro. *Everyone Poops*. Tr. Amanda Mayer Stinchecum. La Jolla, CA: Kane/Miller, 1993.

Grifalconi, Ann. *The Village of Round and Square Houses*. Boston: Little, Brown, 1986.

Hoban, Tana. *Circles, Triangles and Squares*. New York: Macmillan, 1974.

——. *Is It Larger, Is It Smaller?* New York: Greenwillow, 1985.

——. *Push-Pull, Empty-Full*. New York: Macmillan, 1972.

——. *Shapes and Things*. New York: Macmillan, 1970.

Hughes, Shirley. *All Shapes and Sizes*. New York: Lothrop, 1986.

Kohn, Bernice. *How High Is Up?* Illus. Jan Pyk. New York: Putnam, 1971.

Konigsburg, E. L. *Samuel Todd's Book of Great Colors*. New York: Atheneum, 1990.

——. *Samuel Todd's Book of Great Inventions*. New York: Atheneum, 1991.

MacKinnon. *What Shape?* New York: Dial, 1992.

Macmillan, Bruce. *Dry or Wet?* New York: Lothrop, 1988.

——. *Super Super Superwords*. New York: Lothrop, 1989.

Maestro, Betsy, and Guilio Maestro. *Traffic: A Book of Opposites*. New York: Crown, 1981.

Martin, Bill. *Brown Bear, Brown Bear, What Do You See?* New York: Holt, 1983.

McNaughton, Colin. *Autumn*. New York: Dial, 1983.

McPhail, David. *Farm Boy's Year*. New York: Atheneum, 1992.

Oakes, Bill, and Suse MacDonald. *Puzzlers*. New York: Dial, 1989.

Pienkowski, Jan. *Shapes*. New York: Simon & Schuster, 1981.

Reiss, John. *Colors*. New York: Macmillan, 1987.

——. *Shapes*. New York: Macmillian, 1987.

Robbins, Ken. *Tools*. New York: Macmillan, 1983.

Rockwell, Anne, and Harlow Rockwell. *Machines*. New York: Macmillan, 1972.

——. *The Supermarket*. New York: Macmillan, 1979.

Rotner, Shelley, and Richard Olivo. *Close, Closer, Closest*. Photographs by Shelley Rotner. New York: Simon & Schuster, 1997.

Ruben, Patricia. *True or False?* New York: Harper, 1978.

Schwartz, David M. *If You Made a Million*. Illus. Steven Kellogg. Photographs by George Ancona. New York: Lothrop, 1989.

Spier, Peter. *Fast-Slow, High-Low: A Book of Opposites*. New York: Doubleday, 1972.

Tafuri, Nancy. *All Year Long*. New York: Penguin, 1984.

Testa, Fulvia. *If You Look Around You*. New York: Dial, 1983.

Walsh, Ellen Stoll. *Mouse Paint*. New York: Harcourt, 1989.

Walsh, Melanie. *Do Monkeys Tweet?* Boston: Houghton Mifflin, 1997.

Zimmerman, Andrea, and David Clemesha. *Trashy Town*. Illus. Dan Yaccarino. New York: HarperCollins, 1999.

Psychosocial Development

Aliki. *Feelings*. New York: Greenwillow, 1984.

——. *We Are Best Friends*. New York: Greenwillow, 1982.

Anholt, Catherine, and Laurence Anholt. *All about You*. New York: Viking, 1992.

Anno, Mitsumasa. *The King's Flower*. Cleveland: World, 1979.

Aruego, José, and Ariane Dewey. *We Hide, You Seek*. New York: Greenwillow, 1979.

Brenner, Barbara. *Faces*. Photographs by George Ancona. New York: Dutton, 1970.

Cole, Babette. *Mommy Laid an Egg! Or Where Do Babies Come From?* New York: Chronicle, 1996.

Corey, Dorothy. *Tomorrow You Can*. Illus. Lois Axeman. Morton Grove, IL: Whitman, 1977.

Fujikawa, Gyo. *Let's Play!* New York: Grosset, 1975.

Girard, Linda Walvoord. *Alex, the Kid with AIDS*. Morton Grove, IL: A. Whitman, 1990.

——. *Jeremy's First Haircut*. Morton Grove, IL: A. Whitman, 1986.

——. *We Adopted You, Benjamin Koo*. Morton Grove, IL: A. Whitman, 1989.

Maestro, Betsy, and Giulio Maestro. *Where Is My Friend?* New York: Crown, 1976.

Myers, Walter. *Where Does the Day Go?* Illus. Leo Carty. New York: Parents' Magazine, 1969.

Oxenbury, Helen. *Dressing*. New York: Simon & Schuster, 1981.

——. *Shopping Trip*. New York: Dial, 1982.

Rockwell, Harlow. *My Dentist*. New York: Greenwillow, 1975.

——. *My Doctor*. New York: Harper, 1985.

Rosen, Michael J. *Home: A Collaboration of Thirty Distinguished Authors and Illustrators of Children's Books to Aid the Homeless*. New York: Harper, 1992.

Rogers, Fred. *Moving*. Photographs by Jim Judkis. New York: Putnam, 1987.

Zolotow, Charlotte. *The Quarreling Book*. Illus. Arnold Lobel. New York: HarperCollins, 1982.

7

Picture Storybooks

At the beginning of Lewis Carroll's *Alice's Adventures in Wonderland* we are told that Alice "once or twice had peeped into the book her sister was reading, but it had no pictures or conversations in it, 'and what is the use of a book,' thought Alice, 'without pictures or conversations in it?'" This may be the sentiment of all young readers. In this chapter we will look more closely at the stories and illustrations in children's picture books and how they work together to form an artistic whole.

The picture storybook combines the art of storytelling with that of illustration. Despite their apparent simplicity, good picture storybooks are very complex works dealing, as they do, with two distinct art forms. In addition to discussing the storytelling elements, this chapter includes a survey of artistic styles and techniques and a discussion of the design and meaning of picture storybooks. Naturally, the commentary on the artistic style and technique applies equally to most types of picture books.

STORYTELLING ELEMENTS

Picture storybooks are widely varied in content. They may consist of retellings of traditional folktales (*The Three Little Pigs, Cinderella*); original fantasies, such as Beatrix Potter's *The Tale of Peter Rabbit*, and Maurice Sendak's *Where the Wild Things Are*; or realistic stories such as Bernard Waber's *Ira Sleeps Over*. Whatever the type, picture-book stories consist of the same narrative elements of storytelling as described in Chapter 3, that is, point of view, character, plot and conflict, theme, style, and tone.

Picture-book plots tend to be simple and fast-paced. Often picture-book plots rely on repetitive patterns that are particularly suited to the rhythmic nature of the picture-book design. Margaret Wise Brown's *Goodnight Moon*, intended for children around the ages of two to four, is the story of a little bunny who, in a thinly disguised attempt to avoid bedtime, insists on saying "good-night" to virtually everything in his room. The simple and subtly rhythmical text and repetitive pattern can be quickly learned by children so they can help tell the story. At the same time, the gentle, low-key narrative evokes a quieting effect, ideal for bedtime. No more perfect bedtime story has ever been written. Picture books for older children may develop more complicated plots to satisfy the readers' growing sophistication. Robert McCloskey's *Blueberries for Sal* contains two parallel plots in which a little girl and a baby bear are separated from their mothers and wind up getting attached to each other's mother—to the great surprise of both mothers. Picture books also have the added dimension of the illustrations to assist in the storytelling. Sometimes, as in Pat Hutchins's *Rosie's Walk*, the pictures tell an entirely different story from the text. The words of the text constitute a single sentence describing the afternoon walk of Rosie the Hen about the farmyard. It is only from the pictures that we learn that Rosie is being stalked by a hungry fox, who is thwarted in his dastardly attempts by one disaster after another until he is finally chased away by angry bees. Rosie remains blissfully ignorant of the drama that accompanies her stroll, and she arrives home "in time for dinner."

Characterization in picture books is likewise simple, and characters tend to be identified by clearly outlined traits—Peter Rabbit is daring, curious, and impishly rebellious. Sendak's Max (of whom we will hear more later) behaves like a little monster. Outside of these very obvious features, we learn little of their likes or dislikes, their ambitions, and so on. Children tend to identify with characters like themselves, and protagonists in picture books are most often young children or animals (who exhibit childlike qualities). In fact, we can usually determine the age of the intended reader by establishing the age of the protagonist. Sendak's Max appears to be four or five—hence, the intended reader can be assumed to be around four or five. Character motivation in picture books is usually singular—largely because the brevity of the book does not permit complexity. But this does not mean that the characters are simplistic. Bernard Waber's Ira, in *Ira Sleeps Over*, is a boy caught between his desire to grow up and his need for security. It is his first overnighter—he's staying with the boy next door—and it is also his first night without his teddy bear. At last he can no longer contain himself and he admits to his friend that he needs his teddy bear and so he goes home to get it. When he returns, he discovers his friend had been missing his teddy bear all along, too. It is a comical story about a very real childhood dilemma, and we admire Ira for his sensitivity and candor.

Picture-book themes tend to be sharply focused, that is, a single theme clearly dominates a book. However, the range of themes is virtually unlimited. Today few themes are taboo in picture books, and we can find provocative picture books on the Holocaust (Roberto Innocenti and Christophe Gallaz's *Rose Blanche*), the Hiroshima atomic bomb (Toshi Maruki's *Hiroshima No Pika*), social violence (Eve Bunting's *Smoky Night*, about the Los Angeles race riots), and homosexuality (Michael Willhoite's *Daddy's Roommate*). Many of these delicate issues are deftly handled through sensitive illustrations, and usually (but not always) the harsher themes are tempered by an atmosphere of hope at the end of the book. Picture books with these emotionally charged themes seem specifically designed to force meaningful discussion with children—and what better place to have those discussions than in the home in the company of a caring adult?

Since picture books average only about 2,000 words, these words must be carefully chosen indeed. Many rely heavily on dialogue, which can be great fun to read aloud—an important consideration since most picture books are read aloud or are intended to be. Children have a love for language, and are fascinated with repetitive patterns (notice how many stories include refrains, such as the classic "hundreds of cats, thousands of cats, millions and billions and trillions of cats" in Wanda Gág's *Millions of Cats*). Children even like made-up words, such as the jolly tale *Master of All Masters,* retold by Joseph Jacobs, where the maid must learn odd new names for everyday items.

Many picture books are comic in tone, sometimes joyfully slapstick as in Dr. Seuss's work, sometimes the subtle, quiet humor such as that found in the work of Margaret Wise Brown, Robert McCloskey, and Patricia MacLachlan (see Chapter 3 for a more complete discussion of humor in children's literature). Excitement, even suspense such as that found in *The Tale of Peter Rabbit* or in Sendak's *Where the Wild Things Are,* is another staple of the picture book. More serious, reflective books include Lucille Clifton's poetic series about an inner-city African-American boy, Everett Anderson, or Allen Say's *Grandfather's Journey,* a family memoir about Japanese immigrants beginning their lives anew in a strange land. An even more sobering tone is found in the books about the Holocaust, city street violence, and other serious social issues mentioned earlier.

Certainly we should hold picture books to the same high literary standards as we do books for older readers. But picture books are only "literature" in part, and we have to consider how the pictures and the text complement each other to produce the whole.

THE CONVENTIONS OF PICTURE-BOOK ART

Picture-book art is more sophisticated than many people think, and children are often more discerning critics than are adults. It will therefore be helpful if we consider illustration in some detail.

Above all, picture-book art is narrative art; that is, it tells a story. (Even art in alphabet and counting books can be said to be narrative in that it depicts the meaning expressed by the limited text—so on a page illustrating the letter A in *Dr. Seuss's ABC,* we see Aunt Annie riding on the alligator, although a true story does not develop.) As narrative art, picture-book art is, then, a representation of the story as the artist sees it—but this can take in many artistic styles, from purely photographic realism to abstractionism. But as with all art, our understanding depends on our familiarity with the conventions of the artform.

A *convention* is simply a mutually agreed-on rule or method of understanding. A drawing is two-dimensional, but through the artist's use of certain conventions we are able to visualize the third dimension: depth. For instance, making an object smaller and placing it toward the top of the picture can make it seem farther away and thus add depth to an illustration. When we look at Bemelmans's illustration (Figure 7.1) of the twelve little girls leaving for their walk with Miss Clavel, we understand that they are going away from us and not climbing upward. We have accepted the illusion that objects toward the top of the picture are farther away than those at the bottom. In this same illustration, we also accept Bemelmans's childlike depictions of the trees as representations of real trees. Children easily recognize the patterns and designs as "tree-like," and, indeed, the trees they draw probably look rather similar to these. These particular trees seem quite suitable given the cartoonish and comical nature of the rest of the illustration.

To better understand the artist's use of convention, it may be helpful to look briefly at the various artistic elements that constitute an illustration, including line, space, shape, color, texture, composition, and perspective.

Line

Lines are used both to define features and to suggest emotional responses. Lines define objects, but lines can also suggest movement, distance, and even feeling. Curves and circles suggest warmth, coziness, and security (perhaps recalling the safety of the womb and its circular shape). Sharp and zigzagging lines suggest excitement and rapid movement. Horizontal lines suggest calm and stability (recalling firm, solid ground), whereas vertical lines suggest height and distance. The lines in Chris Van Allsburg's *Jumanji* (Figure 7.2) are deliberately angled and crooked, suggesting the havoc created by the monkeys. Bemelmans's very straight lines in the illustration from *Madeline* (Figure 7.1) may be a commentary on the rigid conduct expected at the convent school.

Space

We often do not think of space—literally the empty parts of the page—as an artistic element, but it is, in fact, very powerful. There is an old story about a Japanese artist who, when asked what was the most important part of a painting, replied, "The part that is left out." Space is actually what draws our attention to objects on the page. If a page contains very little empty space, but is instead crowded with images, our attention is necessarily divided—we do not know exactly where to look. The lack of open space on a page may contribute to a claustrophobic or uneasy feeling (see *The Story of Ferdinand*, Figure 7.3) or perhaps confusion or chaos. However, if a page contains a great deal of space surrounding a single object, all our attention goes to that object. Sometimes this generous use of space in a picture suggests quiet serenity, but it may also imply emptiness, loneliness, or isolation. Space may also create the illusion of distance.

Shape

Shape is defined geometrically—circles, ovals, squares, rectangles, triangles, and so on. A good artist is aware of the predominant shapes in an illustration, and these shapes help to elicit emotional reactions. Rounded shapes may suggest emotional reactions similar to

FIGURE 7.1 Ludwig Bemelmans's popular picture storybook *Madeline* is a delightful comedy about a spunky little girl in a Parisian convent school. The illustrations are interesting examples of expressionistic art. Notice the angularity of the figures and the exaggerated height of the nun, Miss Clavel, accompanying the twelve little girls who walk, as we are told, in "two straight lines" (surely a commentary on convent school discipline). The trees are more like ideas of trees; there is no attempt at realistic depiction. There is a carefree jocularity in these pictures that aptly characterizes the mood of the story.

FIGURE 7.2   We, the viewers, are at a child's eye level looking over the table and up at the menacing monkeys (made even more disturbing from this point of view) in this surrealistic pencil drawing from Chris Van Allsburg's *Jumanji*. The figures seem to crowd us, adding an almost claustrophobic feeling, and the whole scene appears to be a moment uncomfortably frozen in time—an appropriate mood for this story of a mysterious board game come to life.

Source: Illustration from *Jumanji* by Chris Van Allsburg. Copyright © 1981 by Chris Van Allsburg. Reprinted by permission of Houghton Mifflin Company.

those of the curved and circular lines, that is, comfort, security, stability (*The Tale of Peter Rabbit*, Figure 7.4, and *Millions of Cats*, Figure 7.5). Squarish, angular shapes may elicit more excitable responses, agitation, alarm, confusion (*Jumanji*, Figure 7.2). Ludwig Bemelmans's illustration for *Madeline* (see Figure 7.1) contrasts the squat shapes of the little girls with their flat, wide-brimmed hats, with the tall, commanding shape of the nun—her figure is nearly as long as the entire line of girls. The geometric shapes of Gerald McDermott's illustrations for the African folktale, *Anansi the Spider*, are playful representations rather than faithful depictions. Still, it would be difficult to misinterpret the shapes—Figure 7.6, for example, is quite clearly a fish swallowing a spider.

He didn't look where he was
sitting and instead of sitting
on the nice cool grass in the
shade he sat on a bumble bee.

FIGURE 7.3   This illustration by Robert Lawson for *The Story of Ferdinand* by Munro Leaf is a good example of the correlation of picture and text (without the text we might not understand what is about to happen to the bee). Notice also how the various textures are depicted–the bull's hair, the bee's body, the clover. We should not overlook the comically expressive eye of the bee as it realizes it is about to be sat upon.

Source: From *The Story of Ferdinand*. Munro Leaf. Illustrated by Robert Lawson, copyright 1936 by Munro Leaf and Robert Lawson, renewed © 1964 by Munro Leaf and John W. Boyd. Used by permission of Viking Penguin, A Division of Penguin Young Readers Group, A Member of Penguin Group (USA) Inc., 345 Hudson Street, New York, NY 10014. All rights reserved.

Color

Color is one of the most emotionally evocative of artistic elements; although in picture books color is chiefly used in a conventional fashion–skies are blue, grass is green, and so on. But color presents far more possibilities than this, and children themselves often prove to be particularly responsive to the subtleties of color. Donnarae MacCann and Olga Richard tell of a seven-year-old who used 32 shades of blue in a painting and asked for the name of each individual shade.

Colors have the ability to evoke emotional responses. Psychologists tell us that reds and yellows are warm or hot colors and suggest excitement, whereas blues and greens are cool or cold colors and suggest calm or quiet. These reactions may be embedded in our responses to the natural world–red and yellow are suggestive of warmth and happiness, and they are also the colors of sunlight and fire; blue we find to be soothing and melancholy perhaps because

FIGURE 7.4   This watercolor from Beatrix Potter's *The Tale of Peter Rabbit* exudes warmth and security, appropriate after Peter's harrowing experience in Mr. McGregor's garden. The original is done in soft warm yellows and earthy browns that complement the gently curved lines and rounded shapes, from the oval mass of Mrs. Rabbit bent before the embracing hearth to the little round tails of each of Peter's sisters. Peter himself, having caught cold from his mischief, is distanced to the right, tucked securely under the folds of his bed blankets.

Source: Beatrix Potter, *The Tale of Peter Rabbit*. London: Warne, 1901.

we associate it with calm waters or the broad expanse of the sky. There are also certain conventional responses to color, purple signifying royalty; green envy or illness, but also life and renewal; red danger, but also boldness; blue depression, but also loyalty and serenity; yellow cowardice, but also cheerfulness; and so on. (Most conventions are cultural phenomena. In imperial China, for example, the color yellow was reserved for the emperor, and throughout Asia white is a traditional color of mourning and brides often wear red.)

Additionally, colors are used to suggest cultural distinctions. When illustrating a Navajo Indian story, *Arrow to the Sun,* Gerald McDermott uses the colors of the Southwest–golds, yellows, desert browns, and oranges. In McDermott's *Anansi the Spider* (Figure 7.6), a traditional folktale of Africa, he turns to the bold, bright reds, greens, and sharply contrasting black reminiscent of the colorful regalia often associated with the folk culture of western Africa.

Before color printing was possible, black and white illustrations were all that could be found in children's books. With the perfection of color printing, color illustrations became commonplace in picture books. Today, the vast majority of picture books are printed in color, but the use of black and white–both photography and pencil and ink drawings–is making a comeback. Professional photographers have long preferred black and white for its evocative subtleties–placing the emphasis on shape, composition, perspective, and texture. Surprisingly, young children seem to enjoy black and white (or monochrome–the use of a single color) just as much as color. It is certainly a mistake to think that children require garish colors in their books or that they will reject books with black and white illustrations. In fact, some of the most popular picture books have been done in black and white, including Wanda Gág's *Millions of Cats* (Figure 7.5), Leaf and Lawson's *The Story of Ferdinand* (Figure 7.3) and Chris Van Allsburg's *Jumanji* (Figure 7.2).

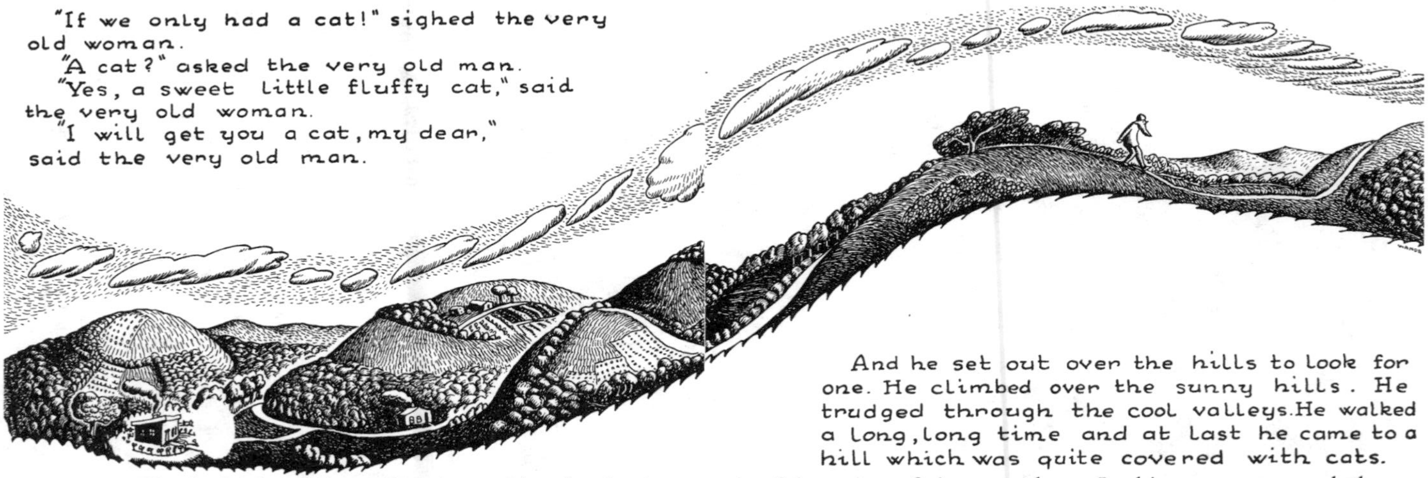

"If we only had a cat," sighed the very old woman.

"A cat?" asked the very old man.

"Yes, a sweet little fluffy cat," said the very old woman.

"I will get you a cat, my dear," said the very old man.

And he set out over the hills to look for one. He climbed over the sunny hills. He trudged through the cool valleys. He walked a long, long time and at last he came to a hill which was quite covered with cats.

FIGURE 7.5 Wanda Gág's *Millions of Cats* is considered a classic example of the union of picture and text. In this two-page spread, the artist captures the lilting rhythm of the words through an almost rhythmic use of shape and flowing design. The layout also emphasizes the concept of the journey on which the old man has embarked to find a cat. The incorporation of various textures adds both depth and interest to the simple and direct illustrations.

Source: From *Millions of Cats* by Wanda Gág, copyright 1928 by Wanda Gág, renewed © 1956 by Robert Janssen. Used by permission of Coward-McCann, A Division of Penguin Young Readers Group, A Member of Penguin Group (USA) Inc., 345 Hudson Street, New York, NY 10014. All rights reserved.

130

FIGURE 7.6 Gerald McDermott's illustrations for the African folktale *Anansi the Spider* were inspired by African folk art. The stylized figures are decorated with geometric shapes and colored boldly in primary colors. Despite the abstract quality of the pictures, children have no difficulty in identifying the scene as that of a fish swallowing a spider.

Source: From *Anansi the Spider* by Gerald McDermott. Copyright © 1972 by Gerald McDermott. Reprinted by permission of Henry Holt and Company, Inc.

Texture

One of the illusions the artist creates is to give a flat surface (the paper) the characteristics of a three-dimensional surface—the suggestion of fur, wood grain, smooth silk, and so on. We refer to this artistic quality as *texture*. An artist who wants to emphasize the realistic quality of a picture may pay great attention to texture. Notice the furry texture achieved in *Jumanji*, Figure 7.2, and *The Story of Ferdinand*, Figure 7.3. However, less realistic styles may make use of texture to enrich the visual experience and to stimulate the viewer's imagination (*Daddy Is a Monster . . . Sometimes*, Figure 7.8). Texture is achieved through the skillful use of the medium—paint layers, brush strokes, pencil marks, and so on.

Composition and Perspective

The *composition* of an illustration refers to the arrangement of the details in the picture. Composition is important to the narrative quality of the picture as well as to its emotional impact. One of the first concerns of composition is the organization of the shapes. For example, grouping many large shapes may suggest stability, enclosure, or confinement, or perhaps awkwardness (*Jumanji,* Figure 7.2). On the other hand, lighter, delicate shapes more loosely grouped may suggest movement, grace, and freedom (*One Morning in Maine,* Figure 7.7).

FIGURE 7.7 The stone lithography of Robert McCloskey's illustrations for *One Morning in Maine* helps to provide the textured appearance—the fine grain we see in the pictures is actually created by the stone surface on which the drawing was made. McCloskey's style is a fine example of representational art; he has, in fact, used himself and his daughters as models in this true-to-life tale.

In addition to the organization of objects, the artist must also consider where best to place the focal point, from what angle the picture is to be viewed, and what mood is to be conveyed. The point of view or *perspective* refers to the vantage point from which we see the objects on the page. The closer we appear to be to the action, the more engaged we are likely to be (*Jumanji,* Figure 7.2 or *The Story of Ferdinand,* Figure 7.3). The farther away we seem to be, the more detached we are (*Millions of Cats,* Figure 7.5). We may view events from a worm's-eye view or a small child's perspective or a bird's-eye view, for example. Van Allsburg uses perspective to heighten the disturbing qualities of his surrealistic tale, *Jumanji.* It is the story of a board game that comes to life with frightening consequences. By using unusual perspectives (as in Figure 7.2), the artist makes us feel uncomfortable—we are viewing the scene from an unreal angle, as if we were hiding behind the table. Films use the same technique to suggest that an unseen person (such as an intruder) is watching a character. The artist may wish to change points of view from illustration to illustration—perhaps to avoid monotony, but more probably to make us see and think about things in specific ways. In fact, Perry Nodelman points out that most picture books give us the "middle shot" (*One Morning in Maine,* Figure 7.7). We see few close-ups and few panoramic views. This is probably because each picture book has only a limited number of "shots"—the typical picture book has approximately 32 pages—and the artist must compromise on the variety of perspectives. Nevertheless, even in a brief picture book, an artist is able to provide a variety of perspectives—from extreme close-ups to long-distance shots. (See Figure 7.3 and 7.5 for examples.)

DESIGN AND MEANING IN PICTURE BOOKS

Crucial to the success of picture-book illustration is the design of the entire book and how that design contributes to the meaning of both the text and pictures, for it is here that the picture book is truly a unique art form. Among the features important to the design and meaning of picture books are rhythm and movement, tension, and page layout.

Rhythm and Movement

John Warren Stewig defines *rhythm* as "controlled repetition in art" (76). Good picture-book design creates a sense of rhythm as we move from page to page—a rhythm that is suited to the nature of the narrative. Among the conventions of picture-book design is the simple fact that we read our books, and therefore our pictures, from left to right. Consequently, it is argued that we tend to identify most closely with objects on the left—protagonists typically appear on the left and antagonists on the right. For example, in the illustration from McDermott's *Anansi the Spider* (Figure 7.6), the spider Anansi, the hero, is on the left. Notice that the movement in Wanda Gág's two-page illustration from *Millions of Cats* (Figure 7.5) is from left to right. But in Van Allsburg's illustration from *Jumanji* (Figure 7.2), the presumed protagonist, the girl in the doorway, is on the right with the unsettling figures of the monkeys on the left. This reversal of the normal order of things may contribute to the apprehensive, unsettling feeling that this illustration evokes–quite suited to the surrealistic story of an innocent game board mysteriously coming to life. (It is interesting to note that the left-to-right orientation is purely conventional. Israeli picture books are designed to be read from right to left, since Hebrew texts are written in reverse of Western texts–right to left, back to front–and as a result the movement in the pictures is also from right to left.)

This movement also suggests another anomaly in the picture book–the interrupted rhythm that occurs when we read it. The movement is not continually forward; rather, we look at the pictures, then we read, then we look at the pictures again. The pictures create a starting and stopping pattern for which the text must accommodate. This is why some picture-book texts sound fairly inane when read without the pictures. (Of course, we should hasten to point out that typically the pictures often make little sense without the text, a problem that the successful wordless picture book must overcome.) Picture books are usually designed so that a natural pause occurs between the turning of pages or so that some tension is set up that invites us to turn the page (either to be surprised or to have our expectations confirmed).

Tension

Good picture books also create what Nodelman refers to as "directed tension"–a tension between what the words say and what the illustrations depict, resulting in our heightened interest and excitement. A book without such tension, where, for example, the pictures do no more than mimic the words or vice versa, soon loses our interest. (For good examples of tension, see Figures 7.2 and 7.6; notice how each picture invites speculation and urges us on to see what will happen next.)

Words in picture books accomplish three things:

1. They indicate how we are to interpret the emotional and narrative content of the pictures.
2. They point out cause-and-effect relationships, either within parts of a single picture or within a series of pictures (for example, the words can indicate the passage of time between two pictures).
3. They explain what is important and what is not (Nodelman 215).

Look at the text and illustration taken from Leaf and Lawson's famous picture book, *The Story of Ferdinand* (Figure 7.3). Without the text, the picture would make little sense. The words explain the bee's wary expression (it is about to be sat upon), they explain what the looming figure at the top of the page is, and, by not mentioning them, they suggest that the building in the background and the clover in the foreground are relatively unimportant. Without the words, as a matter of fact, we might suppose that the bee is the main character who demands our sympathy, when, in reality, the protagonist is Ferdinand, the gentle bull. Finally, the words and pictures together set up a dramatic tension that makes us want to turn the page to see what happens next.

This illustration is also a good example of how the narrative nature of the picture book often prevents the individual pictures from functioning as artistically complete units in themselves. That is, the picture of the bee in Figure 7.3 is only complete when we see it in sequence with the rest of the illustrations in the book, not unlike a cartoon strip, with which picture books have a great deal in common.

Page Layout

Another element of book design is the placement of the pictures and the text on the page: Are all the pictures on the same side of the page? Are they all the same size? Do the placement and size vary from page to page? Is there a good reason for the placement and size; that is, do they reinforce some aspect of the whole story? What size and shape are the pages? For example, most picture books are wider than they are high, and this makes them especially suited to narrative illustration. The characters (whether human or animal) tend to be taller than they are wide, and this gives the artist ample space to depict the setting around the characters, expanding the narrative quality of the pictures (Nodelman 46). On the other hand, books that are tall and narrow usually focus on character and diminish the setting. The size of a book also affects us. We often associate very small books and very large books with the youngest readers—small books are easy for little hands to handle and large books are eye-catching. Medium-sized books, on the other hand, are frequently more complex. These are all issues to be considered by the writer, artist, and editor before a book is produced. And how these issues are handled will affect our response to a book.

Maurice Sendak's *Where the Wild Things Are* provides a good example of the way in which the layout of pictures and text can enrich each other. As the story opens, Max, a rather naughty boy, is causing all manner of havoc about his house (it is significant that we do not actually see Max being destructive, for that might cause us to have less empathy for him—he is, instead, depicted just *about* to pound a nail into the wall or just *about* to pounce on the dog). The initial pictures are small with large white borders around them. Max is then sent to his room for his misbehavior (significantly, we do not see his mother, for the focus is entirely on Max). Soon his room is transformed into a forest, and an ocean tumbles by. Each succeeding picture grows larger and larger on the page and the border recedes in size until it disappears altogether. Eventually the pictures overlap onto the facing page and finally become full-page spreads. The accompanying text describes an apparently extraordinary event. Max steps into his private boat and sails to the land where the Wild Things are, where he becomes their king and presides over a "wild rumpus" during which the creatures all do whatever they like (the dream of every child?). During this rumpus the pictures completely cover the pages and there is no text whatever. In other words, when Max is at his most animal-like, the civilizing aspects of reality (represented by the text and the white border) have vanished. Finally, Max longs to be "where someone loved him best of all," and he sails back to the comfort of his bedroom where he finds his supper waiting for him, "and it was still hot."

The pictures depicting his return gradually recede in size and the border is restored—at the same time that order is restored to Max (or his psyche). At the end of the story, we see Max obviously awakening from a dream and looking very much like a little boy, no longer the wild thing who terrorized the household at the story's beginning. The final words—"and it was still hot"—appear on a page without illustration, causing us to focus entirely on their meaning without pictorial assistance. We are left to ponder the statement, which signifies unconditional parental love and seems to contradict earlier statements in the book about the passage of time. (We are told, for instance, that Max's boat trip took "almost over a year.") The illustrations are far richer than this brief analysis can suggest, but this should provide an idea as to the possibilities that exist in the collaboration of words and pictures.

In another inventive use of picture-book layout, in *Come Away from the Water, Shirley,* John Burningham portrays a day at the beach for the imaginative Shirley and her parents. On the left-hand page, we see the dull routine of the parents portrayed with sparse colors on a large white background. On the right-hand page, we see in vivid colors the lively world of Shirley's imagination as she creates adventures on the beach. The text consists entirely of the mother's words, which are either admonitions to Shirley (which she happily ignores) or empty promises. The contrasting illustrations and the incongruous text make for subtle ironies that will not be lost on many children. Even adult readers must lament the loss of imagination that often comes with maturity.

Of course, we do not always find such powerful symbolism in a book's layout. But the best books remind us that the size and placement of illustrations is not (or should not be) a random process, but rather a carefully conceived plan that carries out the overall intent of the book. Words and pictures work together in a good picture book, and the resulting sum is something far greater and more rewarding than the individual parts.

ARTISTIC MEDIA

The artistic medium is simply the material (or materials—*media*) chosen to produce an illustration. Shall it be drawn with pencil or ink? Shall it be painted in oils or watercolors or tempera? Shall it be cut out on a block of wood or linoleum? We can group media generally into four broad categories: painterly techniques, graphic techniques, photography, and composite techniques.

Painterly Techniques

Painterly techniques are those in which the medium (paint, chalk, ink, and so on) is applied to a surface (usually paper) with an instrument (such as a brush, pen, or pencil). Paint itself consists of pigment (usually powdered) mixed with some liquid or paste to make it spreadable. Many variations are possible depending on the medium used to mix with the pigment.

- *Watercolors*, as their name implies, use water as the medium, resulting in transparent, typically soft, delicate pictures, as in Potter's *The Tale of Peter Rabbit* (Figure 7.4).

- *Tempera* is made by mixing pigments with egg yolk or some other albuminous substance. Tempera is not as transparent as watercolor and can produce some brilliant hues. It was used by Maurice Sendak in his classic *Where the Wild Things Are*.

- *Gouache* is a powdered paint similar to tempera, but mixed with a white base, resulting in a delicate hue. Gouache was the favorite medium of Margot Zemach in such works as *Duffy and the Devil*.

- *Poster color* is a coarser version of gouache and can be found in Jacob Lawrence's *Harriet and the Promised Land*. The colors tend to be bolder than in gouache.

- *Oil paint* typically uses linseed oil as a base and is among the most opaque of media. One of the best examples is found in Paul O. Zelinsky's version of *Rumpelstiltskin*.

- *Acrylics* use a plastic base, a product of twentieth-century technology, and they produce very brilliant colors; Barbara Cooney's illustrations for *Ox-Cart Man* by Donald Hall are excellent examples.

- *Pastels* differ from the rest in that they are typically applied in powdered form (often with the fingers). Chris Van Allsburg used pastels in his *The Wreck of the Zephyr*.

- *Chalk*, *pencil*, and *ink* drawings, while technically not painting, follow the same general principles as painterly techniques. Chris Van Allsburg's *Jumanji* (Figure 7.2) is illustrated with pencil drawings.

- *Crayons* were used by John Burningham in his fanciful story *Come Away from the Water, Shirley*.

- *Scratchboard* illustration is a technique in which the artist first paints a deep, black ink over a smooth board (called, appropriately, a "scratchboard") and then scratches the design onto the surface with a sharp instrument. Leonard Everett Fisher is a master of this technique, using it in his informational books for children (see Figure 12.1).

Each of these media produces differing effects, and two or more may be used in combination as well. Leo and Diane Dillon's illustrations for their alphabet book, *From Ashanti to Zulu*, for example, combine watercolors, pastels, and acrylics.

Graphic Techniques

Graphic techniques refer to those techniques in which the artist prepares blocks or plates that are then inked and imprinted on paper. As with painterly techniques, there are several varieties.

- *Woodblocks* were the very earliest form of reproducible art. The first printed book illustrations—dating from the late middle ages—were made from blocks of wood on which the artist carved away all the areas that were not to be printed. The blocks were inked and paper was pressed onto them, resulting in the transfer of the image from block to paper. Today, wood-block illustrations can still be found in such books as Ed Emberley's *Drummer Hoff* (retold by Barbara Emberley), where stylized wood-block illustrations give an old-fashioned flavor to a folk rhyme.

- *Linocuts* are similar to woodblocks in principle, but the artist uses blocks of linoleum rather than wood. Barbara Cooney's *Dick Whittington and His Cat* is an example.

- *Stone lithography* is a complex process that involves first drawing a design on a smooth, flat stone with a waxy mixture similar to a crayon. As in wood-blocks, the image must be done in reverse. The stone is then treated with a chemical fixative, wetted with water, and finally inked. The ink sticks only to the waxed areas, and when paper is pressed onto the stone, an impression is made. Figure 7.7, Robert McCloskey's *One Morning in Maine,* is an example of stone lithography; if you look closely at the illustration you can detect the grainy surface of the stone imprinted on the paper.

Photography

Photography may be considered an artistic style as much as a technique, but it is nevertheless an art. And the art of photography is the art of composition—of arranging objects within a frame so that the result is intellectually stimulating. In picture story-books, we normally expect something more creative than Polaroid snaps, and when photographs are used to tell stories, it is principally for realistic stories. Photographs can also be especially effective in informational books. Imaginatively used in black and white or in color, photography can be dramatic, beautiful, and highly expressive. Tana Hoban's *Count and See* and *Look Again* demonstrate the uses of photography in concept books for very young children.

Composite Techniques

Composite techniques involve cutting, pasting, and/or assembling of materials to create an artistic whole. *Montage* is the collection and assembling of a variety of different pictures or designs to create a single picture. *Collage* is similar to montage but uses materials other than or in addition to paper—string, cotton, weeds, anything is game. Both have been used effectively in children's picture books, notably in the work of Ezra Jack Keats (*The Snowy Day* and its sequels) and Leo Lionni (*Frederick, Fish Is Fish* and many others).

In addition to these techniques, today's book illustrators are using techniques and media undreamed of by their predecessors. Fabric art, such as the batik used by Patricia MacCarthy in Margaret Mahy's *The Horrendous Hullabaloo,* is becoming popular. And, not surprisingly, computer-generated graphics (in which lies the danger of eliminating the artist's individual touch) have begun to appear in picture books (J. Otto Seibold's *Mr. Lunch Takes a Plane Ride,* for example).

Artistic Styles

Picture-book illustrators are often trained professionals and consummate artists. So it is not surprising that we should find a wide variety of sophisticated artistic styles represented in children's picture books. In the best examples, the artistic style evokes the mood established by the text.

Realism

Realistic or *representational art* portrays the world with faithful attention to lifelike detail. A few artists aim at almost photographic realism, but many, like Robert McCloskey in *One Morning in Maine* (Figure 7.7), prefer to approximate reality. Thus the best representational art carries the individual stamp of the artist. Realistic art can be done in full color or in monochromes (that is, one color, like McCloskey's art), and it is particularly suited to illustrate realistic stories with serious content or themes.

Cartoon Art

Cartoon art is very popular in children's books, probably because of its playful humor. Cartoons consist of exaggerated caricatures that emphasize emotion and movement. They possess no subtlety, but are simple and straightforward, and are a frequent choice for illustrating humorous stories, nonsense, and comical satire. Dr. Seuss's drawings are cartoons at their most outrageous, the colors always bold, the lines distinct. Wanda Gág's illustrations for *Millions of Cats* (Figure 7.5) possess many of the characteristics of cartoon art–although they carry overtones of folk art as well.

Expressionism

Ludwig Bemelmans's *Madeline* (Figure 7.1) is usually regarded as an example of *expressionistic art*. Expressionism was a school of painting that flourished in France toward the end of the nineteenth century. It was a reaction to realism that had long dominated art, but seemed archaic with the development of photography. Painters such as Vincent van Gogh sought new freedom of expression, rejecting traditional uses of line, color, space, and so on. Consequently we see much distortion and experimentalism in this art. Bemelmans refused to depict the landscape realistically and was more interested in shape and design and emotional response. The influence of expressionism is found often in children's picture books in the form of distorted shapes and provocative use of color and line. Another school related to expressionism is *Les Fauves* (the "wild beasts" in French), with its bold lines and almost shimmering quality, best seen in John Steptoe's *Daddy Is a Monster . . . Sometimes* (Figure 7.8). Expressionism is quite versatile and can be used to create fresh perspectives in both serious and humorous stories.

FIGURE 7.8   A child of expressionism, Les Fauves art includes distinctive strong, black lines separating parts of the picture—much like the lines made by the lead framing in stained-glass windows. Also characteristic of this artistic style is a certain vibrance of line that suggests motion—and emotion—as in this illustration from John Steptoe's *Daddy Is a Monster . . . Sometimes,* a story of parent/child relationships.

Impressionism

Another artistic school that has influenced children's illustrators is *impressionism,* also a nineteenth-century French movement. The most influential impressionists were Monet and Cezanne, who wished to convey more of the artist's emotional responses in their paintings. Color is the most distinctive feature of this school, especially the interplay of color and light, often created with splashes, speckles, or dots of paint as opposed to longer brush strokes. The effect is dreamlike, sometimes magical. Impressionism evokes a quiet, pensive mood, such as that found in Maurice Sendak's illustrations for Charlotte Zolotow's *Mr. Rabbit and the Lovely Present.* Related to impressionism is *pointillism,* in which pictures are created entirely from carefully positioned colored dots of equal size. Miroslav Sasek's *This Is New York* is influenced by pointillist art.

Surrealism

Surrealism, whose most famous practitioner was the painter Salvador Dali, is a very intellectual response to a subject. The expressionist and the impressionist make us feel, but the surrealist makes us think. Surrealistic art creates unnatural juxtapositions and bizarre incongruities. The influence of surrealism can be seen in Chris Van Allsburg's illustrations for *Jumanji* (Figure 7.2), which contain haunting images, unusual perspectives, and an eerie quality perfectly suited to a strange tale of a board game come to life. Anthony Browne's *Voices in the Park,* a story of contrasting perceptions—an adult's and a child's—also contains illustrations best described as surrealistic.

Folk Art

Folk art is associated with a specific cultural or social group and is usually decorative in nature, providing ornamentation for everyday utilitarian objects. It is found in such widely varied media as patchwork quilts, clothing designs, jewelry, pottery, and dishes. Because it is culturally specific, folk art is favored in illustrating folktales. Gerald McDermott's *Anansi the Spider* (Figure 7.6) suggests western African influences. Alice and Martin Provensen's primitive illustrations for *A Peaceable Kingdom: The Shaker Abecedarius* suggest the simple ways of the Shaker community.

For the most part, it is safe to say that art in children's picture books is eclectic, combining a wide variety of styles and schools. The best artists learn technique from the masters and then pursue their own creative paths toward a highly personalized expression. Consequently, picture books not only convey a good story, but, as a work of visual art, also refine the young reader's artistic sensibilities.

APPRECIATING THE PICTURE BOOK

Picture books constitute an art form that has become increasingly sophisticated. Understanding the artist's techniques and style can enrich our appreciation of the work as adults and help us to make wiser book selections for children. Additionally, picture books provide us with opportunities for introducing artistic principles, techniques, and styles to young children. Reading good picture books can foster in children an acuity of vision and artistic sensitivity that will serve them well throughout their lives. If we are truly successful, they will not only appreciate beauty in the world, they may wish to preserve and to create it as well.

RECOMMENDED READINGS

Alderson, Brian. *Looking at Picture Books 1973*. New York: Children's Book Council, 1974.

Bader, Barbara. *American Picturebooks from Noah's Ark to the Beast Within*. New York: Macmillan, 1976.

Barrett, Terry, and Kenneth Marantz. "Photographs as Illustrations." *The New Advocate* 17 (Fall 1989): 103–153.

Benedict, Susan, and Leonore Carlisle, eds. *Beyond Words: Picture Books for Older Readers and Writers*. Portsmouth, NH: Heinemann, 1992.

Cianciolo, Patricia. *Picture Books for Children*. 3rd ed. Chicago: American Library Association, 1990.

Cummins, Julie, ed. *Children's Book Illustration and Design*. Glen Cove, NY: PBC International, 1992.

Dooley, Patricia. "The Window in the Book: Conventions in the Illustrations of Children's Books." *Wilson Library Bulletin* October 1980: 108–112.

Freeman, La Verne, and Ruth Sunderlin Freeman. *The Child and His Picture Book*. New York: Century House, 1967.

Gainer, Ruth Straus. "Beyond Illustration: Information about Art in Children's Picture Books." *Art Education* March 1982: 16–19.

Gombrich, E. H. *The Image and the Eye: Further Studies in the Psychology of Pictorial Representation*. Ithaca: Cornell University Press, 1982.

Gottleib, Gerald. *Early Children's Books and Their Illustrations*. Boston: Godine, 1975.

Hubbard, R. *Authors of Pictures, Draughtsmen of Words*. Portsmouth, NH: Heinemann, 1989.

Hurlimann, Bettina. *Picture-Book World*. Cleveland: World, 1969.

Kiefer, Barbara Z. *The Potential of Picturebooks: From Visual Literacy to Aesthetic Understanding*. Columbus, OH: Merrill; Englewood Cliffs, NJ: Prentice-Hall, 1995.

Kingman, Lee, ed. *The Illustrator's Notebook*. Boston: Horn Book, 1978.

Kingman, Lee, Joanna Foster, and Ruth Giles Lontoft, comps. *Illustrators of Children's Books, 1957–1966*. Boston: Horn Book, 1968. (Also, *Illustrators of Children's Books, 1744–1945* and *Illustrators of Children's Books, 1946–1956*.)

Kingman, Lee, Grace Hogarth, and Harriet Quimby. *Illustrators of Children's Books, 1967–1976*. Boston: Horn Book, 1978.

Lacy, L. E. *Art and Design in Children's Books: An Analysis of Caldecott Award Winning Illustrations*. Chicago: American Library Association, 1986.

Lanier, V. *The Visual Arts and the Elementary Child*. New York: Teachers College Press, 1985.

Matthias, Margaret, and Graciela Italiano. "Louder Than a Thousand Words." In *Signposts of Criticism of Children's Literature*. Robert Bator, comp. Chicago: American Library Association, 1983.

Nikolajeva, Maria, and Carol Scott. *How Picture Books Work*. New York: Garland, 2000.

Nodelman, Perry. *Words About Pictures: The Narrative Art of Children's Picture Books*. Athens, GA: University of Georgia Press, 1988.

Pitz, Henry C. *Illustrating Children's Books: History, Technique, Production*. New York: Watson-Guptill, 1963.

Roxburgh, Stephen. "A Picture Equals How Many Words? Narrative Theory and Picture Books for Children." *The Lion and the Unicorn* 7/8 (1983/84): 20–33.

Schwarcz, Joseph H. *Ways of the Illustrator: Visual Communication in Children's Literature*. Chicago: American Library Association, 1982.

Shulevitz, Uri. *Writing with Pictures: How to Write and Illustrate Children's Books*. New York: Watson-Guptin, 1985.

Spitz, Ellen Handler. *Inside Picture Books*. New Haven: Yale University Press, 1999.

Stewig, John Warren. *Looking at Picture Books*. Fort Atkinson, WI: Highsmith Press, 1995.

SELECTED BIBLIOGRAPHY OF PICTURE STORYBOOKS

(See Chapter 5 for a list of multicultural picture books and Chapter 8 for a list of folktales in picture-book format.)

Ackerman, Karen. *Song and Dance Man*. New York: Knopf, 1988.

Adoff, Arnold. *Black Is Brown Is Tan*. Illus. Emily McCully. New York: Harper, 1973.

Ahlberg, Janet, and Allan Ahlberg. *The Jolly Postman*. Illus. Allan Ahlberg. Boston: Little, Brown, 1986.

Aiken, Joan. *The Moon's Revenge*. Illus. Alan Lee. New York: Knopf, 1987.

Akass, Susan. *Number Nine Duckling*. Illus. Alex Ayliffe. Honesdale, PA: Boyds Mills, 1993.

Alexander, Lloyd. *The Fortune-Tellers*. Illus. Trina Schart Hyman. New York: Dutton, 1992.

Alexander, Martha. *Nobody Asked Me If I Wanted a Baby Sister*. New York: Dial, 1971.

Allard, Harry, and James Marshall. *Miss Nelson Is Missing*. Illus. James Marshall. Boston: Houghton Mifflin, 1977.

Allen, Jeffrey. *Mary Alice, Operator Number 9*. Illus. James Marshall. Boston: Little, Brown, 1975.

Ardizzone, Edward. *Little Tim and the Brave Sea Captain*. 1936. New York: Penguin, 1983.

Asch, Frank. *Sand Cake*. New York: Crown, 1987.

Babbitt, Natalie. *Bub: Or, The Very Best Thing*. New York: HarperCollins, 1994.

Bang, Molly. *The Grey Lady and the Strawberry Snatcher*: New York: Four Winds, 1980.

——. *The Paper Crane*. New York: Greenwillow, 1985.

Banks, Kate. *And If the Moon Could Talk*. Illus. Georg Hallensleben. New York: Farrar, Straus & Giroux, 1998.

——. *Baboon*. Illus. Georg Hallensleben. New York: Farrar, Straus & Giroux, 1997.

Bates, Artie Ann. *Ragsale*. Boston: Houghton Mifflin, 1995.

Bedard, Michael. *Emily*. Illus. Barbara Cooney. New York: Doubleday, 1992.

Bemelmans, Ludwig. *Madeline*. New York: Viking, 1937.

——. *Madeline's Rescue*. New York: Penguin, 1953.

Beskow, Elsa. *Pelle's New Suit*. New York: Harper, 1929.

Billout, Guy. *Something's Not Quite Right*. Lincoln, MA: Godine, 2002.

Birney, Betty G. *Tyrannosaurus Rex*. Illus. John O'Brien. Boston: Houghton Mifflin, 1994.

Blos, Joan. *Lottie's Circus*. Illus. Irene Trivas. New York: Morrow, 1989.

Brooke, L. Leslie. *Johnny Crow's Garden*. 1903. London: Warne, 1978.

——. *Johnny Crow's Party*. 1907. London: Warne, 1966.

Brown, Margaret Wise. *The Dead Bird*. Reading, MA: Addison-Wesley, 1958.

——. *Goodnight Moon*. Illus. Clement Hurd. New York: Harper, 1947.

——. *The Little Island*. Illus. Leonard Weisgard. New York: Doubleday, 1946.

——. *The Runaway Bunny*. Illus. Clement Hurd. New York: Harper, 1942.

Browne, Anthony. *Voices in the Park*. New York: DK Ink, 1998.

Bunting, Eve. *Fly Away Home*. Illus. Ronald Himler. New York: Clarion, 1991.

——. *Smoky Night*. Illus. David Diaz. New York: Harcourt, 1994.

——. *So Far from the Sea*. Illus. Chris K. Soenpiet. New York: Clarion, 1998.

Burningham, John. *Come Away from the Water, Shirley*. New York: Harper, 1977.

——. *Mr. Gumpy's Motorcar*. New York: Crowell, 1976.

——. *Mr. Gumpy's Outing*. New York: Holt, 1971.

Burton, Virginia L. *The Little House*. Boston: Houghton Mifflin, 1942.

——. *Mike Mulligan and His Steam Shovel*. Boston: Houghton Mifflin, 1939.

Carrick, Carol. *In the Moonlight, Waiting*. Illus. Donald Carrick. New York: Clarion, 1990.

Chandra, Deborah, and Madeleine Comora. *George Washington's Teeth*. Illus. Brock Cole. New York: Farrar, Straus & Giroux, 2003.

Chorao, Kay. *Little Farm by the Sea*. New York: Holt, 1998.

Clifton, Lucille. *Some of the Days of Everett Anderson*. Illus. Evaline Ness. New York: Holt, 1970.

Collington, Peter. *A Small Miracle*. New York: Knopf, 1997.

Conrad, Pam. *The Tub People*. Illus. Richard Egielski. New York: Harper, 1989.

Cooney, Barbara. *Island Boy*. New York: Viking, 1988.

——. *Miss Rumphius*. New York: Viking, 1982.

Crews, Donald. *Sail Away*. New York: Greenwillow, 1995.

Dana, Doris. *The Elephant and His Secret*. Illus. Antonio Frasconi. New York: Knopf, 1989.

Daugherty, James. *Andy and the Lion*. New York: Viking, 1938.

Dayle, Ann Dodds. *Where's Pup?* Illus. Pierre Pratt. New York: Dial, 2003.

de Angeli, Marguerite. *Thee Hannah!* New York: Doubleday, 1940.

de Brunhoff, Jean. *The Story of Babar, the Little Elephant*. 1933. New York: Knopf, 1989. (The first of a series)

DeFelice, Cynthia. *Willy's Silly Grandma*. Illus. Shelley Jackson. New York: Orchard, 1997.

de Paola, Tomie. *Nana Upstairs, Nana Downstairs*. New York: Penguin, 1978.

De Regniers, Beatrice Schenk. *May I Bring a Friend?* Illus. Beni Montressor. New York: Atheneum, 1964.

Dunrea, Olivier. *The Painter Who Loved Chickens*. New York: Farrar, Straus & Giroux, 1995.

Duvoisin, Roger. *Petunia*. New York: Knopf, 1950.

Ehrlich, Amy. *Parents in the Pigpen, Pigs in the Tub*. Illus. Steven Kellogg. New York: Dial, 1993.

Ets, Marie Hall. *Play with Me*. New York: Penguin, 1955.

Fatio, Louise. *The Happy Lion*. Illus. Roger Duvoisin. 1954. New York: Scholastic, 1986.

Feiffer, Jules. *I Lost My Bear*. New York: Morrow, 1998.

Fitzhugh, Louise, and Sandra Scoppettone. *Bang, Bang, You're Dead*. New York: Harper, 1969.

Flack, Marjorie. *The Story about Ping*. Illus. Kurt Weise. New York: Penguin, 1933.

Fleischman, Sid. *The Scarebird*. Illus. Peter Sis. New York: Greenwillow, 1988.

Ford, Miela. *Little Elephant*. Illus. Tana Hoban. New York: Greenwillow, 1994.

Fox, Mem. *Night Noises*. Illus. Terry Denton. New York: Harcourt, 1989.

Freeman, Don. *Corduroy*. New York: Viking, 1968.

Gág, Wanda. *Millions of Cats*. New York: Coward, McCann, 1928.

Gerstein, Mordicai. *The Man Who Walked Between the Towers*. Brookfield, CT: Millbrook, 2003.

Goble, Paul. *The Girl Who Loved Wild Horses*. New York: Bradbury, 1978.

——. *Hercules*. New York: Putnam, 1960.

Gramatky, Hardie. *Little Toot*. New York: Putnam, 1978.

Hader, Berta, and Elmer Hader. *The Big Snow*. New York: Macmillan, 1948.

Hale, Lucretia. *The Lady Who Put Salt in Her Coffee*. Illus. and adapted by Amy Schwartz. New York: Harcourt, 1989.

Hall, Donald. *Ox-Cart Man*. Illus. Barbara Cooney. New York: Penguin, 1983.

Handforth, Thomas. *Mei Lei*. New York: Doubleday, 1938.

Hawkins, Colin. *Take Away Monsters*. New York: Putnam, 1984.

Hellen, Nancy. *The Bus Stop*. New York: Watts, 1988.

Henkes, Kevin. *Chrysanthemum*. New York: Greenwillow, 1991.

Hoban, Julia. *Amy Loves the Rain*. Illus. Lillian Hoban. New York: Harper, 1989.

Hoestlandt, Jo. *Star of Fear, Star of Hope*. Illus. Johanna Kang. New York: Walker, 1995.

Hoffman, Mary. *Amazing Grace*. Illus. Caroline Binch. New York: Dial, 1991.

Hol, Colby. *A Visit to the Farm*. New York: North-South, 1989.

Holub, Joan. *The Garden That We Grow*. Illus. Hiroe Nakata. New York: Viking, 2001.

Hutchins Pat. *Good-Night Owl*. New York: Macmillan, 1972.

——. *Rosie's Walk*. New York: Macmillan, 1968.

Innocenti, Roberto, and Christophe Gallaz. *Rose Blanche*. New York: Creative Education, 1985.

Johnson, Crockett. *Harold and the Purple Crayon*. New York: Harper, 1955.

——. *Harold's Circus*. New York: Scholastic, 1959.

Johnson, Stephen T. *As the City Sleeps*. New York: Viking, 2002.

Jonell, Lynne. *Mommy Go Away!* Illus. Petra Mathers. New York: Putnam, 1997.

Karas, G. Brian. *The Windy Day*. New York: Simon & Schuster, 1998.

Keats, Ezra Jack. *Peter's Chair*. New York: Harper, 1967.

——. *The Snowy Day*. New York: Viking, 1962.

Keeping, Charles. *Joseph's Yard*. New York: Watts, 1969.

Kellogg, Steven. *The Island of the Skog*. New York: Dial, 1973.

Kraus, Robert. *Leo the Late Bloomer*. Illus. Jose and Ariane Aruego. New York: Simon & Schuster, 1987.

Krauss, Ruth. *The Backward Day*. Illus. Marc Simont. New York: Harper, 1950.

Kuskin, Karla. *The Bear Who Saw the Spring*. New York: Harper, 1961.

Langstaff, John M. *A Frog Went A-Courtin'*. Illus. Feodor Rojankovsky. New York: Scholastic, 1985.

Leaf, Munro. *The Story of Ferdinand*. Illus. Robert Lawson. New York: Viking, 1936.

Lester, Julius. *Black Cowboy, Wild Horses: A True Story*. Illus. Jerry Pinkney. New York: Dial, 1998.

Lionni, Leo. *Fish Is Fish*. New York: Knopf, 1970.

——. *Frederick*. New York: Pantheon, 1967.

Locker, Thomas. *Where the River Begins*. New York: Dial, 1984.

Loomis, Christine. *Cowboy Bunnies*. Illus. Ora Eitan. New York: Putnam, 1997.

MacDonald, Golden (pseud. of Margaret Wise Brown). *The Little Island*. Illus. Leonard Wiesgard. New York: Doubleday, 1946.

MacLachlan, Patricia. *All the Places to Love*. Illus. Mike Wimmer. New York: HarperCollins, 1994.

——. *What You Know First*. Illus. Barry Moser. New York: HarperCollins, 1995.

Mahy, Margaret. *The Horrendous Hullabaloo*. Illus. Patricia MacCarthy. New York: Viking, 1992.

——. *The Rattlebang Picnic*. New York: Dial, 1994.

Martin, Jacqueline Briggs. *Washing the Willow Tree Loon*. Illus. Nancy Carpenter. New York: Simon & Schuster, 1995.

Maruki, Toshi. *Hiroshima No Pika*. Boston: Lothrop, Lee, & Shepard, 1982.

Mathers, Petra. *Lottie's New Beach Towel*. New York: Atheneum, 1998.

Mayer, Mercer. *There's a Nightmare in My Closet*. New York: Dial, 1968.

McCloskey, Robert. *Blueberries for Sal*. New York: Viking, 1948.

——. *Make Way for Ducklings*. New York: Viking, 1941.

——. *Time of Wonder*. New York: Viking, 1957.

McCully, Emily Arnold. *Mirette on the High Wire*. New York: Putnam, 1992.

McMullan, Kate. *I Stink!* Illus. Jim McMullan. New York: HarperCollins, 2002.

Meddaugh, Susan. *Martha Speaks*. Boston: Houghton Mifflin, 1992.

Milhous, Katherine. *The Egg Tree*. New York: Macmillan, 1971.

Mitchell, Margaree King. *Uncle Jed's Barbershop*. Illus. James Ransom. New York: Simon & Schuster, 1993.

Ness, Evaline. *Sam, Bangs & Moonshine*. New York: Holt, 1966.

Patron, Susan. *Dark Cloud Strong Breeze*. Illus. Peter Catalanotto. New York: Watts, 1994.

Pearce, Philippa. *Emily's Own Elephant*. Illus. John Lawrence. New York: Greenwillow, 1988.

Peet, Bill. *Encore for Eleanor*. Boston: Houghton Mifflin, 1985.

Perkins, Lynne Rae. *The Broken Cat*. New York: Greenwillow, 2002.

Peters, Lisa Westberg. *Cold Little Duck, Duck, Duck*. Illus. Sam Williams. New York: Greenwillow, 2000.

Piatti, Celestino. *The Happy Owls*. New York: Atheneum, 1964.

Pinkney, Brian. *JoJo's Flying Side Kick*. New York: Simon & Schuster, 1995.

Pinkney, Gloria Jean. *The Sunday Outing*. Illus. Jerry Pinkney. New York: Dial, 1994.

Politi, Leo. *Song of the Swallows*. New York: Macmillan, 1986.

Potter, Beatrix. *The Tale of Peter Rabbit*. London: Warne, 1901.

Provensen, Alice, and Martin Provensen. *The Glorious Flight: Across the Channel with Louis Bleriot*. New York: Viking, 1983.

Raskin, Ellen. *Nothing Ever Happens on My Block*. New York: Macmillan, 1966.

Rayner, Mary. *Garth Pig Steals the Show*. New York: Dutton, 1993.

Rey, A.H. *Curious George*. Boston: Houghton Mifflin, 1973.

Rylant, Cynthia. *The Relatives Came*. Illus. Stephen Gammell. New York: Bradbury, 1985.

——. *When I Was Young in the Mountains*. Illus. Diane Goode. New York: Dutton, 1982.

Say, Allen. *Tree of Cranes*. Boston: Houghton Mifflin, 1991.

Seibold, J. Otto, and Vivian Walsh. *Mr. Lunch Takes a Plane Ride*. Illus. Otto Seibold, New York: Viking, 1993.

Schwartz, Amy. *What James Likes Best*. New York: Atheneum, 2003.

Sendak, Maurice. *In the Night Kitchen*. New York: Harper, 1970.

——. *Outside Over There*. New York: Harper, 1981.

——. *Where the Wild Things Are*. New York: Harper, 1963.

Seuss, Dr. (pseud. of Theodore Geisel). *And to Think That I Saw It on Mulberry Street*. New York: Vanguard, 1973.

——. *The Cat in the Hat*. New York: Random House, 1957.

——. *Green Eggs and Ham*. New York: Random House, 1960.

Shannon, George. *Tippy-Toe Chick, GO!* Illus. Laura Dronzek. New York: Greenwillow, 2003.

Shannon, Margaret. *Elvira*. Boston: Houghton Mifflin, 1993.

Sheppard, Jeff. *Splash, Splash*. New York: Macmillan, 1994.

Shulevitz, Uri. *Rain, Rain, Rivers*. New York: Farrar, Straus & Giroux, 1969.

Simon, Norma. *The Saddest Time*. Illus. Jacqueline Rogers. Morton Grove, IL: A. Whitman, 1989.

Sis, Peter. *Komodo!* New York: Greenwillow, 1993.

Small, David. *Imogene's Antlers*. New York: Crown, 2000.

Smith, Janice Lee. *The Baby Blues*. Illus. Dick Gackenbach. New York: HarperCollins, 1994.

Soto, Gary. *Chato's Kitchen*. Illus. Susan Guevara. New York: Putnam, 1995.

Steig, William. *Sylvester and the Magic Pebble*. New York: Windmill, 1969.

——. *Wizzil*. Illus. Quentin Blake. New York: Farrar, Straus & Giroux, 2000.

Steptoe, John. *My Daddy Is a Monster . . . Sometimes*. New York: Viking, 1980.

Stewart, Sarah. *The Library*. Illus. David Small. New York: Farrar, Straus & Giroux, 1995.

Stoeke, Janet Morgan. *A Hat for Minerva Louise*. New York: Dutton, 1994.

Suen, Anastasia. *Window Music.* Illus. Wade Zahares. New York: Viking, 1998.

Swift, Hildegarde. *The Little Red Lighthouse and the Great Gray Bridge.* Illus. Lynd Ward. New York: Harcourt, 1974.

Tejima, Keizaburo. *Fox's Dream.* New York: Philomel, 1987.

Thomassie, Tynia. *Feliciana Feydra LeRoux: A Cajun Tall Tale.* Illus. Cat Bowman Smith. Boston: Little, Brown, 1995.

Thurber, James. *Many Moons.* Illus. Marc Simont. New York: Harcourt, 1990.

Titus, Eve. *Anatole in Italy.* Illus. Paul Galdone. New York: McGraw-Hill, 1973.

Tresselt, Alvin. *Hide and Seek Fog.* Illus. Roger Duvoisin. New York: Lothrop, 1965.

——. *White Snow, Bright Snow.* Illus. Roger Duvoisin. New York: Lothrop, 1947.

Turkle, Brinton. *Thy Friend, Obadiah.* New York: Viking, 1967.

Udry, Janice M. *The Moon Jumpers.* Illus. Maurice Sendak. New York: Harper, 1959.

——. *A Tree Is Nice.* Illus. Marc Simont. New York: Harper, 1956.

Ungerer, Tonie. *The Beast of Monsieur Racine.* New York: Farrar, Straus & Giroux, 1971.

Van Allsburg, Chris. *The Garden of Abdul Gasazi.* Boston: Houghton Mifflin, 1979.

——. *Jumanji.* Boston: Houghton Mifflin, 1981.

——. *The Polar Express.* Boston: Houghton Mifflin, 1985.

Viorst, Judith. *Alexander and the Terrible, Horrible, No Good, Very Bad Day.* Illus. Ray Cruz. New York: Atheneum, 1972.

——. *The Tenth Good Thing About Barney.* Illus. Erik Blegvad. New York: Atheneum, 1971.

Waber, Bernard. *The House on East 88th Street.* Boston: Houghton Mifflin, 1975.

——. *Ira Sleeps Over.* Boston: Houghton Mifflin, 1972.

——. *Lyle, Lyle, Crocodile.* Boston: Houghton Mifflin, 1987.

Waddell, Martin. *Hi, Harry!* Illus. Barbara Firth. New York: Candlewick, 2003.

Wandro, Mark, and Joanie Blank. *My Daddy Is a Nurse.* Reading, MA: Addison-Wesley, 1981.

Ward, Lynd K. *The Biggest Bear.* Boston: Houghton Mifflin, 1952.

Watanabe, Shigeo. *It's My Birthday!* Illus. Yasuo Ohtomo. New York: Philomel, 1988.

Wells, Rosemary. *Morris's Disappearing Bag.* New York: Dial, 1978.

——. *Noisy Nora.* New York: Dial, 1980.

Wild, Margaret. *The Queen's Holiday.* New York: Watts, 1992.

Willard, Nancy. *A Visit to William Blake's Inn.* Illus. Alice and Martin Provensen. New York: Harcourt, 1981.

Willhoite, Michael. *Daddy's Roommate.* Boston: Alyson, 1990.

Williams, Vera B. *A Chair for My Mother.* New York: Greenwillow, 1982.

——. *"More More More," Said the Baby: Three Love Stories.* New York: Greenwillow, 1990.

Willis, Val. *The Secret in the Matchbox.* Illus. John Shelley. New York: Farrar, Straus & Giroux, 1988.

Winthrop, Elizabeth. *That's Mine!* Illus. Emily McCully. New York: Holiday, 1977.

Wood, Audrey. *King Bidgood's in the Bathtub.* Illus. Don Wood. New York: Harcourt, 1985.

Yashima, Taro (pseud. of Jun Iwamatsu). *Crow Boy.* New York: Viking, 1955.

Yolen, Jane. *Owl Moon.* Illus. John Schoenherr. New York: Philomel, 1987.

Yorinks, Arthur. *Hey Al.* Illus. Richard Egielski. New York: Farrar, Straus & Giroux, 1988.

Zemach, Margot. *Jake and Honeybunch Go to Heaven.* New York: Farrar, Straus & Giroux, 1982.

Zion, Gene. *Harry, the Dirty Dog.* Illus. Margaret Bloy Graham. New York: Harper, 1956.

——. *Harry and the Lady Next Door.* Illus. Margaret Bloy Graham. New York: Harper, 1960.

Zolotow, Charlotte. *The Moon Was the Best.* Illus. Tana Hoban. New York: Greenwillow, 1993.

——. *Mr. Rabbit and the Lovely Present.* Illus. Maurice Sendak. New York: Harper, 1962.

——. *William's Doll.* Illus. William Pene DuBois. New York: Harper, 1972.

CHAPTER

8

Folk Literature

DEFINITION OF FOLK LITERATURE

Folk literature includes all the myths, legends, fables, and folktales passed down by word of mouth through the generations. These are the oldest stories—some predating the written word—and they have endured because they are entertaining and because they contain fundamental human truths by which people have lived for centuries. In many societies, the tales were passed on by a community storyteller, one who was entrusted with the society's sacred myths, its heroic epics and legends, its moral tales, its history.

These stories are society's attempt to give form and shape to its hopes and fears, reassurance for its doubts, and answers for its questionings. They not only impose order on seemingly random experience, they embody the culture's belief system. Of course, today, we regard many of these old tales as flights of fancy, but their power lingers for they capture our sense of wonder and we recognize their visions as poetic interpretations of the world. These visions are frequently more powerful than the explanations provided by our scientific investigations.

As we might expect, oral tales go through many changes as they pass through the generations and cross cultural boundaries. It has only been in the last two hundred years or so that scholars have begun to record many of these oral tales. In that time, stories have been gathered from the ancient cultures of Africa and the Far East, from pre-Columbian America and Aboriginal Australia—indeed, from all corners of the earth. And they continue to be gathered. What amazed early collectors was the remarkable similarity they found in stories from cultures widely separated by both time and space. The tales tell of heroes of miraculous birth who grow up to save their people from the forces of evil. They tell of wonderful transformations from human to animal or vice versa, of wizards or enchantresses casting their spells, of innocent girls suffering abuse at the hands of a wicked creature, and of strong and handsome warriors defeating powerful demons and dragons. Although the specific details vary from region to region, the general outlines are strikingly similar.

Two explanations have been offered for the similarities in folktales from widely separated cultures—monogenesis and polygenesis. *Monogenesis*—meaning literally "one beginning"—is the theory that all tales were ultimately derived from a single source (such as a Mesopotamian culture) and were gradually disseminated throughout the world. *Polygenesis*—meaning "many beginnings"—is the theory that tales emerged independently of each other in many different places throughout the world. Polygenesis attributes these marked similarities in form and content to the fundamental similarities in the human psyche—people around the world having similar hopes, fears, dreams, physical and emotional needs. Neither theory has yet been absolutely substantiated, and the truth may lie somewhere in between—that some tales emerged independently and others were adopted from neighboring cultures.

Folk literature, regardless of its place of origin, seems clearly to have arisen to meet a variety of human needs:

1. The need to explain the mysteries of the natural world in the absence of scientific information
2. The need to articulate our fears and dreams, thus making them accessible and manageable
3. The need to impose some order on the apparent random, even chaotic, nature of life, thus helping us to understand our place in the universe
4. The need to entertain ourselves and each other

Because folk literature originally served a multitude of purposes, it has assumed many different forms. Folktales and fables, myths, legends, and epics are among the most common. Some stories served as educational tools for preliterate societies, passing on knowledge essential for survival. Others helped to reinforce cultural practices and social mores—the importance of certain virtues, the significance of marriage or of the established social or political order, the superiority of one's clan or tribe over its neighbors, and so on. Vital to nearly all peoples were creation myths: how the world, *their* world, came to be. And we should not forget what must have been one of the driving forces behind the telling of these tales—entertainment. The stories served primitive societies in place of books, plays, movies, and television, and they embodied the popular attitudes, beliefs, and values of the culture. They retain their meaning for us because we still share a great deal more with our ancestors than we at first imagine.

TYPES OF FOLK LITERATURE

Folk literature is of infinite variety; it may be serious or comical, secular or religious, instructional or nonsensical and it holds great appeal for children. Some of the types of tales most popular with children follow.

Animal Tales

The *animal tale* is perhaps the oldest of all tales. Max Lüthi notes that "[a]mong primitive people, animal stories predominate. They are part myth, part fable, part fairy tale. Primitive peoples live in close contact with wild animals: they hunt them, but they also fear them, even revere them, and believe in their powers" (96). So it is not surprising that animals would play significant roles in early stories and legends. In Africa, the tales of Anansi the Spider, a trickster figure, are common. Native Americans tell countless animal tales and include animals in their mythology, as in stories of the Great Turtle, beavers, wolves, coyotes, hawks, and other native creatures. Talking animals also appear in many European folktales–the magic fish in "The Fisherman and His Wife" and the wolf in "Little Red Riding Hood," for example–but in the true animal tale the animals are the main characters and humans, if they appear at all, are merely functional (and often fools). Stories like "The Three Little Pigs" (see Figure 8.1) or "The Three Billy Goats Gruff" depict weaker animals outwitting stronger and fiercer animals–and this is a theme found the world over.

Fables

A *fable* is a brief tale with an explicit moral message. A fable frequently uses talking animals to symbolize human virtues and vices, and it differs from other animal tales in that it is overtly didactic, teaching lessons in moral and social behavior. Hence the old fable, "The Tortoise and the Hare," about the tortoise who wins the race because the overconfident hare dillydallies, concludes with the aphorism, "Slow and steady wins the race." Aesop, a legendary teacher of the ancient Greeks, is credited with the most famous fables, and it is usually assumed that he used them in his teaching. Ironically, even though their form would suggest a strong appeal among young children, many fables demand abstract thinking, and their points are often lost on children.

Märchen or Wonder Tales

The best known of the traditional folktales are the *märchen* or *wonder tales*. These are stories of supernatural wonders typically depicting the conflict between good and evil, usually focused on characters of royal birth. Most conclude with the triumph of virtue and a happy marriage. "Cinderella," "Snow White and the Seven Dwarfs," (see Figures 8.2 and 8.3) and "Sleeping

FIGURE 8.1 H. J. Ford's illustration for "The Three Little Pigs."

Source: From *The Green Fairy Book*, edited by Andrew Lang, London, 1892.

Beauty" are the classic examples. It is largely from these stories that the term "fairy tale" emerged, although few of the stories actually contain fairies. In the *märchen*, the supernatural is a dominant element, whether it be a magical person (a fairy godmother, a wicked witch) or a magical object (a wondrous beanstalk, a talking mirror) or an enchantment (a miraculous sleep that lasts until love's first kiss). Sometimes these stories describe the hero's or heroine's life from childhood through the accomplishment of some great deed and then marriage. Because the protagonists are usually in late adolescence and because matrimony is the end of many of these tales, they seem to be directed toward an older audience. Still they hold appeal for the very young. Their popularity undoubtedly springs from their imaginative characters, their supernatural elements, their focus on action, their simple sense of justice, their happy endings, and from the fundamental wisdom they contain. As Lüthi says, "Fairy tales are unreal but they are not untrue; they reflect essential developments and conditions of man's existence" (70).

Pourquoi Tales

A *pourquoi tale* (the name derives from the French word for "why") seeks to explain natural phenomena–why the beaver has a flat tail, why the mulberry is red, and so on. Pourquoi tales are found throughout the world and are especially popular in African and Native American folklore. A typical Native American tale is that explaining the creation of the Sleeping Bear Dunes on the northwest coast of Michigan's lower peninsula. The massive dunes, according to the tale, cover the body of a mother bear mourning the loss of her two cubs who drowned in Lake Michigan, and North and South Manitou islands, just off the coast, represent the two cubs themselves. Many pourquoi tales—such as creation tales—assume religious significance and are more properly considered myths, discussed below. Still other pourquoi tales are, at the same time, talking animal tales. These are not always exclusive categories.

Noodlehead Tales

A *noodlehead tale* (also termed a *merry, droll,* or *simpleton tale*) is a light-hearted tale about silly people doing silly things. The noodlehead tale is fundamentally that of the underdog. "Hans in Luck," in which the title character successively trades one possession for another of lesser value until he is left with nothing (except happiness), is an excellent example of such a tale. "The Three Wishes" is the story of a poor couple who are granted three wishes by a grateful magical creature whom they helped out of a jam. The foolish pair proceed to waste all three wishes, however, and wind up no better off than they were at the beginning—although they are usually happy in the end. Often noodlehead tales include no supernatural elements, or, if they do, as in "The Three Wishes," they are not the focus of the story. These tales are popular because of their pure nonsense and jocularity, and sometimes we enjoy the triumph of the good-hearted simpleton over the craftier evil characters of the story. Occasionally, the simpleton proves far wiser than anyone else, suggesting it is the world at large that is foolish and unable to recognize true wisdom.

Cumulative Tales

A *cumulative tale* is one in which successive additions are made to a repetitive plot line. Two well-known examples are "The Gingerbread Boy" and "The Turnip," wherein additional characters are summoned to help accomplish some feat, that is, to capture the gingerbread boy or to pull the giant turnip out of the ground. Cumulative tales are generally very simple in plot and brief, else they become tiresome, for with each addition, the entire sequence is repeated. Some of them are set to poetry, such as *Drummer Hoff*, retold by Barbara Emberley and illustrated by Ed Emberley, about the building of a Revolutionary War cannon. The cumulative tale or rhyme appeals to younger children who love the repeated pattern, which tests their memories and allows them to join in the telling.

Tall Tales

Tall tales are comic stories of preposterous exaggeration. In English folklore we find the stories describing the extraordinary exploits of Jack the Giant Killer. But no one loves the tall tale more than Americans. Sometimes the heroes are completely fictional, Paul Bunyan, the giant logger, and his equally impressive blue ox, Babe, being the most famous. Sometimes the heroes are taken from real life—Davy Crockett and Johnny Appleseed—and their stories are amplified well beyond the bounds of fact. Tall tales defy logic and are usually without moral lessons. These tales often are found in series, with each story relating a new and outrageous exploit. Their delight is in their absurdity and in the wildly imaginative yarns, each succeeding one seeming to outdo the last.

Ghost Stories

Most young people enjoy, in the right circumstances, being frightened. The immense popularity of horror movies among teenagers and Halloween celebrations among younger children attests to the appeal of spine tinglers. Telling *ghost stories* around a campfire or beneath the blankets at a pajama party has long been a childhood entertainment. Most cultures have their own versions of chilling tales, ghosts and evil spirits walking the night, or tales that Richard Chase calls "jump tales" because the teller jumps out toward the listeners at the climax to surprise them. Since most children prefer to hear these stories in groups where there is safety in their numbers, and since many of these stories are more effective when delivered orally, ghost stories are perfect examples of the living folktale, told *by* the people *to* the people, with each tale adapted to the specific occasion. But ghost stories also make great reading. Alvin Schwartz's blood-curdling retellings, *Scary Stories to Tell in the Dark*, are great favorites with children.

Myths

Myths are the stories of gods, goddesses, and heroes of a given culture, and these stories serve a variety of purposes, combining science, religion, and even sociology and psychology. Myths perform a number of functions:

1. Myths explain the origin of the world and of human beings—virtually every culture has some creation myth.

FIGURE 8.2 Walter Crane's illustration for "Snow White."

Source: From *Household Stories by the Brothers Grimm*, translated by Lucy Crane, London, 1886.

2. Myths explain the origins of customs and societal beliefs–ancient Greeks and Romans placed coins in the mouths of their dead that they might have the fare for Charon, the mythical creature who would ferry them over the River Styx to the Underworld.

3. Myths provide explanations for natural phenomena–early peoples devised myths to explain the rising and setting of the sun, the changes of the moon, the change of seasons, the occurrence of thunderstorms, and so on.

4. Myths help to define human relationships with the deity or deities–the Judeo-Christian tradition establishes God as a supreme power and an authoritarian father figure, whereas in the Norse tradition, the power of the gods was more restricted.

5. Myths may reinforce cultural values, drawing attention to what the culture sees as primary good and evil; the biblical stories, for example, warn us against over-weening pride or disobedience to parents.

6. Not least, myths help to resolve humanity's fear of the unknown–whether it be thunder and lightning (explained as activities of the gods) or death (typically explained as a passage from one world into another).

CLASSICAL GREEK AND ROMAN MYTHS To people of Western cultures, the most familiar mythology outside the Judeo-Christian tradition is that of ancient Greece and Rome. Our daily lives are imbued with references to their extensive pantheon and the notable heroes of that civilization. Note the names of the planets, stars, and galaxies, and, on a more mundane level, months of the year, body parts (*Achilles tendon*), cleaning agents (*Ajax*), synthetic fibers (*Herculon*), automobiles (*Mercury* and *Saturn*), tires and mapbooks (*Atlas*), athletic games (*Olympics*), and so on. A knowledge of these myths is important to make us aware of our cultural debts, and to help us recognize the multitude of references to Greek and Roman mythology in the modern world. Our interest in these tales might be both entertaining and spiritually uplifting, in that these exciting stories also tell us–as do the folktales–a great deal about human nature. In classical Greece, the gods and goddesses were powerful figures who often struggled against one another for human favor and were pragmatic in their dealings with humans ("I'll do that for you if you do this for me"). The questions of humanity's obedience to a higher power, the relationships of men and women to one another, the power of love, and the strength of parental devotion are all addressed in this body of mythology.

NORSE MYTHS A second important influence on the Western tradition is Norse mythology, which reflects the harsh way of life engendered by the severe, yet dramatically beautiful, Scandinavian lands. In Norse mythology, the gods and goddesses were defenders of humanity against the mighty forces of evil. Like the Greek and Roman gods and goddesses, the Norse deities were anthropomorphic; that is, the gods and goddesses were conceived in human forms (a relatively uncommon practice, when we consider the many monsters, demons, multiarmed deities, feathered serpents, and animal forms worshipped throughout the world). But compared with the Greek deities, the Norse gods and goddesses were a much more serious lot, engaged in a perpetual struggle with the forces of evil, a struggle that they were destined eventually to lose. Individual codes of honor were highly esteemed in this war-conscious society. Among the most familiar images from Norse mythology is the god of thunder, Thor, who is remembered weekly in our own culture, for Thursday was named for him. Tuesday, Wednesday, and Friday were named for other Norse deities: Tuesday for Tiw (the god of war), Wednesday for Woden (the father of the gods), and Friday for Fria (the goddess of fruits). This fascinating mythology still lingers with us.

NATIVE AMERICAN MYTHS The native peoples of the Americas (including North, Central, and South America) lived—and many still do live—in close harmony with the natural world. Indeed, the modern Native American "still lives connected to the nurturing womb of mythology. Mysterious, but real power dwells in nature—in mountains, rivers, rocks, even pebbles" (Erdoes and Ortiz xi). The belief that spirits inhabit natural objects is referred to as *animism,* and it is quite common throughout the world. The stories Native Americans tell are, not surprisingly, stories of nature and the associations between nature and human beings. Among Native Americans, stories are frequently told in chains of episodes—sometimes incomplete—each building on the last. Disorganized by the standards of European folktales, the Native American tales are more spontaneous, largely because they are still relatively close to their oral beginnings. Types of stories found in Native American myths and legends are creation stories, describing the foundation of the world; pourquoi tales, describing the origins of other natural phenomena; and trickster tales, which often combine the animal tale with the heroic legend, the hero being an exasperating and wily character outwitting his compatriots. (The trickster is a familiar character in folk literature, usually being a clever animal, often whimsical and devilish. The trickster delights in bringing havoc to the world and is an ambivalent character, often an antihero and troublemaker who makes life interesting and keeps the rest of us on our toes.) Unlike many of the world's mythical stories, the Native American tales remain part of the living tradition of Native American society.

AFRICAN MYTHS Like Native American mythology, African mythology is widely diverse, with each civilization or society having developed its own set of beliefs. Also like Native American mythology, most African mythology prominently features the natural world, with spirits inhabiting virtually everything. Magic and ancestor worship also form important parts of African religious practice. Most of the tales that have been retold for children are creation stories and stories of animal heroes, including the trickster. Many African myths and legends were carried to America in the seventeenth and eighteenth centuries by Africans who had been sold into slavery. The stories of Anansi the spider are trickster tales that originated in Africa, were later popular in the West Indies, and are now widely disseminated throughout the English-speaking world.

ORIENTAL MYTHS India and the Far East also developed highly complex and sophisticated mythologies. Unlike Greek, Roman, and Norse mythologies with their anthropomorphic deities, the deities of these cultures are frequently polymorphic, combining both human and animal forms. In some oriental religions, as in Hinduism in India, the gods and goddesses take extraordinary forms–humans with many arms, heads, eyes, and so on. The early religions of China and Japan were animistic, much like the Native American and African, but these were supplanted by Buddhism, Confucianism, Shintoism, and Taoism—often in Asian cultures two or more religions are observed simultaneously (in part because they tend to be more ethical than eschatological–in other words, they show people how to live rather than what will happen to them when they die). Each religion has its own stories, for example, the beautiful humanistic tales of the compassionate Buddha or the adventures of the Hindu gods. The mythology of Asian cultures is not particularly well known in the English-speaking world, although in recent years more myths and legends from this region have been published.

What all these disparate mythologies have in common is a need to explain our relationship to the wondrous and mysterious forces that drive the universe, and to give some validity to our existence. These are needs that we have neither outgrown nor entirely satisfied.

Epics and Heroic Legends

Epics and heroic legends initially grew out of mythology, but instead of focusing on gods and goddesses, these stories had human beings as their heroes. Among the most popular of the Greek and Roman heroes are Achilles, Odysseus, Hector, Jason, and Perseus. They were indeed the first superheroes, the prototypes of Superman, Batman, and Wonder Woman. Although Homer's *Iliad* and *Odyssey* were originally intended for adults, they have much appeal for young readers, for they are adventure-filled and wrought with unworldly wonders. Excellent children's versions are available, such as Padraic Colum's *The Children's Homer* and *The Golden Fleece*.

Medieval Europe saw the rise of epic tales derived from Christian sources–King Arthur and the Knights of the Round Table, the Quest for the Holy Grail, and the Life of Charlemagne being the most popular tales. These epics and legends are often more secular than religious, Malory's *The Death of Arthur* and the French epic *The Song of Roland* being among the most famous, and some of these tales have been successfully retold for young readers, for example, Rosemary Sutcliff's story of the Quest for the Holy Grail, *The Light Beyond the Forest*.

Saints' Lives and Local Legends

Also popular in the Middle Ages were the *saints' lives*, stories recounting often apocryphal tales of the lives and miracles of saints. These enjoy little modern popularity, but as late as the early part of the twentieth century, John Foxe's *Book of Martyrs*, a sixteenth-century work about the deaths of persecuted Christians, was still considered fare for children. In a similar fashion, *local legends* emerged, focusing on local secular (as opposed to religious) heroes and typically departing rather dramatically from reality. The typical legend grows up around real people, although the facts are soon lost—George Washington's chopping down the cherry tree, Davy Crockett's frontier exploits, Johnny Appleseed's indefatigable planting of apple trees. Some of these stories, as we have seen, develop into tall tales.

The Literary Fairy Tale

The traditional folktales have inspired modern counterparts—original tales by modern writers that have all the flavor of an old tale. These tales fall somewhere between traditional literature and fantasy. Sometimes, unless we know the origin, it is difficult to distinguish between the *literary fairy tale* (the product of a specific author) and the oral folktale—and perhaps the writers of the literary fairy tales would take that as a sign of their success. Hans Christian Andersen was one of the earliest creators of the literary fairy tale, and he has proved one of the most enduring. His popularity inspired others, and by the last half of the nineteenth century many writers were experimenting with this form. George MacDonald's *The Light Princess, The Princess and the Curdie,* and *The Princess and the Goblin* are all book-length works that we can label literary fairy tales. The literary fairy tale exhibits many of the same features as its oral counterparts: conventional settings in a distant "generic" kingdom, predominantly flat and stereotyped characters, an accepted magical element, and, typically, the requisite happy ending. A modern variation of the literary fairy tale is a spoof or satire, such as James Thurber's delightful *Many Moons,* which contains comic twists on the traditional form. Satire results when writers feel a literary form has been exhausted and that it offers no other serious possibilities; consequently, they begin to poke fun at it and, in doing so, give the form a new lease on life.

FOLKTALE CONVENTIONS

Folktales employ certain conventions, accepted practices common to virtually all tales. The most familiar involve the setting, character, plot, theme and conflict, and style.

Setting

"Once upon a time in a kingdom far, far away" typically defines the time and place. Most folktale settings remove the tale from the real world, taking us to a time and place where animals talk, witches and wizards roam, and magic spells are commonplace. Only occasionally do we find actual place names in tales, and even then we find little that is geographically specific. Naturally, the settings reflect the typical landscape of the tale's culture, whether it be medieval Europe with its forests, castles, and cottages, Africa with its jungles, India with its splendid palaces. Because most folktales were originally told to a community already familiar with the tales, tellers found little need to elaborate on descriptions of time and place. It is characteristic of folktales that the details of time and place are sparse.

Character

If the settings are simple and direct, so are the characters. The characters in folk literature are usually flat, simple, and straightforward. In the folktale, everything is on the surface;

FIGURE 8.3   Lancelot Speed's illustration for "Snowdrop," a variant of "Snow White."

Source: From *The Red Fairy Book*. edited by Andrew Lang, London, 1890.

consequently, characters do not internalize their feelings and seldom are plagued by mental torment. Motivation in folktale characters tends to be singular—that is, the characters are motivated by one overriding desire such as greed, love, fear, hatred, jealousy—unlike characters in novels where motivations are usually more complicated. Stereotypical characters—powerful, wicked stepmothers; weak-willed, ineffectual fathers; jealous siblings; faithful friends—populate most tales. A character is typically either all good or all evil, and it is usually not difficult for the audience to separate the good from the bad. Physical appearance often readily defines a character—wicked witches are ugly, good princesses are beautiful, noble princes are fair, but disguises are common. The Beast in "Beauty and the Beast" has been transformed from his handsome self into a monstrosity by a jealous witch. And in another popular tale a witch transforms a handsome prince into a frog. When the spell is broken, the prince's pleasing appearance is restored. Only rarely do we find a truly beautiful character to be wicked. Snow White's stepmother is an example, but even her beauty is outshone by that of her virtuous stepdaughter, and she performs her most powerful magic when she assumes the disguise of an ugly hag. Truth cannot long remain hidden.

The hero or heroine is often isolated and is usually cast out into the open world or is apparently without any human friends. Evil, on the other hand, seems overwhelming. Consequently, to offset the apparent imbalance, the hero/heroine must be aided by supernatural forces (such as a magical object or an enchanted creature). In short, the folktale hero/heroine is someone very much like we, as young children, pictured ourselves—the helpless victims of evil forces (sometimes appearing in the form of our parents!). And the evil characters symbolize all of our fears and frustrations. The folktales are also wish-fulfilling, for the good triumphs over the evil.

Plot

The plot, or the sequence of events, is among the most identifiable features of folk literature. The action tends to be formulaic. A journey is common (and is usually symbolic of the protagonist's journey to self-discovery). Repetitious patterns are found—twelve tasks, three wishes, four tests, and so on—perhaps suggesting the ritual nature of many tales and perhaps to aid the storyteller in memorization. Suspense and action are far more important to these tales than character development. Conflicts are quickly established and events move swiftly to their conclusion; although there may be subsidiary plots or the events may at times seem to get sidetracked, the action never slows down. Endings are almost always happy.

Theme and Conflict

Themes in most folk literature are usually quite simple, but serious and powerful. Common folktale themes include the following:

1. The struggle to achieve autonomy or to break away from parents ("Beauty and the Beast")

2. The undertaking of a rite of passage—sometimes to sexual maturity ("Rapunzel")

3. The discovery that ultimately we are all alone on our journey to maturity is fraught with struggle and danger ("Hansel and Gretel")

4. The anxiety over the failure to meet a parent's expectations ("Jack and the Beanstalk")

5. The anxiety over one's displacement by another—the "new arrival" ("Cinderella")

These are not the only themes we find in folk literature, but we can easily see why children might be drawn to tales that emphasize these issues, for they are at the very heart of growing up.

If we had to make a general statement about themes in folktales, we might well turn to themes of Greek tragedy: *Wisdom comes through suffering.* For every benefit there is a condition; nothing in life comes without strings attached, responsibilities to be met, and bargains to be kept. And folktale themes—especially in the Western tradition—espouse the virtues of *compassion, generosity,* and *humility* over the vices of *greed, selfishness,* and *excessive* or *overweening pride.*

Style

FORMULA AND REPETITION The style in folktales reflects their oral origins. The language is typically economical, with a minimal amount of description and a heavy reliance on formulaic patterns—conventional openings and closings, for instance ("Once upon a time in a kingdom, far, far away" and "They lived happily ever after"). Repetitious phrases are common; they supply a rhythmical quality desirable in oral tales and perhaps aided in memorizing the stories. Dialogue is frequently used, and in the best-told tales the dialogue captures the nature of the character speaking; hence, a lowly peasant will speak in a folksy manner whereas the speech of a king or princess will be more refined. (The English retellings of Joseph Jacobs admirably capture these differences in speech patterns.)

Folktales also use a technique known as *stylized intensification*, which occurs when, with each repetition, an element is further exaggerated or intensified—with each Billy Goat Gruff we get a larger billy goat, for example, or with each visit Rumpelstiltskin's price for spinning straw into gold increases, and so on. This has the effect of increasing the drama.

MOTIFS AND IMAGERY In art, a motif is a repeated figure or element in a larger design (decorative fads are easily recognized by their motifs—plants, animals, geometric designs, and so on). Similarly, in literature, a motif is a recurring thematic element. Folktale motifs are quite prevalent—they may have served as mnemonic devices when the tales were still passed on orally. The folklorist Stith Thompson, who catalogued thousands of folktale motifs, defines a motif as "the smallest element in a tale having power to persist in tradition." Examples of common motifs include journeys through dark forests, enchanted transformations, magical cures or other spells, encounters with helpful animals or mysterious creatures, trickster antics, foolish bargains, impossible tasks, clever deceptions, and so on. Some motifs are accompanied by powerful visual images by which we readily identify many folktales—a glass slipper, a bean stalk and talking harp, a spinning wheel, a poisoned apple, a bloody handkerchief, a red riding hood. These stark visual elements give the tales their enduring strength.

MAGIC Many folktale motifs are examples of magic—helpful animals, transformations from human to beast and beast to human, granted wishes, and so on. One important stylistic feature of the folktale is that the magic, when it appears, is always greeted by the characters with matter-of-factness. Characters in folktales acknowledge magic as a normal part of life. No one is ever astonished when addressed by a talking animal or when a fairy godmother materializes out of thin air or an elf makes exotic promises. This acquiescent attitude toward magic on the part of every folktale character further distances the folktale from reality, and it provides an important distinction between folk literature and much of literary fantasy. In many literary fantasies (heroic fantasy being one of the exceptions), magical occurrences are not necessarily taken for granted but may even be regarded with surprise, awe, and disbelief. Both Alice and Dorothy, those most famous of child travelers in literary fantasies, are in constant wonder at the characters and circumstances they encounter, whereas Cinderella and Little Red Riding Hood accept the wondrous without batting an eye.

SUBLIMATION Remember Rapunzel, the beautiful girl with the very long hair imprisoned in a tower by the wicked witch? And remember the nightly visits by the handsome prince who learned how to reach the girl's chamber by observing the witch and repeating the chant: "Rapunzel, Rapunzel, let down your hair"? In the Grimm Brothers's retelling, the prince simply asks Rapunzel to take him for her husband, "and she saw that he was young and handsome." Since she thinks he will love her more than the witch, she says yes. After that, the prince makes nightly visits, with her luxuriant, soft hair serving as his access to her (see Figure 8.4). No one explains how they are wed without the benefit of the clergy, nor how they actually spend their nights. But that great tall tower is symbolically suggestive. When their deception (notice the motif) is discovered, the witch cuts off Rapunzel's hair—the source of her beauty and sexuality—and banishes her to the desert. Only after much trial and tribulation are they reunited to live happily ever after (and, incidentally, we are told that in the meantime Rapunzel had given birth to twins).

What is happening in the tale of "Rapunzel" is a process we call "sublimation." To sublimate means to transform something ordinary into something sublime, to lift it up to a higher and more refined level, or to make it more socially acceptable. Hence, the folktale is usually devoid of eroticism, even when it deals with potentially erotic behavior—such as the prince's nightly visits to Rapunzel. All we are told is that "he would come to her every evening." We seldom see true passion in the folktale. Even when a kiss is magical and awakens Sleeping Beauty, for example, it is a dispassionate one. In some cases, the kiss is omitted altogether, as in this version of "Sleeping Beauty":

Finally he entered a chamber completely covered with gold and saw the most lovely sight he had ever looked upon—on a bed with curtains open on each side was a princess who seemed to be about fifteen or sixteen. Her radiant charms gave her such a luminous, supernatural appearance that he approached, trembling and admiring, and knelt down beside her. At that moment the enchantment ended. The princess awoke and bestowed on him a look more tender than a first glance might seem to warrant.

"Is it you, my prince?" she said. "You have been long awaited."

(Zipes, *Beauties, Beasts and Enchantments*, 47–48)

Through the process of sublimation, the folktales lift their heroes and heroines to sublime planes where they remain beautiful, noble, and pure—which is exactly what we ask of our heroes and heroines.

Issues in Folk Literature

Since at least the eighteenth century, people have questioned the suitability of folktales for children. At the heart of most early controversies was the concern over violence and lack of moral instruction in folktales. Today objections are raised over the social attitudes the stories portray. Evidently, the folktales remain as vital as ever.

Violence

Among the issues most often discussed regarding folk literature is the prevalence of violence. Foolish and irresponsible little pigs are devoured, wolves are cooked in boiling water, witches are pushed into hot ovens, characters are mutilated in any number of ways—folktales have their fair share of violent acts. Certainly much of this violence, like the violence in the Mother Goose rhymes, is the product of earlier, less squeamish eras. In Joseph Jacobs's nineteenth-century retelling of "The Rose-Tree," an innocent girl is killed by her stepmother and her liver is cooked and fed to her unsuspecting father. Eventually the girl's brother avenges the brutal crime and the stepmother is herself split in two by an axe. It all sounds very gruesome indeed, but in the whole tale we find no reference to blood or gore. Nor is there a great sense of terror. It is a tale of ultimate evil and the triumph of goodness over adversity. The story is a sad one, but not without hope and not without justice. It is tempting to imagine what a modern storyteller or filmmaker would make of it—blood-curdling screams, sinister shadows, graphic scenes in vivid color.

Yes, many folktales contain violent actions, but few exploit that violence and most leave the details up to the reader's own imagination. And it is probably fair to say that most explicit violence found in the folktales pales when compared with the gratuitous horrors depicted in modern literature and in the cinema. Furthermore, folktale violence is likely

FIGURE 8.4 H. J. Ford's illustration for "Rapunzel."

Source: From *The Red Fairy Book*, edited by Andrew Lang, London, 1890.

quite tame when compared with the acts of pretend violence concocted on the playground. The point is that all children experience hostility, frustration, anger, and fear. They need outlets for these feelings, just as adults do. A folktale may be able to provide just the kind of harmless release children need.

In a controversial study of folktales, *The Uses of Enchantment,* the psychiatrist Bruno Bettelheim argues that the violence in folktales gives children a vicarious means of coping with their inner frustrations (that is, it is better to direct our hatred toward a wicked stepmother or witch in a story than toward our own parent). He further suggests that folktales, through their rich symbolism and evocative story patterns, actually fulfill unconscious psychological needs in some children. Bettelheim's thesis encourages close Freudian readings of folktales and sees them laden with symbolism, particularly sexual—note how many tales end in marriages, suggesting that they are coming-of-age tales, stories of awakening sexual maturity. Bettelheim also advocates that the tales not be tampered with or expurgated in any way and that they not be illustrated (for illustrations can inhibit a child's imagination). Critics of Bettelheim find him too extreme in his Freudian interpretations, but his theories do add an interesting dimension to the study of folktales and should not be summarily dismissed.

We should also consider the reactions of children themselves. Rarely do we find a child who experiences nightmares induced by reading or hearing a folktale. And to imagine that a folktale ever produced a mass killer seems ludicrous. Frankly, it is the children who are not exposed to literature who should concern us. It is interesting that, when given the choice, children most often prefer versions of "Little Red Riding Hood" in which the grandmother is devoured and the wolf is ultimately killed, as opposed to those versions in which the ravenous wolf, after inexplicably tying up the grandmother and tossing her in the closet, is miraculously reformed and promises to be good henceforth. This reaction probably comes not from a love of violence, but from a desire to see evil punished and eradicated from the world once and for all.

Antifeminism

Perhaps more potentially damaging than the violence in the folktales is the depiction of negative female stereotypes (the frail young girl in need of a good man) or the unfortunate deprecation of stepmothers in general. The popular story of "Cinderella" has come under the most severe attack (although "Sleeping Beauty" and "Snow White" are not markedly different). These stories all portray women as rather helpless (beautiful) creatures whose futures depend on the kindness of capable (handsome) men, whom the women must attract by their pleasing appearance and sweet nature (see Figure 8.5). Certainly the most commonly retold folktales present this point of view—a perspective made more prevalent by the animated folktales of Walt Disney, most of whose heroines are helpless maidens longing for their Prince Charming (see Lieberman, Sayers, and Zipes, among others).

This distorted presentation of females should not be surprising given the traditionally patriarchal nature of Western society. Men were the earliest serious collectors of the tales, and the male gender bias is evident in the tales they chose to record. However, in recent

FIGURE 8.5 Walter Crane's illustration for "The Sleeping Beauty."

Source: From *Household Stories by the Brothers Grimm*, translated by Lucy Crane, London, 1886.

years many volumes have been published that reveal positive female role models in stories the world over. The title of Kathleen Ragan's collection, *Fearless Girls, Wise Women, and Beloved Sisters: Heroines in Folktales from Around the World,* suggests the rich variety we can expect to find in folktale heroines. In one story that Ragan includes, titled "Davit" from Georgia in the Caucacus, a young girl, Svetlana, undertakes a heroic quest to save her brother's life. She succeeds admirably, yet Ragan points out that the story itself is told from a male point of view: The story is named "Davit" for her brother; Svetlana as a heroine is self-sacrificing and receives no tangible reward for her success (no husband, no kingdom, no gold); further, she wears stone shoes as a self-imposed penance while on her travels; finally, the storyteller praises her from a male's perspective, noting "In this world, next to a good mother, what can a man have better than a good sister?" (Ragan 80). In these subtle ways, a tale can reinforce dominant male values. Nevertheless, it is good to realize that no longer do Sleeping Beauty's passivity, Cinderella's doting subservience, and Snow White's fragility have to be the primary models for folktale heroines. Although no one would seriously suggest eliminating Cinderella or Sleeping Beauty or Snow White from the experiences of childhood, we should make sure that they are joined by some of their less reticent sisters—Kate Crackernuts, Mollie Whuppie, and Svetlana.

Not only are collectors unearthing forgotten tales that help to elevate the status of women, modern adapters are finding ways of recreating new tales out of the old. Some of the "politically correct" versions, such as Garner's *Politically Correct Bedtime Stories* or Tony Johnston's feminist retelling of "The Princess and the Pea," entitled *The Cowboy and the Black-eyed Pea,* are great fun and actually not out of character with the fluid nature of the oral tale.

COLLECTORS, RETELLERS, AND ADAPTERS

Almost as soon as human beings invented the art of writing, they began to record their oral tales—on stone, on papyrus, and on paper. Ancient Greek literature consists chiefly of renderings and retellings of their myths, legends, and fables. The ancient Romans followed the same practice. The ancient Jews recorded their stories with a rich mixture of history and legend. The Christian Middle Ages built a body of literature on the legendary lives of the saints as well as on the glorified deeds of heroes. But by and large, the vast majority of folktales remained only in oral form, surviving chiefly by word of mouth until the seventeenth and eighteenth centuries when writers began to collect them and put them down on paper.

Among the best known of these writers was the Frenchman Charles Perrault whose *Tales of Mother Goose* made such stories as "Cinderella," "Sleeping Beauty," and "Little Red Riding Hood" standard fare in children's literature. In the early nineteenth century, the famous Grimm brothers gathered together German folktales, which included, not surprisingly, versions of "Cinderella" ("Aschenputtel"), "Little Red Riding Hood" ("Little Red Cap"), and "Snow White and the Seven Dwarfs." Long regarded as the patriarchs of folklore research, the Grimms, we now know, relied largely on literate, middle-class sources and often polished or embellished their tales. But their influence cannot be denied.

Some of the early collections were not especially for children; Jacob Grimm wrote: "The book of fairy tales is . . . not written for children at all, but it is just what they like, and that pleases me" (quoted in Ellis 22). However, since the work of Hans Christian Andersen, Joseph Jacobs, and Andrew Lang in the nineteenth century, folktales have been largely the property of children. It is also worth mentioning that folktales have inspired some of the great illustrators of children's literature. Among the first notable illustrations in this field are the painstakingly detailed engravings of Gustave Doré for the 1867 edition of Perrault's *Fairy Tales*. Doré does not shy away from what many would consider to be the more mature subjects—an ogre cutting the throats of his sleeping babes or a disconcerted Red Riding Hood in bed with the wolf (see Figure 8.6). The celebrated English artist Walter Crane is remembered for his illustrations of an English version of Grimm (see Figure 8.2). Perhaps

FIGURE 8.6 Gustave Doré's celebrated engraving for "Little Red Riding Hood" is typical of the drama—sometimes startling drama—with which he imbued all of his work.

Source: From *Perrault's Fairy Tales*, 1867, reprinted by Dover, 1969.

because the stories may be used freely without copyright infringement and because they are evocative in themselves, folktales are often the subjects of picture books. Among the modern illustrators who have distinguished themselves with their imaginative interpretations of folktales are Marcia Brown, Leo and Diane Dillon, Michael Foreman, Trina Schart Hyman, Errol LeCain, Ed Young, and Margot Zemach. Recent years have seen an explosion in the interest in folklore, and countless collections of tales from all over the world have been published. The most popular modern adaptations have been the animated films of Walt Disney, but they are not without their detractors. Some critics argue that the Disney versions are awash with sentimentality and saccharine sweetness, that they condescend to children, project antifeminism, and lack the power of the original tales. Still others claim that the folktales were intended to be popularized, that their very form invites new adaptations, and that Disney has captured anew some of the magic of the folktales (see Chapter 4).

Folktales have been continually adapted over time to meet the changing needs of society. The parodies of folktales, mentioned in Chapter 3, are recent examples. They are remarkably resilient and, having survived for centuries, will likely endure for generations to come, a testament to their ageless wonder. Pity the child who has been deprived of their irresistible enchantment.

Works Cited

Ellis, John M. *One Fairy Story Too Many*. Chicago: University of Chicago Press, 1983.

Erdoes, Richard, and Alfonso Ortiz, selectors and eds. *American Indian Trickster Tales*. New York: Penguin, 1998.

Lüthi, Max. *Once Upon a Time: On the Nature of Fairy Tales*. Bloomington: Indiana University Press, 1976.

Ragan, Kathleen, ed. *Fearless Girls, Wise Women, and Beloved Sisters: Heroines in Folktales from Around the World*. New York: Norton, 1998.

Zipes, Jack, ed. *Beauties, Beasts and Enchantments: Classic French Fairy Tales*. New York: Penguin, 1991.

Recommended Readings

Bernheimer, Kate, ed. *Mirror, Mirror on the Wall: Women Writers Explore Their Favorite Fairy Tales*. New York: Doubleday, 1998.

Bettelheim, Bruno. *The Uses of Enchantment: The Meaning and Importance of Fairy Tales*. New York: Knopf, 1976.

Bosma, Betty. *Fairy Tales, Fables, Legends, and Myths: Using Folk Literature in Your Classroom*. 2nd ed. New York: Teachers College Press, 1993.

Bottigheimer, Ruth, ed. *Fairy Tales and Society: Illusion, Allusion, and Paradigm*. Philadelphia: University of Pennsylvania Press, 1986.

——. *Grimms' Bad Girls and Bold Boys: The Moral and Social Vision of the Tales*. New Haven: Yale University Press, 1987.

Campbell, Joseph. *The Hero with a Thousand Faces*, 2nd ed. Princeton: Princeton University Press, 1968.

Chase, Richard. *American Folk Tales and Songs*. New York: Dover, 1971.

Cook, Elizabeth. *The Ordinary and the Fabulous*. Cambridge: Cambridge University Press, 1969.

Hettinga, Donald R. *The Brothers Grimm: Two Lives, One Legacy*. New York: Clarion, 2001.

Krappe, Alexander H. *The Science of Folklore*. 1929. New York: Norton, 1964.

Lieberman, Marcia R. "'Some Day My Prince Will Come': Female Acculturation Through the Fairy Tale." *College English* 34:3 (1972): 383–395.

Petrone, Penny. *Native Literature in Canada: From the Oral Tradition to the Present*. Oxford: Oxford University Press, 1990.

Sayers, Frances Clarke, and Charles M. Weisenberg. "Walt Disney Accused." *Horn Book Magazine* 40 (December 1965): 602–611.

Stone, Kay. "Fairy Tales for Adults: Walt Disney's Americanization of the Märchen." *Folklore on Two Continents*. Ed. N. Burlakoff and C. Lindahl. Bloomington: Indiana University Press, 1980.

——. "The Misuses of Enchantment: Controversies on the Significance of Fairy Tales." *Women's Folklore, Women's Culture*. Ed. Rosan A. Jordan and Susan J. Kalicik. Philadelphia: University of Pennsylvania Press, 1985.

——. "Things Walt Disney Never Told Us." *Women and Folklore*. Ed. Claire R. Farrer. Austin: University of Texas Press, 1975.

Storr, Catherine. "Folk and Fairy Tales." *Children's Literature in Education* 17 (Spring 1986): 63–70.

Tatar, Maria. *Off with Their Heads*. Princeton: Princeton University Press, 1992. (Violence and cruelty in fairy tales.)

Thompson, Stith. *The Folktale*. New York: Holt, Rinehart, & Winston, 1951.

Walker, Virginia, and Mary E. Lunz. "Symbols, Fairy Tales and School-Age Children." *The Elementary School Journal* November 1976: 94–100.

Warner, Marina. *From the Beast to the Blonde: On Fairy Tales and Their Tellers*. New York: Farrar, Straus & Giroux, 1995.

Yolen, Jane. *Touch Magic*. New York: Philomel, 1981.

Zipes, Jack. *Breaking the Magic Spell: Radical Theories of Folk and Fairy Tales*. Austin: University of Texas Press, 1979.

——. *Don't Bet on the Prince: Contemporary Feminist Fairy Tales in North America and England*. London: Methuen, 1986.

——. *Fairy Tales and the Art of Subversion: The Classical Genre for Children and the Process of Civilization*. London: Heinemann, 1983.

——. *When Dreams Came True: Classical Fairy Tales and Their Tradition*. New York: Routledge, 1999.

Selected Bibliography of Folk Literature, Myths, and Legends

PICTURE-BOOK VERSIONS

Aardema, Verna. *Bringing the Rain to Kapiti Plain*. Illus. Beatriz Vidal. New York: Dial, 1981.

——. *Subgugugu, the Glutton: A Bantu Tale from Rwanda*. Illus. Nancy Clouse. Grand Rapids, MI: William B. Eerdmans, 1993.

——. *Why Mosquitoes Buzz in People's Ears*. Illus. Leo and Diane Dillon. New York: Dial, 1975.

Andersen, Hans Christian. *The Nightingale*. Trans. Eva LeGallienne. Illus. Nancy Ekholm Burkert. New York: Harper, 1965.

Ashley, Bryan. *Beautiful Blackbird*. New York: Atheneum, 2003.

Bishop, Claire Huchet. *The Five Chinese Brothers*. Illus. Kurt Wiese. New York: Coward, 1938.

Brown, Marcia. *Cinderella*. New York: Scribner's, 1954.

——. *Dick Whittington and His Cat*. New York: Scribner's, 1950.

——. *Once a Mouse*. New York: Scribner's, 1961.

Cendrars, Blaise. *Shadows*. Illus. Marcia Brown. New York: Scribner's, 1982.

Climo, Shirley. *The Egyptian Cinderella*. Illus. Ruth Heller. New York: Crowell, 1989.

Cooney, Barbara. *Chanticleer and the Fox*. New York: Crowell, 1958.

De Paola, Tomi. *Strega Nona*. New York: Prentice-Hall, 1975.

Domanska, Janina. *Little Red Hen*. New York: Macmillan, 1973.

Ehlert, Lois. *Mole's Hill: A Woodland Tale*. New York: Harcourt, 1994.

Emberley, Barbara. *Drummer Hoff*. Illus. Ed Emberley. New York: Prentice-Hall, 1967.

Galdone, Paul. *Hansel and Gretel*. New York: McGraw-Hill, 1982.

Geisert, Arthur. *After the Flood*. Boston: Houghton Mifflin, 1994.

Hodges, Margaret. *The Wave*. Illus. Blair Lent. Boston: Houghton Mifflin, 1964.

——. *Saint George and the Dragon*. Illus. Trina Schart Hyman. Boston: Little, Brown, 1984.

Hogrogian, Nonny. *One Fine Day*. New York: Macmillan, 1971.

Jarrell, Randall, reteller. *Snow White and the Seven Dwarfs*. Illus. Nancy Ekholm Burkert. New York: Farrar, Straus & Giroux, 1972.

Johnston, Tony. *The Cowboy and the Black-eyed Pea*. Illus. Warren Ludwig. New York: Putnam, 1992.

Lester, Julius. *John Henry*. Illus. Jerry Pinkney. New York: Dial, 1994.

Louie, Ai-Ling. *Yeh-Shen: A Cinderella Story from China*. Illus. Ed Young. New York: Philomel, 1982.

Marshall, James. *Red Riding Hood*. New York: Dial, 1987.

McDermott, Gerald. *Anansi the Spider*. New York: Holt, 1972.

——. *Arrow to the Sun*. New York: Viking, 1974.

Minters, Frances. *Cinder-Elly*. Illus. G. Brian Karas. New York: Puffin, 1994.

——. *Sleepless Beauty*. Illus. G. Brian Karas. New York: Puffin, 1996.

Mosel, Arlene. *The Funny Little Woman*. Illus. Blair Lent. New York: Dutton, 1972.

——. *Tikki Tikki Tembo*. Illus. Blair Lent. New York: Holt, 1968.

Moser, Barry, reteller. *The Three Little Pigs*. Boston: Little, Brown, 2001.

Ness, Evaline. *Tom Tit Tot*. New York: Scribner's, 1965.

Nic Leodhas, Sorche (pseudonym of LeClaire G. Alger). *Always Room for One More*. Illus. Nonny Hogrogian. New York: Holt, 1965.

Pinkney, Jerry, reteller. *Aesop's Fables*. New York: SeaStar/North-South, 2000.

Polacco, Patricia. *Babushka Baba Yaga*. New York: Philomel, 1993.

Ransome, Arthur. *The Fool of the World and the Flying Ship*. Illus. Uri Shulevitz. New York: Farrar, Straus & Giroux, 1968.

Robbins, Ruth. *Baboushka and the Three Kings*. Illus. Nicolas Sidjakov. Boston: Houghton Mifflin, 1960.

Root, Phyllis. *Big Momma Make the World*. Illus. Helen Oxenbury. New York: Candlewick, 2003.

San Souci, Robert D., adapter. *Cendrillon: A Caribbean Cinderella*. Illus. Brian Pinkney. New York: Simon & Schuster, 1998.

——. reteller. *Little Gold Star: A Spanish-American Cinderella*. Illus. Sergio Martinez. New York: HarperCollins, 2000.

Sawyer, Ruth. *Journey Cake, Ho!* Illus. Robert McCloskey. New York: Viking, 1953.

Scieszka, John. *The Stinky Cheese Man and Other Fairly Stupid Tales*. Illus. Lane Smith. New York: Viking, 1992.

——. *The True Story of the Three Little Pigs*. Illus. Lane Smith. New York: Viking, 1989.

Shepard, Aaron, reteller. *Master Man: A Tall Tale of Nigeria*. Illus. David Wisniewski. New York: HarperCollins, 2001.

Sierra, Judy. *The Gift of the Crocodile: A Cinderella Story*. Illus. Reynolds Ruffin. New York: Simon and Schuster, 2000.

Singer, Isaac Bashevis. *The Fearsome Inn*. Illus. Nonny Hogrogian. New York: Macmillan, 1984.

Steptoe, John. *Mufaro's Beautiful Daughters: An African Tale*. New York: Lothrop, 1987.

Trivizas, Eugene. *The Three Little Wolves and the Big Bad Pig*. Illus. Helen Oxenbury. New York: Simon and Schuster, 1997.

Weisner, David. *The Three Pigs*. Boston: Houghton Mifflin, 2001.

Young, Ed. *Lon Po Po: A Red Riding Hood Story from China*. New York: Philomel, 1989.

Zelinsky, Paul O. *Rumpelstiltskin*. New York: Dutton, 1986.

Zemach, Harve, reteller. *Duffy and the Devil*. Illus. Margot Zemach. New York: Farrar, Straus & Giroux, 1973.

Zemach, Margot, reteller. *The Little Red Hen*. New York: Farrar, Straus & Giroux, 1983.

——. *The Three Little Pigs*. New York: Farrar, Straus & Giroux, 1988.

FOLKTALE COLLECTIONS

Aesop's Fables. Illus. Fritz Kredel. New York: Grosset, 1947.

Asbjornsen, Peter, and Jorgen Moe. *East O'the Sun and West O'the Moon*. New York: Dover, 1970. (Scandinavian folktales)

Bierhorst, John, ed. *The Dancing Fox: Arctic Folktales*. New York: Morrow, 1997.

——. *Lightning Inside You: And Other Native American Riddles*. New York: Morrow, 1992.

——. *The White Deer and Other Stories Told by the Lenape*. New York: Morrow, 1995.

Bloch, Marie Halun. *Ukrainian Folk Tales*. New York: Coward, McCann, 1964.

Briggs, Katharine. *British Folk Tales*. New York: Pantheon, 1977.

Bushnaq, Inea, trans. *Arab Folktales*. New York: Pantheon, 1986.

Calvino, Italo, ed. *Italian Folktales*. New York: Pantheon, 1980.

Chandler, Robert, trans. *Russian Folk Tales*. New York: Shambhala/Random House, 1980.

Chase, Richard. *The Jack Tales*. Boston: Houghton Mifflin, 1971. (American tall tales)

Cole, Joanna, selector. *Best-Loved Folktales of the World*. Garden City, NY: Doubleday, 1982.

Courlander, Harold. *The Crest and the Hide and Other African Stories of Heroes, Chiefs, Bards, Hunters, Sorcerers and Common People*. New York: Coward, McCann & Geoghegan, 1982.

Demi, adapter. *A Chinese Zoo: Fables and Proverbs*. New York: Harcourt, 1987.

de Wit, Dorothy. *The Talking Stone: An Anthology of Native American Tales and Legends*. New York: Greenwillow, 1979.

Dickinson, Peter, reteller. *City of Gold and Other Stories from the Old Testament*. Illus. Michael Foreman. London: Gollancz, 1992.

Fang, Linda, reteller. *The Ch'i-lin Purse: A Collection of Ancient Chinese Stories*. New York: Farrar, Straus & Giroux, 1995.

Finger, Charles. *Tales from Silver Lands*. New York: Doubleday, 1924. (Central America)

Fuller, O. Muriel. *The Book of Dragons: Tales and Legends from Many Lands*. New York: Dover, 2002.

Gág, Wanda. *Tales from Grimm*. New York: Coward, McCann & Geoghegan, 1981.

Glassie, Henry. *Irish Folk Tales*. New York: Pantheon, 1985.

Grimm, Jakob, and Wilhelm Grimm. *Household Stories*. Trans. Lucy Crane. New York: Dover, 1963. (One of many editions dating from 1812)

Gross, Ila Land. *Cinderella around the World*. New York: L.E.A.P., 2001.

Haley, Gail E, reteller-illustrator. *Mountain Jack Tales*. New York: Penguin, 1992.

Hamilton, Virginia. *In the Beginning: Creation Stories from Around the World*. New York: Harcourt Brace Jovanovich, 1988.

——. *The People Could Fly*. New York: Knopf, 1985. (African American folktales)

Hausman, Gerald, collector-reteller. *How Chipmunk Got Tiny Feet: Native American Origin Stories.* New York: HarperCollins, 1995.

Haviland, Virginia. *Favorite Tales Told in India.* Boston: Little, Brown, 1973.

Hodges, Margaret, reteller. *Hauntings: Ghosts and Ghouls from Around the World.* Boston: Little, Brown, 1991.

Hoogasian-Villa, Susie. *One Hundred Armenian Tales.* Detroit: Wayne State University Press, 1966.

Jacobs, Joseph. *Celtic Fairy Tales.* (1891) New York: Dover, 1968.

——. *English Fairy Tales.* (1890) New York: Dover, 1967.

Jaffe, Nina, and Steve Zeitlin. *While Standing on One Foot: Puzzle Stories and Wisdom Tales from the Jewish Tradition.* Illus. John Segal. New York: Holt, 1993.

Jaffrey, Madhur. *Seasons of Splendour: Tales, Myths & Legends of India.* Illus. Michael Foreman. Harmondsworth, UK: Puffin, 1987.

James, Grace, reteller. *Green Willow and Other Japanese Fairy Tales.* New York: Avenel, 1987.

Joseph, Lynn. *The Mermaid's Twin Sister: More Stories from Trinidad.* New York: Clarion, 1994.

Kherdian, David, reteller. *Feathers and Tails: Animal Fables from around the World.* New York: Putnam, 1992.

Lang, Andrew. *The Blue Fairy Book.* (1889) New York: Dover, 1965. (The first of a series)

Lester, Julius. *Black Folktales.* New York: Richard W. Baron, 1969.

Lyons, Mary E., selector. *Raw Head, Bloody Bones: African-American Tales of the Supernatural.* New York: Scribners, 1991.

Manitonquat (Medicine Story), reteller. *The Children of the Morning Light: Wampanoag Tales.* Illus. Mary F. Arquette. New York: Macmillan, 1994.

Minford, John, trans. *Favourite Folktales of China.* Beijing, China: New World Press, 1983.

Neil, Philip, reteller. *Fairy Tales of Eastern Europe.* Boston: Houghton Mifflin, 1991.

Nic Leodhas, Sorche. *Thistle and Thyme: Tales and Legends from Scotland.* New York: Holt, Rinehart, & Winston, 1962.

Opie, Iona, and Peter Opie. *The Classic Fairy Tales.* New York: Oxford University Press, 1974.

Perrault, Charles. *Perrault's Fairy Tales.* Illus. Gustave Doré. (1867) New York: Dover, 1969.

Phelps, Ethel Johnson. *The Maid of the North: Feminist Folk Tales from Around the World.* New York: Holt, Rinehart, & Winston, 1981.

Ross, Gayle. *How Rabbit Tricked Otter and Other Cherokee Trickster Stories.* Illus. Murv Jacob. New York: HarperCollins, 1994.

Rounds, Glen. *Ol' Paul, the Mighty Logger.* New York: Holiday House, 1936.

Schwartz, Alvin, reteller. *Ghosts!: Ghostly Tales from Folklore.* New York: HarperCollins, 1991.

Schwarz, Howard, and Barbara Rush, retellers. *The Diamond Tree: Jewish Tales from Around the World.* New York: HarperCollins, 1991.

Singer, Isaac Bashevis. *Zlateh the Goat and Other Stories.* New York: Harper, 1966. (Yiddish folktales)

Stoutenburg, Adrien. *American Tall Tales.* New York: Viking, 1966.

Tehranchian, Hassan, adapter. *Kalilah and Dimnah: Fables from the Middle East.* New York: Harmony, 1985.

Thompson, Vivian L. *Hawaiian Tales of Heroes and Champions.* New York: Holiday House, 1971.

Vuong, Lynette Dyer. *The Golden Carp and Other Tales from Vietnam.* Illus. Manabu Saito. New York: Lothrop, 1993.

Wiggin, Kate Douglas, and Nora A. Smith, eds. *The Arabian Nights.* Illus. Maxfield Parrish. New York: Quality Paperback, 1996. (Originally published 1909)

Wolkstein, Diane. *The Magic Orange and Other Haitian Folktales.* New York: Knopf, 1978.

Yeats, W. B., and Lady Gregory. *A Treasury of Irish Myth, Legend, and Folklore.* New York: Avenel, 1986.

Yep, Laurence, reteller. *Tongues of Jade.* New York: HarperCollins, 1991. (Chinese)

Yolen, Jane, ed. *Favorite Folktales from Around the World.* New York: Pantheon, 1986.

Zipes, Jack, trans. *Beauties, Beasts, and Enchantment: Classic French Fairy Tales.* New York: Penguin, 1991.

) EPICS

. *The Illustrated Bulfinch's*
55–1862. Illus. Giovanni Caselli.
ork: Macmillan, 1997.

Colum, Padraic. *The Children's Homer: The Adventures of Odysseus and the Tale of Troy*. 1919. New York: Macmillan, 1982.

———. *The Children of Odin: The Book of Northern Myths*. 1920. New York: Macmillan, 1984.

———. *The Golden Fleece and the Heroes Who Lived Before Achilles*. 1921. New York: Macmillan, 1983.

Coolidge, Olivia. *Greek Myths*. Boston: Houghton Mifflin, 1949.

D'Aulaire, Ingri, and Edgar Parin D'Aulaire. *D'Aulaire's Book of Greek Myths*. New York: Doubleday, 1962.

Erdoes, Richard, and Alfonso Ortiz, eds. *American Indian Myths and Legends*. New York: Pantheon, 1984.

Goldston, Robert, reteller. *The Legend of the Cid*. Indianapolis: Bobbs-Merrill, 1963.

Green, Roger Lancelyn. *Heroes of Greece and Troy: Retold from the Ancient Authors*. Illus. Heather Copley and Christopher Chamberlain. New York: Walck, 1961.

Hieatt, Constance, reteller. *Sir Gawain and the Green Knight*. Illus. Walter Lorraine. New York: Crowell, 1967.

Kingsley, Charles. *The Heroes*. New York: Dutton, 1963.

McCaughrean, Geraldine. *The Bronze Cauldron: Myths and Legends of the World*. New York: Margaret K. McElderry, 1998.

———. *The Crystal Pool: Myths and Legends of the World*. New York: Margaret K. McElderry, 1999.

———. *The Golden Hoard: Myths and Legends of the World*. New York: Margaret K. McElderry, 1996.

———. *The Silver Treasure: Myths and Legends of the World*. New York: Margaret K. McElderry, 1997.

McKinley, Robin. *The Outlaws of Sherwood*. New York: Greenwillow, 1988.

Philip, Neil. *The Tale of Sir Gawain*. Illus. Charles Keeping. New York: Philomel, 1987.

Pyle, Howard. *Some Merry Adventures of Robin Hood*. New York: Scribner's, 1954.

Sherwood, Merriam, trans. *The Song of Roland*. New York: McKay, 1938.

Steig, Jeanne, reteller. *A Gift from Zeus*. Illus. William Steig. New York: HarperCollins, 2001.

Sutcliff, Rosemary. *Beowulf*. London: Bodley Head, 1961. (Later published in the United States as *Dragon Slayer*)

———. *The Light Beyond the Forest: The Quest for the Holy Grail*. New York: Dutton, 1980.

Thompson, Brian. *The Story of Prince Rama*. New York: Viking, 1985.

Westwood, Jennifer, reteller. *Gilgamesh and Other Babylonian Tales*. New York: Coward McCann, 1970.

Zeitlin, Steve. *The Four Corners of the Sky: Creation Stories and Cosmologies from around the World*. New York: Holt, 2000.

LITERARY FAIRY TALES

Andersen, Hans Christian. *The Complete Fairy Tales and Stories*. Trans. Erik Christian Haugaard. New York: Doubleday, 1974.

———. *The Emperor and the Nightingale*. Trans. Eva LeGallienne. Illus. Nancy Burkert. New York: Harper, 1965.

———. *The Steadfast Tin Soldier*. Illus. David Jorgensen. New York: Knopf, 1986.

Bomans, Godfried. *The Wily Witch and All the Other Fairy Tales and Fables*. Illus. Wouter Hoogendijk. Owings Mills, MD: Stemmer, 1977.

Gardner, John. *Dragon, Dragon, and Other Tales*. New York: Knopf, 1975.

MacDonald, George. *At the Back of the North Wind*. (1871) Several modern editions.

——. *The Light Princess*. (1864) Several modern editions.

——. *The Princess and the Curdie*. (1877) Several modern editions.

——. *The Princess and the Goblin*. (1872) Several modern editions.

Thurber, James. *Fables for Our Time*. New York: Harper & Row, 1939.

——. *Many Moons*. New York: Harbrace, 1943.

CHAPTER

Poetry

DEFINITION OF POETRY

"A poem," Robert Frost once wrote, "begins as a lump in the throat, a sense of wrong, a homesickness, a lovesickness ... It finds the thought and the thought finds the words." Poetry is indeed the most emotionally charged means of written expression and it consists of words arranged in patterns of sound and imagery to spark an emotional–and intellectual–response from us. The simplest description of poetry was given to us by the English poet Samuel Taylor Coleridge–"the best words in the best order." And another poet, Paul Roche, once remarked that poetry is like a stained-glass window–it lets the light shine through, but exists for its own beauty.

Poetry is one of the two great classifications of writing–prose being the other. *Prose* is the language of everyday life, of narrative fiction, of informational books (like this textbook). *Poetry* is the language of the imagination, of feelings, of emotional self-expression, of high art. The basic unit of prose is the sentence, which may be long or short, simple or complex. Logic and clarity are the usual guiding principles of prose. The basic unit of the poem is the line, which may be long, short (even a single word), it may rhyme with other lines, it may repeat other lines, and several lines may be organized into a stanza. The guiding principle in the poem is its power to move us, to evoke deep feelings, to satisfy our longing for beauty. Prose explains, but poetry sings.

Take, for example, this prose story:

There was young girl who thought that old people moved slowly and deliberately and had wrinkled faces and veins popping up in their hands just to show that they were special people to be held in awe. Then one day, when an old lady was visiting the house, the girl watched from the stairs as the woman's beads broke and fell all over the floor. The old lady got down on her hands and knees and struggled to pick up all the black beads, and the little girl thought that it reminded her of when she dropped something that scattered all over the floor and she had a hard time picking up all the pieces. She realized that she and the old lady had a lot in common, after all.

Now this is a mildly interesting story—and I emphasize "mildly." But what if it were told this way:

> I used to think that grown-up people chose
> To have stiff backs and wrinkles round their nose,
> And veins like small fat snakes on either hand,
> On purpose to be grand.
> Till through the banisters I watched one day
> My great-aunt Etty's friend who was going away,
> And how her onyx beads had come unstrung.
> I saw her grope to find them as they rolled;
> And then I knew that she was helplessly old,
> As I was helplessly young.
>
> *—Frances Cornford*

We immediately notice that the poem, which is called simply, "Childhood," is an intimate expression told in the first person by the girl herself. We also see that the poem contains only 79 words, whereas the prose passage contains 115 words. But those 79 words leave a more lasting impression and are, in fact, much more specific, more descriptive. References to "stiff backs" and "wrinkles" round noses and veins "like small fat snakes" on hands, to great-aunt Etty's friend and her onyx beads, all make the poem more precise. The language in the poem is musical—it rolls off the tongue without being monotonously singsong. It contains end-rhyme—but not always predictable, as in the rhyming of "young" in the final line with "unstrung" from three lines before. We also find other pleasing, but not heavy-handed, rhymes, such as the repeated long "a" in "veins" and "snakes" or the long "o" in "grope" and "rolled." And the poignant connection the young girl finds between herself and the old woman is expressed through the repetition of the word "helplessly." This use of repetition, rhyme, and rhythm might seem peculiar in a prose passage. But in a poem, these devices transform the experience into something far more memorable; indeed, into something magical. This magic is what poetry is all about.

THE KINDS OF POETRY

When we talk about poetry, it is easy to get bogged down with complex terminology and obscure references, and it is certainly not necessary for children to be able to recognize and label poetic techniques. But if we are to appreciate a poem fully, it is helpful to know something about the poet's craft and to have a vocabulary with which we may discuss poetry. Many different kinds of poetry exist, but we can identify two broad categories—narrative poetry, which tells a story in verse, and lyric poetry, which evokes a musical quality in its sounds and rhythms and typically describes the poet's innermost feelings or candid observations.

Narrative Poetry

Narrative poems are very old. In fact, among the world's earliest literature are the 3,000-year-old Sumerian epic, *Gilgamesh,* and the great narrative poems of Homer, *The Iliad* and *The Odyssey*. These are lengthy stories in verse that were originally intended to be recited to audiences (rather than read by them). A hundred years ago, lengthy narrative poems still enjoyed some popularity, and Robert Browning's "The Pied Piper of Hamelin" and Henry Wadsworth Longfellow's "The Song of Hiawatha" are two nineteenth-century verse narratives still in print today. The early twentieth-century poet Alfred Noyes wrote narrative poems imbued with drama on subjects that appeal to readers in the upper elementary years—"The Highwayman" and "A Song of Sherwood" are examples.

However, for children, perhaps the most accessible narrative poems are *ballads*. Traditional ballads use the so-called "ballad stanza," which contains four lines, each with eight syllables and with the second and fourth lines rhyming, such as in this famous opening stanza to the anonymous ballad, "Barbara Allen's Cruelty":

> In Scarlet town, where I was born,
> There was a fair maid dwellin',
> Made every youth cry Well-a-way!
> Her name was Barbara Allen.

Not all ballads follow this scheme, but all do include a setting, character, and events with a climax. The stories are frequently tragic and plaintive, such as this example of an anonymous ballad from the American West called "The Dying Cowboy" or "The Streets of Laredo":

> Let sixteen gamblers come handle my coffin,
> Let sixteen young cowboys come sing me a song,
> Take me to the green valley and lay the sod o'er me,
> For I'm a poor cowboy and I know I've done wrong.

Occasionally ballads are set to music, such as "The Wreck of the Edmund Fitzgerald" by Gordon Lightfoot, an example of a modern-day shipwreck inspiring a ballad. And country and western music thrives on the ballad form.

Lyric Poetry

Unlike a narrative poem, a lyric poem does not so much tell a story as it does describe the feeling of a moment. But perhaps most importantly, lyrics rely on the musical quality of language–hence, we call song words "lyrics." If lyric poems occasionally tell stories, they seldom include a cast of characters, a setting, or dramatic plots like narrative poems. And lyric poems exhibit an endless variety of forms, with new ones still being created. Below are some of the more popular lyric forms.

HAIKU *Haiku* is of Japanese origin. It typically consists of seventeen syllables divided into three lines and is usually on the subject of nature and our relationship to nature, such as this by Ruby Lytle:

> The moon is a week old–
> A dandelion to blow
> Scattering star seed.

In this haiku, the image of the stars as tiny seeds blown from the moon, a whispery soft dandelion puff gone to seed, brings us closer to the starry night sky and suggests a comforting pattern to all of creation. Haiku in English possesses a subtle rhythm but does not rhyme. Its strength lies in its suggestive imagery. Successful haiku uses metaphor to give us a fresh and imaginative look at something we may view as quite ordinary.

CINQUAIN The *cinquain* is a five-line stanza apparently of medieval origin. The term once seems to have included any five-line poem (*cinq* is French for "five"), but Adelaide Crapsey, in her volume entitled *Verse*, created more precise rules stipulating that the five lines should contain two, four, six, eight, and two syllables, respectively. Her inspiration may have been the Japanese haiku, although little real similarity between the two forms exists. Adelaide Crapsey's cinquain, entitled "November Night," plays on the double meaning of the last word:

> Listen . . .
> With faint dry sound,
> Like steps of passing ghosts,
> The leaves, frost-crisp'd, break from the trees
> And fall.

SONNET A sonnet is a very old form of poetry, having gained prominence during the Renaissance. It is also a very sophisticated form and therefore not found much in poetry for children. Still it remains one of the most famous poetic forms, and virtually all the great English-language poets have experimented with sonnets. A sonnet contains fourteen lines, each line with five iambic feet (or ten syllables). The rhyme scheme usually follows one of two patterns. The Italian sonnet is composed of two quatrains (four-line stanzas) and closes with two triplets (three-line stanzas) with the following rhyme scheme: **abba abba cde cde**. (We use letters to identify end rhymes, thus **a** refers to the first rhyme, **b** the second, and so on. In an Italian sonnet, we find only five end rhymes.) The Shakespearean or English sonnet contains three quatrains and closes with a single couplet with this rhyme scheme: **abab cdcd efef gg**. Few sonnets are written specifically for children, but the following is one that has proved popular among early adolescents. Notice that its rhyme scheme combines characteristics of both the Italian and English sonnets:

High Flight

Oh, I have slipped the surly bonds of earth,
And danced the skies on laughter-silvered wings;
Sunward I've climbed and joined the tumbling mirth
Of sun-split clouds—and done a hundred things
You have not dreamed of—wheeled and soared and swung
High in the sunlit silence. Hov'ring there
I've chased the shouting wind along and flung
My eager craft through footless halls of air.
Up, up the long delirious burning blue
I've topped the wind-swept heights with easy grace,
Where never lark, or even eagle flew;
And, while with silent, lifting mind I've trod
The high untrespassed sanctity of space,
Put out my hand, and touched the face of God.

—*John Gillespie Magee, Jr.*

CONCRETE POETRY When the words of a poem are so arranged that they form a pictorial representation of the poem's subject, we have what is called a *concrete poem*.

These are really not new, for the English metaphysical poets were practicing this sort of poetry in the seventeenth century. George Herbert, for example, wrote "The Altar" so that the lines formed the shape of an altar; also popular were poems in the shapes of crosses and pyramids, and Herbert's "Easter Wings" was designed to suggest angel wings. In the twentieth century, much more liberty has been taken with this sort of thing, such as in an example by Robert Froman, in which the poet defines what he calls "A Seeing Poem."

Robert Froman's "A Seeing Poem."

Reprinted by permission of Mrs. Katherine Froman.

LIMERICK One of the most popular poetic forms among children is the *limerick*, a five-line humorous poem, the first, second, and fifth lines rhyming and the third and fourth rhyming. The fun of the limerick lies in its rollicking rhythm and its broad humor. The following limerick has been attributed to President Woodrow Wilson:

> I sat next to the Duchess at tea;
> It was just as I thought it would be;
> Her rumblings abdominal
> Were simply phenomenal,
> And everyone thought it was me.

The limerick's form is easily imitated, and young children can have a great deal of fun creating their own.

FREE VERSE The twentieth century has popularized *free verse,* which adheres to no predetermined rules, but nevertheless good free verse usually establishes its own intricate patterns of rhyme and rhythm. Free verse is much more demanding on the poet than most readers suppose, and it requires the same thoughtful choice of words and sentence patterns as the more rigid stanza forms. The following example, "The Fog," by Carl Sandburg focuses on a single concrete image:

> The fog comes
> on little cat feet.
> It sits looking

over harbor and city
on silent haunches
and then, moves on.

There are potentially as many stanza forms as there are poets. Perhaps the best we can do for children is to make them aware of the vast array of choices open to them as both readers and writers of poetry, and in this way try to prevent the misconceptions that arise about what a poem is.

THE LANGUAGE OF POETRY

Poetry–like all literature–depends on the effective union of form and content, but poetry is at once more compact than most literature and more reliant on certain literary devices for its effect. As we have already emphasized, the most memorable poems are both pleasing to the ear and stimulating to the mind.

Imagery

Imagery refers simply to mental pictures created by words. Since words are the poem's medium, their selection is the most crucial aspect of the poem's creation.

LITERAL IMAGES   Imagery is said to be *literal* or *direct* when a poet describes something by appealing to one or more of our sensory faculties, as in the following examples:

1. *Visual* images, which are very common in poetry, consist of things we can see, as in this example from Lewis Carroll's nonsense poem, "The Walrus and the Carpenter":

   The sun was shining on the sea,
   Shining with all his might:
   He did his very best to make
   The billows smooth and bright–
   And this was odd, because it was
   The middle of the night.

2. *Tactile* images appeal to our sense of touch as when Walter de la Mare writes "Through the green twilight of a hedge / I peered with cheek on the cool leaves pressed."

3. *Auditory* images suggest the sounds of things, and this usually results in an effect called *onomatopoeia*, when a word's sound imitates its meaning, as when Eve Merriam describes the work of a wrecking ball in her poem, "Bam, Bam, Bam":

Crash goes a chimney,
Pow goes a hall,
Zowie goes a doorway,
Zam goes a wall.

4. *Olfactory* images suggest the smells of things, as in these lines from Shakespeare that mingle sound imagery with that of scent: "[The music] came o'er my ear like the sweet sound / That breathes upon a bank of violets, / Stealing and giving odor!" Dante Gabriel Rosetti suggests another olfactory image: "I know the grass beyond the door / The sweet keen smell."

5. *Kinesthetic* images refer to actions or motions, as do these lines from Alan Cunningham's "At Sea":

A wet sheet and a flowing sea,
A wind that follows fast
And fills the white and rustling sail
And bends the gallant mast

6. And *gustatory* images suggest the tastes of things. These images are less common than others, but it is perhaps taste, texture, and color that Mary O'Neill had in mind when she wrote that "Brown is cinnamon / and morning toast" or that gray is "The bubbling of oatmeal mush." Notice the combination of sensory images in these lines from a nineteenth-century poem entitled "The Mouse and the Cake" by Eliza Cook:

A mouse found a beautiful piece of plum cake,
The richest and sweetest that mortal could make;
'Twas heavy with citron and fragrant with spice,
And covered with sugar all sparkling as ice.
(Iona and Peter Opie, *The Oxford Book of Children's Verse.* Oxford: Oxford University Press, 1973.)

FIGURATIVE IMAGES Images may also be *figurative* or *indirect*, describing one thing by comparing it to something else with which we are more familiar. (It, of course, makes no sense to compare two things neither of which we know or understand.) The three common methods of comparison are through similes, metaphors, and personification.

A *simile* is a stated comparison, employing a connective such as "like" or "as"; take Robert Burns's famous line, "My love is like a red, red rose." The unfamiliar entity, so far as the reader is concerned, is "My love" (presumably the poet's sweetheart), and the familiar is the "red, red rose" (a flower that his audience probably knows). It is true that we, as readers/ listeners, may have different conceptions and attitudes about the "red, red rose" (those who have violent allergies to roses are apt to think of them quite differently from other readers). But most people think of roses as examples of extraordinary delicacy and beauty, and we would certainly have a very different conception of the lover if the poet had written, "My love is like a hardy mum." The point is that the poet's object was not to confuse us (as some readers believe), but, rather, to help us understand his passionate feelings for his lover.

A *metaphor* is implied comparison—one not directly stated with words such as "like" and "as." Metaphors are often more subtle to grasp. In Sandburg's poem "Fog," quoted above, the fog is implicitly compared to a cat—quiet and stealthy. The metaphor succeeds if we see the catlike features in the fog. In a brief poem, "City," by Langston Hughes, the poet implies a comparison of a city in the morning with a songbird:

> In the morning the city
> Spreads its wings
> Making a song
> In stone that sings.

This simple poem gives us an exhilarating feeling about the city. The short, musical lines, with their repeating "s" and "ing" and short "i" sounds, their end rhyme, help to convey a sense of the animated and joyous life in the bustling city. The effective metaphor helps us to understand the poet's message and attitude or tone.

Personification is by its nature metaphorical, although not all metaphors are personification. Personification occurs when a poet gives human qualities to an inanimate object, an abstract idea, or a force of nature. James Stephens is using personification when he writes: "The Night was creeping on the ground! / She crept and did not make a sound. . . ." It is also personification when Eleanor Averitt writes of the November wind that she "has plucked the trees / like pheasants, held / between her knees." Personification appeals to the child's animistic view of the world, in which everything seems imbued with human attributes.

We all use figurative imagery every day of our lives—even children. When we tell a friend she dresses "like a princess" or another that he is fast "as lightning," we are using similes. When we say it's raining "cats and dogs" or that the ground is "blanketed with snow," we are using metaphors. When we refer to "Lady Luck" or a "tired old sofa," we are using personification. Figurative language helps us describe new experiences and new things by allowing us to make connections with what is already familiar. The poet uses figurative language to bring us new experiences, new visions, new ways of looking at the world.

Sound Patterns

Poetry is by its nature musical. Most poems are written to be read aloud, and how they sound is as important as what they mean. Sound patterns consist of two elements—rhythm and rhyme.

RHYTHM *Rhythm* is the pattern of stressed and unstressed syllables in language. Babies respond to rhythmical patterns almost from birth, whether it be swaying or rocking or a simple caressing of the back. Who is to say that our first sensory experience is not, in fact, prenatal–that steady, rhythmical pulsation of our mother's body and the gentle undulations of the embryonic fluids sweeping about us? And, of course, rhythm is ever present in nature, the tides, the orbiting planets and the rhythmical pattern of birth, growth, decline, death, and, eventually, rebirth revealed to us through the changing seasons. Rhythm–be it in nursery rhymes or Shakespeare–is inseparable from poetry.

Rhythmical pattern in poetry is called *meter,* and the smallest unit of rhythmical pattern is called a *foot.* There are many variations of metric feet, each having two or three syllables. The most common are the following:

1. *Iamb* (two syllables with the emphasis on the second: "When **wál**-king **in** a **tí**-ny **ráin**")
2. *Trochee* (two syllables with the emphasis on the first: "**Síng** a **sóng** of **súb**-ways")
3. *Anapest* (three syllables with the emphasis on the last: "In the **mórn**-ing the **cí**-ty")
4. *Dactyl* (three syllables with the emphasis on the first: "**Ský**-scra-per, **ský**-scra-per, **Scrápe** me some **ský**")
5. *Spondee* (two syllables with equally strong emphasis: "**Nó shóp** does the **bírd úse**")
6. *Pyrrhic* (two syllables without emphasis, as in "does the" in the preceding example)

Nursery rhymes tend to have very predictable rhythms: "**Má**-ry **hád** a **lít**-tle **lámb**" (regular trochees). Following their example, much of the verse for the very young repeats similar singsong patterns. But if children are ever to appreciate poetry more fully, they have to be shown that all poetry need not contain such regular, unvaried rhyming and rhythmical patterns. Much poetry combines more than one rhythmical pattern to achieve a particular effect. When we read poetry to children, it is important that we are ourselves aware of any subtleties of rhythm the poem may contain so that we may gain the best effect from our reading.

RHYME *Rhyme,* the second important element of sound patterns, is simply the repetition of similar sounds in two or more words. End rhyme is perhaps the most widely recognized in poetry; it occurs when the last words of two or more lines repeat the same sounds. Too often, end rhyme devolves into trite and unimaginative rhymes, as in that old jingle, "Roses are red, violets are blue,/Sugar is sweet, and so are you." End rhyme is most effective when it is unpredictable, as in this humorous example from Henry Wadsworth Longfellow:

There was a little girl
Who had a little curl
Right in the middle of her forehead.
When she was good

She was very, very good,
But when she was bad she was horrid.

Rhyme, however, can occur anywhere in the poetic line. Wherever a sound is repeated within a reasonably short span, we technically have a rhyme. Other types of rhyme include the following:

1. *Alliteration* is the repetition of initial sounds in two or more words, such as the **b** and **l** sounds in these lines by A. E. Housman:

    By **b**rooks too **b**road for **l**eaping,
    The **l**ightfoot **b**oys are **l**aid.

2. *Assonance* is the repetition of identical vowel sounds, such as the long **a**, long **u**, and long **i** sounds in these lines by Carl Sandburg:

    "Let me be the gr**ea**t n**ai**l holding a sk**y**scr**a**per thr**ough** bl**ue** n**i**ghts into wh**i**te stars."

3. *Consonance* is the repetition of consonant sounds within words, often with a variation in adjoining vowels, such as the **f** and **d** sounds in these lines by William Jay Smith:

    Butter**fl**ies . . .
    Gli**d**ing over **f**iel**d** and stream—
    Like **f**ans un**f**ol**d**ing in a **d**ream.*

Naturally, too much of any repetitive sound pattern becomes noticeable and begins to detract from the content. And certain rhymes result in tongue twisters. The good poet knows just how much to include to make music and just when to stop before the result is tongue-tying racket.

Sharing Poetry with Children

Studies of children's poetry preferences suggest, among other things, that children prefer poetry that they can understand, that they prefer humorous poetry, that they prefer new poems to older ones, and that they do not like serious and contemplative poems (see Terry). However, such studies can be dangerous if we rely on them entirely to determine what poetry we will share with children. This would result in a further narrowing of taste among children and deprive them of many fresh and imaginative poems that they just might enjoy.

*"Butterfly" from *Laughing Time: Collected Nonsense* by William Jay Smith. Copyright © 1990 by William Jay Smith. Reprinted by permission of Farrar, Straus and Giroux, LLC.

Nor should we think that we should give children only the poems they like or think they like. After all, an important part of education is the broadening of experience. It is useful to know what prejudices and preconceptions children may have about poetry, so that we have some idea of where we must go and what we have to overcome.

Too often in school we labor under the misconception that poetry is obscure (a puzzle to be unraveled by English teachers), "pretty" (without any particular meaning), and frivolous. These misconceptions are passed on to children, and by the time they reach adulthood, many have acquired a disdain for poetry. We need to build on the early love of rhythm, rhyme, and figurative language that most children exhibit, and see that poetry continues to be an enjoyable and enriching experience, not a trial or torture.

Reading poetry is ideally a regular part of a child's reading program. Most poetry is best read aloud and—in the classroom, at least—it is best read frequently and not saved up for a weeklong poetry marathon once a year. Poems exist that are suitable for all special occasions (or even ordinary occasions, for instance, poems for a partly cloudy day). A well-presented poem can fill a relatively small time slot in a day and provide some welcome, joyous relief. If we begin to think of poetry in this fashion, we may dispel some of the notions of drudgery and perplexity that currently surround poetry.

An easy way to introduce poetry is through humorous verse. Shel Silverstein's outrageous exaggerations ("Sarah Cynthia Sylvia Stout/Would not take the garbage out" until "it was too late/ . . . The garbage reached from New York to the Golden Gate") and Jack Prelutsky's comic verses are favorites. David McCord, Eve Merriam, and Myra Cohn Livingston are poets with wide range and evocative imagery.

The writing of original poetry may be encouraged and even required (but only after the children have caught the "poetry bug"), and some children will find it fun and rewarding. Encouraging children to form collections of their own favorite poems is also an enriching experience (and every adult presenting poetry to children should do the same). Memorizing is a practice currently frowned on by many teachers, but encouraging children to memorize poems can have happy results. It works best if the children can choose their own poems and if the recitation is kept informal and low-keyed. If the entertaining aspect is emphasized, the exercise need not become the painful experience it is often imagined to be.

Helping children to read their favorite poems effectively is always a worthwhile exercise. Inexperienced readers tend to want to dramatize the rhythm or the rhyme of a poem, to always make a definite pause at the end of a line whether the poet has punctuated it or not, and to overemphasize the singsong quality. Children learn best by example. We can demonstrate the effective reading of poetry, paying close attention to the poet's punctuation, avoiding a lapse into inappropriate nursery-rhyme rhythm, carefully enunciating the words, and emphasizing the meaning of the poem by using natural and not artificial inflections. Reading naturally and remembering not to pause at the end of a line unless the punctuation calls for it are the most helpful suggestions we can give to readers of poetry. Practice in reading poetry is the key to accomplishment. Ideally, the reading of poetry will become a much anticipated part of the daily schedule—both a delight and a refreshment.

SELECTING POEMS AND ANTHOLOGIES

Too often children are asked to read poems that were clearly intended for adults. And then we wonder why the children are confused or bored. The truth is that much of the poetry of our most revered poets speaks about adult emotions and adult perceptions of the world. How can we expect children to identify with these subjects? Plenty of excellent poems for young readers exist; we do not need to raid adult literature for suitable examples.

Every classroom and home should include a generous supply of poetry books, both anthologies and books by individual poets. With the wealth of good poetry available, every child—no matter how resistant to poetry—is bound to find some favorites. The key, of course, is for adults to supply a wide and varied sampling—poems on all subjects, poems representing a myriad of stanza forms and rhyme schemes and rhythms.

A great number of poetry anthologies are available today. It is helpful if we have a few guidelines to help us select an anthology of quality. Following are some of the important characteristics found in the best anthologies (and, of course, the purpose of the anthology must be considered):

1. The selection includes both familiar and new poets.
2. The selection includes a significant number of fresh poems and not simply recycled poems that can already be found in many anthologies.
3. The selection includes a balance of light and serious poems.
4. The poems *show* the reader (through effective imagery, metaphor, personification) rather than *tell* the reader the poet's thoughts.
5. The poems reflect a variety of verse forms.
6. The illustrations (if the book is illustrated) complement the poems without overpowering them.

As with all children's literature, if we wish to instill a love of reading poetry in children, we must begin with ourselves. The poet is a visionary, one who sees the world in fresh and unusual ways and is capable of sharing that vision with the rest of us. It is important that we overcome our own fears and apprehensions about poetry so that we may share in its bounty. But, as with everything else in creation the better we come to know poetry, the richer our experience will be. Few literary forms offer so much in pleasure and knowledge than poetry. Lovers of poetry are not born, but made through patient and careful nurturing.

RECOMMENDED READINGS

Baskin, Barbara Holland, Karen H. Harris, and Coleen C. Salley. "Making the Poetry Connection." *The Reading Teacher* 30 (December 1976): 259–265.

Ciardi, John, and Miller Williams. *How Does a Poem Mean?* 2nd ed. Boston: Houghton Mifflin, 1975.

Fisher, Carol J., and Margaret A. Natarella. "Of Cabbages and Kings: Or What Kinds of Poetry Children Like." *Language Arts* 56:4 (April 1979): 380–385.

Higginson, William J., with Penny Harter. *The Haiku Handbook: How to Write, Share and Teach Haiku.* New York: McGraw-Hill, 1985.

Hopkins, Lee Bennet. *Pass the Poetry Please.* New York: Citation Press, 1972.

Hurst, Carol. "What to Do with a Poem." *Early Years* 11 (February 1980): 28–29, 68.

Kennedy, X. J. "'Go and Get Your Candle Lit!' An Approach to Poetry." *Horn Book Magazine* 57:3 (June 1981): 273–279.

Krogness, Mary Mercer. "Imagery and Image Making." *Elementary English* 51:4 (April 1974): 488–490.

Larrick, Nancy, ed. *Somebody Turned on a Tap in These Kids.* New York: Delacorte, 1971.

Lewis, Marjorie. "Why Is a Poem a Four-Letter Word?" *School Library Journal* 23:9 (May 1977): 38–39.

Livingston, Myra. *Climb into the Bell Tower: Essays on Poetry.* New York: HarperCollins, 1990.

———. *Poem-Making: Ways to Begin Writing Poetry.* New York: HarperCollins, 1991.

Shapiro, Jon E. *Using Literature and Poetry Affectively.* Newark, DE: International Reading Association, 1979.

Steiner, Barbara. "Writing Poetry for Children." *Writer's Digest* February 1986: 34–35.

Terry, Ann. *Children's Poetry Preferences: A National Survey of the Upper Elementary Grades.* Urbana, IL: National Council of Teachers of English, 1984.

SELECTED BIBLIOGRAPHY OF POETRY BOOKS FOR CHILDREN

POETRY ANTHOLOGIES

Abdul, Raoul, ed. *The Magic of Black Poetry.* Illus. Dane Burr. New York: Dodd, 1972.

Adoff, Arnold, ed. *I Am the Darker Brother: An Anthology of Modern Poems by African Americans.* Rev. ed. New York: Simon & Schuster, 1996.

———. *The Poetry of Black America: An Anthology of the 20th Century.* New York: HarperCollins, 1989.

———. *Celebrations: A New Anthology of Black American Poetry.* Chicago: Follett, 1977.

Arbuthnot, May Hill, and Shelton L. Root, eds. *Time for Poetry.* Illus. Arthur Paul. Glenview, IL: Scott, Foresman, 1968.

Blishen, Edward, comp. *Oxford Book of Poetry for Children.* Illus. Brian Wildsmith. New York: Watts, 1963.

Bober, Natalie S., comp. *Let's Pretend: Poems of Flight and Fancy.* Illus. Bill Bell. New York: Viking, 1986.

Bryan, Ashley, selector and illus. *All Night, All Day: A Child's First Book of African-American Spirituals.* New York: Atheneum, 1991.

Carlson, Lori M., ed. *Cool Salsa: Bilingual Poems on Growing Up Latino in the United States.* New York: Holt, 1994.

Carter, Anne, selector. *Birds, Beasts, and Fishes: A Selection of Animal Poems*. New York: Macmillan, 1991.

Cole, William, comp. *Poems of Magic and Spells*. Illus. Peggy Bacon. Cleveland: World, 1960.

——. *A Zooful of Animals*. Illus. Lynn Munsinger. Boston: Houghton Mifflin, 1992.

de Gasztold, Carmen Bernos, selector. *Prayers from the Ark*. Trans. Rumer Godden. Illus. Barry Moser. New York: Viking, 1992.

De La Mare, Walter, ed. *Come Hither*. 3rd ed. Illus. Warren Chappell. New York: Knopf, 1957.

——. *Tom Tiddler's Ground*. Illus. Margery Gill. New York: Knopf, 1962.

Demi, selector and illus. *In the Eyes of the Cat: Japanese Poetry for All Seasons*. Trans. Tze-si Huang. New York: Holt, 1992.

Dunning, Stephen, Edward Lueders, and Hugh Smith, comps. *Reflections on a Gift of Watermelon Pickle*. Glenview, IL: Scott, Foresman, 1967.

——. *Some Haystacks Don't Even Have Any Needle*. Glenview, IL: Scott, Foresman, 1969.

Elledge, Scott, ed. *Wider than the Sky: Poems to Grow Up With*. New York: Harper, 1990.

Esbensen, Barbara Juster, comp. *Swing around the Sun*. Illus. Khee Chee Cheng, Stephen Gammell, and Janice Lee Porter. Minneapolis: Carolrhoda, 2003.

Feelings, Tom, comp. illus. *Soul Looks Back in Wonder*. New York: Dial, 1993.

Gordon, Ruth, selector. *Pierced by a Ray of Sun: Poems about the Times We Feel Alone*. New York: HarperCollins, 1995.

Hopkins, Lee Bennett, ed. *Sports! Sports! Sports!: A Poetry Collection*. Illus. Brian Floca. New York: HarperCollins, 1999.

Houston, James, ed. *Songs of the Dream People*. New York: Atheneum, 1972. (Eskimo and other Native American poems)

Janesczko, Paul B., selector. *Dirty Laundry Pile: Poems in Different Voices*. Illus. Melissa Sweet. New York: HarperCollins, 2001.

——. *Looking for your Name: A Collection of Contemporary Poems*. New York: Jackson/Orchard/Watts, 1993.

——. *The Place My Words Are Looking For: What Poets Say About and Through Their Work*. New York: Bradbury, 1990.

——. *A Poke in the I: A Collection of Concrete Poems*. Illus. Chris Raschka. Cambridge, MA: Candlewick, 2001.

——. *Preposterous: Poems of Youth*. New York: Watts, 1991.

Jones, Hettie, selector. *The Trees Stand Shining: Poetry of the North American Indians*. Illus. Robert Andrew Parker. New York: Dial, 1971.

Kennedy, X. J., and Dorothy Kennedy, eds. *Knock at a Star: A Child's Introduction to Poetry*. Rev. ed. Illus. Karen Lee Baker. Boston: Little Brown, 1999.

Larrick, Nancy, ed. *Piping Down the Valleys Wild*. Illus. Ellen Raskin. 1968. New York: Dell, 1982.

Livingston, Myra Cohn, comp. *Dilly Dilly Piccalilli: Poems for the Very Young*. New York: McElderry, 1989. (Nonsense verse)

——. *Lots of Limericks*. New York: Simon & Schuster, 1991.

Moore, Lilian, ed. *Go with the Poem*. New York: McGraw-Hill, 1979.

——. *Sunflakes: Poems for Children*. Illus. Jan Ormerod. New York: Clarion, 1992.

Moore, Lilian, and Judith Thurman, comps. *To See the World Afresh*. New York: Atheneum, 1974.

Nye, Naomi Shihab, selector. *This Same Sky: A Collection of Poems from around the World*. New York: Macmillan, 1992.

Opie, Iona, and Peter Opie, eds. *The Oxford Book of Children's Verse*. New York: Oxford, 1973.

Orozco, José-Luis, selector-arranger. *De Colores and Other Latin-American Folk Songs for Children*. New York: Dutton, 1994.

Prelutsky, Jack, selector. *The 20th Century Children's Poetry Treasury*. Illus. Meilo So. New York: Knopf, 1999.

Steptoe, Javaka, illus. *In Daddy's Arms I Am Tall: African Americans Celebrating Fathers*. New York: Lee & Low, 1997.

Sullivan, Charles, ed. *Imaginary Gardens: American Poetry and Art for Young People*. New York: Abrams, 1989.

Townsend, John Rowe, comp. *Modern Poetry*. Philadelphia: Lippincott, 1974.

Whipple, Laura, comp. *Animals Animals*. Illus. Eric Carle. New York: Philomel, 1989.

BOOKS BY INDIVIDUAL POETS

Adoff, Arnold. *All the Colors of the Race*. Illus. John Steptoe. New York: Lothrop, 1982.

——. *Street Music: City Poems*. Illus. Karen Barbour. New York: HarperCollins, 1995.

Armour, Richard. *A Dozen Dinosaurs*. Illus. Paul Galdone. New York: McGraw-Hill, 1970.

Berry, James. *Everywhere Faces Everywhere*. Illus. Reynold Ruffins. New York: Simon, 1997.

Blake, William. *Songs of Innocence and Experience*. Illus. Harold Jones. New York: Barnes, 1961.

Bodeker, N. M. *Water Pennies: And Other Poems*. Illus. Erik Blegvad. New York: McElderry, 1991.

Cawthorne, William Alexander. *Who Killed Cockatoo?* Illus. Rodney McRea. New York: Farrar, Straus & Giroux, 1989. (Australian adaptation of "Who Killed Cock Robin?")

Chandra, Deborah. *Balloons and Other Poems*. Illus. Leslie Bowman. New York: Farrar, Straus & Giroux, 1990.

Ciardi, John. *The Man Who Sang the Sillies*. Illus. Edward Gorey. Philadelphia: Lippincott, 1961.

——. *The Reason for the Pelican*. Illus. Madeleine Gekiere. Philadelphia: Lippincott, 1959.

Coatsworth, Elizabeth. *Under the Green Willow*. Illus. Janina Domanska. New York: Macmillan, 1971.

cummings, e. e. *Hist Whist*. Illus. Deborah Kogan Ray. New York: Crown, 1989.

De La Mare, Walter. *Peacock Pie*. Illus. Barbara Cooney. New York: Knopf, 1961.

Dickinson, Emily. *Letter to the World*. Ed. Rumer Godden. Illus. Prudence Seward. New York: Macmillan, 1969.

Eliot, T. S. *Old Possum's Book of Practical Cats*. Illus. Edward Gorey. New York: Harcourt, Brace, Jovanovich, 1982.

Farjeon, Eleanor. *Then There Were Three*. Illus. Isobel and John Morton-Sale. Philadelphia: Lippincott, 1965.

Field, Rachel. *Poems*. New York: Macmillan, 1957.

Fisher, Aileen. *Cricket in a Thicket*. Illus. Feodor Rojankovsky. New York: Scribner's, 1963.

——. *Feathered Ones and Furry*. Illus. Eric Carle. New York: Crowell, 1971.

Fleischman, Paul. *I Am Phoenix: Poems for Two Voices*. Illus. Ken Nutt. New York: Harper, 1985.

——. *A Joyful Noise: Poems for Two Voices*. New York: Harper, 1988.

Fletcher, Ralph. *I Am Wings: Poems about Love*. New York: Macmillan, 1994.

Florian, Douglas. *lizards, frogs, and polliwogs*. New York: Harcourt, 2001.

Froman, Robert. *Seeing Things: A Book of Poems*. New York: Crowell, 1974.

Frost, Robert. *Birches*. Illus. Ed Young. New York: Holt, 1988.

George, Kristine O'Connell. *Little Dog Poems*. Illus. June Otani. New York: Clarion, 1999.

Giovanni, Nikki. *Spin a Soft Black Song*. Illus. George Martins. New York: Hill & Wang, 1985.

Gollub, Matthew. *Cool Melons—Turn to Frogs!: The Life and Poems of Issa*. Illus. Kazuko G. Stone. New York: Lee & Low, 1998.

Greenberg, David T. *Bugs*. Illus. Lyn Munsinger. Boston: Little, Brown, 1997.

Greenfield, Eloise. *Honey, I Love and Other Love Poems*. Illustrated by Diane and Leo Dillon. New York: HarperCollins, 1978.

——. *Night on Neighborhood Street*. Illus. Jan Spivey Gilchrist. New York: Dial, 1991.

Grossman, Bill. *Timothy Tunny Swallowed a Bunny*. Illus. Kevin Hawkes. New York: HarperCollins, 2001.

Hughes, Langston. *The Dream Keeper and Other Poems*. New York: Knopf, 1994.

Hughes, Ted. *Moon-Whales and Other Moon Poems*. Illus. Leonard Baskin. New York: Viking, 1976.

Issa. *A Few Flies and I: Haiku by Issa*. Trans. R. H. Blyth and Nobuyaki Yuasa. Ed. Jean Merrill and Ronni Solbert. New York: Pantheon, 1969.

Janeczko, Paul B. *Brickyard Summer*. New York: Orchard, 1989.

Johnson, Angela. *The Other Side: Shorter Poems*. New York: Orchard, 1998.

——. *Running Back to Ludie*. Illus. Angelo. New York: Orchard/Scholastic, 2001.

Kennedy, X. J. *Chastlies, Goops & Pincushions: Nonsense Verse*. Illus. Ron Barrett. New York: McElderry, 1989.

Kuskin, Karla. *Moon, Have You Met My Mother?* Illus. Sergio Ruzzier. New York: HarperCollins, 2003.

——. *Near the Window Tree*. New York: Harper, 1975.

Lear, Edward. *The Complete Nonsense Book*. Ed. Lady Strachey. New York: Dodd, 1942.

——. *The Quangle-Wangle's Hat*. Illus. Helen Oxenbury. New York: Watts, 1969.

Lee, Dennis. *Bubblegum Delicious*. Illus. David McPhail. New York: HarperCollins, 2001.

Lewis. J. Patrick. *Doodle Dandies: Poems That Take Shape*. Illus. Lisa Desimini. New York: Atheneum, 1998.

——. *A Hippopotamusn't: And Other Animal Verses*. Illus. Victoria Chess. New York: Dial, 1990.

——. *A World of Wonders: Geographic Travels in Verse and Rhyme*. Illus. Alison Jay. New York: Dial, 2002.

Livingston, Myra Cohn. *A Circle of Seasons*. Illus. Leonard Everett Fisher. New York: Holiday House, 1982.

——. *Monkey Puzzle and Other Poems*. Illus. Antonio Frasconi. New York: Atheneum, 1984.

——. *The Way Things Are and Other Poems*. Illus. Jenni Oliver. New York: Atheneum, 1974.

——. *Whispers and Other Poems*. Illus. Jacqueline Chwast. New York: Harcourt, 1958.

McCord, David. *One at a Time: His Collected Poems for the Young*. Illus. Henry Kane. Boston: Little, Brown, 1977.

Mado, Michio. *The Magic Pocket*. Trans. Empress Michiko of Japan. Illus. Mitsumasa Anno. New York: McElderry, 1998.

Margolis, Richard. *Looking for a Place*. Philadelphia: Lippincott, 1969.

Mahy, Margaret. *Nonstop Nonsense*. Illus. Quentin Blake. New York: McElderry, 1989.

Merriam, Eve. *A Sky Full of Poems*. Illustrated by Walter Gaffney-Kessell. New York: Dell, 1986.

——. *The Singing Green: New and Selected Poems for All Seasons*. New York: Morrow, 1992.

——. *There Is No Rhyme for Silver*. Illus. Joseph Schindelman. New York: Atheneum, 1962.

Milne, A. A. *The World of Christopher Robin*. Illus. Ernest Shephard. New York: Dutton, 1924.

Moore, Lilian. *Adam Mouse's Book of Poems*. Illus. Kathleen Garry McCord. New York: Atheneum, 1992.

Myers, Walter Dean. *blues journey*. Illus. Christopher Myers. New York: Holiday, 2003.

Nash, Ogden. *The Adventures of Isabel*. Illus. James Marshall. Boston: Little, Brown, 1991.

——. *Custard and Company: Poems by Ogden Nash*. Comp. and illus. Quentin Blake. Boston: Little, Brown, 1980.

Nelson, Marilyn. *Carver: A Life in Poems*. Asheville, NC: Front Street, 2001.

Nye, Naomi Shihab. *19 Varieties of Gazelle: Poems of the Middle East*. New York: Greenwillow, 2002.

O'Neill, Mary. *Hailstones and Halibut Bones*. Illus. John Wallner. New York: Doubleday, 1989.

Prelutsky, Jack. *The Dragons Are Singing Tonight*. New York: Greenwillow, 1993.

——. *The Frog Wore Red Suspenders*. Illus. Petra Mathers. New York: Greenwillow, 2002.

——. *Ride a Purple Pelican*. New York: Greenwillow, 1986.

——. *The Sheriff of Rottenshot*. Illus. Victoria Chess. New York: Greenwillow, 1982.

——. *Something Big Has Been Here*. Illus. James Stevenson. New York: Greenwillow, 1990.

Richards, Laura. *Tirra Lirra: Rhymes Old and New*. (1932) Illus. Marguerite Davis. Boston: Little, Brown, 1955.

Roethke, Theodore. *Dirty Dinky and Other Creatures*. Selectors Beatrice Roethke and Stephen Lushington. New York: Doubleday, 1973.

Schwartz, Alvin, selector. *And the Green Grass Grew All Around: Folk Poetry from Everyone*. Illus. Sue Truesdell. New York: Harper, 1992.

Seabrooke, Brenda. *Judy Scuppernong*. Illus. Ted Lewin. New York: Dutton, 1990.

Service, Robert W. *The Shooting of Dan McGrew*. Illus. Ted Harrison. Boston: Godine, 1988.

Silverstein, Shel. *A Light in the Attic*. New York: Harper, 1981.

——. *Where the Sidewalk Ends*. New York: Harper, 1974.

Soto, Gary. *Canto Familiar*. San Diego: Harcourt Brace, 1995.

——. *A Fire in My Hands: A Book of Poems*. Illus. James M. Cardillo. New York: Scholastic, 1991.

——. *Neighborhood Odes*. San Diego: Harcourt Brace, 1992.

Starbird, Kaye. *The Covered Bridge House*. Illus. Jim Arnosky. New York: Four Winds, 1979.

Stevenson, James. *Sweet Corn: Poems*. New York: Greenwillow, 1995.

Stevenson, Robert Louis. *A Child's Garden of Verses*. Illus. Jessie Willcox Smith. 1905. New York: Scribner's, 1969.

Swenson, May. *The Complete Poems to Solve*. New York: Macmillan, 1993.

Viorst, Judith. *If I Were in Charge of the World and Other Worries*. Illus. Lyn Cherry. New York: Atheneum, 1969.

Whitman, Walt. *Voyages: Poems by Walt Whitman*. Selector Lee Bennett Hopkins. Illus. Charles Mikolaycak. New York: Harcourt, 1988.

Wilbur, Richard. *Opposites*. New York: Harcourt, 1973.

Willard, Nancy. *Household Tales of Moon and Water*. New York: Harcourt, 1982.

——. *A Visit to William Blake's Inn*. Illus. Alice and Martin Provensen. New York: Harcourt, 1981.

Williams, Vera B. *Amber Was Brave, Essie Was Smart*. New York: Greenwillow, 2001.

Worth, Valerie. *All the Small Poems and Fourteen More*. Illus. Natalie Babbitt. New York: Farrar, Straus & Giroux, 1994.

——. *Peacock and Other Poems*. Illus. Natalie Babbitt. New York: Farrar, 2002.

Wong, Janet S. *A Suitcase of Seaweed and Other Poems*. New York: Simon & Schuster, 1996.

CHAPTER
10

Fantasy

DEFINITION OF FANTASY

The enduring figures of the great fantasies—Alice, Dorothy and her motley companions, the irrepressible Mr. Toad of Toad Hall, Peter Pan, Wilbur the pig and Charlotte the spider—are fixed indelibly on the cultural consciousness of our society and have helped to shape our imaginations. It is difficult to exaggerate the influence that reading fantasy has on young minds.

In the broadest sense, *fantasy* is any story of the impossible. It may include magic, talking animals, time travel, the supernatural, adventures in alternative worlds—any feature that is contrary to the laws of nature as we understand them. Modern fantasy has its roots in traditional folktales—those stories, myths, and legends that have been passed down through a culture for generations. However, modern fantasy is distinctly different from folk literature. The folktales are old stories belonging to the oral tradition, whereas modern fantasy is a new story written by an individual author and its transmission is through the written medium. Although the folktales contain fantastical elements, they are always set in a familiar world; they have stock characters, conventional plots, and traditional motifs (see Chapter 8). The folktales are generally brief because they rely on our prior knowledge of the form to fill in the gaps. The fantasist, on the other hand, is after something original, something unusual. Each writer of fantasy creates a new world with its own possibilities. Consequently, the settings, characters, and plots of a fantasy tend to be much more complex than those of the folktales. One critic has noted that "reading fantasy is not so much an escape *from* something as a liberation *into* something, into openness and possibility and coherence" and that we as readers get perspective on our world "by exploring a strange fictional place and learning how its pieces fit together" (O'Keefe 11–12). It is this challenge in fantasy that attracts its devoted readers.

FIGURE 10.1   Sir John Tenniel's illustration for Lewis Carroll's *Alice's Adventures in Wonderland*. Alice discovers a passage into Wonderland.

The first important fantasies specifically for children appeared in the nineteenth century. Hans Christian Andersen wrote original fairy stories heavily influenced by the folk tradition. But it is Carroll's *Alice's Adventures in Wonderland* (1865) (see Figure 10.1) that is remembered as one of the pioneers in book-length fantasy for children. (It is also considered one of the first children's books written primarily for children's enjoyment without heavy underlying didacticism.) Since that time modern fantasy has prospered, producing some of the most memorable works of children's literature. Other early classics in modern fantasy for children include Carlo Collodi's *The Adventures of Pinocchio* (1881), Jules Verne's popular works of science fiction (*Twenty Thousand Leagues under the Sea* [1869] and others), L. Frank Baum's *The Wonderful Wizard of Oz* (1900), Kenneth Grahame's *The Wind in the Willows* (1908), and A. A. Milne's *Winnie-the-Pooh* (1926).

TYPES OF FANTASY

Like folk literature, modern fantasy comes in many varieties. It may be comical or tragic, it may be frivolous or serious, it may take place in our world or in some imaginary world, it may include talking animals, fire-breathing dragons, or friendly ghosts. Any effort to classify modern fantasy is thwarted by its rich variety; nevertheless, it is helpful to make some tentative generalizations about common fantasy types. Keep in mind that some fantasies simply refuse to fit tidily into categories.

Animal Fantasy

Animal fantasies, in which animals talk and exhibit human emotions, became popular in the early twentieth century. During the nineteenth century, many people still harbored the belief that talking animals were a sacrilege, contrary to the laws of God. By the end of the nineteenth century, young readers might encounter the occasional talking beast—Lewis Carroll includes several in the *Alice* books—but the focus of these stories is still on the human characters. An interesting type of animal fantasy, reaching as far back as the eighteenth century, is the animal autobiography. Dorothy Kilner's *The Life and Perambulations of a Mouse* (1783) is a tale of the importance of obedience to one's parents told from the perspective of the animal. Apparently the weighty moral message made up for the story's suspect narrative style. Several similar moral tales in the form of animal biographies appeared in the nineteenth century. The most famous of these is Anna Sewell's *Black Beauty: The Autobiography of a Horse* (1877), originally for adults but much loved by children. It is one of the first fictional stories to draw attention to the abuse of animals, and it contains a great deal of harsh realism—all related by the horse himself. However, Beatrix Potter's picture-book fantasies—*The Tale of Peter Rabbit, The Tale of Benjamin Bunny*, and many others—are among the first true examples of animal fantasy in which the animals themselves are the chief focus. Potter's little creatures typically wear clothes and speak perfectly good English, but they possess many animal-like traits—the rascal Peter cannot resist raiding Mr. McGregor's garden and he is particularly fond of raw carrots. Kenneth Grahame created similar animal characters in his classic, *The Wind in the Willows*, first published in 1908 (see Figure 10.2). His characters—a water rat, a mole, a badger, and a toad—live in a comfortable pastoral setting where they enjoy well-furnished homes, good cooking, hearty male companionship (the story virtually excludes women), and all the finer things in life. The animals are clearly examples of human types and bear little resemblance to their natural counterparts.

In the 1920s, Hugh Lofting wrote the Doctor Dolittle books, tales of a talented veterinarian who is able to speak the languages of animals. The good doctor is the main character, but the stories revolve entirely about the animals. In the 1930s and 1940s, Walter R. Brooks, an American writer, created the popular stories of Freddy the pig (*Freddy the Detective* and many others) portraying the escapades of affable talking farm animals. Freddy lives in a pig-pen, but he reads books, sometimes dresses up—in other words, he's really very unpiglike. The humans converse with the animals but play minor roles. Perhaps the most famous of all animal fantasies of this sort is E. B. White's *Charlotte's Web*, about Wilbur the pig and his friendship with a spider named Charlotte. Wilbur lives in a barnyard, eats like a pig, and generally has all the habits of a pig. Charlotte, likewise, lives the life of a spider; we see her entrap a fly and suck its blood, an activity that at first horrifies Wilbur. The animals can communicate with each other, but not with the humans on the farm, except for Fern, who saved Wilbur's life when he was born the runt of the litter. Fern, in her youthful innocence,

FIGURE 10.2   Ernest H. Shepard's illustration for Kenneth Grahame's *The Wind in the Willows*. Mole and Water Rat go boating on the River.

can understand the animals, but once she begins to mature and her interests drift to the young boy, Henry Fussy, her role with animals diminishes and she is gradually replaced as their companion by her younger brother. This is a familiar theme in fantasies—the magic only works if one remains childlike and innocent, an attitude inherited from the Romantics of the nineteenth century who celebrated the wise innocence of the young, untainted by the evils of adult society.

Today, animal fantasy is found most frequently in picture books for the young—the tales of Babar the elephant (by the de Brunoffs), of the many animal characters created by William Steig, and, most famously, the cartoon animal creatures that have dominated the film media since the 1930s. In virtually all cases, the animals are imbued with human qualities and serve symbolic roles. We won't learn much about the nature of donkeys by reading William Steig's *Sylvester and the Magic Pebble*, or much about mice by watching Mickey Mouse in action. Animal fantasies for older readers are far less common, but Richard Adams's *Watership Down*, portraying the plight of a society of rabbits forced from their homes by human encroachment, the heroic animal fantasies of Brian Jacques (the *Redwall* series), and Robert O'Brien's *Mrs. Frisby and the Rats of NIMH*, which contains a pointed social message, have proven quite successful.

In all cases of animal fantasy, the premise is that the animals have human feelings, we can empathize with them, and from their behavior we can learn something about ourselves and humanity in general. Consequently, it is possible for us to draw significant conclusions about human behavior from reading either *The Wind in the Willows* or *Charlotte's Web*. Both stories illustrate the importance of friendship, the need for sacrifice, the pleasures of the simple life. By the same token, we learn very little reliable information about animal behavior. In other words, animal fantasy constitutes a form of literary symbolism, the animal characters symbolizing human counterparts, and these fantasies are often vehicles for exploring human emotions, values, and relationships.

Toy Fantasy

In 1883, an Italian author named Carlo Collodi (a pen name for Carlo Lorenzini) wrote *Pinocchio*, the story of a wooden puppet's quest to become a real boy. This was one of the first examples of a toy fantasy—stories of toys come to life—and in a great number of these the animated toys wish to become human. Toy fantasies enjoyed popularity in the 1920s and 1930s with such works as Margery Williams Bianco's *The Velveteen Rabbit*, which remains a perennial favorite. It is not true, however, that all toys in these fantasies are striving for human status. Rachel Field's *Hitty: Her First Hundred Years*, is the first-person narrative of a doll who is reminiscing about her experiences over an entire century, which reveals the peculiar advantages of toy protagonists—they may wear out, but they never die.

A. A. Milne's *Winnie-the-Pooh* and *The House at Pooh Corner* (first published in the 1920s) are among the best-known of toy fantasies—although many readers are apt to see these as animal fantasies (a perfect example of how shaky classification schemes can be). Winnie and his friends are technically toys, although they have many of the characteristics of animals—the owl lives in a tree, the bear lives in a den and loves honey (or "hunny" as he says). But, in fact, the creatures behave like a large, dysfunctional family, each member with a different physical or psychological hang-up—a hyperactive tiger, a manic-depressive donkey, a paranoid pig, a dyslexic owl, a feeble-minded bear (see Manlove 62). The allure of the stories is seeing how these creatures survive through love and loyalty.

Modern toy fantasies are most frequently in picture-book format (Leo Lionni's *Alexander and the Wind-up Mouse* or Don Freeman's *Corduroy*), but Russell Hoban's *The Mouse and His Child* is a serious work of toy fantasy for older readers and is filled with sharp social satire.

Magical Fantasy and Tall Tales

William Steig's picture-book animal fantasy, *Sylvester and the Magic Pebble,* is the story of Sylvester, a young donkey who finds a pebble that will grant his wishes so long as he holds onto it. When he encounters a hungry lion, Sylvester without thinking wishes he were a rock. Sylvester's wish is granted and he is saved from the lion, but the poor donkey has been transformed into a rock and the only way he can be restored is if someone finds the magic pebble and wishes the rock were Sylvester again. This a good example of an animal fantasy that also fits our next category—magical fantasy.

All fantasy stories contain some magic, if by magic we mean any phenomenon contrary to the laws of the natural world as we understand them. But in some fantasies the magic itself—whether a magical object or a character with magical powers—becomes the very subject of the story (rather than simply a means to an end). Take, for example, Astrid Lindgren's *Pippi Longstocking*—a story set in Sweden, perhaps in the 1940s (when it was written), and peopled with very ordinary human beings, except for Pippi herself. Pippi is a young girl, apparently orphaned, who lives by herself and does as she pleases. Her behavior is quite outrageous—which is why children love her. We do not worry about her being alone because she possesses superhuman strength (for which no explanation is ever given). Her magical strength makes her impervious to any danger and puts her on a superior footing to the adults in the story.

Another example is P. L. Travers's *Mary Poppins*, the story of an unconventional nanny who has magical powers. She moves in with the Banks family—a rather stiff bunch of Londoners—and brings wonder into their lives, enabling them to finally find happiness. In both *Pippi Longstocking* and *Mary Poppins*, the magic helps give readers a fresh view of the world. These fantasies are typically set in the modern world and we are constantly aware of the incongruity of the magical element (often the "normal" characters have to be convinced that the magic is real). This is quite different from the magic in folktales, which is always taken for granted as a part of the way of the world.

It is important to note that in these tales of magic, the magic itself is always conditional. We find similar restrictions in the folktales, whose creators knew that most things in life come with strings attached. Sylvester cannot be transformed back into a donkey unless someone touches the magic pebble and wishes it so. Only Pippi and Mary Poppins possess the magic. And, in E. Nesbit's *Five Children and It*, the children are granted a new wish every day, but the wish ends with each sunset. The magic always operates according to some established rule or rules (and these are established, of course, by the author). We tend to be very uncomfortable when fantasies seem to have no rules.

Closely related to magical tales are tall tales. In fact, *Pippi Longstocking* is little different from the characters in American tall tales like Paul Bunyan, except that in the tall tale the exaggeration is taken to absurdity. Paul Bunyan and his blue ox, Babe, are of stupendous size and their feats include creating new rivers and canyons and leveling mountains. Tall tales seem to be largely an American phenomenon, characteristic of the American love of overstatement. The characters are outlandish, their feats quite unbelievable. Sid Fleischman's McBroom series for younger readers appears to have been inspired by the Paul Bunyan tales, and his stories for older readers, such as *The Ghost in the Noonday Sun* and *Chancy and the Grand Rascal*, are comical yarns set in nineteenth-century America and filled with eccentric characters. In another form of the tall tale, Lucretia Hale's *The Peterkin Papers*, which was written in the nineteenth century, describe the misadventures of a completely inept family. In the twentieth century, Harry Allard wrote a series of picture books illustrated by James Marshall about the Stupids (Stupid being their family name) who find themselves in one absurd situation after another. In *The Stupids Die*, an electrical failure leads them to believe they are dead—a situation remedied when their cat (the brains in the family) repairs the blown fuse.

Enchanted Journeys and Alternative Worlds

This is another amorphous category, but a very useful one. In many fantasies we see the protagonists undertaking journeys, quite often to some secondary or fantasy world–some call it an alternative world. Realistic stories also use the journey motif, but only in fantasy journeys do magical things occur.

The journey motif is one of the oldest in literature, going back to Homer's *Odyssey* and beyond. The great advantage to sending fictional characters on a journey is that the possibilities for plot variations are virtually endless. Everyone is familiar with those fantasies that take a character–almost always a child–from the Real World into an Other World, a sort of never-never land of magic or enchantment. These fantasies are especially popular with younger readers, and some of these tales include the most famous books of childhood–Carroll's *Alice's Adventures in Wonderland,* L. Frank Baum's *The Wonderful Wizard of Oz* (see Figure 10.3), and James Barrie's *Peter Pan.* Enchanted journeys typically begin in the real world (called the primary world) and then, by some device–such as a cyclone or a rabbit hole–the principal character is allowed to enter the enchanted realm (called the secondary world).

The journey may have some purpose (Dorothy wants to find the Emerald City and ultimately a way back home; Alice wants to find the Queen's Garden), but that purpose is usually overshadowed by the thrill and delight offered by the extraordinary events that can happen in the secondary world. The credibility of these stories is typically aided by the fact that the fanciful events can happen only in the secondary world and not in the primary world–the Wicked Witch has no authority in Kansas. The plots of these tales are frequently quite loose, sometimes episodic, simply stringing together a series of adventures, and we rely on the central character (the child human) to be our touchstone with reality. Alice and Dorothy judge everything they see in Wonderland and Oz, respectively, by the standards they knew at home.

In a similar vein are those fantasies that take place largely in the secondary world. Currently the most famous of these are J. K. Rowlings's Harry Potter stories, which begin in London, but quickly take us to Hogwarts, a school for children with magical powers where all the action is set. Tove Jansson, the Finnish writer, created a magical secondary world in her series about the exploits of the gentle Moomins and their peculiar friends in Moominvalley. (The series begins with *Comet in Moominland* and includes many sequels.)

Another type of secondary world is the land of miniaturized characters. Jonathan Swift's work is usually singled out as the prototype for this form, with his description of the journey to Lilliput in the first book of *Gulliver's Travels;* however, the adventures of the diminutive folktale hero, Tom Thumb, predate Swift. Modern examples include L. Frank Baum's depiction of the Munchkins in *The Wonderful Wizard of Oz* and Mary Norton's *The Borrowers,* a tale of a family of miniature people living in the walls of a house (they are the ones responsible for all those items that inexplicably disappear). Carol Kendall's *The Gammage Cup,* about the struggles of the Minnipin society against their ancient enemies, the Mushroom People, contains many of the features of the heroic fantasy, just on a smaller

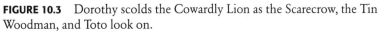

FIGURE 10.3 Dorothy scolds the Cowardly Lion as the Scarecrow, the Tin Woodman, and Toto look on.

Source: From W. W. Denslow's original illustrations for *The Wonderful Wizard of Oz*, New York: Hill, 1900.

scale. Young readers are attracted to these miniature worlds because they can identify with the diminutive characters and because these stories often depict the clever triumph of the small and weak characters over the larger, but duller, bullies of the world.

These fantasies are not always lighthearted, however. Lois Lowry's *The Giver* (and its two sequels) depicts a future society (some might argue this makes these books science fiction) in which all human emotion has been eradicated in order to "perfect" the community. The people are without pain, sorrow, and hate—but they are also without pleasure, joy, and love. The result is a *dystopia,* a society gone awry where people are dehumanized, and freedom and individuality are unknown (in other words, the opposite of a *utopia,* a perfect society). Such a fantasy can result in much thought-provoking discussion.

Whether the characters are on an enchanted journey or already live in an enchanted land, their wondrous experiences can open new horizons for readers. In either case, the author is required to provide enough details that we might understand the peculiarities of these characters and lands.

Heroic or Quest Fantasy

Alice and Dorothy, although they perform several acts that might be interpreted as heroic, remain clearly grounded in the primary world, which is the touchstone against which the wonders of the fantasy world are measured. However, in the *heroic fantasy* (sometimes referred to as *quest fantasy* or *high fantasy*), we share the heroic exploits of a hero or heroine engaged in a monumental struggle against a seemingly all-powerful evil, and the fate of an entire civilization often depends on the outcome of the struggle. Whereas the enchanted journey is often episodic, the heroic fantasy is usually more tightly woven, with all the action directed toward a single purpose—the triumph of good over evil.

Primary and secondary worlds are variously treated in heroic fantasies. In some heroic fantasies, the story begins with characters in the primary world who find some passage to the secondary world. C. S. Lewis's *The Lion, the Witch and the Wardrobe,* part of his Narnia chronicles, is among the best-known examples, the children getting to the secondary world of Narnia through the back of an old wardrobe. Many heroic fantasies, such as Ursula Le Guin's Earthsea cycle, Lloyd Alexander's Pyrdain chronicles, and J. R. R. Tolkien's *Lord of the Rings* trilogy, takes place entirely in alternative worlds inhabited by imaginary creatures (some human-like, some not). In rare instances, such as Susan Cooper's *The Dark Is Rising* series, the fantasies are set in the real (or primary) world, which is threatened by dark forces. Here the secondary world is really another plane of reality, outside of time, where the dark forces reside. Cooper draws on the old Arthurian heroic legends for much of her inspiration.

Heroic fantasies are most often structured around the hero's or heroine's *quest*—this frequently turns out to be a quest for identity, although the hero or heroine usually does not realize that at first. The fate of a nation or a people is often dependent on the success or failure of the quest, and the hero or heroine becomes a figure of adulation and may even be rewarded with a crown by the story's end. The central character acts decisively, is altruistic, and eventually becomes the savior of a people. The plot typically consists of a series of remarkable *adventures*–usually impediments that the central character must overcome to achieve the quest. Because of the seriousness of the themes–the necessity for good to overcome evil, the defense of an entire society, the search for the rightful ruler, and so on–humor is either absent or a decidedly secondary element in heroic fantasy. (Lloyd Alexander's Prydain chronicles, based on Welsh legend, is a good example of heroic fantasy employing humorous elements, usually in the form of comic characters. The hero, however, if sympathetic, is always quite serious.) Most heroic fantasies do not shy away from tragedy, and the message is frequently that good is not accomplished without some significant sacrifice. Heroic fantasy owes a great deal to the ancient myths, legends, and traditional folktales, from which are derived themes, plot structures, even characters and settings.

Supernatural and Time-Shift Fantasy

Supernatural and *time-shift fantasies* are among the most popular of fantasy types, including ghost and witch stories, stories of mysterious and unexplained occurrences, and stories of time travel. All are set in the primary world, and the fantasy element is often seen as an aberration that must be corrected before the story ends. Ghost stories are perennial favorites with many young people. Robert Bright's *Georgie and the Robbers* is a picture book about a shy ghost, and the cartoon figure of Casper the Friendly Ghost (also a popular film) has a long history. But older children generally prefer more threatening ghosts; indeed, the more horrifying and gruesome the story is, the better some seem to like it. Many people have deep within them something of the ambulance chaser. Nevertheless, the most thrilling tales of the supernatural are not those that dramatize and glamorize the blood and horror, but those that leave something for our imaginations. Penelope Lively's *The Ghost of Thomas Kempe* is a popular and well-told example of a modern ghost story. Devoid of any grisly horror, Lively's novel explores the potential problems that a ghost from an earlier time might have in the modern world.

Related to the supernatural tales are those stories that involve tricks with time–a ghost, after all, is simply a human presence moving about in a time other than that in which it lived. Philippa Pearce's *Tom's Midnight Garden* explores movement in and out of time and deals sensitively and seriously with human relationships. In a similar vein are Lucy Boston's *Green Knowe* books and Alan Garner's *Owl Service,* the latter of which is a somewhat sophisticated tale of the occult, drawing on mysterious ancient powers.

Science Fiction and Space Fantasy

Closely related to supernatural and time-shift fantasies are science fiction and space fantasy. Mary Shelley's *Frankenstein* (1818) is usually credited with being the first true work of *science fiction,* followed by the works of Jules Verne, *Twenty Thousand Leagues Under the Sea* and *From Earth to the Moon Direct,* which achieved great popularity in the mid-nineteenth century. Today science fiction has a following among young readers who make up in enthusiasm what they may lack in actual numbers. Science fiction is speculative writing usually focusing on life in the future, either on earth or on some other planet. The principal types of science fiction include stories about aliens from outer space, many of which are set in the present or near future (John Christopher's *When the Tripods Came*); stories about the future, often on other planets (Sylvia Engdahl's *Enchantress from the Stars*); and stories about space travel or time-dimensional travel (Madeleine L'Engle's *A Wrinkle in Time*). Many variations on these patterns exist.

Much of science fiction is devoted to dramatizing the wonders of technology (although science fiction is usually not especially scientific). Science fiction, in fact, closely resembles heroic fantasy, with magic replaced by technology, and the plots focused on mighty struggles between the forces of good and evil and with the fate of civilization hanging in the balance. As one critic notes, "How different, after all, is a wizard with a magic wand from a scientist with a microminiaturized matter-transformer? The reader does not know how either gadget works" (Roberts 90).

Science fiction seldom contains much humor because the science fiction writer usually wants to create the illusion of reality, or at least of possibility. Any flippancy or lightheartedness would threaten to undercut this serious tone. (The exception may be science fiction written for the younger reader; these works are largely space travel adventures–Ruthven Todd's *Space Cat*–or perhaps robot stories–Lester Del Rey's *The Runaway Robot*.)

Some works we categorize as science fiction may be better termed *space fantasy*. This is the term preferred by Sylvia Engdahl, whose *Enchantress from the Stars* and *The Far Side of Evil*, among other works, are set in the future on distant planets but otherwise are little concerned with scientific or technological achievements. Engdahl's works, despite their futuristic setting, are usually preferred by readers who are not science fiction buffs. Engdahl treats her futuristic setting as simply the framework through which she conveys her sense of the development of human civilization, socially and psychologically rather than scientifically and technologically.

A strong didactic strain runs through most science fiction, and many works deal with ethical problems facing humanity as science and technology outpaces our development as human beings. Consequently, the question as to whether technological discoveries will be used for humanity's benefit or its destruction frequently becomes a theme of science fiction. Madeleine L'Engle, best known for *A Wrinkle in Time*, addresses such issues in her science fiction.

SPECIAL QUALITIES OF FANTASY

Zilpha Snyder suggests that, regardless of the type, children demand two things from fantasy–that it contain *no nonsense* and that it contain *no treachery* (230). These, at first, may appear to be curious requirements, but they are quite important. Even though fantasy presents situations that we know to be impossible, we do expect them to be presented as if they *were* possible. Consequently, children insist that writers of fantasy establish certain rules that operate within the fantasy world itself and that the writers abide by those rules.

Also, children insist that the fantasy not be unfairly taken away at the book's end (such as pretending that it never happened, that it was all a dream, and so on). Such a betrayal on the writer's behalf usually generates a groan from readers. After all, part of the readers' delight in fantasy is being completely absorbed into the fantasy, and, once having made that commitment, readers do not like to find out that it has all been a trick or an elaborate deception. For example, the implication at the end of the MGM movie, *The Wizard of Oz,* is that the entire adventure was just a dream, but in the book Baum played no such trick on his readers. In the book, Dorothy *really* went to Oz and returned to Kansas. Baum wants us to believe in that magical land, and so do we want to believe.

Dreams, however, have long been an important tool of fantasy. Typically, the dream is only the means for the fantasy world to connect with the characters in the real world—such as the use of dreams in Pearce's *Tom's Midnight Garden.* Ian McEwan's *The Daydreamer* is an example in which the protagonist is frequently lost in his daydreams, imagining all sorts of extraordinary things—usually as a means of escaping the mundane world. It is the technique used by the humorist James Thurber in his short story, "The Secret Life of Walter Mitty," about a henpecked husband who escapes his wife's carping through fantastic daydreams.

Originality

In addition to the general characteristics that we expect of all fiction, we expect good fantasy to meet some special requirements. Perhaps above all, we expect fantasy to be *original, fresh, bold.* From a stylistic point of view, neither *The Wonderful Wizard of Oz* nor *Peter Pan* is particularly well written, but the ideas in these works are so imaginative and so unusual that the stories remain with us throughout our lives. The characters of good fantasy—Alice, Mr. Toad of Toad Hall, Winnie-the-Pooh, the Scarecrow and the Tin Woodsman—remain indelibly marked in our minds, and we inevitably measure new characters in our fantasy reading against these highly original figures.

One of the most original of recent fantasy writers was the late Roald Dahl, who was voted Britain's most popular writer in 2000—ten years after his death. Certainly among the reasons for his popularity is his extraordinary originality—who could have dreamed up a giant peach coming to the rescue of an unhappy and neglected boy (*James and the Giant Peach*), or another desolate boy inheriting a vast chocolate-making establishment (*Charlie and the Chocolate Factory*)? Another writer of great originality is Finland's Tove Jansson, mentioned earlier, who created the lovable and wondrous Moomins, small creatures with rounded bodies, long tails, and snouts resembling a hippopotamus's. The Moomins have numerous, equally bizarre friends, with whom they enjoy enchanted adventures. If a fantasy does not possess some strikingly original feature, it is not likely to endure.

Believability

Secondly, we expect good fantasy to be *believable.* This may sound contradictory, but, in fact, a fantasy may have to seem more believable than a realistic work. Readers want to believe in the fantasy, and we often resent it when a writer includes something that we immediately recognize as silly. ("Silly" is, of course, a relative term. We tolerate certain behavior in a toy fantasy such as *Winnie-the-Pooh* that we would not tolerate in C. S. Lewis's heroic fantasy *The Lion, the Witch, and the Wardrobe*. And the silliness of the Stupids is their appeal. It is the writer who, in the creation of the fantasy, sets the limits of silliness, and those limits must not be overstepped.) A good writer achieves believability in fantasy by several means.

1. *The massing of detail* provides us with vivid descriptions of characters, setting, and action. This is one area where folktales and fantasies tend to differ. Folktales contain few descriptive details, whereas fantasies are often lush with description. Fantasy writers make their stories believable by giving us the colors, sounds, textures, tastes, and smells of their fantasy worlds, and thus these worlds are made to seem real.

2. *Restraining the fantastic* simply means that all fantasies must have their limits or else they devolve into nonsense. A fantasy in which "anything goes" is really no fun. (When children invent games during their play, one of the first things they do is set up the "rules.") The wizards in Le Guin's Earthsea cycle possess magical powers, but those powers are made more believable because they have their limitations. Pippi Longstocking is an extraordinary child who has superhuman strength and takes care of herself. Her friends, Tommy and Annika, are very ordinary children, however, and they are the touchstones to reality. In *Alice's Adventures in Wonderland,* the fantastic elements seem to have no limits, except, thankfully, that the nonsense can only happen in Wonderland. It would be very disturbing if the chaos of the secondary world began to overtake the primary world.

3. *Maintaining consistency* is essential in good fantasy. Rules are established for every secondary world. For example, there is only one way into the fantasy world, drinking from a certain fountain bestows immortality, the villain can be killed only by a special sword, ghosts can be seen only by certain people, and so on. The writer must abide by whatever rules he or she creates, and any violation of the rules is likely to seem unfair and spoil the fantasy experience for the reader.

4. Finally, good fantasy is *rooted in reality and in human nature*. Even if the characters are not human or not of this world, the good fantasist realizes that readers are human and that the fantasy characters must exhibit human traits—even if they are not human themselves. Mr. Toad of Toad Hall may look like a toad, but he acts like a human and has human weaknesses. Winnie-the-Pooh, toy though he is, is capable of human adventures and even human responses to those adventures (despite his protest that he is only a "bear of little brain"). Most fantasy, despite its wondrous dress, is imbued with a strong sense of reality and a deep seriousness. The imaginary world captures us; its underlying reality moves us.

Fantasy and the Imagination

Fantasy, like all literature, changes with the tastes of a culture. Victorian fantasy tended to be written for children of all ages and the Victorians–Lewis Carroll aside–preferred stories with pointed morals and usually with some magical element intruding on the real world. The early twentieth century was the heyday of escapist fantasy–animal fantasies, toy and doll fantasies, and magical stories for younger readers–all perhaps a reaction to the upheaval caused by two World Wars and a great worldwide economic depression. Beginning in about the 1950s came a shift toward fantasy for increasingly older children. (Animal fantasies remain popular in children's picture books, except that the stories themselves are often realistic and not magical–except that the animals talk.)

More and more fantasies today deal with horrifying menaces. The rational fantasy world–such as that created by C. S. Lewis–has given way to a world in which irrational evil presents a constant threat. Psychological thrillers–done so successfully by the adult fantasist, Stephen King–are now common among fantasies for children (R. L. Stine has written dozens of these types of fantasies). And the fantasy audience has grown older and many fantasies are now written for teenagers, who seem to demand more and more chilling tales. The works of J. K. Rowling (*Harry Potter and the Sorcerer's Stone* and its sequels) would seem to be an exception, for they are clearly intended for younger audiences (despite their great length). They are lighter reading fare and much more traditional in their approach, and it is this familiarity that undoubtedly makes them so popular.

This brief chapter can only skim the surface of the rich world of fantasy literature. Fantasy holds many treasures for us, not the least of which is the stimulation of our imaginations. Fantasy writer Joan Aiken, in an essay entitled "On Imagination," has summarized what she sees to be the practical value of a developed imagination. In addition to amusing us, Aiken points out, our imagination keeps us hopeful, enabling us to see the myriad possibilities that life offers. It helps us to solve problems by allowing us to see things from a variety of perspectives. It helps us to see the points of view of others and serves as a check to fanaticism.

Aiken goes further to suggest that the imagination is a bit like a muscle–if we do not exercise it, it becomes weak and ineffectual. Reading is the best way of exercising our imagination. Although Aiken does not suggest that reading fantasy is a better exercise of the imagination than reading realism or nonfiction, we can safely say that fantasy does make special demands of readers. Fantasy creates not only its own characters and plots, but also its own peculiar set of laws with which readers must become acquainted.

Through the medium of fantasy, writers are able to explore complex ideas on a symbolic level that would be difficult to convey to young readers otherwise. Natalie Babbitt's *Tuck Everlasting* can cause us to think of the implications of immortality on earth, its advantages and disadvantages, in a way that would be impossible for a realistic story and tedious in a nonfictional treatise. Fantasy is perfectly suited to the thoughtful exploration of philosophical issues at a level that can be understood and appreciated by the child reader. Fantasy

FIGURE 10.4   What Makes Good Fantasy?

1. The fantasy element is fresh and original.

2. The characters are engaging and believable; the protagonist possesses a clearly defined (and perhaps complex) personality and exhibits growth during the course of the story.

3. The fantasy or secondary world, if there is one, is vividly and convincingly described—regardless of how fantastical it may be.

4. The primary world, if it is included, is true to life.

5. The fantasy rules are clearly drawn and the author does not violate them.

6. The plot makes good use of the fantasy elements—they are not simply decoration.

7. The resolution makes sense within the realm of the fantasy world or the rules of the fantasy.

8. The writer makes us want to believe in the fantasy that is created.

9. The writer's theme grows naturally out of the action and characters—the writer does not preach at us.

deliberately challenges our perceptions of reality and forces us to explore new, uncharted realms of thought. These additional demands make fantasy a bit too difficult for readers who lack the patience and the necessary concentration to enter and embrace the fantasy world. It is, after all, easier to read about the familiar and the everyday. But the readers who accept the challenge find whole new worlds opened up for them and their lives enriched beyond measure.

The great psychologist, Carl Gustav Jung, wrote this of the importance of fantasy and its impact on the imagination and our lives:

> The dynamic principle of fantasy is play, which belongs also to the child, and as such it appears to be inconsistent with the principle of serious work. But without this playing with fantasy no creative work has ever yet come to birth. The debt we owe to the play of the imagination is incalculable. (82)

Works Cited

Aiken, Joan. "On Imagination." *The Horn Book* November/December, 1984: 735–741.

Jung, Carl Gustav, *Psychological Types*. New York: Harcourt, Brace, 1923.

O'Keefe, Deborah. *Readers in Wonderland: The Liberating Worlds of Fantasy Fiction*. New York: Continuum, 2003.

Roberts, Thomas J. "Science Fiction and the Adolescent." *Children's Literature: The Great Excluded* 2 (1973): 87–91.

Snyder, Zilpha Keatley. "Afterword." *Tom's Midnight Garden* by Philippa Pearce. New York: Dell, 1986: 230–232.

RECOMMENDED READINGS

Alexander, Lloyd. "High Fantasy and Heroic Romance." *Horn Book Magazine* 47:6 (Dec. 1971): 577–584.

Attebery, Brian. *The Fantasy Tradition in American Literature: From Irving to Le Guin*. Bloomington: Indiana University Press, 1980.

Babbitt, Natalie. "Fantasy and the Classic Hero." *School Library Journal* October 1987: 25–29.

Brennan, Geraldine, Kevin McCarron, and Kimberly Reynolds. *Frightening Fiction*. New York: Continuum, 2001.

Cameron, Eleanor. *The Green and Burning Tree*. Boston: Little, Brown, 1969.

Cooper, Susan. *Dreams and Wishes: Essays on Writing for Children*. New York: McElderry, 1996.

Dickinson, Peter. "Fantasy: The Need for Realism." *Children's Literature in Education* 17:1 (1986): 39–51.

Egoff, Sheila. *Worlds Within: Children's Fantasy from the Middle Ages to Today*. Chicago: American Library Association, 1988.

Engdahl, Sylvia. "The Changing Role of Science Fiction in Children's Literature." *Horn Book Magazine* 47:5 (Oct. 1971): 449–455.

Hume, Kathryn. *Fantasy and Mimesis*. New York and London: Methuen, 1984.

Kuznets, Lois. *When Toys Come Alive: Narratives of Animations, Metamorphosis and Development*. New Haven: Yale University Press, 1994.

Le Guin, Ursula. *The Language of the Night*. Ed. Susan Wood. New York: G. P. Putnam's Sons, 1979.

Lewis, C. S. "Three Ways of Writing for Children." *Horn Book Magazine* 39:5 (October 1963): 459–469.

Manlove, Colin. *From Alice to Harry Potter: Children's Fantasy in England*. Christchurch, New Zealand: Cybereditions, 2003.

Marcus, Leonard S. "Picture Book Animals: How Natural a History?" *The Lion and the Unicorn* 7/8 (1983/84): 127–139.

Raynor, Mary. "Some Thoughts on Animals in Children's Books" *Signal* 29 (May 1979): 81–87.

Sale, Roger. *Fairy Tales and After: From Snow White to E. B. White*. Cambridge, MA: Harvard University Press, 1978.

Singer, Jerome. "Fantasy: The Foundation of Serenity." *Psychology Today* July 1976: 33–37.

Smith, Karen Patricia. *The Fabulous Realm*. Lanham, MD: Scarecrow, 1993.

Sullivan, C. W. *Science Fiction for Young Readers*. New York: Greenwood, 1993.

Swinfen, Ann. *In Defence of Fantasy: A Study of the Genre in English and American Literature since 1945*. New York: Routledge, 1984.

Tolkien, J. R. R. *Tree and Leaf*. Boston: Houghton Mifflin, 1965.

Waggoner, Diana. *The Hills of Faraway: A Guide to Fantasy*. New York: Atheneum, 1978.

Westfahl, Gary. *Science Fiction, Children's Literature, and Popular Culture: Coming of Age in Fantasyland*. New York: Greenwood, 2000.

Wood, Michael. "Coffee Break for Sisyphus: The Point of Science Fiction." *New York Review of Books 2* (October 1975): 3–4, 6–7.

Wullschläger, Jackie. *Inventing Wonderland: The Lives and Fantasies of Lewis Carroll, Edward Lear, J. M. Barrie, Kenneth Grahame, and A. A. Milne*. New York: Free Press, 1996.

SELECTED BIBLIOGRAPHY OF FANTASY FICTION

ANIMAL FANTASIES

Books for Younger Readers (Grades K–4)

Bond, Michael. *A Bear Called Paddington*. Boston: Houghton Mifflin, 1960.

——. *Paddington at Large*. Boston: Houghton Mifflin, 1963.

Brooks, Walter R. *Freddy the Detective*. New York: Knopf, 1932.

——. *To and Again*. New York: Knopf, 1927. Reissued as *Freddy Goes to Florida*. 1949.

Cleary, Beverly. *Runaway Ralph*. New York: Morrow, 1970.

Ets, Marie Hall. *Mister Penny*. New York: Viking, 1935.

Hoban, Lillian. *Arthur's Birthday Party*. New York: HarperCollins, 1999.

Jarrell, Randall. *The Gingerbread Rabbit*. New York: Macmillan, 1964.

King-Smith, Dick. *Babe, the Gallant Pig*. New York: Random House, 1983.

——. *The Water Horse*. New York: Crown, 1998.

Kipling, Rudyard. *Just So Stories*. (1902) Illus. Barry Moser. New York: Morrow, 1996.

Lawson, Robert. *Ben and Me*. Boston: Little, Brown, 1939.

——. *Rabbit Hill*. New York: Viking, 1944.

——. *The Tough Winter*. New York: Viking, 1970.

Lobel, Arnold. *Frog and Toad Are Friends*. New York: Harper, 1970.

——. *Frog and Toad Together*. New York: Harper, 1972.

Lofting, Hugh. *The Story of Dr. Dolittle*. New York: Stokes, 1920.

——. *The Voyages of Dr. Dolittle*. New York: Stokes, 1922.

Marshall, James. *Rats on the Roof and Other Stories*. New York: Dial, 1991.

Proimos, James. *The Many Adventures of Johnny Mutton*. New York: Harcourt, 2001.

Reid Banks, Lynn. *The Magic Hare*. New York: Morrow, 1993.

Selden, George. *The Cricket in Times Square*. Illus. Garth Williams. New York: Farrar, Straus & Giroux, 1960.

Sharp, Margery. *Miss Bianca*. Boston: Little, Brown, 1962.

——. *The Rescuers*. Boston: Little, Brown, 1959.

Steig, William. *Abel's Island*. New York: Farrar, Straus & Giroux, 1976.

——. *Dominic*. New York: Farrar, Straus & Giroux, 1972.

Titus, Eve. *Basil in Mexico*. Illus. Paul Galdone. New York: McGraw-Hill, 1976.

White, E. B. *Charlotte's Web*. New York: Harper, 1952.

——. *Stuart Little*. New York: Harper, 1945.

——. *The Trumpet of the Swan*. New York: Harper, 1970.

Books for Older Readers (Grades 5 and Up)

Adams, Richard. *Watership Down*. New York: Macmillan, 1974.

Corbett, W. J. *The Song of Pentacost*. New York: Dutton, 1983.

Delaney, Michael. *Birdbrain Amos*. New York: Philomel, 2002.

Grahame, Kenneth. *The Wind in the Willows*. (1908) Several modern editions.

Jacques, Brian. *Marell of Redwall*. New York: Philomel, 1992.

——. *Mattimeo*. New York: Philomel, 1990.

——. *Mossflower*. New York: Philomel, 1988.

——. *Redwall*. New York: Philomel, 1987.

Jarrell, Randall. *The Animal Family*. Illus. Maurice Sendak. New York: Pantheon, 1965.

——. *The Bat-Poet*. New York: Macmillan, 1964.

Jennings, Richard. *Orwell's Luck*. Boston: Houghton Mifflin, 2000.

Lisle, Janet Taylor. *Forest*. New York: Jackson, 1993.

O'Brien, Robert. *Mrs. Frisby and the Rats of NIMH*. New York: Atheneum, 1971.

Salton, Felix. *Bambi*. New York: Simon & Schuster, 1929.

TOY FANTASIES

Books for Younger Readers (Grades K–4)

Bailey, Caroline Sherwin. *Miss Hickory*. New York: Viking, 1968.

Field, Rachel. *Hitty, Her First Hundred Years*. New York: Macmillan, 1929.

Godden, Rumer. *The Doll's House*. New York: Viking, 1962.

——. *Impunity Jane*. New York: Viking, 1964.

Lionni, Leo. *Alexander and the Wind-Up Mouse*. New York: Pantheon, 1969.

Milne, A. A. *The House at Pooh Corner*. (1928) Illus. Ernest Shepard. New York: Dutton, 1961.

——. *Winnie-the-Pooh*. (1926) Illus. Ernest Shepard. New York: Dutton, 1961.

Williams, Margery. *The Velveteen Rabbit*. (1922) Illus. Michael Hague. New York: Holt, Rinehart & Winston, 1983.

Books for Older Readers (Grades 5 and Up)

Clarke, Pauline. *The Return of the Twelves*. New York: Coward-McCann, 1964. (British title: *The Twelve and the Genii*)

Collodi, Carlo (pseudonym for Carlo Lorenzini). *The Adventures of Pinocchio*. (1883) Several modern editions.

Gardam, Jane. *Through the Doll's House Door*. New York: Greenwillow, 1987.

Griffith, Helen V. *Caitlin's Holiday*. New York: Greenwillow, 1990.

Hoban, Russell. *The Mouse and His Child*. New York: Harper, 1967.

Kennedy, Richard. *Amy's Eyes*. New York: Harper, 1985.

Reid Banks, Lynn. *The Indian in the Cupboard*. New York: Doubleday, 1981.

——. *The Secret of the Indian*. New York: Doubleday, 1989.

Winthrop, Elizabeth. *The Castle in the Attic*. New York: Holiday, 1985.

MAGICAL FANTASY AND TALL TALES

Books for Younger Readers (Grades K–4)

Allard, Harry. *The Stupids Die*. Illus. James Marshall. Boston: Houghton Mifflin, 1981.

——. *The Stupids Step Out*. Illus. James Marshall. Boston: Houghton Mifflin, 1974.

Atwater, Richard, and Florence Atwater. *Mr. Popper's Penguins*. Illus. Robert Lawson. Boston: Little, Brown, 1938.

Dahl, Roald. *Charlie and the Chocolate Factory*. New York: Knopf, 1964.

——. *James and the Giant Peach*. New York: Knopf, 1961.

——. *Matilda*. New York: Viking, 1988.

Fleishman, Sid. *McBroom Tells a Lie*. Boston: Little, Brown, 1976.

Kastner, Erich. *The Little Man*. Trans. James Kirkup. Illus. Rick Schreiter. New York: Knopf, 1966.

Lindgren, Astrid. *Pippi Longstocking*. New York: Viking, 1950.

Norton, Mary. *The Borrowers*. New York: Harcourt, 1953.

——. *The Borrowers Afield*. New York: Harcourt, 1955.

Parish, Peggy. *Amelia Bedelia*. New York: Harper, 1963.

Thomas, Shelley Moore. *Get Well, Good Knight*. Illus. Jennifer Plecar. New York: Dutton, 2002.

Travers, P. L. *Mary Poppins*. New York: Harcourt, 1934.

Books for Older Readers (Grades 5 and Up)

DuBois, William Pene. *Twenty-One Balloons*. New York: Viking, 1947.

Du Prau, Jeanne. *The City of Ember*. New York: Random, 2003.

Fleischman, Sid. *Chancy and the Grand Rascal*. Boston: Little, Brown, 1966.

——. *The Ghost in the Noonday Sun*. Boston: Little, Brown, 1965.

——. *Humbug Mountain*. Boston: Little, Brown, 1978.

Garner, Alan. *The Owl Service*. New York: Walck, 1968.

Hale, Lucretia P. *The Peterkin Papers*. 1886. New York: Dover, 1963.

Kipling, Rudyard. *Puck of Pook's Hill*. (1906) Various modern editions.

McCaughrean, Geraldine. *A Pack of Lies*. New York: Scholastic, 1988.

Merrill, Jean. *The Pushcart War*. Reading, MA: Scott/Addison, 1964.

Nesbit, E. *The Enchanted Castle*. (1907). Several modern editions.

——. *Five Children and It*. (1902). Several modern editions.

——. *The Phoenix and the Carpet*. (1904) Several modern editions.

——. *The Story of the Amulet*. (1906) Several modern editions.

Norton, Mary. *The Magic Bedknob*. (1945) New York: Odyssey, 2000. (With *Bonfires and Broomsticks*.)

Pierce, Tamora. *Shatterglass*. New York: Scholastic, 2003.

Pratchett, Terry. *The Wee Free Man*. New York: HarperCollins, 2003.

Rodgers, Mary. *Freaky Friday*. New York: Harper, 1972.

——. *Summer Switch*. New York: Harper, 1982.

Wyke-Smith, E. A. *The Marvelous Land of Snergs*. 1928. Baltimore: Old Earth, 1996.

Yolen, Jane. *Sword of the Rightful King: A Novel of King Arthur*. New York: Harcourt, 2003.

ENCHANTED JOURNEYS AND ALTERNATIVE WORLDS

Books for Younger Readers (Grades K–4)

Babbitt, Natalie. *Kneeknock Rise*. New York: Farrar, Straus & Giroux, 1970.

——. *The Search for Delicious*. New York: Farrar, Straus & Giroux, 1969.

Barrie, Sir James. *Peter Pan*. New York: Scribner's, 1950.

Baum, L. Frank. *The Wonderful Wizard of Oz*. (1900) Several modern editions.

Carroll, Lewis. *Alice's Adventures in Wonderland*. Illus. John Tenniel. (1865) Several modern editions.

Fleischman, Sid. *The Midnight Horse*. New York: Morrow, 1990.

——. *The Whipping Boy*. New York: Morrow, 1986.

Books for Older Readers (Grades 5 and Up)

Aiken, Joan. *Black Hearts in Battersea*. New York: Doubleday, 1964.

——. *The Wolves of Willoughby Chase*. New York: Doubleday, 1963.

Cresswell, Helen. *The Night-Watchmen*. London: Puffin, 1988.

——. *The Outlanders*. London: Faber, 1978.

Dickinson, Peter. *The Blue Hawk*. New York: Ballantine, 1977.

Farjeon, Eleanor. *Martin Pippin in the Apple Orchard*. (1921)

Farmer, Penelope. *The Summer Birds*. New York: Harcourt, 1962.

Goudge, Elizabeth. *The Little White Horse*. (1946) New York: Dell, 1992.

Janssen, Tove. *Comet in Moominland*. Trans. Elizabeth Portch. (1961) New York: Farrar, Straus & Giroux, 1990.

——. *Finn Family Moomintroll*. (1948) Trans. Elizabeth Portch. New York: Farrar, Straus & Giroux, 1989.

——. *Moominsummer Madness*. Trans. Thomas Warburton. (1964) New York: Farrar, Straus & Giroux, 1991.

Juster, Norton. *The Phantom Tollbooth*. New York: Random, 1961.

Kendall, Carol. *The Gammage Cup*. New York: Harcourt, 1959.

Lagerlof, Selma. *The Wonderful Adventures of Nils*. (1906) Several modern editions.

Lively, Penelope. *The House in Nordam Gardens*. New York: Dutton, 1974.

——. *A Stitch in Time*. London: Heinemann, 1976.

Lowry, Lois. *Gathering Blue*. New York: Houghton Mifflin, 2000.

——. *The Giver*. Boston: Houghton Mifflin, 1993.

McKinley, Robin. *A Knot in the Grain and Other Stories*. New York: Greenwillow, 1994.

Pope, Elizabeth Marie. *The Perilous Gard*. New York: Puffin, 1962.

Rowling, J. K. *Harry Potter and the Chamber of Secrets*. London: Bloomsbury, 1998.

——. *Harry Potter and the Order of the Phoenix*. London: Bloomsbury, 2003.

——. *Harry Potter and the Prisoner of Azkaban*. London: Bloomsbury, 1999.

——. *Harry Potter and the Sorcerer's Stone*. London: Bloomsbury, 1997.

Snyder, Zilpha Keatley. *Song of the Gargoyle*. New York: Delacorte, 1991.

Steele, Mary Q. *Journey Outside*. New York: Viking, 1969.

Townsend, John Rowe. *The Fortunate Isles*. New York: Lippincott, 1989.

Wein, Elizabeth E. *The Winter Prince*. New York: Atheneum, 1993.

HEROIC FANTASIES

Books for Older Readers (Grades 5 and Up)

Alexander, Lloyd. *Prydain* chronicles, (New York: Holt): *The Book of Three* (1964); *The Black Cauldron* (1965); *The Castle of Llyr* (1965); *Taran Wanderer* (1967); *The High King* (1968).

Cooper, Susan. *"The Dark Is Rising"* series, (New York: Atheneum): *Over Sea, Under Stone* (1966); *The Dark Is Rising* (1973); *Greenwitch* (1974); *The Grey King* (1975); *The Silver on the Tree* (1977).

Doyle, Debra, and James D. Macdonald. *Knight's Wyrd*. New York: Harcourt, 1992.

Garner, Alan. *The Moon of Gomrath*. London: Puffin, 1965.

——. *The Weirdstone of Brisingamen*. London: Puffin, 1963.

Le Guin, Ursula. *Earthsea* cycle, (New York: Atheneum): *A Wizard of Earthsea* (1968); *The Tombs of Atuan* (1971); *The Farthest Shore* (1972); *Tehanu: The Last Book of Earthsea* (1990).

Lewis, C. S. The *Narnia* chronicles (New York: Macmillan): *The Lion, the Witch and the Wardrobe* (1950); *Prince Caspian, The Return to Narnia* (1951); *The Voyage of the "Dawn Treader"* (1952); *The Silver Chair* (1953); *The Horse and His Boy* (1954); *The Magician's Nephew* (1954); *The Last Battle* (1956).

McCaffrey, Anne. *Dragondrums*. New York: Atheneum, 1979.

——. *Dragonsinger*. New York: Atheneum, 1977.

——. *Dragonsong*. New York: Atheneum, 1976.

McKinley, Robin. *The Blue Sword*. New York: Greenwillow, 1982.

——. *The Hero and the Crown*. New York: Greenwillow, 1985.

Mayne, William. *Antar and the Eagles*. New York: Delacorte, 1990.

Nix, Garth. *Sabriel*. New York: HarperCollins, 1996.

Pullman, Philip. *The Golden Compass*. New York: Knopf, 1996. (Published in UK as *Northern Lights*, 1995)

Tolkien, J. R. R. *The Hobbit*. Boston: Houghton Mifflin, 1938. (Followed by the *Lord of the Rings* trilogy)

Yolen, Jane. *Dragon's Blood*. New York: Delacorte, 1982.

SUPERNATURAL AND TIME-SHIFT FANTASIES

Books for Younger Readers (Grades K–4)

Aiken, Joan. *A Foot in the Grave*. New York: Viking, 1992.

Babbitt, Natalie. *Tuck Everlasting*. New York: Farrar, Straus & Giroux, 1975.

Norton, Mary. *Bed-Knob and Broomstick*. Illus. Erik Blegvad. New York: Harcourt, 1957.

Yolen, Jane, and Martin H. Greenberg, eds. *Things That Go Bump in the Night: A Collection of Original Stories*. New York: Harper, 1989.

Books for Older Readers (Grades 5 and Up)

Boston, Lucy. *The Children of Greene Knowe*. New York: Harcourt, 1964.

Cameron, Eleanor. *The Court of the Stone Children*. New York: Dutton, 1973.

Cobalt, Martin (pseudonym for William Mayne). *Pool of Swallows*. New York: Nelson, 1974.

Dunlop, Eileen. *Elizabeth, Elizabeth*. New York: Holt, 1977.

——. *The Valley of Deer*. New York: Holiday, 1989.

Farmer, Penelope. *A Castle of Bone*. New York: Philomel, 1982.

——. *Charlotte Sometimes*. New York: Harcourt, 1969.

Garfield, Leon. *Mister Corbett's Ghost*. New York: Pantheon, 1968.

——. *The Restless Ghost: Three Stories*. New York: Pantheon, 1969.

Griffin, Peni R. *The Ghost Sitter*. New York: Dutton, 2001.

Hamilton, Virginia. *Sweet Whispers, Brother Rush*. New York: Philomel, 1982.

Hunter, Mollie. *The Haunted Mountain*. New York: Harper, 1972.

Ibbotson, Eva. *Dial-a-Ghost*. Illus. Kevin Hawkes. New York: Dutton, 2001.

Jones, Diana Wynne. *Cart and Cwidder*. London: Macmillan, 1975.

——. *Drowned Ammet*. New York: Beech Tree, 1995.

——. *The Spellcoats*. New York: Beech Tree, 1995.

Lindbergh, Anne. *Nick of Time*. Boston: Little, Brown, 1994.

Lively, Penelope. *The Ghost of Thomas Kempe*. Illus. Antony Maitland. New York: Dutton, 1973.

Lunn, Janet. *The Root Cellar*. New York: Scribner's, 1983.

Mayne, William. *Earthfasts*. New York: Dutton, 1967.

——. *A Game of Dark*. New York: Dutton, 1971.

——. *Over the Hills and Far Away*. (1968) London: Hodder, 1997.

Morgan, Helen. *The Witch Doll*. New York: Viking, 1992.

Pearce, Philippa. *Tom's Midnight Garden*. New York: Dell, 1986.

Pearson, Kit. *A Handful of Time*. New York: Viking, 1988.

Price, Susan. *Ghost Song*. New York: Farrar, Straus & Giroux, 1992.

Prince, Maggie. *The House on Hound Hill*. Boston: Houghton Mifflin, 1998.

Pullman, Philip. *Clockwork*. New York: Scholastic, 1998.

Schmidt, Annie M. G. *Minnie*. New York: Milkweed, 1994.

Vande Velde, Vivian. *Ghost of a Hanged Man*. New York: Cavendish, 1998.

Walsh, Jill Paton. *A Chance Child*. New York: Farrar, Straus & Giroux, 1978.

Waugh, Sylvia. *The Mennyms*. New York: Random House, 1994.

Westall, Robert. *The Devil on the Road*. New York: Greenwillow, 1979.

———. *Gulf*. New York: Scholastic, 1992.

———. *The Scarecrows*. London: Puffin, 1983.

Woodruff, Elvira. *The Magnificent Mummy Maker*. New York: Scholastic, 1994.

Yee, Paul. *Dead Man's Gold and Other Stories*. Toronto: Groundwood, 2002.

SCIENCE FICTION AND SPACE FANTASY

Books for Younger Readers (Grades K–4)

Cameron, Eleanor. *Wonderful Flight to the Mushroom Planet*. Illus. Robert Henneberger. Boston: Little, Brown, 1954.

Del Rey, Lester. *The Runaway Robot*. Philadelphia: Westminster, 1965.

Todd, Ruthven. *Space Cat*. Illus. Paul Galdone. New York: Scribner's, 1952.

Books for Older Readers (Grades 5 and Up)

Christopher, John. *Beyond the Burning Lands*. New York: Macmillan, 1971.

———. *When the Tripods Came*. New York: Dutton, 1988.

———. *The White Mountains*. New York: Macmillan, 1967.

Clarke, Arthur C. *Dolphin Island*. New York: Holt, 1963.

Conley, Jane Leslie. *The Rudest Alien on Earth*. New York: Holt, 2002.

Cresswell, Helen. *The Watchers: A Mystery of Alton Towers*. New York: Macmillan, 1994.

Dickinson, Peter. *Eva*. New York: Delacorte, 1989.

Engdahl, Sylvia. *Enchantress from the Stars*. New York: Macmillan, 1970.

———. *The Far Side of Evil*. New York: Macmillan, 1971.

Hamilton, Virginia. *Justice and Her Brothers*. New York: Greenwillow, 1978.

Hautman, Pete. *Hole in the Sky*. New York: Simon & Schuster, 2001.

Heinlein, Robert. *Have Space Suit—Will Travel*. New York: Scribner's, 1958.

Lawrence, Louise. *Moonwind*. New York: Harper, 1986.

L'Engle, Madeleine. *A Wrinkle in Time*. New York: Farrar, Straus & Giroux, 1962.

———. *A Ring of Endless Light*. New York: Farrar, Straus, & Giroux, 1980.

———. *A Swiftly Tilting Planet*. New York: Farrar, Straus, & Giroux, 1978.

Norton, Andre. *Moon of Three Rings*. New York: Viking, 1966.

Oppel, Kenneth. *Dead Water Zone*. New York: Joy Street, 1993.

Rubenstein, Gillian. *Beyond the Labyrinth*. New York: Watts, 1990.

Sleator, William. *Strange Attractors*. New York: Dutton, 1989.

Verne, Jules. *Twenty Thousand Leagues Under the Sea*. (1864) New York: Penguin, 1987.

Waugh, Sylvia. *Earthborn*. New York: Delacorte, 2002.

Wells, H. G. *The Time Machine* (1895). New York: Bantam, 1982.

———. *War of the Worlds* (1898). New York: Putnam, 1978.

CHAPTER

II

Realistic Fiction:
Contemporary and Historical

DEFINITION OF REALISTIC FICTION

Realistic fiction attempts to portray the world as it is. Realistic fiction contains no fantasy, no supernatural elements, and it usually depicts ordinary people going about the business of daily living, with all its joys, sorrows, successes, and failures. Some writers present a world that seems happier than the one we live in—we call this romance. Other writers portray a darker, harsher world; one that is, sadly, more true to life. Over the past 150 years, children's literature has gradually moved from a romantic view of the world toward a more realistic view. Subjects that were once taboo in realistic fiction are now commonplace, and language and character development are presented with greater candor and boldness.

This chapter discusses both contemporary realism—stories set in the present day—and historical realism—stories set in the past. Naturally, in time, all stories become stories set in the past (a book written in the 1950s about the 1950s is now set in the past). However, when an author sets out to write a book about the past rather than his or her own present, some very different considerations come into play—Louisa May Alcott's *Little Women,* set in the 1860s or L. M. Montgomery's *Anne of Green Gables,* set in the early 1900s, both of which were written as contemporary fiction, would be different stories if written today as historical fiction, which will be discussed in the second half of this chapter.

CHARACTERISTICS OF REALISTIC FICTION

The Coming-of-Age Theme

Many realistic stories depict their protagonist growing up or coming of age (this characteristic is not restricted to realistic fiction, for many heroic or quest fantasies do the same thing). The Germans coined the term *bildungsroman* for a book that describes the trials and tribulations of a young person coming into maturity. These coming-of-age stories typically trace the protagonist's growth from a self-absorbed, immature individual into an expansive, mature human being concerned with the welfare of others, and his or her place in the world scheme. In children's stories, the protagonist usually reaches a higher level of maturity and a greater sense of self-awareness by the book's end, but has not achieved adulthood.

A classic example of the coming-of-age story is Frances Hodgson Burnett's *The Secret Garden,* which first appeared in 1909. The heroine, Mary Lennox, is initially a rather unpleasant child, having been raised by wealthy parents in India where she was waited on hand and foot. She is self-centered, arrogant, and disagreeable. Then she is suddenly orphaned and sent to live with a wealthy, but mysterious, uncle in England. Her uncle's household is grim and depressing and filled with miserable people. But Mary, partly through her own forceful personality and partly through the influence of characters she meets, transforms the gloomy house into a place of warmth and happiness. Mary's own growth as a human being who becomes more concerned with those around her than with herself is mirrored by the growth of the secret garden she carefully nurtures.

In good fiction–and this is often true for fantasy as well as realism–we find main characters who grow in self-awareness, who are wiser people at the end than they were at the beginning of the story. And usually this wisdom, this self-awareness, comes with struggling, pain, even suffering–there is no free lunch in life or literature.

Humor in Realistic Fiction

Of course, we find humor in all types of children's stories and many fantasies contain humor. However, in fantasies the humor is often the humor of the absurd. In realistic fiction, humor is frequently used to break the tension in sensitive situations. Judy Blume's *Are You There, God? It's Me, Margaret* is the story of a middle-school girl awaiting her first menstrual cycle and confronting serious religious doubts–two very weighty subjects for a children's book. But by introducing the issues with humor–in language, character development, and situation–Blume is able to reassure the reader that Margaret's emotional traumas are, indeed, quite normal and quite manageable. Jerry Spinelli effectively uses humor in *Maniac Magee* to explore the serious issue of racism in a divided community.

Laughter can be redemptive, and our ability to laugh may be largely responsible for our survival in today's complex society. Humor is extremely versatile. It may be reactionary, as when it attacks the outsider in an ethnic joke, or it may be revolutionary, as when it ridicules the status quo in a political joke. In either case, humor is a form of self-preservation, of coping. Humor can be cruel (again, the ethnic joke), but it can also be liberating and therapeutic (see also pages 45–46). In realistic fiction, humor usually takes one of three forms:

1. *The humor of character.* This depends on the antics of an eccentric personality (a clown or buffoon, a nonconformist, a curmudgeon, a neurotic, and so on). Betsy Byars's eccentric, quirky, and accident-prone Blossom family in *The Not-Just-Anybody Family* and its sequels are good examples.

2. *The humor of situation.* Surprising, awkward, or ridiculous actions or situations are among the most common sources of children's humor. In Robert McCloskey's *Homer Price*, a doughnut machine goes wild and cannot stop making doughnuts. Young children delight in this sort of wild exaggeration.

3. *The humor of language.* Plays on words, verbal irony, malapropisms (the misuse of words), misunderstandings, all contribute to verbal humor. In Beverly Cleary's *Ramona the Pest*, young Ramona misunderstands the words to the national anthem–"dawnzer lee light"–which leads to the conclusion that a "dawnzer" is "another word for a lamp."

New Realism

Beginning in the 1960s, a movement called New Realism emerged that reacted against the romantic and sentimental children's books that had dominated the market for so long. The New Realism sought to bring more honest emotions, franker language, and bolder ideas to literature for children. It opened an entirely new range of subjects, and little remained that was taboo. Stories began appearing on a wide variety of issues formerly avoided in children's literature: racial prejudice (works by Mildred Taylor and Virginia Hamilton), teenage gangs (S. E. Hinton's *The Outsiders* and Walter Dean Myers's *Scorpions*), drug abuse (Alice Childress's *A Hero Ain't Nothin' But a Sandwich*), homosexuality (M. E. Kerr's *"Hello," I Lied*), child abuse (Mirjam Pressler's *Halinka*), mental illness (Zibby Oneal's *The Language of Goldfish*), sexual abuse (Cynthia Voigt's *When She Hollers*), and many others.

An inevitable result of New Realism was a phenomenon known as the *problem novel*, which focuses on a singular, "hot" issue that affects the protagonist. The problem novel is always set in contemporary times and aims at a naturalistic portrayal of a problem plaguing young teens–ranging from sexuality to drug abuse to parental problems to psychological disorders–the list is endless. Problem novels are directed to older readers and focus on the individual's emotional response to life's experience. Judy Blume's name has long been associated with the problem novel. Her *Forever* was one of the first books for young readers to deal frankly with sex (which also got it banned), and her *Blubber* describes the cruelty inflicted by children on an overweight girl.

Too often problem novels contain predictable plots, shallow characters, and trite dialogue. Sometimes they are sensationalized and devolve into melodrama–they are the soap operas of young adult literature. At times they imply that teenage problems have simplistic solutions. Of course, their predictability and easy answers make them very popular with young readers, as evidenced by the success of the Sweet Valley High series and the Baby-sitters Club series. But at their best, problem novels explore significant psychological and sociological issues with sensitivity, and they give us vivid, complex characters. Judy Blume's *Tiger Eyes,* for young adult readers, is a good example.

Problem novels have also been used as part of *bibliotherapy,* a process by which young people cope with personal problems through directed reading. However, some critics have held that problem novels themselves often encourage a self-indulgence that only makes matters worse (see, especially, Nodelman, 1981). Teenagers, according to this theory, read only about other teenagers just like themselves who suffer the same traumas as they do, and this results in an inflated view of their problems. In other words, rather than giving them a fresh outlook on the problems, the books encourage them to wallow in self-pity that narrows instead of widens their world. But teenagers often have an inflated view of their own tribulations—the books they read do not create that dilemma. Perhaps a truly effective bibliotherapy is that which expands the reader's experiences, broadens the reader's mind, and thus multiplies the reader's possible responses to problems. (See Figure 11.2 for guidelines to realistic fiction.)

Types of Contemporary Realism

FAMILY STORIES Family stories—also called domestic stories—have been around since Victorian days when they were the mainstay of a girl's reading. Most childhood experiences involve home and family, so it is not surprising that young readers are drawn to these familiar subjects. Family stories frequently rely on episodic plots, since they are built around the daily details and activities, the squabblings, the schemings, the reconciliations, in which families are normally engaged.

The early family stories were unabashedly sentimental; however, Louisa May Alcott's *Little Women* (1867), one of the earliest family stories, presents us with a realistic portrayal of mid-nineteenth-century American family life with all its ups and downs (see Figure 11.1). But Alcott's successors, such as Margaret Sidney, author of the once enormously popular *The Five Little Peppers and How They Grew,* plumbed the depths of Victorian sentimentalism. The Pepper family is destitute but virtuous, the self-sacrificing and dutiful children always ready to do more than their fair share for the family's well-being, and their widowed mother draws strength from their unfailing togetherness. The sentimental story portrays life as the author wishes it were, not necessarily how it is.

In early family stories, the family was a haven from the troubles of the world, whereas modern family stories often portray the family as the source of trouble. Today's family is characterized by working parents, single parents, neglectful parents, ungrateful children, sibling rivalry, and a general breakdown in communications. Writers of family stories now prefer to face these issues head-on. Beverly Cleary's *Dear Mr. Henshaw,* written as a series of letters and journal entries, shows us a young boy coping with his parents' divorce. Katherine

FIGURE 11.1 J. S. Eland's sentimental illustration for an early edition of Louisa May Alcott's popular domestic story, *Little Women*, depicts Amy playing dress up, a typical pastime for middle-class, nineteenth-century girls.

Source: From George Routledge and Sons, London, n.d.

Paterson's *The Great Gilly Hopkins* is a realistic portrayal of a troubled child placed in a foster home. Cynthia Voigt's *Homecoming* and its sequels trace the difficulties faced by four siblings, abandoned by their emotionally unstable mother, making their way across several states in search of their grandmother whom they have never met. The message of the modern family story remains positive, but it does suggest that the definition of "family" extends beyond those individuals related by blood, and that happy families are the result of a great deal of effort on everyone's behalf.

STORIES OF SOCIAL REALISM Recent studies about human growth and development suggest that our peers are among our greatest influences—in some ways, our friends are even more influential than our families. After all, few children want to grow up to be like their parents—they want to grow up to be like their friends. So we might expect that many realistic novels for young people deal with friendships. And, of course, our friendships lead us into the larger society. Mark Twain's *The Adventures of Huckleberry Finn*—to be sure, not exactly a children's book, but a good example just the same—helped to set the standard for books about young people struggling with unlikely friendships (Huck makes friends with the runaway slave, Jim) and dealing with a troubled society (Huck meets social misfits, criminals, neurotics, phonies, and every other human type imaginable).

Perhaps the most salient feature of growing up is the movement away from a preoccupation with self toward a concern for others. The result of this progression is inevitably the discovery of one's own identity. Modern realistic fiction pursues this theme by presenting to young readers a multi-faceted view of society. Books like Sharon Creech's *Granny Torrelli Makes Soup* (about friendship with a blind boy), Lois Lowry's *A Summer to Die* (about the death of a sibling), and Richard Peck's *Remembering the Good Times* (about a friend's suicide) all portry young people coming to terms with complex personal issues.

Modern authors are not afraid to broach the most delicate social issues. Jerry Spinelli's *Maniac Magee* is a charming and amusing story about the healing of a racially divided city. And the works of Walter Dean Myers depict the triumphs and struggles of African American children in the inner city. Even more serious are the books of Robert Cormier (such as *The Chocolate War* and *I Am the Cheese*) which reveal the seamier side of human nature and often have unhappy endings, depicting society as hopelessly corrupt and people as selfish and unprincipled. Cormier's works have been criticized by adults as being too dark, but many young readers are drawn to them, indicating that young people are far more aware of their surroundings than adults sometimes imagine. Recent subjects for novels of social inquiry are child abuse (as in Cynthia Voigt's *When She Hollers*) and homosexuality (as in Jean Ferris's *Eight Seconds* or Alex Sanchez's *Rainbow Boys*) and sexual abuse (as in Laurie Halse Anderson's *Speak*).

The common ground of all these books is that their authors believe it is far better for young readers to learn about the harsh subjects of life from a capable and sensitive writer than from ill-informed friends or a bad experience.

ADVENTURE AND SURVIVAL STORIES Adventure stories, which tend to be romantic in the broad sense of the word, have long been popular with children. Robert Louis Stevenson's *Treasure Island* (1883), the classic swashbuckling pirate tale, is an early example of the adventure story, with its exotic setting, its mysterious characters, and its action-packed plot. Although most early adventure stories were written expressly for boys, today writers generally recognize that males hold no monopoly on the love of excitement. Many adventure stories are, in fact, *survival stories,* which depict an individual or individuals pitted against the forces of nature or, in many modern works, the forces of a cruel, insensitive society, which the protagonist must either outwit or (more likely) cooperate with in order to survive. As with many children's books, survival stories are invariably coming-of-age stories. Daniel Defoe's *Robinson Crusoe* (1719) is often regarded as the granddaddy of the survival story, and the Swiss writer Johann David Wyss modeled his *The Swiss Family Robinson* (1812) on Defoe's work, as did R. M. Ballantyne in his popular *The Coral Island* (1857). These authors have their heroes taming the wild tropical paradise in which they find themselves and carving out lives of considerable comfort; however, modern versions of the survival story depict their heroes or heroines humbled before the forces of nature. Rather than taming the wild and forcing the environment to conform to human whims, modern-day heroes of survival stories adapt their lifestyles to their surroundings. Scott O'Dell's *Island of the Blue Dolphins,* a work of historical fiction, was one of the first modern survival stories to adopt this new and far more realistic approach to survival narratives. Whereas Defoe, Wyss, and Ballantyne wrote stories that are fanciful at best, O'Dell sought realism (his story is, in fact, based on a historical incident). O'Dell wished to convey the message that in real life survival means sacrifice, suffering, adaptation, and often loneliness. Jean Craighead George (*Julie of the Wolves* and *My Side of the Mountain*) and Harry Mazer (*Snowbound* and *The Island Keeper*) are writers of survival stories who have followed O'Dell's example, portraying heroes and heroines who learn to live in harmony with the natural world and who often come to respect nature above the civilizing forces of humanity.

Felice Holman's *Slake's Limbo* portrays the hero surviving not in some isolated wilderness, but in the grim world of the New York City subway system. In a time when technology and impersonal bureaucracy threaten our identity and, it seems, even the nature of society and civilization as we know it, we may well feel that growing up in a city slum is as much a challenge as being abandoned on a desert island or in the frozen Arctic reaches. One key element in any survival story is its detailing of the means of survival—the protagonist's locating food, providing shelter from the elements, and securing protection from threatening forces. Sharon Creech's *The Wanderer,* the story of a family on a small boat in the Atlantic, brilliantly depicts the triumph of the human spirit against overwhelming odds. The survival story, however, at its heart is the story of individuals rising above adversity, facing forces that are greater and more formidable than they are, and discovering themselves.

MYSTERY OR DETECTIVE STORIES The mystery or detective story is a form of romance, escapist fiction creating a world somehow more exciting, more dangerous, and more beautiful than we imagine our own to be. The *mystery,* first popularized in the early nineteenth century by Edgar Allan Poe and later refined by Arthur Conan Doyle, the creator of Sherlock Holmes, has long been a favorite of young readers. Such serial detectives as Nancy Drew, the Hardy Boys, the Bobbsey Twins, and Donald Sobol's Encyclopedia Brown are enormously popular. The mystery always involves the solving of a puzzle—usually a crime. The success of a mystery depends on the clever planting of clues and the ingenuity of the puzzle and its solution. The puzzle must not be too easily solved or the reader will lose interest. And the solution to the mystery must seem logical once all the pieces are put together or the reader will feel deceived. The mystery writer must keep a delicate balance, knowing just how much to reveal and when.

Among the fine mysteries for young readers is E. L. Konigsburg's *From the Mixed-Up Files of Mrs. Basil E. Frankweiler,* which recounts the exploits of young brother and sister detectives as they follow clues to the unraveling of a mystery, largely set in the Metropolitan Museum of Art. Ellen Raskin's *The Westing Game* likewise depicts a young detective searching out the word clues of a cleverly devised puzzle, containing numerous surprising twists. Virginia Hamilton's *The House of Dies Drear* may be regarded as a mystery of sorts, weaving suspense into a tale of the discovery of African-American heritage. Hamilton has the uncanny ability to take seemingly ordinary people and places and weave an almost magical story. Her characters are so richly developed that we come to believe in even the most bizarre of them.

ANIMAL STORIES—REAL OR ROMANTIC It is nearly impossible to have a completely realistic animal story, since, to retain the reader's interest, the fictional story must hinge on the premise that the animal characters share certain human traits—the capacity for love, loyalty, jealousy, fear, and so on. Fortunately, for readers drawn to animal stories, such a leap of faith is not difficult.

Realistic animal stories first appeared in the late nineteenth and early twentieth centuries, and they were most popular in North America. The Canadians Ernest Thompson Seton (*Wild Animals I Have Known*) and Charles G. D. Roberts (*Red Fox*), wrote stories depicting animals realistically, but giving them personalities. Jack London's popular *White Fang* and *Call of the Wild* soon followed. The animals in these stories live as animals, behave as animals, and do not talk (although some readers may argue they are given human emotions). A modern example of this type is Sheila Burnford's *The Incredible Journey,* in which a cat and two dogs undertake a hazardous trip across the Canadian wilderness. Some readers feel that Burnford oversteps the limits of credulity, with the animals assuming too much of human nature to be totally believable animals. This criticism brings us back to our first point about animal stories—the difficulty of writing a full-length novel about an animal and not imbuing the animal characters with human traits. But for many readers, making the animal characters too human is a minor technical flaw that detracts very little from the story's appeal.

Young readers have always had soft spots for animals of all kinds, and animal stories have proved to be among the most enduring of modern children's literature and are the frequent inspirations for the cinema. Stories often portray the relationship between an animal and a youthful human companion, such as in Marjorie Kinnan Rawlings' *The Yearling* (about a fawn), Mary O'Hara's *My Friend Flicka* (about a horse), and Eric Knight's *Lassie Come Home,* the popular story of a heroic collie. One of the most loved of all is Wilson Rawls' *Where the Red Fern Grows,* about two hunting dogs and their boy master. Unfortunately, animal stories have the reputation for being tearjerkers and, as such, lack appeal for older readers who like to think of themselves as beyond such sentimentality. However, one serious theme recurring in many animal stories—is that of animals falling prey to the savage insensitivity of human beings, as in Phyllis Reynolds Naylor's Newbery-Award-winning *Shiloh.*

SPORTS STORIES Very popular among an important group of readers is the sports story, which actually has its origin in the boys' magazines of the nineteenth century. As full-blown books, however, they are a twentieth-century phenomenon.

One of the most popular of the early sports writers was Clair Bee—himself a noted athlete, he lettered in three high-school sports and went on to become a celebrated basketball coach and an inductee into the Basketball Hall of Fame. Bee's books, beginning with *Touchdown Pass* in 1948, are all about a high-school athlete, Chip Hilton (who also letters in three sports). The stories promote high moral character and good sportsmanship. The series is still being reprinted today, although the books have been revised for the modern reader, much to the chagrin of purists and those who grew up with Chip Hilton.

FIGURE 11.2 What Makes Good Realistic Fiction?

1. The characters are engaging and believable; the protagonist possesses a clearly defined (and perhaps complex) personality and exhibits growth during the course of the story.

2. The dialogue is believable.

3. The plot is fresh and original; the writer avoids clichés or worn-out patterns.

4. The setting is true to life; the description not only gives us a clear picture of where the action takes place, but it helps set the tone for the story.

5. The resolution makes sense, given the characters and the background of the story.

6. The writer avoids sentimentalism or emotionalism for its own sake.

7. The writer avoids sensationalism or lurid details for their own sake.

8. The writer is honest in the portrayal of the problems faced by the characters; sugarcoating is avoided.

9. The writer's theme grows naturally out of the action and characters—the writer does not preach at us.

Sports tales are usually coming-of-age stories, particularly when the protagonist gains self-knowledge through participation in sports, as in the works of Matt Christopher (*The Fox Steals Home*, and others). Most sports stories hinge on the excitement of the game, the necessity for teamwork and fair sportsmanship, and the interpersonal problems that develop between the players. They are popular because of their subject matter, although too often the plots are predictable, the characters are stereotyped, and the dialogue is trite—faults that do not deter eager fans. But in the hands of a talented writer such as Chris Crutcher (*Athletic Shorts* and others), the sports story can be a compelling study of human nature.

Historical Fiction

Definition of Historical Fiction

Historical fiction is more than just a story set in the past. If that were so, then, eventually, all fictional works would become historical fiction. Rather, historical fiction is set in a time period that is earlier from the time the work was written—most experts believe it should be at least a generation (about twenty years) earlier. This means that the writer of historical fiction is aware that his or her readers may not be familiar with the time period of the story and that at least some historical background information will have to be introduced. Also, a writer of historical fiction does not assume that the reader understands the prevailing social, moral, religious, or political attitudes of the time period being portrayed—as a writer of contemporary fiction well might assume. Good historical fiction therefore requires research and careful attention to the details of the earlier time period so that it might faithfully recreate the cultural, social, and intellectual atmosphere in which the story is set.

The Development of Historical Fiction

Historical fiction was almost single-handedly invented in the early nineteenth century by Sir Walter Scott with such novels as *Ivanhoe*, a romantic tale of the Middle Ages, and *Waverley*, about a Scottish rebellion against the English in 1745. Early historical fiction sprang from the Romantic Movement and appealed to the Romantic desire to escape from the frantic pace of modern life. In the later nineteenth century, historical fiction became popular with young readers who were drawn in by the exotic settings, colorful adventures, and heroic figures of the early historical novels. Popular historical novels included Charlotte Yonge's *The Dove in the Eagle's Nest* (1866) and writers such as G. A. Henty and R. L. Stevenson were widely read. In the United States, nineteenth-century writers of historical fiction generally looked to American history for their inspiration; however, the most famous of them all, Howard Pyle, drew on medieval settings in *The Merry Adventures of Robin Hood* and *Otto of the Silver Hand* (see Figure 11.3).

FIGURE 11.3   An illustration by Howard Pyle for his historical novel, *Otto of the Silver Hand,* an adventure romance set in the European Middle Ages.

With the First World War, historical fiction fell into decline, perhaps this is because during war, people pin their hopes on the future, and World War I brought great disillusionment in the old ways. A revival of historical fiction occurred in the 1930s, and for the next thirty or more years historical fiction flourished. It became more eclectic, drawing on the histories of various cultures from ancient Ethiopia (Elizabeth Coatsworth's *The Princess and the Lion*) to Roman Britain (Rosemary Sutcliff's *The Lantern Bearers*) to the Spanish explorations of sixteenth-century America (Scott O'Dell's *The King's Fifth*). Many historical novels won major book awards and enjoyed great popularity.

The 1970s saw the youth rebellion and the subsequent rejection of the past and an insistence on "relevance." All this cast shadows on history in general and on the historical novel in particular. The genre is now recovering its former popularity, and some very fine historical fiction is being written for children today, with an emphasis on reassessing and understanding the past, rather than extolling it. For example, in contrast to celebrating the patriotic glory of the Revolutionary War, Christopher and James Lincoln Collier paint a far more realistic (some would say cynical) picture in *My Brother Sam Is Dead*. Mildred Taylor reveals the ugliness of racial injustice in the South of the 1930s in *Roll of Thunder, Hear My Cry*. And many powerful stories of the inhumanity and sacrilege of the Second World War have been published, some of them fiction (Lois Lowry's *Number the Stars* and Hans Richter's *Friedrich*) and others based on firsthand accounts (Aranka Siegal's *Upon the Head of the Goat: A Childhood in Hungary, 1939–1944*).

The Requirements of Historical Fiction

We distinguish historical fiction from realistic fiction because historical fiction requires specialized treatment, much as does cross-cultural realism (as discussed in Chapter 5). Naturally, we expect historical fiction to contain interesting characters that are convincingly developed, an engaging plot and setting, a thoughtful theme, and carefully crafted language. It is important to remember that historical realistic fiction is *not* history and that the author is not obligated by a dogged adherence to historical facts. But by the same token we do expect historical fiction to recreate an accurate feeling of the past. With that in mind, we can review some of the challenges of historical fiction (see Figure 11.4).

RECREATING THE HISTORICAL PERIOD A good piece of historical fiction faithfully recreates the historical period, and the setting avoids anachronisms. An anachronism is anything that is out of place in a time period, such as a wristwatch in a story of the Middle Ages or eyeglasses in a tale of ancient Rome. An anachronism in a historical novel suggests carelessness in research and casts suspicion on historical accuracy. It is like watching a film portraying a medieval battle scene with armored knights on horses and glimpsing a modern minivan driving down a road off in the distance. (Such cinematic errors have happened.) It destroys the illusion. The political and social structures described should be true to the period. For example, we would not expect to find modern democratic attitudes being touted in a story of the Renaissance. One danger writers occasionally fall prey to is giving historical figures modern-day attitudes. We can hardly expect a medieval woman to act like a twentieth-century feminist, a criticism that has been directed toward the title character of Karen Cushman's Newbery Honor book, *Catherine, Called Birdy*. Birdy is a willful thirteenth-century girl whose attitudes toward the men in her life have a distinctive feminist ring to them. Another example is found in Avi's *True Confessions of Charlotte Doyle*, also a Newbery Honor book. Set in 1832, it is the story of a thirteen-year-old girl sailing to America, who proves herself the equal of any sailor in her strength and daring. She outmaneuvers the ship's wicked captain and ultimately replaces him at the helm. Anne Scott MacLeod, although admitting the story is a "fine vicarious adventure story," calls it also "preposterous." MacLeod goes on to note that many recent historical novels are guilty of evading "the common realities of the societies they write about" (see MacLeod 29–31).

FIGURE 11.4   What Makes Good Historical Fiction?

1. The historical setting is faithfully portrayed and gives us a clear sense of what it was like to live in that time period.

2. The historical details do not overshadow the story itself but are unobtrusively included in the description.

3. The characters seem to be products of their own time and not modern individuals living in the past; their values, beliefs, and attitudes are faithful to historical period.

4. The dialogue seems suited to the time period as far as it is reasonably possible (for it must be intelligible to us).

5. The protagonist possesses a clearly defined (and perhaps complex) personality and exhibits growth during the course of the story.

6. The plot is fresh and original and grows out of the historical period (otherwise it might as well be a contemporary story).

7. The resolution makes sense, given the characters and the historical background of the story.

8. The writer's theme grows naturally out of the action and characters–the writer does not preach at us.

9. The writer provides a carefully balanced view of the historical period, depicting all sides of the issues if possible, and avoiding stereotypes or hasty generalizations.

We usually want an author of historical fiction to give us enough details to suggest the flavor of the period. One distinction between historical and contemporary realistic fiction is that in historical fiction many everyday things may need to be explained for the modern reader. For instance, a writer of contemporary realism need not explain modern methods of preserving food for us, because most of us already know that we just throw it in the freezer. But when writing about the American frontier of the mid-nineteenth century, a writer might have to describe an ice house or the methods of preserving meat, such as salting or smoking. The more remote and unfamiliar the historical period, the more background the author must supply, including political and social history, customs, and even psychological attitudes. However, readers usually prefer these details to be introduced in small doses. In just a few words Marguerite de Angeli sets the stage for her novel of Medieval England, *The Door in the Wall:* "Robin drew the coverlet close about his head and turned his face to the wall. He covered his ears and shut his eyes, for the sound of the bells was deafening. All the bells of London were ringing the hour of Nones" (7).

UNOBTRUSIVE HISTORY If the everyday details described in historical fiction should be accurate, the skillful writer also knows that readers are not reading the book primarily to learn about such things. The good writer tries to include such information as unobtrusively as possible. Joan Blos, herself a writer of some fine historical fiction (*A Gathering of Days* and *Brothers of the Heart*), has noted some of the pitfalls writers of historical fiction should avoid:

1. Overloading the text with historical background information
2. Having characters reveal this information in an artificial and inappropriate fashion
3. Using language unsuited to the historical time. ("The Overstuffed Sentence" 38–39)

The apparatus of writing, in other words, should never get in the way of the story. In fact, if the author errs, it should probably be on the side of dramatic interest rather than historical completeness or accuracy. Readers may forgive an anachronism; they will not forgive a boring story.

Karen Hesse's Newbery-Award–winning *Out of the Dust* is written as a diary of a young girl struggling in Oklahoma during the worst of the Depression in the mid-1930s. Through this device we learn a great deal about the relentless sand storms and the vacillation between courage and desperation so characteristic of impoverished, struggling people. All is told in a child's simple, straight-forward manner, engaging and moving. Hesse gives us enough information that we understand the plight, but not so much that we feel as if we were reading a history textbook.

CREDIBLE DIALOGUE Part of the flavor of a period is the language the people speak. We know that nineteenth-century Americans did not speak the same way that Americans of today speak (indeed teenagers of the 1950s did not speak like the teenagers of today). The following brief passage from Irene Hunt's Civil War story, *Across Five Aprils,* clearly shows how certain language is acceptable and even appropriate in historical fiction that would be out of place in a contemporary story:

> The young man got to his feet grinning. "Sure, Red, glad to oblige. Hear you been blowin' off at the mouth at some of the cracker-barrel heroes agin."
>
> Milton shrugged. "Word gets around fast."
>
> "Ben Harris was in fer a minute." The young man shook his head. "You jest ain't goin' to be happy till you git dressed up in tar and feathers, are you, Red?" (78)

The passage refers, of course, to an actual nineteenth-century practice of covering victims with tar and feathers–a not-too-subtle means of public chastisement. The use of words rarely used today like "oblige" and "cracker-barrel heroes," as well as of clipped and carelessly pronounced words lends an aura of realism to the scene and the characters.

SENSITIVITY AND OBJECTIVITY Finally, an issue of growing importance is the need for writers to view history with both objectivity and sensitivity. White supremacy and nineteenth-century imperialism are no longer the accepted norms. The day is past when we can excuse insensitive American Westerns depicting idealized cowboys pitted against savage, dehumanized Indians, for example. The capable writer of historical fiction recognizes the nature of the historical period and, rather than romanticizing it, provides a balanced and intelligent viewpoint. Patricia Reilly Giff's *Lily's Crossing* is a World War II story set in America, giving us a view of the home front. The American protagonist, young Lily, is exposed to several facets of warfare. One friend loses a brother in the fighting, Lily's own father is sent overseas, and she befriends a refugee who has lost most of his family. As with Hesse's *Out of the Dust*, this story emphasizes the strength that can come through adversity.

Of course, ignorance and prejudice have no place in any writing for children, but they can be especially unfortunate in historical fiction. Historical fiction ought to broaden our perspectives. It is regrettable that we find few works of historical fiction about the lands and peoples outside of Europe and North America. Historical novels set in Asia, Africa, South America, or India are exceedingly rare. Perhaps in the future, budding writers will see the unexplored possibilities in this field.

The Importance of Historical Fiction

Historical fiction deals with the same themes as contemporary realism and fantasy—coming of age, family relationships, friendships, societal issues, and so on. We read historical fiction because we are interested in the lives of the characters—their loves, fears, likes, dislikes, struggles, and triumphs. What we invariably learn from historical fiction—and what we learn from history as well—is that human beings of different times and places have a great deal in common. This is an important concept if we are to get along in this world, for our natural survival instinct tells us to be wary of strangers or anyone different from us. Ignorance is the root of hatred, of prejudice and bigotry, of conflict and war. One way to overcome our narrow biases—perhaps the only way—is to learn to know people different from us. And, ironically, we invariably learn that they are not so different after all.

Historical fiction is one way to broaden our horizons, to learn more about the people and places of our world by reading about the past—where we all came from. There is another equally important reason for reading historical fiction: We are told that we can learn from the past, that we can avoid the mistakes of the past. The philosopher George Santayana said, "Those who cannot remember the past are condemned to repeat it." This is why it is important for us to read about the ugliness of American slavery (Paula Fox's *The Slave Dancer*), or about the brutal treatment by the white Americans of the American Indians (Scott O'Dell's *Sing Down the Moon*), or about the racial bigotry in twentieth-century America (Mildred Taylor's *Roll of Thunder, Hear My Cry*), or about the ghastly crimes of the Holocaust (Hans

Richter's *Friedrich*). We read about them because we know that covering up our past sins will not erase them, and that ignorance of the past only leaves us unprepared for the future. But good historical fiction not only bares for us the transgressions of the past, it shows us the glory as well. Sometimes this shines in unexpected places as we discover in Lois Lowry's moving story of the Nazi occupation of Denmark in World World II, *Number the Stars*. In the face of Nazi bigotry and hatred, the Danish people boldly undertook to save 7,000 Danish Jews from the concentration camps. Their astonishing success is a testament to humanity's noblest spirit. Our past, littered with violence and iniquity and the ridiculous, is also strewn with examples of honor and hope and the sublime.

WORKS CITED

Blos, Joan. "The Overstuffed Sentence and Other Means for Assessing Historical Fiction for Children." *School Library Journal* 31 (November 1985): 38–39.

de Angeli, Marguerite. *The Door in the Wall*. New York: Doubleday, 1949.

Hunt, Irene. *Across Five Aprils*. New York: Follett, 1964.

MacLeod, Anne Scott. "Writing Backward: Modern Models in Historical Fiction." *The Horn Book Magazine* January/February 1998: 26–33.

RECOMMENDED READINGS

Abrahamson, Jane. "Still Playing It Safe: Restricted Realism in Teen Novels." *School Library Journal* 22 (May 1976): 38–39.

Dickinson, Peter. "In Defense of Rubbish." *Children's Literature in Education* 3 (November 1970): 7–10.

Ellis, Anne W. *The Family Story in the 1960's*. New York: Archon, 1970.

Frye, Northrup. *The Educated Imagination*. Bloomington: Indiana University Press, 1964.

Hinton, S. E. "Teenagers Are for Real." *New York Times Book Review* 27 August 1967: 26–29.

Hipple, T., and B. Bartholomew. "The Novels College Freshmen Have Read." *ALAN Review* Winter 1982: 8–10.

Kingston, Carolyn. *The Tragic Mode in Children's Literature*. New York: Teachers College Press, 1974.

McDowell, Miles. "Fiction for Children and Adults: Some Essential Differences." *Children's Literature in Education* 10 (March 1973): 50–63.

Mertz, Maia Pank, and David A. England. "The Legitimacy of American Adolescent Fiction." *School Library Journal* 29 (October 1983): 119–123.

Moorman, Charles. *Kings & Captains: Variations on a Heroic Theme*. Louisville: University of Kentucky Press, 1971.

Moran, Barbara B., and Susan Stienfirst. "Why Johnny (and Jane) Read Whodunits in Series." *School Library Journal* March 1985: 113–117.

Nixon, Joan Lowry. "Clues to the Juvenile Mystery." *The Writer* 90 (February 1977): 23–26.

Nodelman, Perry. "How Typical Children Read Typical Books." *Children's Literature in Education* 12 (Winter 1981): 177–185.

Paterson, Katherine. *Gates of Excellence: On Reading and Writing Books for Children*. New York: Elsevier/Nelson, 1981.

Peck, Richard. "Some Thoughts on Adolescent Literature." *News from ALAN* September/October 1975: 4–7.

Rees, David. *The Marble in the Water*. Boston: The Horn Book, 1980.

——. *Painted Desert, Green Shade: Essays on Contemporary Writers for Children and Young Adults*. Boston: The Horn Book, 1984.

Soderbergh, Peter A. "The Stratemeyer Strain: Educators and the Juvenile Series Book, 1900–1980." In *Only Connect*. Ed. Sheila Egoff, G. T. Stubbs, and L. F. Ashely. 2nd ed. New York: Oxford, 1980: 63–73.

Wilkin, Binnie Tate. *Survival Themes in Fiction for Children and Young People*. New York: Scarecrow, 1978.

SELECTED BIBLIOGRAPHY OF REALISTIC FICTION

(The following lists are merely representative of the wealth of realistic fiction for young readers. The best books are not easily classified into tidy pigeonholes and the classifications are suggestive only. Supplement these lists with those at the ends of Chapters 5 and 7 as well, which contain more examples of realistic fiction.)

FAMILY STORIES

Books for Younger Readers (Grades K–4)

Aiken, Joan. *Cold Shoulder Road*. New York: Delacorte, 1996.

Blume, Judy. *Tales of a Fourth Grade Nothing*. New York: Dutton, 1972.

Burnett, Francis Hodgson. *The Secret Garden*, 1909. Various modern editions.

Byars, Betsy. *The Blossoms Meet the Vulture Lady*. New York: Delacorte, 1986.

——. *The Not-Just-Anybody Family*. New York: Delacorte, 1986.

——. *Wanted . . . Mud Blossom*. New York: Delacorte Press, 1991.

Cleary, Beverly. *Ellen Tebbits*. New York: Morrow, 1951.

——. *Henry Huggins*. New York: Morrow, 1950.

——. *Ramona the Brave*. New York: Morrow, 1975.

——. *Ramona the Pest*. New York: Morrow, 1968.

Enright, Elizabeth. *Thimble Summer*. New York: Holt, 1938.

Estes, Eleanor. *The Moffats*. New York: Harcourt, 1941.

Fine, Anne. *Alias, Madame Doubtfire*. Boston: Little, Brown, 1988. (Humor)

——. *The Jamie and Angus Stories*. Cambridge, MA: Candlewick, 2002.

Gates, Doris. *Blue Willow*. New York: Viking, 1940.

Gautier, Gail. *A Year with Butch and Spike*. New York: Putnam, 1998. (Humor)

Henkes, Karen. *The Birthday Room*. New York: Greenwillow, 1999.

Lowry, Lois. *Anastasia Again!* Boston: Houghton Mifflin, 1981.

——. *Anastasia Has the Answers*. Boston: Houghton Mifflin, 1986.

——. *Anastasia Krupnik*. Boston: Houghton Mifflin, 1979.

——. *Attaboy, Sam!* Boston: Houghton Mifflin, 1992.

McCloskey, Robert. *Centerburg Tales*. New York: Viking, 1951.

——. *Homer Price*. New York: Viking, 1943.

——. *Lentil*. New York: Viking, 1940.

MacLachlan, Patricia. *Sarah, Plain and Tall*. New York: Harper, 1985.

Pinkwater, Daniel. *The Education of Robert Nifkin*. New York: Farrar, Straus & Giroux, 1998.

Sawyer, Ruth. *Roller Skates*. New York: Viking, 1936.

Sidney, Margaret. *The Five Little Peppers and How They Grew* (1880). Various modern editions.

Sorenson, Virginia. *Miracles on Maple Hill*. New York: Harcourt, 1956.

Taylor, Sidney. *All-of-a-Kind Family*. New York: Follett, 1951.

Wiggin, Kate Douglas. *Rebecca of Sunnybrook Farm*. New York: Grosset and Dunlap, 1903.

Books for Older Readers (Grades 5 and Up)

Alcott, Louisa May. *Little Women*. 1868–1869. Various modern editions.

Bawden, Nina. *The Real Plato Jones*. New York: Clarion, 1993.

Blume, Judy. *Tiger Eyes*. Scarsdale, NY: Bradbury, 1981.

Byars, Betsy. *The Night Swimmers*. New York: Delacorte, 1980.

———. *The Summer of the Swans*. New York: Viking, 1970.

Cleary, Beverly. *Dear Mr. Henshaw*. New York: Morrow, 1983.

Cleaver, Bill, and Vera Cleaver. *Where the Lilies Bloom*. Philadelphia: Lippincott, 1969.

Creech, Sharon. *Walk Two Moons*. New York: Harper, 1994.

Dorris, Michael. *The Window*. New York: Hyperion, 1997.

Ellis, Sarah. *Out of the Blue*. New York: McElderry, 1995.

Fitzhugh, Louise. *Harriet the Spy*. New York: Harper, 1964.

Hermes, Patricia. *Mama, Let's Dance*. Boston: Little, 1991.

Hickman, Janet. *Jericho*. New York: Greenwillow, 1994.

Hunter, Mollie. *A Sound of Chariots*. New York: Harper, 1972.

Killingsworth, Monte. *Equinox*. New York: Holt, 2001.

Klein, Norma. *Mom, the Wolfman and Me*. New York: Pantheon, 1972.

L'Engle, Madeleine. *Meet the Austins*. New York: Vanguard, 1960.

Lowry, Lois. *A Summer to Die*. Boston: Houghton Mifflin, 1977.

MacLachlan, Patricia. *Baby*. New York: Delacorte, 1993.

———. *Cassie Binegar*. HarperCollins, 1982.

———. *Journey*. New York: Delacorte, 1991.

Montgomery, L. L. *Anne of Green Gables*. 1908. Various modern editions.

Namioka, Lensey. *Yang the Youngest and His Terrible Ear*. Boston: Little, Brown, 1992.

Oneal, Zibby. *The Language of Goldfish*. New York: Random House, 1980.

———. *In Summer Light*. New York: Viking, 1985.

Paterson, Katherine. *The Great Gilly Hopkins*. New York: Crowell, 1978.

———. *Jacob Have I Loved*. New York: Crowell, 1980.

Peck, Robert. *A Day No Pigs Would Die*. New York: Knopf, 1972.

Porter, Eleanor. *Pollyanna*. (1913). Various modern editions.

Raskin, Ellen. *Figgs & Phantoms*. New York: Dutton, 1974.

Shannon, George. *Unlived Affections*. New York: Harper, 1989.

Voight, Cynthia. *Dicey's Song*. New York: Atheneum, 1982.

———. *Homecoming*. New York: Atheneum, 1981.

———. *A Solitary Blue*. New York: Atheneum, 1983.

Withrow, Sarah. *Box Girl*. Vancouver, BC: Douglas and McIntyre, 2002.

STORIES OF SOCIAL REALISM

Books for Younger Readers (Grades K–4)

Blue, Rose. *Me and Einstein*. New York: Human Sciences, 1979. (Learning disability–dyslexia)

Byars, Betsy. *The Cybil War*. New York: Viking, 1981. (Friendship)

Greene, Bette. *Philip Hall Likes Me. I Reckon Maybe*. New York: Dial, 1974. (Boy-girl relationships)

Greene, Constance. *The Ears of Louis*. New York: Viking, 1974. (Self-acceptance)

Hanson, Joyce. *Yellow Bird and Me*. New York: Houghton, 1986. (Learning disability)

Konigsburg, E. L. *Jennifer, Hecate, Macbeth, William McKinley, and Me, Elizabeth*. New York: Atheneum, 1967. (Friendship)

Little, Jean. *Emma's Magic Winter*. Illus. Plecas. New York: HarperCollins, 1998. (Shyness)

Marek, Margot. *Different, Not Dumb*. New York: Watts, 1985. (Learning disability)

Myers, Walter Dean. *Me, Mop, and the Moondance Kid*. New York: Dell, 1985. (Adoption)

Naylor, Phyllis Reynolds. *Alice In Rapture, Sort Of*. New York: Atheneum, 1989. (Boy-girl friendship)

Smith, Doris Buchanan. *A Taste of Blackberries*. New York: Crowell, 1973. (Death of a friend)

Books for Older Readers (Grades 5 and Up)

Anderson, Laurie Halse. *Speak*. New York: Farrar, Straus & Giroux, 1999. (Sexual abuse)

Avi. *Nothing but the Truth: A Documentary Novel*. New York: Watts, 1991.

Bauer, Marion Dane. *Am I Blue?: Coming Out of the Silence*. New York: HarperCollins, 1994. (Homosexuality)

Bawden, Nina. *Humbug*. New York: Clarion, 1992. (Personal issues and the elderly)

Bennett, James. *I Can Hear the Mourning Dove*. Boston: Houghton Mifflin, 1990. (Emotional illness)

Block, Francesca Lia. *Weetzie Bat*. New York: HarperCollins, 1989. (Alternative lifestyles in a work of surrealism)

Blume, Judy. *Are You There, God? It's Me, Margaret*. New York: Bradbury, 1970. (Sexuality)

Brooks, Jerome. *Uncle Mike's Boy*. New York: Harper, 1973. (Emotional illness)

Brooks, Martha. *True Confessions of a Heartless Girl*. New York: Farrar, Straus & Giroux, 2003. (Teenage pregnancy and relationships)

Bunting, Eve. *Summer Wheels*. San Diego: Harcourt Brace Jovanovich, 1992. (Aging)

Carrick, Carol. *Stay Away from Simon*. New York: Clarion, 1985. (Mental retardation)

Childress, Alice. *A Hero Ain't Nothin' but a Sandwich*. New York: Coward, 1973. (Drugs)

Clymer, Eleanor. *The Get-Away Car*. New York: Dutton, 1978. (Aging)

Cole, Brock. *Celine*. New York: Farrar, Straus & Giroux, 1989. (Personal relationships)

——. *The Goats*. New York: Farrar, Straus & Giroux, 1987. (Personal relationships)

Cormier, Robert. *Beyond the Chocolate War*. New York: Knopf, 1985. (Social corruption)

——. *The Bumblebee Flies Anyway*. New York: Pantheon, 1983. (Terminal illness)

——. *The Chocolate War*. New York: Pantheon, 1974. (Social corruption)

——. *I Am the Cheese*. New York: Bell, 1987. (Government corruption)

——. *Tenderness*. New York: Delacorte, 1997. (Serial murderer)

Creech, Sharon. *Chasing Redbird*. New York: HarperCollins, 1997. (Self-acceptance)

——. *Granny Torrelli Makes Soup*. New York: Harper, 2003. (Friend with a disability)

Crutcher, Chris. *Staying Fat for Sarah Byrnes*. New York: Morrow, 1993. (Child abuse)

Daly, Maureen. *Seventeenth Summer*. New York: Dodd, 1942. (First love)

Danziger, Paula. *The Cat Ate My Gymsuit*. New York: Delacorte, 1974. (Personal relationships)

Donovan, John. *I'll Get There. It Better Be Worth the Trip*. New York: Harper, 1969. (Homosexuality)

Ferris, Jean. *Eight Seconds*. New York: Penguin, 2002. (Homosexuality)

Fine, Anne. *Flour Babies*. Boston: Little, 1994. (Personal responsibility)

——. *The Tulip Touch*. Boston: Little, 1997. (Coming of age)

Fleischman, Paul. *The Half-a-Moon Inn*. New York: Harper, 1980. (Muteness)

Foreman, Michael. *Seal Surfer*. Orlando: Harcourt Brace, 1997. (Physical disability)

Fox, Paula. *The Eagle Kite*. New York: Jackson/Orchard, 1995. (Homosexuality)

Garden, Nancy. *Annie on My Mind*. New York: Farrar, Straus & Giroux, 1982. (Lesbianism)

Greene, Bette. *Summer of My German Soldier*. New York: Dial, 1973. (Ethnic prejudice)

Hamilton, Virginia. *The Planet of Junior Brown*. New York: Macmillan, 1971. (Emotional problems)

Hinton, S. E. *The Outsiders*. New York: Viking, 1967. (Teenage gangs)

Howe, James. *The Watcher*. New York: Atheneum, 1997. (Child abuse)

Hunt, Irene. *Up a Road Slowly*. New York: Follett, 1967. (Coming of age)

Hunter, Kristen. *Soul Brothers and Sister Lou*. New York: Scribner's, 1958. (Race)

Hunter, Mollie. *A Sound of Chariots*. New York: Harper, 1972. (Death of a parent)

Johnson, Angela. *Gone from Home: Short Takes*. New York: DK Ink, 1998. (Coming of age)

Johnston, Julie. *The Only Outcast*. Toronto: Tundra, 1998. (Physical disability)

Kerr, M. E. *Deliver Us from Evie*. New York: HarperCollins, 1994. (Homosexuality)

——. *"Hello," I Lied*. New York: HarperCollins, 1997. (Homosexuality)

Konigsburg, E. L. *The View from Saturday*. New York: Atheneum, 1996. (Personal relationships)

Levoy, Myron C. *A Shadow Like a Leopard*. New York: Harper, 1981. (Aging)

Lipsyte, Robert. *One Fat Summer*. New York: Harper, 1977. (Obesity)

Lowry, Lois. *A Summer to Die*. Boston: Houghton Mifflin, 1977. (Terminal illness)

Marsden, John. *Letters from the Inside*. Boston: Houghton Mifflin, 1994.

Martin, Ann M. *A Corner of the Universe*. New York: Scholastic, 2002. (Friendship)

Meyer, Carolyn. *Killing the Kudu*. New York: Macmillan, 1990. (Disability–mobility)

Murrow, Liza Ketchum. *Twelve Days in August*. New York: Holiday House, 1993. (Sexuality)

Myers, Walter Dean. *It Ain't All for Nothin'*. New York: Viking, 1978. (Crime)

——. *Scorpions*. New York: Harper, 1988. (Gangs)

Naylor, Phyllis Reynolds. *Reluctantly Alice*. New York: Atheneum, 1991. (Sexuality)

Nelson, Theresa. *Earthshine*. New York: Jackson, 1994. (AIDS)

Paterson, Katherine. *Bridge to Terabithia*. New York: Crowell, 1977. (Death of a friend)

——. *Come Sing, Jimmy Jo*. New York: Dutton, 1985. (Self-acceptance)

Peck, Richard. *Remembering the Good Times*. New York: Delacorte, 1985. (Friend's suicide)

——. *Secrets of the Shopping Mall*. New York: Delacorte, 1979. (Running away)

——. *Those Summer Girls I Never Met*. New York: Delacorte, 1988. (Aging)

Perkins, Lynne Rae. *All Alone in the Universe*. New York: Greenwillow, 1999. (Friendship)

Potok, Chaim. *Zebra and Other Stories*. New York: Knopf, 1998. (Coming of age)

Pressler, Mirjam. *Halinka*. Trans. Elizabeth D. Crawford. New York: Holt, 1998. (Child abuse)

Rapp, Adam. *The Buffalo Tree*. Arden, NC: Front Street, 1997. (Juvenile detention center)

Roberts, Ken. *The Thumb in the Box*. Toronto: Groundwood, 2001. (Humor)

Ryan, Sara. *Empress of the World*. New York: Viking, 2001. (Lesbianism)

Rylant, Cynthia. *A Couple of Kooks and Other Stories about Love*. New York: Orchard, 1990. (Love and sexuality)

——. *A Fine White Dust*. New York: Bradbury, 1986. (Religious faith)

Sachar, Louis. *Holes*. New York: Farrar, Straus & Giroux, 1998. (Friendship)

Salisbury, Graham. *Lord of the Deep*. New York: Delacorte, 2001. (Coming of age)

Sanchez, Alex. *Rainbow Boys*. New York: Simon & Schuster, 2001. (Homosexuality)

Scoppettone, Sandra. *Trying Hard to Hear You*. New York: Harper, 1981. (Homosexuality)

Skinner, David. *The Wrecker*. New York: Simon, 1995. (Social misfit)

Spinelli, Jerry. *Maniac Magee*. Boston: Little, Brown, 1990. (Race)

Thomas, Rob. *Slave Day*. New York: Simon, 1997. (Social interaction)

Twain, Mark. *The Adventures of Tom Sawyer*. (1876). Various modern editions.

——. *The Adventures of Huckleberry Finn*. (1884). Various modern editions.

Voigt, Cynthia. *When She Hollers*. New York: Scholastic, 1994. (Sexual abuse)

Woodson, Jacqueline. *Locomotion*. New York: Putnam, 2003. (Personal tragedy)

Wojciechowska, Maia. *Shadow of a Bull*. New York: Atheneum, 1964. (Coming of age)

Woodson, Jacqueline. *I Hadn't Meant to Tell You This*. New York: Delacorte, 1994. (Sexual abuse)

Wright, Betty Ren. *Getting Rid of Marjorie*. New York: Holiday House, 1981. (Aging)

Wynne-Jones, Tim. *Some of the Kinder Planets*. New York: Kroupa, 1995. (Short stories about relationships and various themes)

Zindel, Paul. *The Pigman*. New York: Harper, 1968. (Old age)

ADVENTURE, SURVIVAL, MYSTERY, AND SPORTS STORIES

Books for Older Readers (Grades 5 and Up)

Bee, Clair. *Touchdown Pass*. New York: Grosset and Dunlap, 1948.

Brooks, Bruce. *The Moves Make the Man*. New York: Harper & Row, 1984. (Sports)

Christopher, Matt. *Football Fugitive*. Boston: Little, Brown, 1976. (Sports)

——. *The Fox Steals Home*. Boston: Little, Brown, 1978. (Sports)

Corcoran, Barbara. *A Star to the North*. Philadelphia: Lippincott, 1970. (Survival)

Creech, Sharon. *The Wanderer*. New York: Harper, 2000. (Adventure/survival)

Cross, Gillian. *On the Edge*. New York: Holiday House, 1985. (Mystery, suspense)

Crutcher, Chris. *Athletic Shorts*. New York: Greenwillow, 1991. (Sports)

Dyer, T. A. *A Way of His Own*. Boston: Houghton Mifflin, 1981. (Survival)

Fenner, Carol. *The King of Dragons*. New York: Simon & Schuster, 1998. (Survival)

George, Jean Craighead. *Julie of the Wolves*. New York: Harper, 1972. (Survival)

——. *My Side of the Mountain*. New York: Dutton, 1959. (Survival)

Holman, Felice. *Slake's Limbo*. New York: Scribner's, 1974. (Survival)

Houston, James. *Frozen Fire*. New York: Atheneum, 1977. (Survival)

——. *Long Claw: An Arctic Adventure*. New York: Atheneum, 1981. (Survival)

Konigsburg, E. L. *From the Mixed-Up Files of Mrs. Basil E. Frankweiler*. New York: Atheneum, 1967. (Mystery)

Mazer, Harry. *The Island Keeper*. New York: Delacorte, 1981. (Survival)

——. *Snowbound*. New York: Dell, 1973. (Survival)

Morpurgo, Michael. *Kensuke's Kingdom*. New York: Scholastic, 2003.

Paulsen, Gary. *Hatchet*. New York: Bradbury, 1987. (Survival)

Phipson, Joan. *Hit and Run*. New York: Atheneum, 1985. (Survival)

Powell, Randy. *My Underrated Year*. New York: Farrar, Straus & Giroux, 1988. (Sports)

Raskin, Ellen. *The Mysterious Disappearance of Leon (I Mean Noel)*. New York: Dutton, 1971. (Mystery)

——. *The Westing Game*. New York: Dutton, 1978. (Mystery)

Shecter, Ben. *Inspector Rose*. New York: Harper, 1969. (Mystery)

Slote, Alfred. *The Trading Game*. Philadelphia: Lippincott, 1990. (Sports)

Sobol, Donald. *Encyclopedia Brown Saves the Day*. Nashville, TN: Nelson, 1970. (Mystery)

Speare, Elizabeth George. *The Sign of the Beaver*. Boston: Houghton Mifflin, 1983. (Survival)

Stevenson, Robert Louis. *Treasure Island*. 1883. Various modern editions.

Streiber, Whitley. *Wolf of Shadows*. New York: Knopf, 1985. (Survival)

Taylor, Theodore. *The Cay*. New York: Doubleday, 1969. (Survival)

Watson, Harvey. *Bob War and Poke*. Boston: Houghton Mifflin, 1991.

Westall, Robert. *The Kingdom by the Sea*. New York: Farrar, 1991. (Mystery)

——. *A Place to Hide*. New York: Scholastic, 1994. (Mystery)

Wynne-Jones, Tim. *The Maestro*. New York: Orchard, 1996. (Survival)

ANIMAL STORIES FOR ALL AGES

Burnford, Sheila. *The Incredible Journey*. Boston: Little, Brown, 1961.

Byars, Betsy. *The Midnight Fox*. New York: Viking, 1968.

Cleary, Beverly. *Socks*. New York: Morrow, 1973.

DeJong, Meindert. *Hurry Home, Candy*. New York: Harper, 1953.

Eckert, Allan W. *Incident at Hawk's Hill*. Boston: Little, Brown, 1971.

Farley, Walter. *The Black Stallion*. New York: Random House, 1944.

——. *The Black Stallion Returns*. New York: Random House, 1945.

Gates, Doris. *Little Vic*. New York: Viking, 1951.

George, Jean. *The Cry of the Crow*. New York: Harper, 1980.

Gipson, Fred. *Old Yeller*. New York: Harper, 1956.

Griffiths, Helen. *The Greyhound*. New York: Doubleday, 1964.

——. *The Wild Heart*. New York: Doubleday, 1963.

Henry, Marguerite. *King of the Wind*. New York: Rand, 1948.

——. *Misty of Chincoteague*. New York: Rand, 1947.

James, Will. *Smoky, the Cow Horse*. New York: Scribner's, 1926.

Kjelgaard, Jim. *Big Red*. New York: Holiday, 1956.

Knight, Eric. *Lassie Come Home*. Philadelphia: Winston, 1940.

London, Jack. *The Call of the Wild*. 1903. Various modern editions.

Mowat, Farley. *Owls in the Family*. Boston: Little, Brown, 1962.

Mukerji, Dhan Gopal. *Gay-Neck*. New York: Dutton, 1927.

Naylor, Phyllis Reynolds. *Shiloh*. New York: Atheneum, 1991.

O'Hara, Mary. *My Friend Flicka*. New York: Lippincott, 1941.

Rawlings, Marjorie Kinnan. *The Yearling*. New York: Scribner's, 1938.

Rawis, Wilson. *Where the Red Fern Grows*. New York: Doubleday, 1961.

Reaver, Chap. *Bill*. New York: Delacorte, 1994.

Rodowsky, Colby. *Not My Dog*. New York: Farrar, Straus & Giroux, 1999.

Sewell, Anna. *Black Beauty: The Autobiography of a Horse*. 1877. Various modern editions.

Taylor, William. *Agnes the Sheep*. New York: Scholastic, 1991.

SELECTED BIBLIOGRAPHY OF HISTORICAL FICTION

(This list has been restricted to fictional works that emphasize the historical details of their setting. They are classified according to the time period and geographical region. These works are suitable for young readers of about the fourth or fifth grade level and older. See the booklist in Chapter 12 for nonfiction works on historical subjects.)

ANCIENT, MEDIEVAL, AND RENAISSANCE EUROPEAN HISTORY

Avi. *Crispin: The Cross of Lead*. New York: Hyperion, 2002. (Medieval England)

Behn, Harry. *The Faraway Lurs*. New York: Putnam, 1963. (Ancient World)

Brennan, J. H. *Shiva: An Adventure of the Ice Age*. New York: Lippincott, 1989.

Cheaney, J. B. *The True Prince*. New York: Knopf, 2002. (Renaissance England)

Chute, Marchette. *The Innocent Wayfaring*. New York: Dutton, 1955. (Medieval England)

Cushman, Karen. *Catherine, Called Birdy*. New York: Clarion, 1994. (Medieval England)

——. *Matilda Bone*. New York: Random House, 2000. (Medieval England)

——. *The Midwife's Apprentice*. New York: Clarion, 1995. (Medieval England)

de Angeli, Marguerite. *The Door in the Wall*. New York: Doubleday, 1949. (Medieval England)

Ellis, Deborah. *A Company of Fools*. Markham, Ontario: Fitzhenry and Whiteside, 2002. (Medieval England)

Gray, Elizabeth Janet. *Adam of the Road*. New York: Viking, 1942. (Medieval England)

Haugaard, Erik Christian. *Leif the Unlucky*. Boston: Houghton Mifflin, 1982. (Medieval Norse)

——. *Orphans of the Wind*. New York: Dell, 1966. (Medieval Norse)

——. *Hakon of Rogen's Saga*. Boston: Houghton Mifflin, 1963. (Medieval Norse)

Hunter, Mollie. *The Spanish Letters*. New York: Funk, 1967. (Renaissance England)

——. *The Stronghold*. New York: Harper, 1974. (The Bronze Age)

Ish-Kishor, Sulamith. *A Boy of Old Prague*. New York: Pantheon, 1963.

Kelly, Eric P. *The Trumpeter of Krakov*. New York: Macmillan, 1928. (Medieval Poland)

McGraw, Eloise Jarvis. *Mara, Daughter of the Nile*. New York: Coward, 1961. (Ancient Egypt)

Oliver, Jane, *Faraway Princess*. New York: St. Martin's, 1962. (Medieval Britain)

Pilar, Molina Llorente. *The Apprentice*. New York: Farrar, Straus & Giroux, 1993. (Renaissance Florence)

Pyle, Howard. *Men of Iron*. (1890). Various modern editions. (Medieval England)

——. *Otto of the Silver Hand*. (1888) Various modern editions. (Medieval Germany)

Speare, Elizabeth George. *The Bronze Bow*. Boston: Houghton Mifflin, 1961. (Ancient Rome)

Stolz, Mary. *Zekmet the Stone Carver: A Tale of Ancient Egypt*. Illus. by Deborah Nourse Lattimore, New York: Harcourt, 1988.

Sutcliff, Rosemary. *The Eagle of the Ninth*. New York: Walck, 1954. (Roman Britain)

——. *The Lantern Bearers*. New York: Walck, 1959. (Roman Britain)

——. *The Mark of the Horse Lord*. New York: Walck, 1965. (Roman Britain)

Tarr, Judith. *His Majesty's Elephant*. New York: Harcourt, 1993. (Early Medieval France)

Treace, Geoffrey. *The Red Towers of Granada*. New York: Vanguard, 1967. (Medieval Spain)

Treece, Henry. *The Centurion*. Illus. Mary Russon. New York: Meredith, 1967. (Ancient Rome)

——. *Viking's Dawn*. New York: Criterion, 1956.

Vining, Elizabeth Gray. *Adam of the Road*. New York: Viking, 1942. (Medieval England)

Walsh, Jill Paton. *The Emperor's Winding Sheet*. New York: Farrar, Straus & Giroux, 1974. (Medieval Constantinople)

Wein, Elizabeth E. *A Coalition of Lions*. New York: Viking, 2003. (Very early Britain)

Yolen, Jane, and Robert J. Harris. *Girl in a Cage*. New York: Philomel, 2002. (Medieval Scotland)

MODERN EUROPEAN HISTORY SINCE THE RENAISSANCE

Anderson, Rachel. *Black Water*. New York: Holt, 1995. (Victorian England)

Avery, Gillian. *Maria Escapes*. New York: Simon, 1992. (Originally published in 1957 in England as *The Warden's Niece*) (Victorian England)

Avi. *The True Confessions of Charlotte Doyle*. New York: Orchard, 1990. (Nineteenth-century high seas)

Burton, Hester. *Time of Trial*. Cleveland: World, 1964. (Eighteenth-century England)

Dumas, Alexandre. *The Three Musketeers*. (1844) Several modern editions. (Seventeenth-century France)

Garfield, John. *December Rose*. New York: Viking, 1986. (Eighteenth-century England)

——. *Smith*. New York: Pantheon, 1967. (Eighteenth-century England)

——. *The Sound of Coaches*. New York: Viking, 1974. (Eighteenth-century England)

Hesse, Karen. *Letters from Rifka*. New York: Holt, 1992. (Russian immigrants to U.S., early twentieth century)

Holman, Felice. *The Wild Children*. New York: Scribner's, 1983. (Russian revolution)

Hughes, Dean. *Soldier Boys*. New York: Atheneum, 2001. (World War II)

Kerr, Judith. *When Hitler Stole Pink Rabbit*. New York: Coward, 1972. (World War II)

Lowry, Lois. *Number the Stars*. Boston: Houghton Mifflin, 1989. (World War II)

McCaughrean, Geraldine. *The Pirate's Son*. New York: Scholastic, 1998. (Eighteenth-century England)

Minard, Rosemary. *Long Meg*. New York: Pantheon, 1982. (Sixteenth-century Holland)

Monjo, Ferdinand. *The Sea Beggar's Son*. New York: Coward, 1975. (Seventeenth-century Holland)

O'Dell, Scott. *The Hawk That Dare Not Hunt by Day*. Boston: Houghton Mifflin, 1975. (Sixteenth-century Europe)

Orczy, Baroness Emmuska. *The Scarlet Pimpernel*. (1905) Several modern editions. (French Revolution)

Orlev, Uri. *The Island on Bird Street*. Trans. Hillel Halkin. Boston: Houghton Mifflin, 1984. (World War II)

Pelgrom, Els. *The Winter When Time Was Frozen*. Trans. Maryka and Rafael Rudnik. New York: Morrow, 1980. (World War II)

Peyton, K. M. *Flambards*. Oxford: Oxford University Press, 1967. (Pre-World War I England)

Pressler, Mirjam. *Malka*. Tr. Brian Murdoch. New York: Philomel, 2003. (Holocaust)

Richter, Hans Peter. *Friedrich*. New York: Holt, 1970. (World War II)

Schmidt, Gary D. *Anson's Way*. New York: Clarion, 1999. (Eighteenth-century Ireland)

Serraillier, Ian. *The Silver Sword*. New York: Criterion, 1959. (World War II)

Stevenson, Robert Louis. *Kidnapped*. (1886) Several modern editions. (Eighteenth-century Scotland)

Suhl, Yuri. *The Merrymaker*. New York: Four Winds, 1975. (Early twentieth-century Eastern Europe)

NORTH AMERICAN AND NATIVE AMERICAN HISTORY

Anderson, Laurie Halse. *Fever 1793*. New York: Simon and Schuster, 2000. (Eighteenth-century America)

Armer, Laura Adams. *Waterless Mountain*. New York: McKay, 1931. (Navajo)

Avi. *The Barn*. New York: Jackson, 1994. (Nineteenth century)

——. *Encounter at Easton*. New York: Pantheon, 1980. (Eighteenth century)

Banks, Sara Harrell. *Abraham's Battle: A Novel of Gettysburg*. New York: Antheneum, 1999. (Civil War)

Bawdin, Nina. *Carrie's War*. New York: Lippincott, 1973. (World War II)

Beatty, Patricia. *Jayhawker*. New York: Morrow, 1991. (Civil War)

Blos, Joan. *A Gathering of Days*. New York: Scribner's, 1979. (Early nineteenth century)

Brink, Carol Ryrie. *Caddie Woodlawn*. 1936. Various modern editions. (Nineteenth century)

Bulla, Clyde. *A Lion to Guard Us*. New York: Crowell, 1978. (Seventeenth century)

Cannon, A. E. *Charlotte's Rose*. New York: Random House, 2002. (Nineteenth-century Mormons in Utah)

Collier, James Lincoln and Christopher. *My Brother Sam Is Dead*. New York: Four Winds Press, 1974. (American Revolution)

Donnelly, Jennifer. *A Northern Light*. San Diego, CA: Harcourt, 2003. (Early twentieth-century)

Dorris, Michael. *Guests*. New York: Hyperion, 1994. (Pre-Columbian America)

———. *Morning Girl*. New York: Hyperion, 1992. (Pre-Columbian America)

Fleischman, Paul. *The Borning Room*. New York: Harper, 1991. (Nineteenth century)

Forbes, Esther. *Johnny Tremain*. Boston: Houghton Mifflin, 1946. (American Revolution)

Fox, Paula. *The Slave Dancer*. New York: Bradbury, 1973. (Early nineteenth century)

Fritz, Jean. *The Cabin Faced West*. New York: Coward, 1958. (Late eighteenth century)

Giff, Patricia Reilly. *Lily's Crossing*. New York: Delacorte, 1997. (World War II)

Hahn, Mary Downing. *Hear the Wind Blow: A Novel of the Civil War*. New York: Clarion, 2003.

Hesse, Karen. *Out of the Dust*. New York: Scholastic, 1997. (1930s)

Hickman, Janet. *Susannah*. New York: Greenwillow, 1998. (Nineteenth century)

Hudson, Jan. *Sweetgrass*. New York: Philomel, 1989. (Native Canadian)

Hunt, Irene. *Across Five Aprils*. New York: Follett, 1964. (Civil War)

Hurwitz, Johanna. *Faraway Summer*. Illus. Mary Azarian. New York: Morrow, 1998. (Late nineteenth century)

Isaacs, Anne. *Treehouse Tales*. New York: Dutton, 1997. (1880s)

Kerr, M. E. *Slap Your Sides*. New York: Harper-Collins, 2001. (World War II)

Lasky, Kathryn. *Beyond the Burning Time*. New York: Scholastic, 1994. (Colonial)

Leviton, Sonia. *Clem's Chances*. New York: Scholastic, 2001. (Nineteenth century)

Lyons, Mary E. *Letters from a Slave Girl: The Story of Harriet Jacobs*. New York: Scribner's, 1992. (Nineteenth century)

Myers, Walter Dean. *The Glory Field*. New York: Scholastic, 1994. (Eighteenth century to the present)

O'Dell, Scott. *Island of the Blue Dolphins*. Boston: Houghton Mifflin, 1960. (Early nineteenth-century Native American)

———. *The King's Fifth*. Boston: Houghton Mifflin, 1966. (Sixteenth-century Spanish America)

———. *Sing Down the Moon*. Boston: Houghton Mifflin, 1970. (Navajo)

Paterson, Katherine. *Jip: His Story*. New York: Lodestar, 1996. (Nineteenth-century New England)

Peck, Richard. *Fair Weather*. New York: Dial, 2001. (Late nineteenth century)

———. *A Long Way from Chicago*. New York: Dial, 1998. (The Great Depression)

———. *A Year Down Yonder*. New York: Dial, 2000. (The Great Depression)

Perez, N. A. *The Slopes of War: A Novel of Gettysburg*. Boston: Houghton Mifflin, 1984. (Civil War)

Pellowski, Anne. *Winding Valley Farm: Annie's Story*. New York: Philomel, 1982. (Late nineteenth century)

Petry, Ann. *Tituba of Salem Village*. New York: Crowell, 1964. (Colonial)

Pinkney, Andrea Davis. *Silent Thunder: A Civil War Story*. New York: Hyperion, 1999.

Reeder, Carolyn. *Shades of Gray*. New York: Macmillan, 1989. (Civil War)

Richter, Conrad. *The Light in the Forest*. New York: Knopf, 1953. (Nineteenth century)

Rostokowski, Margaret I. *After the Dancing Days*. New York: Harper, 1986. (World War I)

Sebestyen, Ouida. *Words by Heart*. Boston: Little, Brown, 1979. (Early twentieth century)

Speare, Elizabeth George. *The Sign of the Beaver*. Boston: Houghton Mifflin, 1983. (Eighteenth century)

———. *The Witch of Blackbird Pond*. Boston: Houghton Mifflin, 1958. (Colonial)

Taylor, Mildred. *Let the Circle Be Unbroken*. New York: Dial, 1981. (The 1930s)

———. *Roll of Thunder, Hear My Cry*. New York: Dial, 1976. (The 1930s)

Watts, Leander. *Stonecutter*. Boston: Houghton Mifflin, 2002. (Early nineteenth century)

Wilder, Laura Ingalls. *By the Shores of Silver Lake*. New York: Harper, 1939. (Nineteenth century)

———. *Farmer Boy*. New York: Harper, 1933.

———. *The First Four Years*. New York: Harper, 1971.

——. *Little House in the Big Woods*. New York: Harper, 1932.

——. *Little House on the Prairie*. New York: Harper, 1935.

——. *Little Town on the Prairie*. New York: Harper, 1941.

——. *The Long Winter*. New York: Harper, 1940.

——. *On the Banks of Plum Creek*. New York: Harper, 1937.

——. *Those Happy Golden Years*. New York: Harper, 1943.

Wolf, Virginia Euwer. *Bat 6*. New York: Scholastic, 1998. (The 1940s)

OTHER TIMES AND PLACES

Aldridge, James. *The True Story of Spit MacPhee*. New York: Viking, 1986. (1920s Australia)

Bosse, Malcolm. *The Examination*. New York: Farrar, Straus & Giroux, 1994. (Medieval China)

Choi, Sook-Nyul. *Year of Impossible Goodbyes*. Boston: Houghton Mifflin, 1991. (World War II Korea)

De Jenkins, Lyll Becerra. *The Honorable Prison*. New York: Lodestar, 1988. (South America)

DeJong, Meindert. *The House of Sixty Fathers*. New York: Harper, 1956. (China)

Dickinson, Peter. *The Dancing Bear*. Boston: Little, Brown, 1972. (Byzantium)

Disher, Gary. *The Bamboo Flute*. Boston: Houghton Mifflin, 1993. (1930s Australia)

Hautzig, Esther. *The Endless Steppe: A Girl in Exile*. New York: Harper, 1968.

Ho Minfong. *The Clay Marble*. New York: Farrar, Straus & Giroux, 1991. (Cambodia)

Holman, Felice. *Wild Children*. New York: Scribner's, 1983. (Russia)

Lewis, Elizabeth Foreman. *Young Fu of the Upper Yangtze*. New York: Holt, 1932. (China)

Maruki, Toshi. *Hiroshima No Pika*. New York: Lothrop, 1982. (World War II Japan)

Namioka, Lensey. *Island of Ogres*. New York: Harper, 1989. (Japan)

——. *Village of the Vampire Cat*. New York: Delacorte, 1981. (Medieval Japan)

O'Dell, Scott. *My Name Is Not Angelica*. Boston: Houghton Mifflin, 1989. (Eighteenth-century West Indies)

Park, Linda Sue. *A Single Shard*. New York: Dell, 2001. (Twelfth-century Korea)

——. *When My Name Was Keoko*. Boston: Houghton Mifflin, 2002. (World War II Korea)

Paterson, Katherine. *The Master Puppeteer*. New York: T. Crowell, 1976. (Japan)

——. *Of Nightingales That Weep*. New York: T. Crowell, 1974. (Japan)

——. *Rebels of the Heavenly Kingdom*. New York: T. Crowell, 1983. (China)

——. *The Sign of the Chrysanthemum*. New York: T. Crowell, 1973. (Japan)

Ritchie, Rita. *The Golden Hawks of Genghis Khan*. New York: Dutton, 1958.

——. *Secret Beyond the Mountains*. New York: Dutton, 1960. (China)

——. *The Year of the Horse*. New York: Dutton, 1957. (China)

Yep, Laurence. *Hiroshima*. New York: Scholastic, 1995. (World War II Japan)

——. *The Serpent's Children*. New York: Harper, 1984. (China)

12

Biography and Information Books

Biographies, histories, travel books, science and technology books all belong to that great amorphous class often referred to as nonfiction. Too often, adults view nonfiction works as merely functional, their purpose being to inform rather than to entertain or inspire. But in children's literature the distinction has always been fuzzier, perhaps because children themselves do not compartmentalize their reading. Joanna Cole's very popular Magic School Bus series includes picture books about an unconventional science teacher who believes in hands-on experience and has at her disposal a school bus capable of taking the class to unusual places, such as the center of the earth, for example, to study rocks (in *The Magic School Bus: Inside the Earth*). It is a good example of presenting factual information in an entertaining way.

In this chapter, we will consider first biography and autobiography and then examine the broad spectrum of children's information books. Our theme, however, is that nonfiction can and ought to be just as exciting and as pleasurable as fiction.

BIOGRAPHY

The biographer Paul Murray Kendall notes that biography lies between history and literature— and has never been fully embraced by either (3). Because of this peculiar position of biography and because biography is so popular with many young readers, we will examine its characteristics in some detail.

Definition and Purpose

A *biography* is a literary work describing the life–or part of the life–of an individual. When someone writes the story of his or her own life, we call the work an *autobiography*. In addition to giving us fascinating stories, biographies can inspire us with portraits of the indomitable human spirit or arouse us from complacency with portraits of human malice and insensitivity. Perhaps most of all, biographies are reminders of the common thread of humanity running through us all.

Early biographies written for children were, not surprisingly, didactic in nature. Charlotte Yonge's *Book of Golden Deeds of All Time* (1864) is one of the earliest examples and its title suggests its purpose. Children were given biographies of the saints and noble men and women who were intended to set good examples for them. Unfortunately, these early biographies tended to be very one-sided, portraying untouchable heroes or dastardly villains, with little aim toward creating real-life characters. Children's biography remained in this mode for many years. Edgar and Ingri Parin D'Aulaire, a husband-and-wife team, and James Daugherty were notable biographers for young readers from the 1930s through the 1970s. Their books are beautifully illustrated, but contain only noncontroversial material and straightforward facts. They are without bibliographies or indexes, which was typical of all children's information books of the day. But this absence of apparent research leaves the impression that the material in the books is not to be questioned, that there is just one story to be told.

In 1987, Russell Freedman's *Lincoln: A Photobiography* won the Newbery Medal and went a long way toward changing the perception and practice of biographical writing for children. Freedman's work is characterized by a lively writing style, accuracy, attention to detail, and boldness in confronting controversy. He also includes actual period photographs for a more authentic view of the era, and he provides both a list of resources and an index. These features have now become almost standard not only in biographies for children, but in all information books. They suggest a new respect for the young reader. The results have been an increasing number of information books of higher quality than ever before–information books that are not only more accurate, but more interesting to read and to look at. The entire genre has been elevated.

Types of Biography

Biography for children takes one of three forms: one, the *authentic biography*, values faithful adherence to facts; a second, the *fictionalized biography*, values dramatic narrative; and a third, *biographical fiction*, values a good story over hard facts. Each has its peculiar strengths and appeal.

AUTHENTIC BIOGRAPHY If a biography attempts to convey the factual information of a person's life and times faithfully, we call it an authentic biography. An authentic biography, such as Freedman's *Lincoln: A Photobiography,* uses only facts that can be supported by evidence. Consequently, if dialogue is used (which is not common in authentic biography) it has to be supported by historical documents (such as letters or diaries) or verifiable personal recollections. Although authentic biography attempts to be accurate in its use of facts, even the most thorough and honest biographer is not wholly objective or free from bias. By ignoring some facts and highlighting others, writers impose their own points of view on their subjects.

FICTIONALIZED BIOGRAPHY In writing for young people, some biographers have found it inviting to dramatize certain events—to make up lively dialogue or to invent dramatic scenes—presumably to make the story more interesting. These fictionalized biographies are often recognizable by their use of dialogue. That is, if we are reading a biography of Benjamin Franklin and find extended conversations between young Franklin and his brother or his parents, we can be fairly certain that the author has invented these discussions because it is unlikely that such details are recorded in any surviving records. A sound fictionalized biography, however, will not tamper with the basic facts of history. Jean Lee Latham's *Carry on, Mr. Bowditch* is an example of fictionalized biography. Most of this book consists of dramatized scenes depicting events that occurred in the late eighteenth century—scenes with dialogue obviously invented by the writer. Naturally, it cannot be regarded with the same reliability as authentic biography, but fictionalized biography makes good leisure reading and can stimulate a reader's curiosity to pursue the facts.

BIOGRAPHICAL FICTION In biographical fiction, an author builds a story around a character's life, altering facts to suit the narrative needs. In other words, the story becomes more important than the truth. The result does not even have to be realistic, as evidenced by Robert Lawson's several fantasy biographies—of the pirate Captain Kidd (*Captain Kidd's Cat*), of Christopher Columbus (*I Discover Columbus*), of Benjamin Franklin (*Ben and Me*)—all told by animals who knew them. They are great fun, but they are not history.

A more serious work of biographical fiction is E. L. Konigsberg's *A Proud Taste for Scarlet and Miniver,* a life of the great medieval English queen Eleanor of Aquitaine. Eleanor's story is related by some of the principal figures in her life, a churchman, a nobleman, and her mother-in-law, all from their point of view in heaven. The story is both entertaining and historically quite accurate—an example of the often hazy division between the genres of fiction and nonfiction.

COMPLETE, PARTIAL, AND COLLECTIVE BIOGRAPHIES In addition to these differences in approach, biographies differ in the degree of biographical coverage. A *complete biography* covers a subject's entire life, from cradle to grave. A complete biography may be simple—such as Aliki's charming picture-book biographies (*The Story of Johnny Appleseed,* for example)–or it may be more extensive as in the Freedman's *Lincoln: A Photobiography*. A *partial biography* covers only one phase of the subject's life and allows the author to focus more clearly on a specific theme or issue. For instance, Johanna Johnston's fictionalized biography of Harriet Beecher Stowe, *Harriet and the Runaway Book*, focuses chiefly on Mrs. Stowe's writing of *Uncle Tom's Cabin*. Younger children have difficulty identifying with the activities and accomplishments of adult life, and they enjoy partial biographies concentrating on the childhoods of famous people. One example is Max Bolliger's *David*, which explores the youth of King David up until he became King of Israel. Of course, each of these types can be either authentic or fictionalized.

A *collective biography* provides a view into the lives of several people who are linked by a common thread: scientists, First Ladies, sports figures, musicians, and so on. Collective biographies may take two general forms. Most commonly, brief biographical sketches are provided for each individual included, forming a collection of short biographies. Henrietta Buckmaster's *Women Who Shaped History* deals with such influential women as Dorothea Dix, Harriet Tubman, and Mary Baker Eddy. One of the most famous of all collective biographies is President John F. Kennedy's best-selling *Profiles in Courage,* which has been edited for younger audiences. The collective biography emphasizes the theme of an individual's life and work, and it further allows readers to place that theme in a larger perspective. Another type of collective biography examines the lives of people who were themselves closely associated, such as Jane Goodsell's *The Mayo Brothers,* about the famous physicians who founded the clinic that bears their name, or Mike Venezia's *Beatles,* about the legendary rock group.

Autobiography

Autobiography has some special characteristics that set it apart from biography. Obviously, autobiographies are not complete lives–since they are written in the midst of one's life. Often, an autobiographer will write about only one part of his or her life, childhood and adolescence, for example, or early adult years, or specific career experiences. Autobiography is usually more informal than biography, sometimes appearing in the form of memoirs or reminiscences. Individuals often feel they have no need to research their own lives and therefore rely on their memories to supply them with information. Consequently, specific dates are frequently missing from autobiographies, and seldom do we find any documentation. After all, the authors undoubtedly think, who should know their lives better than they themselves?

However, we must be wary of what someone says in an autobiography, for it is difficult to find a more potentially biased source on an individual's life than the individual himself or herself. This does not mean that the autobiographers always put themselves in the best light. Henry Adams' famous autobiography for adult readers, *The Education of Henry Adams,* is remarkably self-effacing and modest. He dwells so much on his failures and disappointments that readers would hardly guess that the writer was a highly respected teacher, scholar, and public servant.

Even though autobiographies are often not particularly reliable sources of facts about people, they can be indispensable sources for discovering an individual's character traits, likes and dislikes, innermost feelings—these things are not easily hidden. The unique personal perspective of the autobiography can tell us things about a person we will find no place else. It also has the advantage—if it is well written—of immediacy, of making us feel as if we are right there with the subject, sharing his or her life experiences.

Not surprising, few autobiographies are written especially for children, since individuals who feel their lives are worth recording usually prefer to write for adult readers. In recent years, however, we have seen more and more autobiographies for young readers. The series of autobiographical picture books about famous children's illustrators, including *Self-Portrait: Margot Zemach* and *Self-Portrait: Eric Blegvad*, provides an interesting variation on the autobiography whereby artists not only tell their own life stories, they illustrate them as well. We can also find some good, brief autobiographies for children by their favorite authors, including Betsy Byars's *The Moon and I*, Phyllis Reynolds Naylor's *How I Came to Be a Writer*, and Roald Dahl's *Boy: Tales of Childhood*. Aside from providing positive role models and uplifting examples, autobiographies are excellent sources for encouraging children to think about their own life experiences and to record those experiences in a diary or journal. Both biography and autobiography can inspire us all to examine our own lives and bring us to a deeper understanding of ourselves.

Information Books

Definition and Purpose

Since Comenius's *Orbis Pictus* in the seventeenth century, information books have been a staple in children's reading. Information or nonfiction books were initially for instruction, but the best authors have always known that factual information can also be entertaining. Information writing is important for children because they are so receptive to new ideas, so eager to learn. This need can be early met with concept books (see Chapter 6). But soon they are ready for meatier fare.

Types of Information Books

For the sake of convenience, we will divide information books into four, admittedly sweeping, categories: History and Culture; Science and Nature; Humanities, Arts, and Leisure; and Human Development and Behavior.

HISTORY AND CULTURE This is a very large category, but most of the books fit into one of the following subcategories: history, geography, social and cultural studies, or religion.

Consider how many of the world's problems have resulted from our failure to understand and empathize with the other people who share this planet. We only dimly understand our own culture, let alone the cultures of distant foreign peoples. Being introduced to other cultures, other civilizations, we not only learn about them, we also learn more about ourselves. Additionally, tolerance is often a happy by-product of this knowledge. Bigotry and hatred are usually the results of ignorance. Any book that makes young readers aware of the world and the people around them may contribute positively to global understanding.

As we have seen in the preceding chapters, we can learn a great deal about people and places through well-written realistic fiction or through the traditional folktales. However, along with these fictional works, children must necessarily read factual accounts to gain a fuller understanding of and appreciation for a culture. The recent popular trend of using true-to-life stories as the bases for both books and films (the so-called docudramas) suggests that nonfiction works possess tremendous appeal for audiences of all ages.

Children as early as first and second grade can be drawn into historical subjects, and Aliki has been among the most consistently successful in bringing stories of history and world cultures to children in the lower grades. One of the secrets to Aliki's success in this area is that she recognizes the natural curiosity children have about virtually everything. Particularly interesting is her *Mummies Made in Egypt,* which describes in words and pictures the lengthy and complicated process by which the ancient Egyptians embalmed their dead. The colorful illustrations help capture the feeling of early Egyptian civilization, and the minute details will satisfy even the most curious.

Of course, books about history, geography, and cultures figure even more prominently in reading for children in the middle elementary years. These books are characterized by fuller texts and are illustrated books rather than picture books. Leonard Everett Fisher (see Figure 12.1) has created two outstanding series of first-rate informational books—one on colonial American crafts (*The Schoolmasters, The Tanners,* and others) and one on nineteenth-century American commerce and industry (*The Factories, The Railroads,* and others). Fisher gives us a clear text and powerful illustrations, two of the most important features in any informational book for young readers.

Until recently, writers of children's nonfiction tended to sugarcoat the past or to omit the unsavory elements. This sanitizing process gave young readers an inaccurate view of history, an uncritical approach to life, and unrealistic expectations for the future. Today, the best writers prefer to depict the past faithfully, including the controversies and the unpleasantries. Indeed, children are better equipped to handle the truth than most adults give them credit for. Milton Meltzer is one writer who has been committed to portraying the past accurately for his young audience, and he has tackled some difficult facets of American history. His books include *In Their Own Words: A History of the American Negro; Brother Can You Spare a Dime? The Great Depression: 1929–1933;* and *Bread and Roses: The Struggle of American Labor, 1865–1915.* Meltzer's works are distinguished by their thorough scholarship. He treats his young readers with great respect, and never condescends to them; he includes bibliographies and indexes; and he prefers to use period photographs to illustrate his works (a feature that gives them a great deal of authenticity).

Russell Freedman (whose noteworthy biographies were mentioned above) has written such historical works as *Cowboys of the Wild West,* presenting a fascinating history that

George Washington opens the Philadelphia Convention

FIGURE 12.1 Leonard Everett Fisher's dramatic scratchboard illustration of George Washington opening the Constitutional Convention. Washington is depicted as a commanding figure, towering over everything and everyone else. The large window helps to frame the illustration, but also is a source of light, and thus symbolic of the bold new venture about to begin.

Source: From Richard B. Morris's *The First Book of the Constitution* (New York: Franklin Watts, Inc., 1958).

corrects some of our misconceptions about cowboys. Through his use of photographs and an exciting writing style, Freedman suggests that the reality was even more interesting than the myth—as so often turns out to be the case. Jim Murphy has written equally compelling studies of some rather specific aspects of American history, such as the infamous nineteenth-century emigrant trains in *Across America on an Emigrant Train,* the whaling industry in *Gone A-Whaling: The Lure of the Sea and the Hunt for the Great Whale,* and the story of the Chicago fire in *The Great Fire.* Murphy's books all include thorough bibliographies, indexes, and period photographs. Modern social concerns are documented in Brent Ashabranner's *Children of the Maya,* a photo essay about Central American natives attempting to rebuild their lives in Florida after escaping from persecution in their homeland. Books such as Walter Dean Myers's *Now Is Your Time!: The African-American Struggle for Freedom* seek to address the inadequacy that has plagued us so long in books about African Americans and their contribution to American society.

Religion is a sensitive area for many people, and writers on religious subjects are wise to be mindful of religion's delicate nature. Nevertheless, if approached purely from an informational point of view, books on religion can help children learn about their own heritage as well as about religions and cultures around the world. Some of the most serious problems we face today result from religious differences and people's failure to understand or to respect the beliefs of others. All children can benefit from books such as Howard Greenfield's *Passover* and *Rosh Hashanah and Yom Kippur* or Karla Kuskin's *Jerusalem, Shining Still,* all about Judaism. Anton Powell's *The Rise of Islam* describes the earlier history of that important world religion. And Elizabeth Seeger's *Eastern Religions* explores the religious faiths of Asia. In an age when religion is still capable of firing passions to violence, the more knowledge we have of other faiths, the more likely we are to learn tolerance for them.

SCIENCE AND NATURE Books about science and nature include the following topics: animals and plants; the earth, the environment, and the weather; technology; and astronomy and mathematics.

As might be expected, information books about animals are among the most popular of the science books, particularly with younger readers. We are told that the most frequently consulted entry in a young people's encyclopedia is "*dogs.*" Children from the very youngest find almost any book about animals appealing. In recent years a number of very good books have appeared on unusual or threatened animal species, including the puffin, the panda, the bald eagle, and some obscure species, such as the hoiho in Adele Vernon's *The Hoiho: New Zealand's Yellow-Eyed Penguin.* Catherine Paladino's *Our Vanishing Farm Animals* describes several breeds of American farm animals close to extinction. The best animal books describe the animals' appearance, life cycles, and habits, and some also show us the animals' importance in the larger frame of creation.

The plant world can be equally fascinating to younger children, as demonstrated in such books as Carol Gibbons's *From Seed to Plant* and Ruth Heller's *The Reason for a Flower.* Both books illustrate one of nature's most elemental tales, the growth of a plant from a tiny seed, and they invite hands-on experiences. Plants, of course, are not naturally cuddly, nor do they have expressive personalities (except possibly for the Venus's flytrap). A writer must therefore make the subject appealing, perhaps by showing its importance to us and our ecosystem. It is not only the animal world that is threatened with extinction, and we are beginning to see books alerting young children to the potential disappearance of our plant life as well. Barbara Taylor's series, including *Coral Life, Desert Life, Pond Life,* and *Rain Forests,* introduces the very young to the concept of the ecosystem—plants and animals working together to maintain the balance of nature and ensure the survival of the planet.

Laurence Pringle's *Living in a Risky World* encourages young readers to think about modern civilization and the implications of our lifestyle, particularly the effects of pollutants (acid rain, carcinogens, and other environmental hazards). A book such as this demonstrates that science is not divorced from our everyday world or from the complicated ethical issues that face humanity. Pringle's work pointedly examines the ethics of science and technology in the modern world—the title suggests both the substance and the theme. As we face the ethical dilemma of humanity's responsibility to the earth and as pollution, overpopulation, and reckless development take their toll, children need to learn about the delicate ecosystem in which we all must live out our lives.

Books about the earth sciences include such works as Joanna Cole's *The Magic School Bus: Inside the Earth,* mentioned earlier, and Seymour Simon's *Earthquake,* which provides not only elementary scientific information on the description and cause of earthquakes but also practical information, such as what to do in the event of one. Franklyn Branley's *Light and Darkness* and Claire Llewellyn's *My First Book of Time* both focus on physics at a fundamental level. Probably the most popular of these types of books are those not about earth at all, but about outer space. Astronaut Sally Ride in *To Space and Back* (coauthored with Susan Okie) describes her experiences on the space shuttle flight, and this book serves the dual purpose of presenting fascinating, up-to-date information and dispelling feminine stereotyping in career choices.

The abstract science of physics can best be brought home to young readers through a discussion of technology. David Macaulay's near monumental *The Way Things Work* (originally published in 1988 but expanded and updated in 1998 in *The New Way Things Work*) explores all the realms of the earth sciences—mechanics, physics (even nuclear physics), electronics, and chemistry. With amazing clarity and simplicity and with the help of hundreds of clever drawings, Macaulay explains a phenomenal number of complex ideas and processes. This book has enormous appeal for adults as well as young people.

Even abstract mathematical subjects have been successfully presented in children's books, such as Mitsumasa Anno's imaginatively illustrated *Anno's Math Games* in two volumes and Jane Jonas Srivastava's *Statistics,* an introduction for middle elementary school children. Given the highly publicized math deficiency of most American children, this is a field ripe for imaginative writers and illustrators.

Sometimes a science book skirts the boundaries between science and art. Jim Arnosky's *Secrets of a Wildlife Watcher* is a firsthand account of ways to locate and observe animals in the wild. This work is also an example of how science writing can be brought to a practical level.

HUMANITIES, ARTS, AND LEISURE This category includes a wide variety of books covering everything from cooking to watching movies to playing football. These works may be roughly categorized into four broad subject areas:

1. Performing arts (music, dance, theater)
2. Graphic arts (drawing, painting, photography)
3. Plastic arts (sculpture, architecture)
4. Sports and entertainment

Unfortunately, modern society has typically regarded these activities as luxuries or pastimes. When school budgets are cut, art programs are often the first to go. But art feeds the soul as well as the mind and is an indispensable part of a child's education. As with anything else, most people find art more meaningful when they can participate in it—perform the music or the dance, act in the play, paint the picture, form the sculpture. But books can expand experiences, pique curiosity, and develop taste. Historical surveys of the various art forms provide useful perspectives—it is always important to know what has gone before us. Marc Aronson's *Art Attack: A Short Cultural History of the Avant-Garde*, for example, describes a specific modern movement in art. Some books instruct on various aspects of the art, such as Cheryl Walsh Bellville's *Theater Magic: Behind the Scenes at a Children's Theater*. And some books actually teach the techniques of the art form, such as Miriam Cooper's *Snap! Photography*.

Author/illustrator David Macaulay has made a career of bringing the complex world of architecture to young readers. His picture books describe the building of some of the world's great monuments, from the Egyptian pyramids (*Pyramid*) to medieval castles and cathedrals (*Castle* and *Cathedral*) to modern skyscrapers (*Unbuilding*). In addition to their attention to technical detail, his books also convey information about human society, including lifestyles and cultural beliefs. His book *Mosque* attempts to bridge the gap that has long existed between the Judeo-Christian and Muslim cultures, and provides the kind of understanding needed to help mend the wounds of generations of misunderstanding.

Leisure activities and sports consume a great deal of a child's time, and many books have been written to introduce and explain the history, techniques, and importance of these subjects. For example, ice skating, as described in Jonah and Laura Kalb's *The Easy Ice Skating Book*, has developed into a highly refined performing art. One sport in particular has long captured the imagination of writers, and that is fishing. Jim Arnosky's *Fish in a Flash?: A Personal Guide to Spin-Fishing* is just one of the more recent in a long line of books for fishing enthusiasts, reaching back to Renaissance England. Combining sports and the art of writing is William Jaspersohn's *Magazine: Behind the Scenes at* Sports Illustrated. This photo essay may have an immediate appeal to sports buffs, but its focus is actually on the writing, editing, illustrating, and printing of a magazine. Of course, young readers can also turn to the growing number of biographies of athletes, musicians, artists, writers, and others.

HUMAN DEVELOPMENT AND BEHAVIOR   Books about human development and behavior are the most recent addition to informational writing for children. They include the following types:

1. Sexual growth and development
2. Death and dying
3. Family relationships
4. Friendship and human interaction
5. Physical and emotional challenges

These issues are treated frequently in picture storybooks (Martha Alexander's *Nobody Asked Me If I Wanted a Baby Sister* and Judith Viorst's book about the death of a pet, *The Tenth Good Thing About Barney,* are two good examples) and in problem novels (see Chapter 11). However, these works are still fiction and cannot technically be considered *information* books, the primary purpose of which is to impart facts; however, fiction is probably the most effective way of conveying complex psychological concepts to young readers. But for older readers, stories of human behavior have a great impact if they are factual.

Nonfiction works in this area tend to be documentary. In Jill Krementz's . . . *How It Feels When Parents Divorce,* children of divorced parents share their emotional responses to this childhood trauma. Appropriately, the book is illustrated with photographs, intensifying the reality of the subject. Eda Le Shan's *What Makes Me Feel This Way?* is written for upper elementary-aged children and deals with personal emotions. Physical disabilities are too frequently ignored in books for children, and Ron Roy's *Move Over, Wheelchairs Coming Through!* helps to fill a significant gap. Subtitled *Several Young People in Wheelchairs Talk About Their Lives,* the book treats the subject with both frankness and sensitivity.

Self-help books, long popular among adults, are now making their way into children's literature. These works, with their obvious titles, such as Laurie Krasny and Marc Brown's *How to Be a Friend: A Guide to Making Friends and Keeping Them,* are clearly designed as instructional books on the art of living. As mentioned in Chapter 5, there is virtually no limit to the sort of psychological or sociological problems that children's literature might discuss. An important example is Susan Terkel and Janice Rench's *Feeling Safe, Feeling Strong: How to Avoid Sexual Abuse and What to Do If It Happens to You.* Our society's penchant for therapy has at last spilled over into the realm of children's books, and although we may regret the need for such books for children, we should be glad that capable and sensitive writers have taken up the cause.

An increasing number of books on sexuality and bodily functions have raised much controversy. Robert Harris's *It's Perfectly Normal,* with Michael Emberley's bold cartoon drawings depicting aspects of puberty and sex, earned both awards and censorship. (See Chapter 6 for other examples of such books for the very young, including Taro Gomi's *Everyone Poops.*)

Another example of this more open approach to sexuality is Babette Cole's *Mommy*

Laid an Egg! Or, Where Do Babies Come From? This humorous, boldly accurate, picture-book account for children in the primary grades even includes cartoon drawings of sexual intercourse. At first, many adults are reluctant (or embarrassed) to share such details with young children, and it is surely unnecessary information for preschoolers. However, children in the primary grades do raise questions about these matters, and it is better for them to learn the facts from sensitive, intelligently written books aimed at their reading level than from ill-informed friends on the playground. Our not telling children about these things will not keep them from finding out. Usually, the best protection anyone can have is accurate information.

THE CHARACTERISTICS OF GOOD INFORMATION WRITING

A good biography or information book includes at least five features: (1) a clear purpose and identifiable audience, (2) authenticity and accuracy, (3) balance and objectivity, (4) an accessible and polished style, and (5) a clear and appropriate format and organization. (See Figures 12.2 and 12.3.)

Purpose and Audience

It is important to take into account the author's stated or implied purpose for writing a book. Why did the author choose this particular subject? Or, to put it another way, what is so important about this individual or this subject that we should consider reading a whole book? Part and parcel of the purpose is the author's intended audience. Aliki's *The King's Day* is a story of Louis XIV of France, but it is for very young readers. Consequently, Aliki concentrates on a typical single day in the king's life, showing us the customs, manners, and day-to-day details. Accompanying the simple text are richly detailed and colorful pictures—certainly appropriate to the portrayal of the glamorous life in the palace of Versailles. Naturally, information books for older readers are more complex, usually divided into chapters, and they assume the reader comes with some background knowledge. An author cannot always be faulted for the readers' inadequacies. Consequently, an adolescent reader who has never read a book on astronomy may be wise to look at the works of Seymour Simon or Franklyn Branley before tackling something more sophisticated. Even adults can learn a great deal of useful information from a good children's book.

Authenticity and Accuracy

Since biographies and information books presumably present the truth, authenticity and accuracy are crucial. For example, in a good biography we can feel what it was like to live during the subject's lifetime. A good biographer makes us savor the period. The good biographer gives us background information about the subject and explores the subject's influences,

FIGURE 12.2   What Makes a Good Biography?

1. The material is suitably adapted for the intended audience's age level.

2. The writer gives a fair and balanced presentation of the subject's life, including both character strengths and weaknesses.

3. The necessary background information about the society and times in which the subject lived is provided in an interesting fashion.

4. The biography includes illustrations that add to the information and are appropriate to the overall tone of the work; the illustrations have artistic merit or historical significance.

5. The writer uses specific details to support general claims about the subject and to add interest to the work.

6. The organization, usually chronological, is easy to follow and traces the subject's development.

7. The writer maintains a consistency of approach throughout the work, whether it is authentic biography, fictionalized biography, or biographical fiction; the forms are not mixed.

8. Dialogue, if it is used, conveys some of the flavor of the period (and, of course, in authentic biography, dialogue is not used unless the words can be corroborated in historical records).

9. The writing style is clear, direct, and appropriate for the audience.

10. If the work is for older readers, suitable supplemental materials, such as a table of contents, glossary, bibliography, and index, are included.

motives, successes, failures, and legacy. Jean Fritz's biographies for upper-elementary children provide in a few words the kind of detail that gives us the flavor of the time. Take this passage from Fritz's *And Then What Happened, Paul Revere?*:

> To make extra money, [Paul Revere] took a job ringing the bells in Christ Church. In Boston, church bells were rung not just on Sundays but three times a day on weekdays, at special hours on holidays and anniversaries, for fires and emergencies, whenever a member of the congregation died, and whenever there was especially good news or especially bad news to announce. Sometimes at a moment's notice word would come that the bells were to be rung, and off Paul would run, his hat clapped to his head, his coattails flying. (10)

Thus, Fritz describes a long-lost custom as she builds the character of Paul Revere.

Accuracy is important, particularly in science books. However, as Millicent Selsam, a noted science writer for children, said, "a good science book is not just a collection of facts"

FIGURE 12.3   What Makes a Good Information Book?

1. The material is suitably adapted for the intended audience's age level.

2. All terms are clearly defined.

3. Specific details are used to illustrate the most important points.

4. The details are accurate and up to date.

5. The details are organized in a logical and easy-to-follow pattern: in the case of ideas, from simple to complex; in the case of processes, from start to finish.

6. The illustrations are clear and help to explain the subject; the illustrations have artistic merit (or historical significance).

7. When appropriate, the writer provides all sides or points of view of an issue.

8. The writing style is clear, direct, and appropriate for the audience.

9. If the work is for older readers, suitable supplemental materials, such as a table of contents, maps, charts, glossary, bibliography, and index, are included.

---

(62). A good science book conveys, in Selsam's words, "something of the beauty and excitement of science" (65). Science books for children deal with many subjects, including animals and plants, the earth and our environment, the weather, astronomy, mathematics, and technology. The challenge of the science book writer is to explain complex and factual material in an accurate, but easy-to-understand and engaging, way.

Accuracy is a complicated issue. If a book is nothing but accurate facts, it is likely to be dull—which is the greatest sin in writing. In children's science books, accuracy is, of course, crucial, and we should avoid books with blatant factual errors in them. But because the child's science book is necessarily simplified—which means something has been left out or it has been expressed in metaphorical or less subtle terms to make it more understandable to the child reader—thorough accuracy is not always achievable. Sometimes, oversimplification leads to inaccuracy. Simplified drawings of plant or animal life can be misleading—they never seem to look quite like the real thing.

As important as accuracy is clarity of expression. It does not matter how accurate the text is if we cannot understand what it's saying. Terms need to be identified in a language young readers can grasp. Here is where the language of metaphor comes in handy. When Selsam describes the white spots on a baby deer's coat as looking "like spots of sunlight on the forest floor" (*Hidden Animals*), she is making a comparison to help us visualize the subject. Clarity can also be achieved through the use of charts, diagrams, and figures—although, of course, they themselves must be clearly presented. All children's science books contain illustrations—usually drawings or photographs—but these should be more than mere decoration. The illustrations ought to help us understand the concepts. Sometimes this can be done humorously, as in Joanna Cole's Magic School Bus series, about a classroom of children who go on fantastic adventures with their science teacher (into the core of the earth, into outer space, and so on). The science-book illustrator has to be careful not to trivialize or sentimentalize the subject, which may be why so many turn to photographs or serious drawings and paintings. It is important that the illustrations contain captions so we know exactly what we are looking at and what we are supposed to see.

Sophie Webb has written a fascinating personal account, *My Season with Penguins: An Antarctic Journal,* which shows us another important feature of the science book—the human dimension. Science books about scientists and how they discover knowledge are excellent introductions for young readers. Science is a process of discovery; it is not an end unto itself. Sharing the stories of dedicated scientists in pursuit of knowledge—people actually getting their hands dirty in the field, meeting with discouragement but pressing forward—can be inspiring. Danielle Ford, a scientist and writer, sums it up, "A good book models for children the nature of scientific thinking, provides opportunities for them to engage in this thinking while reading the book, and uses text, images, and graphics to best convey scientific information" (271). But, she goes on to say that the most important element in a good science book is that it is filled "with passion for science and nature, and invites readers to engage with, imagine, and experience science in ways they may never have thought of before" (271).

Balance and Objectivity

As suggested above, good biographies and information books are as free as possible from bias and present a balanced view of their subjects. When it comes to biographies, few people are saints or sinners; rather, they land somewhere in between. They make errors in judgment, they possess personality flaws, peculiar habits, and eccentric ideas. When these are included in biographies, we usually do not think less of the subjects, but we develop a greater sympathy and understanding for them. This does not mean that we want our heroes debunked—a fault that is found often in popular biographies for adults (which focus on the perversions, sexual escapades, and criminal activities of public officials, sports heroes, movie stars, and so on). Young people want heroes or heroines to believe in. But to portray them as godlike figures without fault is to do an injustice to them and to set impossible standards for the rest of us to emulate. Abraham Lincoln, for instance, was self-conscious about his appearance. Russell Freedman tells us in *Lincoln: A Photobiography* that once "[w]hen a rival called him 'two-faced' during a political debate, Lincoln replied: 'I leave it to my audience. If I had another face, do you think I'd wear this one?'" (1). What sets heroes apart from everyone else is not that they have no weaknesses, but that they triumph despite their weaknesses.

One critic remarks: "Children's biography does not always present the whole truth about a subject. If a life contains tragic or unsavory aspects, these are generally omitted" (Gottlieb 174). There is disagreement over this issue: some feel that children may not have the emotional and intellectual capacity to handle certain themes, and others believe that the implied dishonesty in omitting these elements is a worse offense. Most biographers of

Benjamin Franklin, for example, do not make a point of mentioning that his son was illegitimate, but Jean Fritz, in her biography *What's the Big Idea, Ben Franklin?*, explains in an endnote that we do not know who the son's mother was, a bold admission in a book for elementary children. Fritz's solution seems reasonable, combining honesty with discretion. A good biography generally aims to reveal the real person, without either debunking or deifying.

To be objective is to consider all sides. The wise author weighs all the available evidence, including conflicting viewpoints, and draws conclusions based on that evidence. Jim Murphy's account of the Chicago fire, *The Great Fire*, is a good example of a book that provides a variety of viewpoints, including firsthand reports. Additionally, Murphy carefully examines the various problems the city faced in fighting the fire—human error, inefficient organization of the firefighters, and so on—problems that prevented a successful response. Murphy's book shows us that a historical account can be balanced and faithful to the facts as well as exciting to read. The old saying has it that truth is stranger than fiction, and if that is true the writer of nonfiction should not have to embellish the facts.

One final issue regarding balance and objectivity relates to changing social and political attitudes. Information books, as we have noted, can become quickly dated—science books become outdated when new discoveries and theories supersede the old; books about history, art, and human behavior become outdated as new material is uncovered and as our attitudes change, causing us to reinterpret the facts. A survey of books on Christopher Columbus will reveal a marked change in society's attitude. Early books (such as Ingri and Edgar Parin d'Aulaire's *Columbus*, 1955) depict Columbus in an unabashedly heroic light, whereas more recent studies (notably David Adler's *Christopher Columbus, Great Explorer*, 1991, and Milton Meltzer's *Christopher Columbus and the World Around Him*, 1990) reveal Columbus's mercenary side as well as his heinous treatment of the native American population. History itself may not change, but what we know about it does, as does how we view it.

Style and Tone

A lively writing style can make any topic interesting. Take biography, for example. It is possible to find a very dull book on a very interesting person. The biographer's task is to present the subject in an interesting manner by choosing the right facts and expressing them in an engaging way. In the good biography, for instance, necessary background material (which can be tedious) is carefully woven into the narrative—young people generally prefer action and dialogue to lengthy description. Dialogue, when it is used, is believable and authentic to the period. Eighteenth-century farm boys are not to sound like twenty-first-century urbanites.

In his brief biography for younger readers, *Mark Twain? What Kind of Name Is That?*, Robert Quackenbush opens with a folksy, light-hearted tone that seems quite appropriate when writing about America's favorite humorist:

> Samuel Langhorne Clemens—river pilot, gold miner, frontier reporter, humorist, and this nation's best-loved author—claimed that two important events took place

on November 30, 1835. One was the appearance in the night sky of Halley's Comet—an event that comes only once every seventy-five years—and the other was his birth in Florida, Missouri. Sam loved telling jokes and playing tricks. He claimed that he couldn't remember what his first lie was, but he told his second lie when he was only nine days old. He had pretended that a diaper pin was sticking him, and he'd hollered as loud as he could. This brought him extra loving attention—until his trickery was found out, that is. Sam's mother thought he might get hit by a bolt of lightning one day, on account of all the mischief he caused as he was growing up in Hannibal, Missouri, with his older brother Orion, his older sister Pamela, his younger brother Henry, and nineteen cats. (9)

Yes, much is omitted about young Sam Clemens' childhood, but in this short paragraph we learn several facts, we get a good idea of his character, and most of us would be anxious to read further. It is just what we want from an information book.

Jim Arnosky, in *Watching Desert Wildlife*, shares with the reader his detailed observations about birds, snakes, lizards, deer, and other desert wildlife. At the conclusion of his work, he is able to beautifully sum up his experience and its meaning:

I went to the desert to feel the heat of the desert sun and breathe the dry air. I went to the desert to see its wide open places. I went with my eyes open wide, watchful for snakes and scorpions, and alert, ready to see all the wonderful wild animals who make their homes amid the thorns and spines.

I came home from the desert with a fresh new outlook on nature and wildlife. I felt bigger and broader, happy in the knowledge that I had discovered another world. (n. pag.)

The good writer of information books is often something of a poet—sharing in beautiful words the wondrous things of life.

Perhaps the first virtue of any information book is clarity of style—without this, the book is a failure. But an information book, not only through its choice of facts, but through its choice of words (diction) and sentence structure (syntax), can be stimulating reading. A good writer will suit both diction and syntax to the intended audience's age level. (Remember that boredom results from the material or the style being either too simple or too difficult for the reader.)

Where it is appropriate, humor can add enjoyment to information books, so long as it neither mocks nor obscures an issue. And humor can help to make the material less intimidating. Appropriate similes and metaphors not only make interesting reading, they can also clarify complicated or unfamiliar ideas. David Macaulay's *The Way Things Work* treats some extremely complicated concepts, but he ties the entire work together by using cartoon figures of woolly mammoths to demonstrate the various properties and scientific principles involved. For example, the mammoths are used to represent "force" or "effort." (The cartoon figures, incidentally, do not trivialize the subject matter in this case; instead they clarify complex ideas–such as jet propulsion and the operation of computers.) In this way, Macaulay makes use of metaphor to illustrate an abstract concept and of humor to make his explanations understandable and enjoyable, and the ideas approachable. The comical cartoons in Joanna Cole's Magic School Bus books depict wisecracking students at the mercy of their eccentric teacher, Ms. Frizzle. Humor is a tool that helps many people learn material more quickly and remember it more easily, and it is difficult to understand why it appears so seldom in biography and information books.

Format and Organization

A book that is well laid out can go a long way toward making the information less intimidating for young readers. Readers (young and old) prefer books that are easy to follow, but a book does not have to be simplistic to be accessible. We look for clear and logical organization: in biographies or histories, the organization is usually chronological; in science or art books, the information is usually presented from simplest to most complex. Organizational aids, such as headings and subheadings, and supplementary aids, such as a table of contents, a glossary, an index, and a bibliography, are especially desirable in more complex books for older children.

Sometimes, a topic requires a great deal of ingenuity in order to make it understandable for the reader. Science writer Terence Dickinson describes the immense size of the solar system with an extended metaphor:

> A model of the solar system gives an idea of its size and the sizes of its various members. Let's use a major-league baseball stadium located in the centre of a large city for the model. The sun, the size of a baseball, rests on home plate. Mercury, Venus, Earth and Mars, each about the dimensions of the ball in a ball-point pen, are, respectively, $\frac{1}{8}$, $\frac{1}{5}$, $\frac{1}{3}$ and $\frac{1}{2}$ of the way to the pitcher's mound. A pea near second base is Jupiter. In shallow centre field is a smaller pea, Saturn. Uranus, the size of this letter O, is at the fence off in deep centre field. Neptune and Pluto, a letter O and a grain of salt in our model, are just outside the park. (*Exploring the Night Sky* 26)

Perhaps even more dramatic is Dickinson's explanation that, continuing with the baseball field metaphor, the nearest star to our solar system "would be a baseball in another city more than 1,000 miles away" (26). The use of this metaphoric language is far more powerful than merely rattling off numbers that readers could not begin to imagine.

Illustrations juxtaposed with the text they are illustrating make the most sense. In many informational books, the illustrations are accompanied by captions–brief textual remarks that explain the illustration, clarify its purpose, or identify specific points we should be noting in the illustration. The best illustrations both increase our knowledge and provide aesthetic pleasure. As has been pointed out, photographs are frequently used to illustrate information books, and photographs give the works a keen sense of authenticity and, of course, accuracy.

In information picture books for younger readers, particularly, we can find some very stunning artwork, such as that in David Macaulay's work (*Castle, Cathedral,* and others) and Peter Sis's *Starry Messenger: Galileo Galilei,* a richly illustrated life of the great astronomer and his times with artwork that is at times whimsical, at times surreal, and always wonderfully evocative of the Italian Renaissance. The illustrations in the best information books are inspired by the subject and therefore suited to it. They neither trivialize nor sentimentalize the subject, but present it imaginatively and with respect for the child audience.

The Importance of Biography and Information Books

Finally, the good biography or information book not only reveals to us the facts about the subject, but it also contributes to our broader and deeper understanding of life in general. In other words, when we are finished reading a nonfiction work we should feel that we know more not only about the subject itself, but also about people or perhaps about the nature of the universe. Just as in novels, the best of biographies and information books are unified by a significant theme. The theme or the writer's point of view, for example, may shed new light on what the author sees as old misunderstandings or provide direction for the future. The point is that a well-constructed nonfiction work is not simply a loose collection of facts (something like a *Guinness Book of Records*—interesting to read in bits and pieces, but hardly a gripping story). The best nonfiction is built on profound themes that speak to the strength and resilience of the human spirit and to the unending wonder of the universe.

Works Cited

Arnosky, Jim. *Watching Desert Wildlife*. Washington, DC: National Geographic Society, 1998.

Dickinson, Terence. *Exploring the Night Sky*. Willowdale, Ontario: Firefly, 1987.

Ford, Danielle. "More than the Facts: Reviewing Science Books." *The Horn Book Magazine* 78, 3 (May/June 2002): 265–71.

Freedman, Russell. *Lincoln: A Photobiography*. New York: Clarion, 1987.

Fritz, Jean. *And Then What Happened, Paul Revere?* New York: Coward, McCann & Geoghegan, 1973.

Gottleib, Robin. "On Nonfiction Books for Children: Tradition & Dissent." *Wilson Library Journal* October 1974: 174–177.

Kendall, Paul Murray. *The Art of Biography*. 1965. New York: Norton, 1985.

Quackenbush, Robert. *Mark Twain? What Kind of Name Is That?: A Story of Samuel Langhorne Clemens*. New York: Simon and Schuster, 1984.

Selsam, Millicent E. "Writing About Science for Children." In *Beyond Fact: Nonfiction for Children and Young People*. Ed. Jo Carr. Chicago: American Library Association, 1982: 61–65.

RECOMMENDED READINGS

Aiken, Joan. "Interpreting the Past." *Children's Literature in Education* 16 (Summer 1985): 67–83.

Bacon, Betty. "The Art of Nonfiction." *Children's Literature in Education* 14 (Spring 1981): 3–14.

Berry, Thomas Elliott, ed. *The Biographer's Craft.* New York: Odyssey, 1967.

Blenz-Clucas, Beth. "History's Forgotten Heroes: Women on the Frontier." *School Library Journal* 39 (March 1993): 118–123.

Blos, Joan. "The Overstuffed Sentence and Other Means for Assessing Historical Fiction for Children." *School Library Journal* 31 (November 1985): 38–39.

Bowen, Catherine Drinker. *Biography: The Craft and the Calling.* Boston: Little, Brown, 1968.

Burton, Hester. "The Writing of Historical Novels." In *Children and Literature: Views and Reviews.* Ed. Virginia Haviland. Glenview, IL: Scott, Foresman, 1973: 299–304.

Carr, Jo. "What Do We Do About Bad Biographies?" In *Beyond Fact.* Ed. Jo Carr. Chicago: American Library Association, 1982: 119–128.

Carr, Jo, ed. *Beyond Fact: Nonfiction for Children and Young People.* Chicago: American Library Association, 1982.

Carter, Betty, and Richard F. Abrahamson. *Nonfiction for Young Adults: From Delight to Wisdom.* Phoenix: Oryx Press, 1991.

Chamberlain, Larry. "Enchantment Isn't Everything: A New Way of Looking at Lands and Peoples." *School Library Journal* (1978): 25–26.

Coolidge, Olivia. "My Struggle with Facts." *Wilson Library Bulletin* October 1974: 146–151.

Dempsey, Frank J. "Russell Freedman." *The Horn Book* (July/August 1988): 452–456.

Epstein, William H. "Introducing Biography." *Children's Literature Association Quarterly* 12 (Winter 1987): 177–179.

Fisher, Margery. "Life Course or Screaming Force." *Children's Literature in Education* 8 (Autumn 1976): 107–127.

——. *Matters of Fact: Aspects of Non-fiction for Children.* New York: Crowell, 1972.

Fleming, Margaret, and Jo McGionnis. *Portraits: Biography and Autobiography in the Secondary School.* Urbana, IL: National Council of Teachers of English, 1985.

Forman, Jack. "Biography for Children: More Facts, Less Fiction." *Library Journal* 97 (September 15, 1972): 2968–2969.

Fritz, Jean. "George Washington, My Father, and Walt Disney." *Horn Book Magazine* 52 (April 1976): 191–198.

Garfield, Leon. "Historical Fiction for Our Global Times." *The Horn Book* November/December 1988: 736–742.

Groff, Patrick. "Biography: The Bad or the Bountiful." *Top of the News* April 1973: 210–217.

Herman, Gertrude B. "'Footnotes on the Sands of Time': Biography for Children." *Children's Literature in Education* 9 (Summer 1977): 85–94.

Higgins, Judith. "Biographies They Can Read." *School Library Journal* 18 (April 1971): 33–34.

Jurich, Marilyn. "What's Left Out of Biography for Children?" *Children's Literature* 1 (1972): 143–151.

Kobrin, Beverly. *Eyeopeners! How to Choose and Use Children's Books About Real People, Places, and Things.* New York: Viking, 1988.

Lochhead, Marion. "Clio Junior: Historical Novels for Children." In *Only Connect*, 2nd ed. Ed. Sheila Egoff, G. T. Stubbs, and L. F. Ashely. New York: Oxford University Press, 1980: 17–27.

Long, Joanna Rudge. "Eloquent Visions: Perspectives in Picture Book Biographies." *School Library Journal* 43 (April 1997): 48–49.

Mallet, Margaret. *Making Facts Matter: Reading Non-fiction 5–11.* London: Paul Chapman, 1992.

Marcus, Leonard. "Life Drawing: Some Notes on Children's Picture Book Biographies." *The Lion and the Unicorn* 4 (Summer 1980): 15–31.

Meltzer, Milton. "Where Do All the Prizes Go? The Case for Nonfiction." *Horn Book Magazine* 52 (February 1976): 17–23.

Moore, Ann W. "A Question of Accuracy: Errors in Children's Biographies." *School Library Journal* 31 (February 1985): 34–35.

Morman, Charles. *Kings & Captains: Variations on a Heroic Theme.* Louisville: University of Kentucky Press, 1971.

Norris, Lynn. "Extending Curiosity: Children's Informational Books." *Idaho Librarian* October 1975: 126–128.

Rahn, Suzanne. "An Evolving Past: The Story of Historical Fiction and Nonfiction for Children." *The Lion and the Unicorn* 15 (June 1991): 1–26.

Segel, Elizabeth. "In Biographies for Young Readers, Nothing Is Impossible." *The Lion and the Unicorn* 4 (Summer 1980): 4–14.

Stott, Jon. C. "Biographies of Sports Heroes and the American Dream." *Children's Literature in Education* 10 (Winter 1979): 174–185.

Sutherland, Zena. "Information Pleases— Sometimes." *Wilson Library Journal* 49 (October 1974): 17–23.

——. "Science as Literature." *Literary Trends* 22:4 (April 1974): 485–489.

Weinberg, Steve. "Biography: Telling the Untold Story." *The Writer* (February 1993): 23–25.

Wilms, Denise M. "An Evaluation of Biography." In *Jump Over the Moon.* Ed. Pamela Barron and Jennifer Burley. New York: Holt, Rinehart, & Winston, 1984: 220–225.

SELECTED BIBLIOGRAPHY OF BIOGRAPHIES AND AUTOBIOGRAPHIES

(Since many writers specialize in biographical writing, look for other biographies by many of the writers represented on this list. If the subject of the biography is not obvious from the title, it has been supplied in parentheses next to the entry. The recommended reading levels are only approximations since every young reader develops at a different pace.)

BIOGRAPHIES FOR YOUNGER READERS (GRADES K–4)

Adler, David A. *Christopher Columbus, Great Explorer.* New York: Holiday House, 1991.

——. *Lou Gehrig: The Luckiest Man Alive.* Illus. Terry Widener. New York: Harcourt, 1997.

Aliki (pseud. of Aliki Brandenburg). *The Story of Johnny Appleseed.* Englewood Cliffs, NJ: Prentice-Hall, 1963.

——. *A Weed Is a Flower: The Life of George Washington Carver.* Englewood Cliffs, NJ: Prentice-Hall, 1965.

——. *William Shakespeare and the Globe.* New York: HarperCollins, 1999.

Anderson, M. T. *Handel, Who Knew What He Liked.* Illus. Kevin Hawkes. Cambridge, MA: Candlewick, 2001.

——. *Strange Mr. Satie.* Illus. Peter Mathers. New York: Viking, 2003. (Composer Erik Satie)

Andronik, Catherine M. *Hatshepsut, His Majesty, Herself.* New York: Atheneum, 2001. (Ancient Egypt's only female pharaoh)

Bolliger, Max. *David.* Illus. Edith Schindler. New York: Delacorte, 1967.

Bulla, Clyde. *Songs of St. Francis.* Illus. Valenti Angelo. New York: Crowell, 1952. (St. Francis of Assisi)

——. *Squanto, Friend of the Pilgrims.* Illus. Peter Burchard. New York: Crowell, 1954.

——. *Washington's Birthday.* Illus. Don Bolognese. New York: Crowell, 1957.

Carlson, Laurie. *Boss of the Plains: The Hat That Won the West.* New York: DK Ink, 1998. (Hatmaker John Stetson)

Christensen, Bonnie. *Woody Guthrie: Poet of the People.* New York: Knopf, 2001.

Clouse, Nancy L. *Perugino's Path: The Journey of a Renaissance Painter*. Grand Rapids, MI: Wm. B. Eerdmans, 1997.

Daugherty, James. *Abraham Lincoln*. New York: Viking, 1943.

——. *Daniel Boone*. New York: Viking, 1939.

d'Aulaire, Ingri, and Edgar Parin d'Aulaire. *Abraham Lincoln*. New York: Doubleday, 1939.

——. *Columbus*. New York: Doubleday, 1959.

Demi. *Ghandi*. New York: McElderry, 2001.

Faber, Doris. *Eleanor Roosevelt: First Lady of the World*. New York: Viking, 1985.

Fritz, Jean. *Bully for You, Teddy Roosevelt!* New York: Putnam, 1991.

——. *Can't You Make Them Behave, King George?* Illus. Tomie da Paola. New York: Coward-McCann, 1977. (King George III)

——. *Where Was Patrick Henry on the 29th of May?* Illus. Margot Tomes. New York: Coward-McCann, 1975.

Gerstein, Mordicai. *What Charlie Heard*. New York: Farrar, Straus & Giroux, 2002. (American Composer Charles Ives)

Gish, Lillian, and Selma Lanes. *An Actor's Life for Me*. New York: Viking, 1987.

Goodsell, Jane. *Eleanor Roosevelt*. New York: Crowell, 1970.

——. *The Mayo Brothers*. New York: Crowell, 1972.

Greenfield, Eloise. *Mary McLeod Bethune*. New York: Crowell, 1977.

——. *Rosa Parks*. New York: Crowell, 1973.

Hyman, Trina Schart. *Self-Portrait: Trina Schart Hyman*. (1981). New York: HarperCollins, 1989.

Johnson, Johanna. *Harriet and the Runaway Book: The Story of Harriet Beecher Stowe and Uncle Tom's Cabin*. New York: Harper, 1977.

Judson, Clara Ingram. *Abraham Lincoln, Friend of the People*. Chicago: Wilcox and Follett, 1950.

——. *Admiral Christopher Columbus*. Chicago: Follett, 1965.

Lasker, Joe. *The Great Alexander the Great*. New York: Viking, 1983.

Lawrence, Jacob. *Harriet and the Promised Land*. New York: Windmill, 1968. (One-time slave and heroine of the underground railroad Harriet Tubman)

Monjo, F. N. *The One Bad Thing About Father*. New York: Harper, 1970. (Theodore Roosevelt)

——. *Poor Richard in France*. New York: Holt, 1973. (Benjamin Franklin)

Mora, Pat. *A Library for Juana: The World of Sor Juana Inéz*. Illus. Beatriz Vidal. New York: Knopf, 2002. (Seventeenth-century woman scholar of Mexico)

Oneal, Zibby. *Grandma Moses: Painter of Rural America*. New York: Viking, 1986.

Parks, Rosa, with Jim Haskins. *I Am Rosa Parks*. Illus. Wil Clay. New York: Dial, 1997.

Peet, Bill. *Bill Peet: An Autobiography*. Boston: Houghton Mifflin, 1989.

Poole, Josephine. *Joan of Arc*. Illus. Angela Barret. New York: Knopf, 1998.

Provensen, Alice, and Martin Provensen. *The Glorious Flight: Across the Channel with Louis Bleriot*. New York: Viking, 1983.

Raboff, Ernest. *Marc Chagall*. New York: Doubleday, 1968.

——. *Pablo Picasso*. New York: Doubleday, 1968.

Shippen, Katherine. *Leif Eriksson: First Voyager to America*. New York: Harper, 1951.

Stanley, Diane. *Joan of Arc*. New York: Morrow, 1998.

——. *Leonardo da Vinci*. New York: Morrow, 1996.

——. *Peter the Great*. New York: Four Winds, 1986.

Stanley, Diane, and Peter Vennema. *Good Queen Bess: The Story of Elizabeth I of England*. New York: Four Winds, 1990.

——. *Shaka: King of the Zulus*. New York: Morrow, 1988.

Steig, William. *When Everybody Wore a Hat*. New York: HarperCollins, 2003.

Venezia, Mike. *Beatles*. New York: Scholastic, 1997.

——. *Johann Sebastian Bach*. New York: Scholastic, 1998.

——. *Ludwig von Beethoven*. New York: Scholastic, 1996.

Wallner, Alexander. *Laura Ingalls Wilder*. New York: Holiday, 1997.

BIOGRAPHIES FOR OLDER READERS (GRADES 5 AND UP)

Adoff, Arnold. *Malcolm X*. Illus. John Wilson. New York: Crowell, 1970.

Asimov, Isaac. *Breakthroughs in Science*. Boston: Houghton Mifflin, 1960.

Bitton-Jackson, Livia. *I Have Lived a Thousand Years: Growing Up in the Holocaust*. New York: Simon & Schuster, 1997.

Blegvad, Erik. *Self-Portrait: Erick Blegvad*. Reading, MA: Addison-Wesley, 1979.

Brooks, Polly Schoyer. *Queen Eleanor: Independent Spirit of the Medieval World*. Philadelphia: Lippincott, 1983.

Bruchac, Joseph. *A Boy Called Slow: The True Story of Sitting Bull*. New York: Philomel, 1995.

Buckminster, Henrietta. *Women Who Shaped History*. New York: Macmillan, 1966.

Burleigh, Robert. *Flight: The Journey of Charles Lindbergh*. New York: Philomel, 1991.

Carter, Dorothy S. *Queen Hatshepsut*. Illus. Cecil Leslie. New York: Faber, 1978.

Clayton, Ed. *Martin Luther King: The Peaceful Warrior*. Englewood Cliffs, NJ: Prentice-Hall, 1968.

Cleary, Beverly. *A Girl from Yamhill: A Memoir*. New York: Morrow, 1988.

Coolidge, Olivia. *Tom Paine: Revolutionary*. New York: Scribner's, 1969.

——. *Winston Churchill and the Story of Two World Wars*. Boston: Houghton, 1960.

Dahl, Roald. *Boy: Tales of Childhood*. New York: Farrar, Straus & Giroux, 1984.

Davidson, Margaret. *The Story of Eleanor Roosevelt*. New York: Four Winds, 1969.

De Trevino, Elizabeth Borton. *I, Juan de Pareja*. New York: Farrar, Straus & Giroux, 1965.

Duncan, Lois. *Chapters: My Growth as a Writer*. Boston: Little, Brown, 1982.

Eaton, Jeanette. *America's Own Mark Twain*. Illus. Leonard Everett Fisher. New York: Morrow, 1958.

Ferris, Jeri. *Native American Doctor: The Story of Susan LaFlesche Picotte*. Minneapolis: Carolrhoda, 1991.

Fisher, Leonard Everett. *Galileo*. New York: Macmillan, 1992.

Fleischman, Sid. *The Abracadabra Kid: A Writer's Life*. New York: Greenwillow, 1996.

Frank, Anne. *The Diary of a Young Girl: The Definitive Edition*. Edited by Otto H. Frank and Mirjam Pressler. Translated by Susan Massotty. New York: Doubleday, 1995.

Freedman, Russell. *Eleanor Roosevelt: A Life of Discovery*. New York: Clarion, 1993.

——. *Franklin Delano Roosevelt*. New York: Clarion, 1990.

——. *Indian Chiefs*. New York: Holiday House, 1987.

——. *The Life and Death of Crazy Horse*. New York: Holiday House, 1996.

——. *Lincoln: A Photobiography*. New York: Clarion, 1987.

——. *Martha Graham: A Dancer's Life*. New York: Clarion, 1998.

——. *The Wright Brothers: How They Invented the Airplane*. New York: Holiday, 1991.

Fritz, Jean. *The Double Life of Pocahontas*. New York: Putnam, 1983.

——. *Homesick: My Own Story*. New York: Putnam, 1982. (Autobiography)

——. *Make Way for Sam Houston*. New York: Putnam, 1986.

Gibbin, James Cross. *Charles A. Lindbergh: A Human Hero*. New York: Clarion, 1998.

Hamilton, Virginia. *W. E. B. DuBois: A Biography*. New York: Crowell, 1972.

Hanff, Helene. *Queen of England: The Story of Elizabeth I*. New York: Doubleday, 1969.

Haskins, James. *The Story of Stevie Wonder*. New York: Lothrop, 1976.

Henry, Marguerite, and Wesley Dennis. *Benjamin West and His Cat Grimalkin*. Illus. Wesley Dennis. Indianapolis: Bobbs-Merrill, 1947. (Early American artist Benjamin West)

Hoyt-Goldsmith, Diane. *Hoang Anh: A Vietnamese-American Boy*. New York: Holiday, 1992.

Kennedy, John F. *Profiles in Courage.* New York: Harper, 1964. (Abridged for young readers; stories of courageous Americans)

Kherdian, David. *The Road from Home: The Story of an Armenian Girl.* New York: Greenwillow, 1979.

Komroff, Manuel. *Mozart.* Illus. Warren Chappell. New York: Knopf, 1956.

Konigsburg, E. L. *A Proud Taste for Scarlet and Miniver.* New York: Dell, 1973. (Fictionalized account of the life of Eleanor of Aquitaine)

——. *The Second Mrs. Giaconda.* New York: Macmillan, 1975. (Leonardo da Vinci)

Krull, Kathleen. *Lives of the Athletes: Thrills, Spills (and What the Neighbors Thought).* Illus. Kathryn Hewitt. Orlando: Harcourt, 1997.

——. *Lives of the Presidents: Fame, Shame (and What the Neighbors Thought).* Illus. Kathryn Hewitt. Orlando: Harcourt, 1998.

Lacy, Leslie Alexander. *Cheer the Lonesome Traveler: The Life of W. E. B. DuBois.* New York: Dial, 1970.

Lanier, Shannon, and Jane Feldman. *Jefferson's Children: The Story of One American Family.* New York: Random House, 2000.

Latham, Jean Lee. *Carry On, Mr. Bowditch.* Boston: Houghton Mifflin, 1955.

Littlefield, Bill. *Champions: Stories of Ten Remarkable Athletes.* Boston: Little, Brown, 1993.

McKissack, Patricia C. *Jesse Jackson: A Biography.* New York: Scholastic, 1989.

McNeer, May. *America's Mark Twain.* Illus. Lynd Ward. Boston: Houghton Mifflin, 1962.

Marrin, Albert. *George Washington and the Founding of a Nation.* New York: Dutton, 2001.

Mathis, Sharon Bell. *Ray Charles.* New York: Crowell, 1973.

Meigs, Cornelia. *Invincible Louisa.* Boston: Little, Brown, 1968.

Meltzer, Milton. *Benjamin Franklin: The New American.* New York: Watts, 1984.

——. *Dorothea Lange: Life Through the Camera.* New York: Viking, 1985.

——. *Langston Hughes: A Biography.* New York: Crowell, 1968.

Mitchison, Naomi. *African Heroes.* New York: Farrar, Straus & Giroux, 1969.

Myers, Walter Dean. *At Her Majesty's Request: An African Princess in Victorian England.* New York: Scholastic, 1999.

Naylor, Phyllis Reynolds. *How I Came to Be a Writer.* (1978) New York: Aladdin, 1987.

Oneal, Zibby. *Grandma Moses: Painter of Rural America.* New York: Viking, 1986.

Reef, Catherine. *Walt Whitman.* New York: Clarion, 1995.

Reich, Susanna. *Clara Schumann: Piano Virtuoso.* New York: Clarion, 1999.

Reiss, Joanna. *The Upstairs Room.* New York: Crowell, 1972.

Rylant, Cynthia. *Best Wishes.* Photographs Carlo Ontal. Katonah, NY: Richard C. Owen, 1992. (Autobiography)

Sandburg, Carl. *Abe Lincoln Grows Up.* Illus. James Daugherty. New York: Harcourt, 1928.

Severance, John B. *Gandhi: Great Soul.* New York: Clarion, 1997.

——. *Winston Churchill.* New York: Clarion, 1996.

Shiels, Barbara. *Winners: Women and the Nobel Prize.* Minneapolis: Dillon, 1985.

Siegal, Aranka. *Upon the Head of a Goat: A Childhood in Hungary, 1939–1944.* New York: Farrar, Straus & Giroux, 1985.

Sills, Leslie. *Inspirations: Stories about Women Artists.* Morton Grove, IL: Whitman, 1989.

Singer, Isaac Bashevis. *A Day of Pleasures: Stories of a Boy Growing Up in Warsaw.* New York: Farrar, Straus & Giroux, 1969.

Sis, Peter. *Follow the Dream.* New York: Knopf, 1991. (Christopher Columbus)

——. *Starry Messenger: Galileo Galilei.* New York: Farrar, Straus & Giroux, 1996.

Stanley, Fay. *The Last Princess: The Story of Princess Ka'iulani of Hawai'i.* New York: Four Winds, 1991.

Stanley, Jerry. *I Am an American: A True Story of Japanese Internment.* New York: Crown, 1994.

Stoddard, Hope. *Famous American Women.* New York: Crowell, 1970.

Swift, Hildegarde. *From the Eagle's Wing: A Biography of John Muir*: Illus. Lynd Ward. New York: Morrow, 1962.

Szabo, Corinne. *Sky Pioneer: A Photobiography of Amelia Earhart*. Washington, DC: National Geographic, 1997.

Thomas, Jane Resh. *Behind the Mask: The Life of Queen Elizabeth I*. New York: Clarion, 1998.

Tillage, Leon Walter. *Leon's Story*. Illus. Susan L. Roth. New York: Farrar, Straus & Giroux, 1997. (Autobiographical account of an African American's struggle in the mid-twentieth century)

Tobias, Tobi. *Marian Anderson*. New York: Crowell, 1972.

Turner, Robyn Montana. *Georgia O'Keeffe*. Boston: Little, Brown 1991.

——. *Rosa Bonheur*. Boston: Little, Brown 1991.

van der Rol, Ruud, and Rian Verhoeven. *Anne Frank: Beyond the Diary*. New York: Viking, 1993.

Wadsworth, Ginger. *Rachel Carson: Voice for the Earth*. Minneapolis: Lerner, 1992.

Weidhorn, Manfred. *Jackie Robinson*. New York: Atheneum, 1993.

Yates, Elizabeth. *Amos Fortune, Free Man*. New York: Dutton, 1950.

Yolen, Jane. *A Letter from Phoenix Farm*. Photographs Jason Stemple. Katonah, NY: Richard C. Owens, 1992. (Autobiography)

Zemach, Margot. *Self-Portrait: Margot Zemach*. Reading, MA: Addison-Wesley, 1978.

SELECTED BIBLIOGRAPHY OF INFORMATION BOOKS

(The books in this list simply represent a cross-section of the wealth of nonfiction reading available for young readers. The books in this list are categorized according to the four broad classifications outlined in this chapter; however, these are only general guidelines and frequently books cross boundaries. This list is also in addition to those concept books listed at the end of Chapter 6.)

HISTORY AND CULTURE

Books for Younger Readers (Grades K–4)

Aliki (pseudonym for Aliki Brandenburg). *Corn Is Maise—The Gift of the Indians*. New York: Crowell, 1976.

——. *The King's Day: Louis XIV of France*. New York: Crowell, 1989.

——. *A Medieval Feast*. New York: Crowell, 1983.

——. *Mummies Made in Egypt*. New York: Crowell, 1979.

Baylor, Byrd. *When Clay Sings*. Illustrated by Tom Bakhi. New York: Scribner's, 1972.

Branley, Franklyn. *The Mystery of Stonehenge*. New York: Crowell, 1969.

Commager, Henry Steele. *The First Book of American History*. Illus. Leonard Everett Fisher. New York: Watts, 1957.

Coolidge, Olivia. *Tales of the Crusades*. Boston: Houghton Mifflin, 1970.

Fisher, Leonard Everett. *The Hospitals*. New York: Watts, 1980.

——. *The Factories*. New York: Holiday, 1979.

——. *The Peddlers*. New York: Watts, 1968.

——. *The Railroads*. New York: Holiday, 1979.

——. *The Schoolmasters*. New York: Watts, 1967.

Foster, Genevieve. *The World of William Penn*. New York: Scribner's, 1973.

——. *The Year of the Pilgrims—1620*. New York: Scribner's, 1969.

Frank, John. *The Tomb of the Boy King*. Illus. Tom Pohrt. New York: Farrar, Straus & Giroux, 2001. (Tutankhamen)

Herbst, Judith. *The Mystery of UFO's*. Illus. Greg Clarke. New York: Atheneum, 1997.

Hoyt-Goldsmith, Diane. *Celebrating Ramadan*. Photographs by Lawrence Migdale. New York: Holiday, 2001.

Keegan, Marcia. *Pueblo Boy: Growing Up in Two Worlds*. New York: Dutton, 1991.

Kuskin, Karla. *Jerusalem, Shining Still*. New York: Harper, 1987.

Smith, David J. *If the World Were a Village: A Book about the World's People*. Illus. Shelagh Armstrong. Toronto: Kids Can, 2002.

Books for Older Readers (Grades 5 and Up)

Armstrong, Carol. *Women of the Bible*. New York: Simon & Schuster, 1998.

Ashabranner, Brent. *Children of the Maya*. New York: Dodd, Mead & Co., 1986.

——. *Land of Yesterday, Land of Tomorrow: Discovering Chinese Central Asia*. New York: Cobblehill, 1992.

Atkin, S. Beth. *Voices from the Streets: Young Former Gang Members Tell Their Stories*. Boston: Little, Brown, 1996.

Bach, Alice, and J. Cheryl Exum. *Miriam's Well: Stories about Women in the Bible*. New York: Delacorte, 1991.

Bartoletti, Susan Campbell. *Black Potatoes: The Story of the Great Irish Famine*. Boston: Houghton Mifflin, 2001.

——. *Growing Up in Coal Country*. Boston: Houghton Mifflin, 1996.

Bealer, Alex W. *Only the Names Remain: The Cherokees and the Trail of Tears*. Boston: Little, Brown, 1972.

Berck, Judith. *No Place to Be: Voices of Homeless Children*. Boston: Houghton Mifflin, 1991.

Bial, Raymond. *Cajun Home*. Boston: Houghton Mifflin, 1998.

Bontemps, Arna. *Story of the Negro*. 3rd ed. New York: Knopf, 1958.

Britton-Jackson, Livia. *I Have Lived a Thousand Years: Growing Up in the Holocaust*. New York: Simon & Schuster, 1997.

Caselli, Giovanni. *The First Civilizations*. New York: Bedrick, 1985.

Chaikin, Miriam. *Clouds of Glory*. Illus. David Frampton. New York: Clarion, 1998.

——. adapter. *Exodus*. Illus. Charles Mikolaycak. New York: Holiday, 1987.

——. *Sound the Shofar: The Story and Meaning of Rosh Hashanah and Yom Kippur*. Boston: Houghton Mifflin, 1986.

Chang, Ina. *A Separate Battle: Women and the Civil War*. New York: Dutton, 1991.

Chubb, Thomas Caldecot. *The Byzantines*. Cleveland: World, 1959.

Colman, Penny. *Corpses, Coffins, and Crypts: A History of Burial*. New York: Holt, 1997.

——. *Rosie the Riveter: Women Working on the Home Front in World War II*. New York: Crown, 1995.

Cooper, Ilene. *The Dead Sea Scrolls*. Illus. John Thompson. New York: Morrow, 1997.

Cooper, Margaret. *Exploring the Ice Age*. New York: Atheneum, 2001.

Freedman, Russell. *Cowboys of the Wild West*. New York: Tickner & Fields, 1985.

——. *Immigrant Kids*. New York: Dutton, 1980.

——. *An Indian Winter*. New York: Holiday, 1992.

Greenfeld, Howard. *Chanukah*. New York: Holt, 1976.

——. *The Hidden Children*. New York: Clarion, 1993.

——. *Passover*. New York: Holt, 1978.

——. *Rosh Hashanab and Yom Kippur*. New York: Holt, 1979.

Hughes, Langston. *The First Book of Africa*. Rev. ed. New York: Watts, 1964.

Ippisch, Hanneke. *Sky: A True Story of Resistance During World War II*. New York: Simon & Schuster, 1996.

Jacobs, Francine. *The Tainos: The People Who Welcomed Columbus*. New York: Putnam, 1992.

Kantar, Andrew. *29 Missing: The True and Tragic Story of the Disappearance of the S. S. Edmund Fitzgerald*.

East Lansing: Michigan State University Press, 1998.

Kimmel, Eric A. *Bar Mitzvah: A Jewish Boy's Coming of Age*. New York: Viking, 1995.

Meltzer, Milton, ed. *The Black Americans: A History in Their Own Words, 1619–1983*. New York: Crowell, 1984.

——. *Brother Can You Spare Dime? The Great Depression: 1929–1933*. New York: New American Library, 1977.

——. *Columbus and the World Around Him*. New York: Watts, 1990.

——. *The Hispanic Americans*. New York: Crowell, 1982.

Murphy, Jim. *Across America on an Emigrant Train*. New York: Clarion, 1993.

——. *Gone A-Whaling: The Lure of the Sea and the Hunt for the Great Whale*. New York: Clarion, 1998.

——. *The Great Fire*. New York: Scholastic, 1995. (The Chicago fire)

Myers, Walter Dean. *Now Is Your Time!: The African-American Struggle for Freedom*. New York: HarperCollins, 1991.

Philbrick, Nathaniel. *Revenge of the Whale: The True Story of the Whaleship* Essex. New York: Putnam, 2002.

Price, Christine. *Made in Ancient Egypt*. New York: Dutton, 1970.

Rylant, Cynthia. *Appalachia: The Voices of Sleeping Birds*. New York: Harcourt, 1991.

Schwartz, Alvin. *The City and Its People: The Story of One City's Government*. New York: Dutton, 1967.

Seeger, Elizabeth. *Eastern Religions*. New York: T. Crowell, 1973.

Snelling, John. *Buddhism*. New York: Watts, 1986.

Stanley, Jerry. *I Am an American: A True Story of Japanese Internment*. New York: Crown, 1994.

Van Loon, Hendrik Willem. *The Story of Mankind*. Updated by John Merriman. New York: Liveright, 1999. Originally published 1921.

SCIENCE AND NATURE

Books for Younger Readers (Grades K–4)

Anno, Mitsumasa. *Anno's Math Games*. New York: Philomel, 1987.

——. *Anno's Math Games II*. New York: Philomel, 1987.

Bang, Molly. *Common Ground: The Water, Earth, and Air We Share*. New York: Scholastic, 1997.

Branley, Franklyn. *Air Is All Around You*. New York: Crowell, 1986.

——. *The International Space Station*. Illus. True Kelley. New York: HarperCollins, 2000.

——. *Light and Darkness*. New York: Crowell, 1975.

——. *Uranus*. New York: Crowell, 1988.

Brown, Laurie Krasny, and Marc Brown. *Dinosaurs to the Rescue!: A Guide to Protecting Our Planet*. Boston: Little, Brown, 1992.

Cobb, Vicki. *The Scoop of Ice Cream*. Boston: Little, Brown, 1985.

——. *I Face the Wind*. New York: HarperCollins, 2003.

——. *Sneakers Meet Your Feet*. Boston: Little, Brown, 1985.

Cole, Joanna. *The Magic School Bus and the Electric Field Trip*. Illus. Bruce Degen. New York: Scholastic, 1997.

——. *The Magic School Bus: Inside the Earth*. Illus. Bruce Degen. New York: Scholastic, 1987.

Cowley, Joy. *Red-Eyed Tree Frog*. Photographs by Nic Bishop. New York: Scholastic, 1999.

Curlee, Lynn. *Brooklyn Bridge*. New York: Simon & Schuster, 2001.

Ehlert, Lois. *Waiting for Wings*. San Diego: Harcourt, 2001. (Butterflies)

Facklam, Margery. *Spiders and Their Web Sites*. Boston: Little, Brown, 2001.

——. *Bugs for Lunch*. Illus. Sylvia Long. Watertown, MA: Charlesbridge, 1999.

Gibbons, Gail. *Exploring the Deep, Dark Sea*. Boston: Little, Brown, 1999.

——. *From Seed to Plant*. New York: Holiday, 1991.

——. *The Puffins Are Back!* New York: HarperCollins, 1991.

——. *Recycle!: A Handbook for Kids.* Boston: Little, Brown, 1992.

Heller, Ruth. *The Reason for a Flower.* New York: Scholastic, 1983.

Henderson, Douglas, *Asteroid Impact.* New York: Penguin, 2001.

Herbst, Judith. *The Mystery of UFOs.* Illus. Greg Clarke. New York: Simon, 1997.

Jenkins, Martin. *Fly Traps!: Plants That Bite Back.* Illus. David Parkins. New York: Candlewick, 1996.

Jenkins, Steve. *Life on Earth: The Story of Evolution.* Boston: Houghton Mifflin, 2002.

Lauber, Patricia. *The Friendly Dolphins.* New York: Random, 1963.

——. *Summer of Fire: Yellowstone 1988.* New York: Watts, 1991.

——. *Tales Mummies Tell.* New York: Crowell, 1985.

Llewellyn, Claire. *My First Book of Time.* Boston: Houghton, 1992.

Markle, Sandra. *Outside and Inside Bats.* New York: Atheneum, 1992.

Mendoza, George. *The Digger Wasp.* New York: Dial, 1969.

Paladino, Catherine. *Our Vanishing Farm Animals: Saving America's Rare Breeds.* Boston: Little, Brown, 1991.

Patent, Dorothy Hinshaw. *Where the Bald Eagles Gather.* Photographs by William Munoz. Boston: Houghton Mifflin, 1984.

Peters, Lisa Westberg. *Water's Way.* New York: Arcade, 1991.

Ride, Sally, and Susan Okie. *To Space and Back.* New York: Lothrop, 1986.

Schwartz, David M. *Millions to Measure.* Illus. Steven Kellogg. New York: HarperCollins, 2003.

Simon, Seymour. *Destination: Space.* New York: HarperCollins, 2002.

——. *Earthquakes.* New York: Morrow, 1991.

——. *Mars.* New York: Morrow, 1987.

——. *Uranus.* New York: Morrow, 1987.

Srivastava, Jane Jonas. *Statistics.* New York: Crowell, 1973.

Taylor, Barbara. *Coral Reef.* Boston: Houghton, 1992.

——. *Desert Life.* Boston: Houghton, 1992.

——. *Pond Life.* Boston: Houghton, 1992.

——. *Rain Forest.* Boston: Houghton, 1992.

Vernon, Adele. *The Hoiho: New Zealand's Yellow-Eyed Penguin.* New York: Putnam, 1991.

Wick, Walter. *Walter Wick's Optical Tricks.* New York: Scholastic, 1998.

Zoehfeld, Kathleen Weidner. *What Is the World Made Of?: All about Solids, Liquids, and Gases.* Illus. Paul Meisel. New York: Harper, 1998.

Books for Older Readers (Grades 5 and Up)

Anderson, Joan. *Earth Keepers.* New York: Harcourt, 1993.

Arnosky, Jim. *Secrets of a Wildlife Watcher.* New York: Lothrop, 1983.

——. *Watching Desert Wildlife.* Washington, DC: National Geographic, 1998.

Brandenburg, Jim. *An American Safari: Adventures on the North American Prairie.* New York: Walker, 1995.

Dickinson, Terence. *Exploring the Night Sky.* Buffalo, NY: Firefly, 1987.

Farrell, Jeanette. *Invisible Enemies: Stories of Infectious Disease.* New York: Farrar, Straus & Giroux, 1998.

George, Jean Craighead. *Spring Comes to the Ocean.* New York: Crowell, 1965.

Gross, Ruth Belov. *A Book about Pandas.* New York: Scholastic, 1974.

——. *Snakes.* New York: Four Winds, 1975.

Lewin, Ted. *Tooth and Claw: Animal Adventures in the Wild.* New York: HarperCollins, 2003.

Macaulay, David. *The New Way Things Work.* Boston: Houghton Mifflin, 1998.

Masoff, Joy. *Fire!* New York: Scholastic, 1998.

Montgomery, Sy. *The Man-Eating Tigers of Sundarbans.* Photographs by Eleanor Briggs. Boston: Houghton Mifflin, 2001.

Patent, Dorothy Hinshaw. *Quetzel: Sacred Bird of the Cloud Forest.* Illus. Neil Waldman. New York: Morrow, 1996.

Pringle, Laurence. *City and Suburbs: Exploring Ecosystems.* New York: Macmillan, 1975.

——. *The Hidden World: Life Under a Rock*. New York: Macmillan, 1977.

——. *Living in a Risky World*. New York: Morrow, 1989.

Scott, Elaine. *Close Encounters: Exploring the Universe with the Hubble Space Telescope*. New York: Hyperion, 1998.

St. George, Judith. *The Brooklyn Bridge: They Said It Couldn't Be Built*. New York: Putnam, 1982.

——. *The Panama Canal: Gateway to the World*. New York: Putnam, 1989.

Skurzynski, Gloria. *Waves: The Electromagnetic Universe*. Washington, DC: National Geographic, 1996.

Walker, Sally M. *Fossil Fish Found Alive: Discovering the Coelacanth*. Minneapolis: Carolrhoda, 2002.

Webb, Sophie. *My Season with Penguins: An Antarctic Journal*. Boston: Houghton Mifflin, 2000.

HUMANITIES, ARTS, AND LEISURE

Books for Younger Readers (Grades K–4)

Ancona, George. *Cutters, Carvers, and the Cathedral*. New York: Lothrop, 1995. (St. John the Divine, New York City)

Bellville, Cheryl Walsh. *Theater Magic: Behind the Scenes at a Children's Theater*. Minneapolis: Carolrhoda, 1986.

Brown, Marc. *Your First Garden Book*. Boston: Little, Brown, 1981.

Cooper, Elisha. *Dance!* New York: Greenwillow, 2001.

Florian, Douglas. *A Carpenter*. New York: Greenwillow, 1991.

——. *A Potter*. New York: Greenwillow, 1991.

Heller, Ruth. *A Cache of Jewels and Other Collective Nouns*. New York: Grosset, 1987.

——. *Merry-Go-Round: A Book about Nouns*. New York: Grosset, 1990.

——. *Mine, All Mine: A Book about Pronouns*. New York: Grosset, 1997.

Jones, Bill T., and Susan Kuklin. *Dance*. Photographs by Susan Kuklin. New York: Hyperion, 1998.

Kalb, Jonah, and Laura Kalb. *The Easy Ice Skating Book*. Illus. Sandy Kossin. Boston: Houghton Mifflin, 1981.

Krementz, Jill. *A Very Young Rider*. New York: Knopf, 1977.

Lasky, Kathryn. *Puppeteer*. New York: Macmillan, 1985.

Marks, Mickey K. *OP-Tricks: Creating Kinetic Art*. Philadelphia: Lippincott, 1972.

Pulver, Robin. *Punctuation Takes a Vacation*. Illus. Lynn Rowe Reed. New York: Holiday, 2003.

Rodari, Florian. *A Weekend with Picasso*. New York: Rizzoli, 1991.

Skira-Venturi, Rosabianca. *A Weekend with Van Gogh*. New York: Rizzoli, 1994.

——. *A Weekend with Renoir*. New York: Rizzoli, 1991.

Streatfield, Noel. *A Young Person's Guide to Ballet*. London: Warne, 1985.

Books for Older Readers (Grades 5 and Up)

Aliki. *Ah, Music!* New York: HarperCollins, 2003.

Anderson, Dave. *The Story of Golf*. New York: Morrow, 1998.

Arnosky, Jim. *Fish in a Flash!: A Personal Guide to Spin-Fishing*. New York: Bradbury, 1991.

——. *Sketching Outdoors in Spring*. New York: Lothrop, 1987.

Aronson, Marc. *Art Attack: A Short Cultural History of the Avant-Garde*. New York: Clarion, 1998.

Batterberry, Ariane, and Michael Batterberry. *The Pantheon Story of American Art for Young People*. New York: Pantheon, 1976.

Beardsley, John. *Pablo Picasso*. New York: Abrams, 1991.

Bierhorst, John. *A Cry from the Earth: Music of the North American Indians*. New York: Four Winds, 1979.

Carter, David A., and James Diaz. *The Elements of Pop-Up*. New York: Simon & Schuster, 1999.

Cone, Ferne Geller. *Crazy Crocheting*. Illus. Rachel Osterlof. Photographs. J. Morton Cone. New York: Atheneum, 1981.

Cooper, Miriam. *Snap! Photography*. New York: Messner, 1981.

Duncan, Lois. *The Circus Comes Home: When the Greatest Show on Earth Rode the Rails*. New York: Doubleday, 1993.

Fisher, Leonard Everett. *Alphabet Art*. New York: Four Winds, 1978.

———. *Calendar Art*. New York: Four Winds, 1987.

Greenberg, Jan, and Sandra Jordan. *The Painter's Eye: Learning to Look at Contemporary American Art*. New York: Delacorte, 1991.

Haskell, Arnold. *The Wonderful World of Dance*. New York: Doubleday, 1969.

Hofsinde, Robert (Gray-Wolf). *Indian Arts*. New York: Morrow, 1971.

Hughes, Langston. *The First Book of Jazz*. New York: Watts, 1955.

Jaspersohn, William. *Magazine: Behind the Scenes at Sports Illustrated*. Boston: Little, Brown, 1983.

Kohl, Herbert. *A Book of Puzzlements: Play and Invention with Language*. New York: Schocken, 1981.

Macaulay; David. *Castle*. Boston: Houghton Mifflin, 1983.

———. *Cathedral: The Story of Its Construction*. Boston: Houghton Mifflin, 1974.

———. *Mosque*. Boston: Houghton Mifflin, 2003.

———. *Pyramid*. Boston: Houghton Mifflin, 1977.

———. *Unbuilding*. Boston: Houghton Mifflin, 1986.

Naylor, Penelope. *Black Images: The Art of West Africa*. New York: Doubleday, 1973.

Thomson, Peggy, with Barbara Moore. *The Nine-Ton Cat: Behind the Scenes at an Art Museum*. Boston: Houghton, 1997.

Tinkelman, Murray. *Rodeo: The Great American Sport*. New York: Greenwillow, 1982.

Weiss, Harvey. *How to Make Your Own Books*. New York: Crowell, 1974.

Wolf, Diane. *Chinese Writing*. New York: Holt, Rinehart & Winston, 1975.

HUMAN DEVELOPMENT AND BEHAVIOR

Books for Younger Readers (Grades K–4)

Banish, Roslyn. *A Forever Family*. New York: HarperCollins, 1992.

Bernstein, Joanne, and Stephen Gullo. *When People Die*. New York: Dutton, 1977.

Brown, Laurie Krasny, and Marc Brown. *What's the Big Secret?: Talking about Sex with Girls and Boys*. Illus. Marc Brown. Boston: Little, 1997.

———. *How to Be a Friend: A Guide to Making Friends and Keeping Them*. Boston: Little Brown, 1998.

Cole, Babette. *Mommy Laid an Egg! Or, Where Do Babies Come From?* San Francisco: Chronicle Books, 1993.

Cole, Joanna. *The New Baby at Your House*. New York: Morrow, 1985.

Engel, Joel. *Handwriting Analysis Self-Taught*. New York: Elsevier/Nelson, 1980.

Giblin, James Cross. *From Hand to Mouth: Or How We Invented Knives, Forks, Spoons, and Chopsticks & the Table Manners to Go with Them*. New York: Crowell, 1987.

Kamien, Janet. *What If You Couldn't . . . ?* New York: Scribner's, 1979.

LeShan, Eda. *What's Going to Happen to Me? When Parents Separate or Divorce*. New York: Four Winds, 1978.

———. *When a Parent Is Very Sick*. New York: Atlantic, 1986.

Perl, Lila. *The Great Ancestor Hunt: The Fun of Finding Out Who You Are*. Boston: Houghton Mifflin, 1989.

Rofes, Eric E. *The Kids' Book About Death and Dying*. Boston: Little, Brown, 1985.

Books for Older Readers (Grades 5 and Up)

Bode, Janet. *Death Is Hard to Live With: Teenagers and How They Cope with Loss*. New York: Delacorte, 1993.

Brooks, Bruce. *Boys Will Be*. New York: Holt, 1993.

Dee, Catherine. *The Girls' Guide to Life: How to Take Charge of the Issues That Affect You.* Illus. Cynthia Jabar. Photos. Carol Palmer. Boston: Little, Brown, 1997.

Gravelle, Karen, and Nick and Chava Castro. *What's Going on Down There?: Answers to Questions Boys Find Hard to Ask.* Illus. Robert Leighton. New York: Walker, 1997.

Harris, Robie H. *It's Perfectly Normal: A Book about Changing Bodies, Growing Up, Sex, and Sexual Health.* Cambridge, MA: Candlewick, 1994.

Jennes, Aylette. *Families: A Celebration of Diversity, Commitment, and Love.* Boston: Houghton Mifflin, 1990.

Machotka, Hana. *Breathtaking Noses.* New York: Morrow, 1992.

——. *What Neat Feet!* New York: Morrow, 1991.

Meltzer, Milton. *The Landscape of Memory.* New York: Viking, 1987.

Schwartz, Alvin. *Telling Fortunes: Love Magic, Dream Signs, and Other Ways to Learn the Future.* Philadelphia: Lippincott, 1987.

Sutton, Roger. *Hearing Us Out: Voices from the Gay and Lesbian Community.* Boston: Little, Brown, 1994.

Terkel, Susan N., and Janice Rench. *Feeling Safe, Feeling Strong: How to Avoid Sexual Abuse and What to Do If It Happens to You.* Minneapolis: Lerner, 1984.

Children's Book Awards

Every year numerous book awards are presented to works of children's literature, both for writing and for illustration. These awards are sponsored by various organizations, each with its own set of criteria. In addition, several awards are presented to individuals recognizing lifetime achievement in children's literature. Included here are some, but not all, of the more prestigious awards. The award-selection process is not infallible, and often some very excellent works have been overlooked, whereas some award-winning works have not altogether successfully stood the test of time. In general, these lists can suggest—in addition to specific titles—authors and illustrators who produce works of high quality, but we should by no means be slaves to book award lists.

Included in the following lists are awards presented not only to writers in English, but also some international awards. It is good that we make a concerted effort to acquaint ourselves not only with American and English children's authors, but with writers the world over. Perhaps in time, more of these foreign language books for children will be available in translation as we realize how important intercultural communication is to global understanding.

AMERICAN BOOK AWARDS

The Newbery Medal

The Newbery Medal was named for John Newbery, the British entrepreneur who pioneered children's book publishing in the eighteenth century. The award is, however, an American award, presented annually by the American Library Association to the most distinguished contribution to children's literature published in the United States. Runners-up are termed Honor Books. As with any such award, there has not always been general agreement with the decisions. However, the list does include some of the finest writing for young people over the past eighty years.

> 1922   *The Story of Mankind* by Hendrik Willem van Loon, Liveright
> Honor Books: *The Great Quest* by Charles Hawes, Little, Brown; *Cedric the Forester* by Bernard Marshall, Appleton; *The Old Tobacco Shop: A True Account of What Befell a Little Boy in Search of Adventure* by William Bowen, Macmillan; *The Golden Fleece and the Heroes Who Lived before Achilles* by Padraic Colum, Macmillan; *Windy Hill* by Cornelia Meigs, Macmillan

1923   *The Voyages of Doctor Dolittle* by Hugh Lofting, Lippincott
Honor Books: No record

1924   *The Dark Frigate* by Charles Hawes, Little, Brown
Honor Books: No record

1925   *Tales from Silver Lands* by Charles Finger, Doubleday
Honor Books: *Nicholas: A Manhattan Christmas Story* by Anne Carroll Moore, Putnam; *Dream Coach* by Anne Parrish, Macmillan

1926   *Shen of the Sea* by Arthur Bowie Chrisman, Dutton
Honor Book: *Voyagers: Being Legends and Romances of Atlantic Discovery* by Padraic Colum, Macmillan

1927   *Smoky, The Cowhorse* by Will James, Scribner's
Honor Books: No record

1928   *Gayneck, The Story of a Pigeon* by Dhan Gopal Mukerji, Dutton
Honor Books: *The Wonder Smith and His Son: A Tale from the Golden Childhood of the World* by Elia Young, Longmans; *Downright Dencey* by Caroline Snedeker, Doubleday

1929   *The Trumpeter of Krakow* by Eric P. Kelly, Macmillan
Honor Books: *Pigtail of Ah Lee Ben Loo* by John Bennett, Longmans, Green (McKay); *Millions of Cats* by Wanda Gág, Coward, McCann & Geoghegan; *The Boy Who Was* by Grace Hallock, Dutton; *Clearing Weather* by Cornelia Meigs, Little, Brown; *Runaway Papoose* by Grace Moon, Doubleday; *Tod of the Fens* by Elinor Whitney, Macmillan

1930   *Hitty, Her First Hundred Years* by Rachel Field, Macmillan
Honor Books: *Daughter of the Seine: The Life of Madame Roland* by Jeanette Eaton, Harper; *Pran of Albania* by Elizabeth Miller, Doubleday; *Jumping-off Place* by Marian Hurd McNeely, Longmans, Green (McKay); *Tangle-coated Horse and Other Tales: Episodes from the Fionn Saga* by Ella Young, Longmans, Green (McKay); *Vaino: A Boy of New England* by Julia Davis Adams, Dutton; *Little Blacknose* by Hildegarde Swift, Harcourt Brace Jovanovich

1931   *The Cat Who Went to Heaven* by Elizabeth Coatsworth, Macmillan
Honor Books: *Floating Island* by Anne Parrish, Harper; *The Dark Star of Itza: The Story of a Pagan Princess* by Alida Malkus, Harcourt Brace Jovanovich; *Queer Person* by Ralph Hubbard, Doubleday; *Mountains Are Free* by Julia Davis Adams, Dutton; *Spice and the Devil's Cave* by Agnes Hewes, Knopf; *Meggy MacIntosh* by Elizabeth Janet Gray, Doubleday; *Garram the Hunter: A Boy of the Hill Tribes* by Herbert Best, Doubleday; *Ood-Le-Uk the Wanderer* by Alice Lide and Margaret Johansen, Little, Brown

1932   *Waterless Mountain* by Laura Adams Armer, Longmans, Green (McKay)
Honor Books: *The Fairy Circus* by Dorothy P. Lathrop, Macmillan; *Calico Bush* by Rachel Field, Macmillan; *Boy of the South Seas* by Eunice Tietjens, Coward, McCann & Geoghegan; *Out of the Flame* by Eloise Lownsbery, Longmans, Green (McKay); *Jane's Island* by Marjorie Allee, Houghton Mifflin; *Truce of the Wolf and Other Tales of Old Italy* by Mary Gould Davis, Harcourt Brace Jovanovich

1933   *Young Fu of the Upper Yangtze* by Elizabeth Foreman Lewis, Winston
Honor Books: *Swift Rivers* by Cornelia Meigs, Little, Brown; *The Railroad to Freedom: A Story of the Civil War* by Hildegarde Swift, Harcourt Brace Jovanovich; *Children of the Soil: A Story of Scandinavia* by Nora Burglon, Doubleday

1934   *Invincible Louisa: The Story of the Author of* Little Women by Cornelia Meigs, Little, Brown
Honor Books: *The Forgotten Daughter* by Caroline Snedeker, Doubleday; *Swords of Steel* by Elsie Singmaster, Houghton Mifflin; *ABC Bunny* by Wanda Gág, Coward, McCann & Geoghegan; *Winged Girl of Knossos* by Erik Berry, Appleton; *New Land* by Sarah Schmidt, McBride; *Big Tree*

of Bunlaby: Stories of My Own Countryside by Padraic Colum, Macmillan; *Glory of the Seas* by Agnes Hewes, Knopf; *Apprentice of Florence* by Ann Kyle, Houghton Mifflin

1935   *Dobry* by Monica Shannon, Viking
Honor Books: *Pageant of Chinese History* by Elizabeth Seeger, Longmans, Green (McKay); *Davy Crockett* by Constance Rourke, Harcourt Brace Jovanovich; *Day on Skates: The Story of a Dutch Picnic* by Hilda Van Stockum, Harper

1936   *Caddie Woodlawn* by Carol Ryrie Brink, Macmillan
Honor Books: *Honk, the Moose* by Phil Strong, Dodd, Mead; *The Good Master* by Kate Seredy, Viking; *Young Walter Scott* by Elizabeth Janet Gray, Viking; *All Sail Set: A Romance of the* "Flying Cloud" by Armstrong Sperry, Winston

1937   *Roller Skates* by Ruth Sawyer, Viking
Honor Books: *Phoebe Fairchild: Her Book* by Lois Lenski, Stokes; *Whistler's Van* by Idwal Jones, Viking; *Golden Basket* by Ludwig Bemelmans, Viking; *Winterbound* by Margery Bianco, Viking; *Audubon* by Constance Rourke, Harcourt Brace Jovanovich; *The Codfish Musket* by Agnes Hewes, Doubleday

1938   *The White Stag* by Kate Seredy, Viking
Honor Books: *Pecos Bill* by James Cloyd Bowman, Little, Brown; *Bright Island* by Mabel Robinson, Random House; *On the Banks of Plum Creek* by Laura Ingalls Wilder, Harper

1939   *Thimble Summer* by Elizabeth Enright, Holt, Rinehart & Winston
Honor Books: *Nino* by Valenti Angelo, Viking; *Mr. Popper's Penguins* by Richard and Florence Atwater, Little, Brown; *"Hello the Boat!"* by Phillis Crawford, Holt, Rinehart & Winston; *Leader by Destiny: George Washington, Man and Patriot* by Jeanette Eaton, Harcourt Brace Jovanovich; *Penn* by Elizabeth Janet Gray, Viking

1940   *Daniel Boone* by James Daugherty, Viking
Honor Books: *The Singing Tree* by Kate Seredy, Viking; *Runner of the Mountain Tops: The Life of Louis Agassiz* by Mabel Robinson, Random House; *By the Shores of Silver Lake* by Laura Ingalls Wilder, Harper; *Boy with a Pack* by Stephen W. Meader, Harcourt Brace Jovanovich

1941   *Call It Courage* by Armstrong Sperry, Macmillan
Honor Books: *Blue Willow* by Doris Gates, Viking; *Young Mac of Fort Vancouver* by Mary Jane Carr, Crowell; *The Long Winter* by Laura Ingalls Wilder, Harper; *Nansen* by Anna Gertrude Hall, Viking

1942   *The Matchlock Gun* by Walter D. Edmonds, Dodd, Mead
Honor Books: *Little Town on the Prairie* by Laura Ingalls Wilder, Harper; *George Washington's World* by Genevieve Foster, Scribner; *Indian Captive: The Story of Mary Jemison* by Lois Lenski, Lippincott; *Down Ryton Water* by Eva Roe Gaggin, Viking

1943   *Adam of the Road* by Elizabeth Janet Gray, Viking
Honor Books: *The Middle Moffat* by Eleanor Estes, Harcourt Brace Jovanovich; *Have You Seen Tom Thumb?* by Mabel Leigh Hunt, Lippincott

1944   *Johnny Tremain* by Esther Forbes, Houghton Mifflin
Honor Books: *These Happy Golden Years* by Laura Ingalls Wilder, Harper; *Fog Magic* by Julia Sauer, Viking; *Rufus M.* by Eleanor Estes, Harcourt Brace Jovanovich; *Mountain Born* by Elizabeth Yates, Coward, McCann & Geoghegan

1945   *Rabbit Hill* by Robert Lawson, Viking
Honor Books: *The Hundred Dresses* by Eleanor Estes, Harcourt Brace Jovanovich; *The Silver Pencil* by Alice Dalgliesh, Scribner's; *Abraham Lincoln's World* by Genevieve Foster, Scribner's; *Lone Journey: The Life of Roger Williams* by Jeanette Eaton, Harcourt Brace Jovanovich

1946   *Strawberry Girl* by Lois Lenski, Lippincott
        Honor Books: *Justin Morgan Had a Horse* by Marguerite Henry, Rand McNally; *The Moved-Outers* by Florence Crannell Means, Houghton Mifflin; *Bhimsa, the Dancing Bear* by Christine Weston, Scribner; *New Found World* by Katherine Shippen, Viking

1947   *Miss Hickory* by Carolyn Sherwin Bailey, Viking
        Honor Books: *Wonderful Year* by Nancy Barnes, Messner; *Big Tree* by Mary and Conrad Buff, Viking; *The Heavenly Tenants* by William Maxwell, Harper; *The Avion My Uncle Flew* by Cyrus Fisher, Appleton; *The Hidden Treasure of Glaston* by Eleanore Jewett, Viking

1948   *The Twenty-One Balloons* by William Pene du Bois, Viking
        Honor Books: *Pancakes-Paris* by Claire Huchet Bishop, Viking; *Le Lun, Lad of Courage* by Carolyn Treffinger, Abingdon; *The Quaint and Curious Quest of Johnny Longfoot, The Shoe-King's Son* by Catherine Besterman, Bobbs-Merrill; *The Cow-Tail Switch, and Other West African Stories* by Harold Courlander, Holt, Rinehart & Winston; *Misty of Chincoteague* by Marguerite Henry, Rand McNally

1949   *King of the Wind* by Marguerite Henry, Rand McNally
        Honor Books: *Seabird* by Holling C. Holling, Houghton Mifflin; *Daughter of the Mountains* by Louise Rankin, Viking; *My Father's Dragon* by Ruth S. Gannett, Random House; *Story of the Negro* by Arna Bontemps, Knopf

1950   *The Door in the Wall* by Marguerite de Angeli, Doubleday
        Honor Books: *Tree of Freedom* by Rebecca Caudill, Viking; *The Blue Cat of Castle Town* by Catherine Coblentz, Longmans, Green (McKay); *Kildee House* by Rutherford Montgomery, Doubleday; *George Washington* by Genevieve Foster, Scribner's; *Song of the Pines: A Story of Norwegian Lumbering in Wisconsin* by Walter and Marion Havighurst, Winston

1951   *Amos Fortune, Free Man* by Elizabeth Yates, Aladdin
        Honor Books: *Better Known as Johnny Appleseed* by Mabel Leigh Hunt, Lippincott; *Gandhi, Fighter without a Sword* by Jeanette Eaton, Morrow; *Abraham Lincoln, Friend of the People* by Clara Ingram Judson, Follett; *The Story of Appleby Capple* by Anne Parrish, Harper

1952   *Ginger Pye* by Eleanor Estes, Harcourt Brace Jovanovich
        Honor Books: *Americans before Columbus* by Elizabeth Baity, Viking; *Minn of the Mississippi* by Holling C. Holling, Houghton Mifflin; *The Defender* by Nicholas Kalashnikoff, Scribner's; *The Light at Tern Rock* by Julia Sauer, Viking; *The Apple and the Arrow* by Mary and Conrad Buff, Houghton Mifflin

1953   *Secret of the Andes* by Ann Nolan Clark, Viking
        Honor Brooks: *Charlotte's Web* by E. B. White, Harper; *Moccasin Trail* by Eloise McGraw, Coward, McCann & Geoghegan; *Red Sails to Capri* by Ann Well, Viking; *The Bears on Hemlock Mountain* by Alice Dalgliesh, Scribner; *Birthdays of Freedom, Vol. 1*, by Genevieve Foster, Scribner

1954   *. . . and Now Miguel* by Joseph Krumgold, Crowell
        Honor Books: *All Alone* by Claire Huchet Bishop, Viking; *Shadrach* by Meindert DeJong, Harper, *Hurry Home Candy* by Meindert DeJong, Harper; *Theodore Roosevelt, Fighting Patriot* by Clara Ingram Judson, Follett; *Magic Maize* by Mary and Conrad Buff, Houghton Mifflin

1955   *The Wheel on the School* by Meindert DeJong, Harper
        Honor Books: *The Courage of Sarah Noble* by Alice Dalgliesh, Scribner's; *Banner in the Sky* by James Ullman, Lippincott

1956   *Carry On, Mr. Bowditch* by Jean Lee Latham, Houghton Mifflin
        Honor Books: *The Secret River* by Marjorie Kinnan Rawlings. Scribner's; *The Golden Name Day* by Jennie Linquist, Harper; *Men, Microscopes, and Living Things* by Katherine Shippen, Viking.

1957   *Miracles on Maple Hill* by Virginia Sorensen, Harcourt Brace Jovanovich
Honor Books: *Old Yeller* by Fred Gipson, Harper; *The House of Sixty Fathers* by Meindert DeJong, Harper; *Mr. Justice Holmes* by Clara Ingram Judson, Follett; *The Corn Grows Ripe* by Dorothy Rhoads, Viking; *Black Fox of Lorne* by Marguerite de Angeli, Doubleday

1958   *Rifles for Watie* by Harold Keith, Crowell
Honor Books: *The Horsecatcher* by Mari Sandoz, Westminster; *Gone-Away Lake* by Elizabeth Enright, Harcourt Brace Jovanovich; *The Great Wheel* by Robert Lawson, Viking; *Tom Paine, Freedom's Apostle* by Leo Gurko, Crowell

1959   *The Witch of Blackbird Pond* by Elizabeth George Speare, Houghton Mifflin
Honor Books: *The Family under the Bridge* by Natalie Savage Carlson, Harper; *Along Came a Dog* by Meindert DeJong, Harper; *Chúcaro: Wild Pony of the Pampas* by Francis Kalnay, Harcourt Brace Jovanovich; *The Perilous Road* by William O. Steele, Harcourt Brace Jovanovich

1960   *Onion John* by Joseph Krumgold, Crowell
Honor Books: *My Side of the Mountain* by Jean George, Dutton; *America Is Born* by Gerald W. Johnson, Morrow; *The Gammage Cup* by Carol Kendall, Harcourt Brace Jovanovich

1961   *Island of the Blue Dolphins* by Scott O'Dell, Houghton Mifflin
Honor Books: *America Moves Forward* by Gerald W. Johnson, Morrow; *Old Ramon* by Jack Schaefer, Houghton Mifflin; *The Cricket in Times Square* by George Selden, Farrar, Straus & Giroux

1962   *The Bronze Bow* by Elizabeth George Speare, Houghton Mifflin
Honor Books: *Frontier Living* by Edwin Tunis, World; *The Golden Goblet* by Eloise McCraw, Coward, McCann & Geoghegan; *Belling the Tiger* by Mary Stolz, Harper

1963   *A Wrinkle in Time* by Madeline L'Engle, Farrar, Straus & Giroux
Honor Books: *Thistle and Thyme: Tales and Legends from Scotland* by Sorche Nic Leodhas, Holt, Rinehart & Winston; *Men of Athens* by Olivia Coolidge, Houghton Mifflin

1964   *It's Like This, Cat* by Emily Cheney Neville, Harper
Honor Books: *Rascal* by Sterling North, Dutton; *The Loner* by Ester Wier, McKay

1965   *Shadow of a Bull* by Maia Wojciechowska, Atheneum
Honor Book: *Across Five Aprils* by Irene Hunt, Follett

1966   *I, Juan de Pareja* by Elizabeth Borten de Trevino, Farrar, Straus & Giroux
Honor Books: *The Black Cauldron* by Lloyd Alexander, Holt, Rinehart & Winston; *The Animal Family* by Randall Jarrell, Pantheon; *The Noonday Friends* by Mary Stolz, Harper

1967   *Up a Road Slowly* by Irene Hunt, Follett
Honor Books: *The King's Fifth* by Scott O'Dell, Houghton Mifflin; *Zlateh the Goat and Other Stories* by Isaac Bashevis Singer, Harper; *The Jazz Man* by Mark H. Weik, Atheneum

1968   *From the Mixed-Up Files of Mrs. Basil E. Frankweiler* by E. L. Konigsburg, Atheneum
Honor Books: *Jennifer, Hecate, Macbeth, William McKinley, and Me, Elizabeth* by E. L. Konigsburg, Atheneum; *The Black Pearl* by Scott O'Dell, Houghton Mifflin; *The Fearsome Inn* by Isaac Bashevis Singer, Scribner; *The Egypt Game* by Zilpha Keatley Snyder, Atheneum

1969   *The High King* by Lloyd Alexander, Holt, Rinehart & Winston
Honor Books: *To Be a Slave* by Julius Lester, Dial Press; *When Shlemiel Went to Warsaw and Other Stories* by Isaac Bashevis Singer, Farrar, Straus & Giroux

1970   *Sounder* by William H. Armstrong, Harper
Honor Books: *Our Eddie* by Sulamith Ish-Kishor, Pantheon; *The Many Ways of Seeing: An Introduction to the Pleasures of Art* by Janet Gaylord Moore, World; *Journey Outside* by Mary Q. Steele, Viking

1971   *Summer of the Swans* by Betsy Byars, Viking
Honor Books: *Kneeknock Rise* by Natalie Babbitt, Farrar, Straus & Giroux; *Enchantress from the Stars* by Sylvia Louise Engdahl, Atheneum; *Sing Down the Moon* by Scott O'Dell, Houghton Mifflin

1972   *Mrs. Frisby and the Rats of NIMH* by Robert C. O'Brien, Atheneum
Honor Books: *Incident at Hawk's Hill* by Allan W. Eckert, Little, Brown; *The Planet of Junior Brown* by Virginia Hamilton, Macmillan; *The Tombs of Atuan* by Ursula K. Le Guin, Atheneum; *Annie and the Old One* by Miska Miles, Little, Brown; *The Headless Cupid* by Zilpha Keatley Snyder, Atheneum

1973   *Julie of the Wolves* by Jean Craighead George, Harper
Honor Books: *Frog and Toad Together* by Arnold Lobel, Harper; *The Upstairs Room* by Johanna Reiss, Crowell; *The Witches of Worm* by Zilpha Keatley Snyder, Atheneum

1974   *The Slave Dancer* by Paula Fox, Bradbury
Honor Book: *The Dark Is Rising* by Susan Cooper, Atheneum

1975   *M. C. Higgins, the Great* by Virginia Hamilton, Macmillan
Honor Books: *Figgs & Phantoms* by Ellen Raskin, Dutton; *My Brother Sam Is Dead* by James Lincoln Collier and Christopher Collier, Four Winds: *The Perilous Gard* by Elizabeth Marie Pope, Houghton Mifflin; *Philip Hall Likes Me. I Reckon Maybe* by Bette Greene, Dial Press

1976   *The Grey King* by Susan Cooper, Atheneum
Honor Books: *The Hundred Penny Box* by Sharon Bell Mathis, Viking; *Dragonwings* by Laurence Yep, Harper

1977   *Roll of Thunder, Hear My Cry* by Mildred D. Taylor, Dial Press
Honor Books: *Abel's Island* by William Steig, Farrar, Straus & Giroux; *A String in the Harp* by Nancy Bond, Atheneum

1978   *Bridge to Terabithia* by Katherine Paterson, Crowell
Honor Books: *Ramona and Her Father* by Beverly Cleary, Morrow; *Anpao: An American Indian Odyssey* by Jamake Highwater, Lippincott

1979   *The Westing Game* by Ellen Raskin, Dutton
Honor Book: *The Great Gilly Hopkins* by Katherine Paterson, Crowell

1980   *A Gathering of Days: A New England Girl's Journal 1830–32* by Joan Blos, Scribner's
Honor Book: *The Road from Home: The Story of an Armenian Girl* by David Kherdian, Greenwillow (Morrow)

1981   *Jacob Have I Loved* by Katherine Paterson, Cromwell
Honor Books: *The Fledgling* by Jane Langton, Harper; *A Ring of Endless Light* by Madeleine L'Engle, Farrar, Straus & Giroux

1982   *A Visit to William Blake's Inn: Poems for Innocent and Experienced Travelers* by Nancy Willard, Harcourt Brace Jovanovich
Honor Books: *Ramona Quimby, Age 8* by Beverly Cleary, Morrow; *Upon the Head of the Goat: A Childhood in Hungary, 1939–1944* by Aranka Siegal, Farrar, Straus & Giroux

1983   *Dicey's Song* by Cynthia Voigt, Atheneum
Honor Books: *Blue Sword* by Robin McKinley, Morrow; *Dr. DeSoto* by William Steig, Farrar, Straus & Giroux; *Graven Images* by Paul Fleischman, Harper; *Homesick: My Own Story* by Jean Fritz, Putnam; *Sweet Whisper, Brother Rush* by Virginia Hamilton, Philomel (Putnam)

1984   *Dear Mr. Henshaw* by Beverly Cleary, Morrow
Honor Books: *The Wish Giver* by Bill Brittain, Harper; *Sugaring Time* by Kathryn Lasky, Macmillan; *The Sign of the Beaver* by Elizabeth George Speare, Houghton Mifflin; *A Solitary Blue* by Cynthia Voigt, Atheneum

1985   *The Hero and the Crown* by Robin McKinley, Greenwillow (Morrow)
Honor Books: *The Moves Make the Man* by Bruce Brooks, Harper; *One-Eyed Cat* by Paula Fox, Bradbury; *Like Jake and Me* by Mavis Jukes, Knopf

1986   *Sarah, Plain and Tall* by Patricia MacLachlan, Harper
Honor Books: *Commodore Perry in the Land of the Shogun* by Rhoda Blumberg, Lothrop; *Dogsong* by Gary Paulsen, Bradbury

1987   *The Whipping Boy* by Sid Fleischman, Greenwillow (Morrow)
Honor Books: *On My Honor* by D. Bauer, Clarion; *Volcano: The Eruption and Healing of Mount St. Helens* by Patricia Lauber, Bradbury; *A Fine White Dust* by Cynthia Rylant, Bradbury

1988   *Lincoln: A Photobiography* by Russell Freedman, Clarion/Houghton Mifflin
Honor Books: *After the Rain* by Norma Fox Mazer, Morrow; *Hatchet* by Gary Paulsen, Bradbury

1989   *Joyful Noise: Poems for Two Voices* by Paul Fleischman, Harper
Honor Books: *In the Beginning* by Virginia Hamilton, Harcourt Brace Jovanovich; *Scorpions* by Walter Dean Myers, Harper

1990   *Number the Stars* by Lois Lowry, Houghton Mifflin
Honor Books: *Afternoon of the Elves* by Janet Taylor Lisle, Orchard Books/Watts; *The Winter Room* by Gary Paulsen, Orchard Books/Watts; *Shabanu: Daughter of the Wind* by Suzanne Fisher Staples, Knopf

1991   *Maniac Magee* by Jerry Spinelli, Little, Brown
Honor Book: *The True Confessions of Charlotte Doyle* by Avi, Orchard

1992   *Shiloh* by Phillis Reynolds Naylor, Atheneum
Honor Books: *Nothing But the Truth* by Avi, Orchard; *The Wright Brothers: How They Invented the Airplane* by Russell Freedman, Holiday

1993   *Missing May* by Cynthia Ryland, Orchard
Honor Books: *The Dark-Thirty: Southern Tales of the Supernatural* by Patricia McKissack, Knopf; *Somewhere in the Darkness* by Walter Dean Myers, Scholastic; *What Hearts* by Bruce Brooks, HarperCollins

1994   *The Giver* by Lois Lowry, Houghton Mifflin
Honor Books: *Eleanor Roosevelt: A Life of Discovery* by Russell Freedman, Clarion/Houghton Mifflin; *Dragon's Gate* by Laurence Yep, HarperCollins; *Crazy Lady* by Jane Leslie Conly, HarperCollins

1995   *Walk Two Moons* by Sharon Creech, HarperCollins
Honor Books: *Catherine, Called Birdy* by Karen Cushman, Clarion; *The Ear, the Eye, and the Arm* by Nancy Farmer, Orchard

1996   *The Midwife's Apprentice* by Karen Cushman, Houghton Mifflin
Honor Books: *What Jamie Saw* by Carolyn Coman, Front Street; *The Watsons Go to Birmingham—1963* by Christopher Paul Curtis, Delacorte; *Yolanda's Genius* by Carol Fenner, Simon; *The Great Fire* by Jim Murphy, Scholastic

1997   *The View from Saturday* by E. L. Konigsburg, Atheneum
Honor Books: *A Girl Named Disaster* by Nancy Farmer, Orchard; *Moorchild* by Eloise McGraw, McElderry; *The Thief* by Whalen Turner, Greenwillow; *Belle Prater's Boy* by Ruth White, Farrar

1998   *Out of the Dust* by Karen Hesse, Scholastic
Honor Books: *Ella Enchanted* by Gail Carson Levine, HarperCollins; *Lily's Crossing* by Patricia Reilly Giff, Delacorte; *Wringer* by Jerry Spinelli, HarperCollins

1999   *Holes* by Louis Sachar, Farrar, Straus & Giroux
Honor Books: *A Long Way Home* by Richard Peck, Dial

2000   *Bud, Not Buddy* by Christopher Paul Curtis, Delacorte
Honor Books: *Getting Near to Baby* by Audrey Couloumbis, Putnam; *26 Fairmount Avenue* by Tomie de Paola, Putnam; *Our Only May Amelia* by Jennifer L. Holm, HarperCollins

2001   *A Year Down Yonder* by Richard Peck, Dial
Honor Books: *Hope Was Here* by Joan Bauer, Putnam; *The Wanderer* by Sharon Creech, HarperCollins; *Because of Winn-Dixie* by Kate DiCamillo, Candlewick; *Joey Pigza Loses Control* by Jack Gantos, Farrar

2002   *A Single Shard* by Linda Sue Park, Houghton Mifflin
Honor Books: *Everything on a Waffle* by Polly Horvath, Farrar, Straus & Giroux; *Carver: A Life in Poems* by Marilyn Nelson, Front Street

2003   *Crispin: The Cross of Lead* by Avi, Hyperion
Honor Books: *The House of the Scorpion* by Nancy Farmer, Atheneum; *Pictures of Hollis Woods* by Patricia Reilly Giff, Random House; *Hoot* by Carl Hiaasen, Knopf; *A Corner of the Universe* by Ann M. Martin, Scholastic; *Surviving the Applewhites* by Stephanie S. Tolan, HarperCollins

2004   *The Tale of Despereaux: Being the Story of a Mouse, a Princess, Some Soup, and a Spool of Thread* by Kate DiCamillo, Candlewick Press
Honor Books: *Olive's Ocean* by Kevin Henkes, Greenwillow; *An American Plague: The True and Terrifying Story of the Yellow Fever Epidemic of 1793* by Jim Murphy, Clarion

The Caldecott Medal

Named for the British illustrator Randolph Caldecott, the Caldecott Medal has been awarded annually since 1938 by the American Library Association to the most distinguished picture book published in America. Runners-up are given Honor Awards. Although the passage of time has not always validated the awards and many fine books have been overlooked, the awards list does provide a roll call of some of the best in children's books. The Caldecott Award is given to the illustrator and honors the pictorial art rather than the text. Unless indicated otherwise, the illustrator is the author.

1938   *Animals of the Bible* by Helen Dean Fish, illustrated by Dorothy P. Lathrop, Stokes
Honor Books: *Seven Simeons: A Russian Tale* by Boris Artzybasheff, Viking; *Four and Twenty Blackbirds: Nursery Rhymes of Yesterday Recalled for Children of To-Day* by Helen Dean Fish, illustrated by Robert Lawson, Stokes

1939   *Mei Li* by Thomas Handforth, Doubleday
Honor Books: *The Forest Pool* by Laura Adams Arner, Longmans, Green (McKay); *Wee Gillis* by Munro Leaf, illustrated by Robert Lawson, Viking; *Snow White and the Seven Dwarfs* by Wanda Gág, Coward, McCann & Geoghegan; *Barkis* by Clare Newberry, Harper; *Andy and the Lion: A Tale of Kindness Remembered or the Power of Gratitude* by James Daugherty, Viking

1940   *Abraham Lincoln* by Ingri and Edgar Parin d'Aulaire, Doubleday
Honor Books: *Cock-a-Doodle Doo: The Story of a Little Red Rooster* by Berta and Elmer Hader, Macmillan; *Madeline* by Ludwig Bemelmans, Simon & Schuster; *The Ageless Story* by Lauren Ford, Dodd, Mead

1941   *They Were Strong and Good* by Robert Lawson, Viking
Honor Book: *April's Kittens* by Clare Newberry, Harper

1942   *Make Way for Ducklings* by Robert McCloskey, Viking
Honor Books: *An American ABC* by Maud and Miska Petersham, Macmillan; *In My Mother's House* by Ann Nolan Clark, illustrated by Velino Herrera, Viking; *Paddle-to-the-Sea*

by Holling C. Holling, Houghton Mifflin; *Nothing at All* by Wanda Gág, Coward, McCann & Geoghegan

1943   *The Little House* by Virginia Lee Burton, Houghton Mifflin
Honor Books: *Dash and Dart* by Mary and Conrad Buff, Viking; *Marshmallow* by Clare Newberry, Harper

1944   *Many Moons* by James Thurber, illustrated by Louis Slobodkin, Harcourt Brace Jovanovich
Honor Books: *Small Rain: Verses from the Bible* selected by Jessie Orton Jones, illustrated by Elizabeth Orton Jones, Viking; *Pierre Pigeon* by Lee Kingman, illustrated by Arnold E. Bare, Houghton Mifflin; *The Mighty Hunter* by Berta and Elmer Hader, Macmillan; *A Child's Good Night Book* by Margaret Wise Brown, illustrated by Jean Chariot, W. R. Scott; *Good Luck Horse* by Chih-Yi Chan, illustrated by Plato Chan, Whittlesey

1945   *Prayer for a Child* by Rachel Field, illustrated by Elizabeth Orton Jones, Macmillan
Honor Books: *Mother Goose: Seventy-Seven Verses with Pictures,* illustrated by Tasha Tudor, Walck; *In the Forest* by Marie Hall Ets, Viking; *Yonie Wondernose* by Marguerite de Angeli, Doubleday; *The Christmas Anna Angel* by Ruth Sawyer, illustrated by Kate Seredy, Viking

1946   *The Rooster Crows . . . ,* illustrated by Maud and Miska Petersham, Macmillan
Honor Books: *Little Lost Lamb* by Golden MacDonald, illustrated by Leonard Weisgard, Doubleday; *Sing Mother Goose* by Opal Wheeler, illustrated by Marjorie Torrey, Dutton; *My Mother Is the Most Beautiful Woman in the World* by Becky Reyher, illustrated by Ruth Gannett, Lothrop; *You Can Write Chinese* by Kurt Wiese, Viking

1947   *The Little Island* by Golden MacDonald, illustrated by Leonard Weisgard, Doubleday
Honor Books: *Rain Drop Splash* by Alvin Tresselt, illustrated by Leonard Weisgard, Lothrop; *Boats on the River* by Marjorie Flack, illustrated by Jay Hyde Barnum, Viking; *Timothy Turtle* by Al Graham, illustrated by Tony Palazzo, Viking; *Pedro, The Angel of Olvera Street* by Leo Politi, Scribner's; *Sing in Praise: A Collection of the Best Loved Hymns* by Opal Wheeler, illustrated by Marjorie Torrey, Dutton

1948   *White Snow, Bright Snow* by Alvin Tresselt, illustrated by Roger Duvoisin, Lothrop
Honor Books: *Stone Soup: An Old Tale* by Marcia Brown, Scribner's; *McElligot's Pool* by Dr. Seuss, Random House; *Bambino the Clown* by George Schreiber, Viking; *Roger and the Fox* by Lavinia Davis, illustrated by Hildegard Woodward, Doubleday; *Song of Robin Hood* edited by Anne Malcolmson, illustrated by Virginia Lee Burton, Houghton Mifflin

1949   *The Big Snow* by Berta and Elmer Hader, Macmillan
Honor Books: *Blueberries for Sal* by Robert McCloskey, Viking; *All Around the Town* by Phyllis McGinley, illustrated by Helen Stone, Lippincott; *Juanita* by Leo Politi, Scribner's; *Fish in the Air* by Kurt Wiese, Viking

1950   *Song of the Swallows* by Leo Politi, Scribner's
Honor Books: *America's Ethan Allen* by Stewart Holbrook, illustrated by Lynd Ward, Houghton Mifflin; *The Wild Birthday Cake* by Lavinia Davis, illustrated by Hildegard Woodward, Doubleday; *The Happy Day* by Ruth Krauss, illustrated by Marc Simont, Harper; *Bartholomew and the Oobleck* by Dr. Seuss, Random House; *Henry Fisherman* by Marcia Brown, Scribner's

1951   *The Egg Tree* by Katherine Milhouse, Scribner's
Honor Books: *Dick Whittington and His Cat* by Marcia Brown, Scribner's; *The Two Reds* by William Lipkind, illustrated by Nicholas Mordvinoff, Harcourt Brace Jovanovich; *If I Ran the Zoo* by Dr. Seuss, Random House; *The Most Wonderful Doll in the World* by Phyllis McGinley, illustrated by Helen Stone, Lippincott; *T-Bone, the Baby Sitter* by Clare Newberry, Harper

1952   *Finders Keepers* by William Lipkind, illustrated by Nicholas Mordvinoff, Harcourt Brace Jovanovich
Honor Books: *Mr. T. W. Anthony Woo: The Story of a Cat and a Dog and a Mouse* by Marie Hall Ets, Viking; *Skipper John's Cook* by Marcia Brown, Scribner's; *All Falling Down* by Gene Zion, illustrated by Margaret Bloy Graham, Harper; *Bear Party* by William Pene du Bois, Viking; *Feather Mountain* by Elizabeth Olds, Houghton Mifflin

1953   *The Biggest Bear* by Lynd Ward, Houghton Mifflin
Honor Books: *Puss in Boots* by Charles Perrault, illustrated and translated by Marcia Brown, Scribner's; *One Morning in Maine* by Robert McCloskey, Viking; *Ape in a Cape: An Alphabet of Odd Animals* by Fritz Eichenberg, Harcourt Brace Jovanovich; *The Storm Book* by Charlotte Zolotow, illustrated by Margaret Bloy Graham, Harper; *Five Little Monkeys* by Juliet Kepes, Houghton Mifflin

1954   *Madeline's Rescue* by Ludwig Bemelmans, Viking
Honor Books: *Journey Cake, Ho!* by Ruth Sawyer, illustrated by Robert McCloskey, Viking; *When Will the World Be Mine?* by Miriam Schlein, illustrated by Jean Charlot, W. R. Scott; *The Steadfast Tin Soldier* by Hans Christian Andersen, illustrated by Marcia Brown, Scribner's; *A Very Special House* by Ruth Krauss, illustrated by Maurice Sendak, Harper; *Green Eyes* by A. Birnbaum, Capitol

1955   *Cinderella, or the Little Glass Slipper* by Charles Perrault, translated and illustrated by Marcia Brown, Scribner's
Honor Books: *Book of Nursery and Mother Goose Rhymes*, illustrated by Marguerite de Angeli, Doubleday; *Wheel on the Chimney* by Margaret Wise Brown, illustrated by Tibor Gergely, Lippincott; *The Thanksgiving Story* by Alice Dalgliesh, illustrated by Helen Sewell, Scribner's

1956   *Frog Went A-Courtin* edited by John Langstaff, illustrated by Feodor Rojankovsky, Harcourt Brace Jovanovich
Honor Books: *Play with Me* by Marie Hall Ets, Viking; *Crow Boy* by Taro Yashima, Viking

1957   *A Tree Is Nice* by Janice May Udry, illustrated by Marc Simont, Harper
Honor Books: *Mr. Penny's Race Horse* by Marie Hall Ets, Viking; *1 is One* by Tasha Tudor, Walck; *Anatole* by Eve Titus, illustrated by Paul Galdone, McGraw-Hill; *Gillespie and the Guards* by Benjamin Elkin, illustrated by James Daugherty, Viking; *Lion* by William Pene du Bois, Viking

1958   *Time of Wonder* by Robert McCloskey, Viking
Honor Books: *Fly High, Fly Low* by Don Freeman, Viking; *Anatole and the Cat* by Eve Titus, illustrated by Paul Galdone, McGraw-Hill

1959   *Chanticleer and the Fox* adapted from Chaucer and illustrated by Barbara Cooney, Crowell
Honor Books: *The House That Jack Built: A Picture Book in Two Languages* by Antonio Frasconi, Harcourt Brace Jovanovich; *What Do You Say, Dear?* by Sesyle Joslin, illustrated by Maurice Sendak, Scott; *Umbrella* by Taro Yashima, Viking

1960   *Nine Days to Christmas* by Marie Hall Ets and Aurora Labastida, illustrated by Marie Hall Ets, Viking
Honor Books: *Houses from the Sea* by Alice E. Goudey, illustrated by Adrienne Adams, Scribner's; *The Moon Jumpers* by Janice May Udry, illustrated by Maurice Sendak, Harper

1961   *Baboushka and the Three Kings* by Ruth Robbins, illustrated by Nicolas Sidjakov, Parnassus
Honor Book: *Inch by Inch* by Leo Lionni, Obolensky

1962   *Once a Mouse . . .* by Marcia Brown, Scribner's
Honor Books: *The Fox Went Out on a Chilly Night: An Old Song* by Peter Spier, Doubleday; *Little Bear's Visit* by Else Holmelund Minarik, illustrated by Maurice Sendak, Harper; *The Day We Saw the Sun Come Up* by Alice E. Goudey, illustrated by Adrienne Adams, Scribner's

1963   *The Snowy Day* by Ezra Jack Keats, Viking
        Honor Books: *The Sun Is a Golden Earring* by Natalia M. Belting, illustrated by Bernarda Bryson, Holt, Rinehart & Winston; *Mr. Rabbit and the Lovely Present* by Charlotte Zolotow, illustrated by Maurice Sendak, Harper

1964   *Where the Wild Things Are* by Maurice Sendak, Harper
        Honor Books: *Swimmy* by Leo Lionni, Pantheon Books; *All in the Morning Early* by Sorche Nic Leodhas, illustrated by Evaline Ness, Holt, Rinehart & Winston; *Mother Goose and Nursery Rhymes* illustrated by Philip Reed, Atheneum

1965   *May I Bring a Friend?* by Beatrice Schenk de Regniers, illustrated by Beni Montresor, Atheneum
        Honor Books: *Rain Makes Applesauce* by Julian Scheer, illustrated by Marvin Bileck, Holiday; *The Wave* by Margaret Hodges, illustrated by Blair Lent, Houghton Mifflin; *A Pocketful of Cricket* by Rebecca Caudill, illustrated by Evaline Ness, Holt, Rinehart & Winston

1966   *Always Room for One More* by Sorche Nic Leodhas, illustrated by Nonny Hogrogian, Holt, Rinehart & Winston
        Honor Books: *Hide and Seek Fog* by Alvin Tresselt, illustrated by Roger Duvoisin, Lothrop; *Just Me* by Marie Hall Ets, Viking; *Tom Tit Tot* by Evaline Ness, Scribner's

1967   *Sam, Bangs & Moonshine* by Evaline Ness, Holt, Rinehart & Winston
        Honor Book: *One Wide River to Cross* by Barbara Emberley, illustrated by Ed Emberley, Prentice-Hall

1968   *Drummer Hoff* by Barbara Emberley, illustrated by Ed Emberley, Prentice-Hall
        Honor Books: *Frederick* by Leo Lionni, Pantheon; *Seashore Story* by Taro Yashima, Viking; *The Emperor and the Kite* by Jane Yolen, illustrated by Ed Young, World

1969   *The Fool of the World and the Flying Ship* by Arthur Ransome, illustrated by Uri Shulevitz, Farrar, Straus & Giroux
        Honor Book: *Why the Sun and the Moon Live in the Sky: An African Folktale* by Elphinstone Dayrell, illustrated by Blair Lent, Houghton Mifflin

1970   *Sylvester and the Magic Pebble* by William Steig, Windmill (Simon & Schuster)
        Honor Books: *Goggles!* by Ezra Jack Keats, Macmillan; *Alexander and the Wind-Up Mouse* by Leo Lionni, Pantheon; *Pop Corn and Ma Goodness* by Edna Mitchell Preston, illustrated by Robert Andrew Parker, Viking; *Thy Friend, Obadiah* by Brinton Turkle, Viking; *The Judge: An Untrue Tale* by Harve Zemach, illustrated by Margot Zemach, Farrar, Straus & Giroux

1971   *A Story—A Story: An African Tale* by Gail E. Haley, Atheneum
        Honor Books: *The Angry Moon* by William Sleator, illustrated by Blair Lent, Little, Brown; *Frog and Toad Are Friends* by Arnold Lobel, Harper; *In the Night Kitchen* by Maurice Sendak, Harper

1972   *One Fine Day* by Nonny Hogrogian, Macmillan
        Honor Books: *If All the Seas Were One Sea* by Janina Domanska, Macmillan; *Moja Means One: Swahili Counting Book* by Muriel Feelings, illustrated by Tom Feelings, Dial Press; *Hildilid's Night* by Cheli Duran Ryan, illustrated by Arnold Lobel, Macmillan

1973   *The Funny Little Woman* retold by Arlene Mosel, illustrated by Blair Lent, Dutton
        Honor Books: *Anansi the Spider: A Tale from the Ashanti* adapted and illustrated by Gerald McDermott, Holt, Rinehart & Winston; *Hosie's Alphabet* by Hosea Tobias and Lisa Baskin, illustrated by Leonard Baskin, Viking; *Snow White and the Seven Dwarfs* translated by Randall Jarrell, illustrated by Nancy Elkholm Burkert, Farrar, Straus & Giroux; *When Clay Sings* by Byrd Baylor, illustrated by Tom Bahti, Scribner's

1974   *Duffy and the Devil* by Harve Zemach, illustrated by Margot Zemach, Farrar, Straus & Giroux
        Honor Book: *Three Jovial Huntsmen* by Susan Jeffers, Bradbury; *Cathedral: The Story of Its Construction* by David Macaulay, Houghton Mifflin

1975   *Arrow to the Sun* adapted and illustrated by Gerald McDermott, Viking
Honor Book: *Jambo Means Hello: A Swahili Alphabet Book* by Muriel Feelings, illustrated by Tom Feelings, Dial Press

1976   *Why Mosquitoes Buzz in People's Ears* retold by Verna Aardema, illustrated by Leo and Diane Dillon, Dial Press
Honor Books: *The Desert Is Theirs* by Byrd Baylor, illustrated by Peter Parnall, Scribner's; *Strega Nona* retold and illustrated by Tomie de Paola, Prentice-Hall

1977   *Ashanti to Zulu: African Traditions* by Margaret Musgrove, illustrated by Leo and Diane Dillon, Dial Press
Honor Books: *The Amazing Bone* by William Steig, Farrar, Straus & Giroux; *The Contest* retold and illustrated by Nonny Hogrogian, Greenwillow (Morrow); *Fish for Supper* by M. B. Goffstein, Dial Press; *The Golem: A Jewish Legend* by Beverly Brodsky McDermott, Lippincott; *Hawk, I'm Your Brother* by Byrd Baylor, illustrated by Peter Parnall, Scribner's

1978   *Noah's Ark* by Peter Spier, Doubleday
Honor Books: *Castle* by David Macaulay, Houghton Mifflin; *It Could Always Be Worse* retold and illustrated by Margot Zemach, Farrar, Straus & Giroux

1979   *The Girl Who Loved Wild Horses* by Paul Goble, Bradbury
Honor Books: *Freight Train* by Donald Crews, Greenwillow (Morrow); *The Way to Start a Day* by Byrd Baylor, illustrated by Peter Parnall, Scribner's

1980   *Ox-Cart Man* by Donald Hall, illustrated by Barbara Cooney, Viking
Honor Books: *Ben's Trumpet* by Rachel Isadora, Greenwillow (Morrow); *The Treasure* by Uri Shulevitz, Farrar, Straus & Giroux; *The Garden of Abdul Gasazi* by Chris Van Allsburg, Houghton Mifflin

1981   *Fables* by Arnold Lobel, Harper
Honor Books: *The Bremen-Town Musicians* by Ilse Plume, Doubleday; *The Grey Lady and the Strawberry Snatcher* by Molly Bang, Four Winds; *Mice Twice* by Joseph Low, Atheneum; *Truck* by Donald Crews, Greenwillow (Morrow)

1982   *Jumanji* by Chris Van Allsburg, Houghton Mifflin
Honor Books: *A Visit to William Blake's Inn: Poems for Innocent and Experienced Travelers* by Nancy Willard, illustrated by Alice and Martin Provensen, Harcourt Brace Jovanovich; *Where the Buffaloes Begin* by Olaf Baker, illustrated by Stephen Gammell, Warne; *On Market Street* by Arnold Lobel, illustrated by Anita Lobel, Greenwillow (Morrow); *Outside Over There* by Maurice Sendak, Harper

1983   *Shadow* by Blaise Cendrars, illustrated by Marcia Brown, Scribner's
Honor Books: *When I Was Young in the Mountains* by Cynthia Rylant, illustrated by Diane Goode, Dutton; *Chair for My Mother* by Vera B. Williams, Morrow

1984   *The Glorious Flight: Across the Channel with Louis Blériot July 25, 1909* by Alice and Martin Provenson, Viking
Honor Books: *Ten, Nine, Eight* by Molly Bang, Greenwillow (Morrow); *Little Red Riding Hood* by Trina Schart Hyman, Holiday House

1985   *Saint George and the Dragon* by Margaret Hodges, illustrated by Trina Schart Hyman, Little, Brown
Honor Books: *Hansel and Gretel* by Rika Lesser, illustrated by Paul O. Zelinsky, Dodd, Mead; *The Story of the Jumping Mouse* by John Steptoe, Lothrop; *Have You Seen My Duckling?* by Nancy Tafuri, Greenwillow (Morrow)

1986   *The Polar Express* by Chris van Allsburg, Houghton Mifflin
Honor Books: *The Relatives Came* by Cynthia Rylant, illustrated by Stephen Gammell, Bradbury; *King Bidgood's in the Bathtub* by Audrey Wood, illustrated by Don Wood, Harcourt Brace Jovanovich

1987   *Hey, Al* by Arthur Yorinks, illustrated by Richard Egielski, Farrar, Straus & Giroux
Honor Books: *The Village of Round and Square Houses* by Ann Grifalconi, Little, Brown; *Alphabatics* by Suse MacDonald, Bradbury; *Rumpelstiltskin* by Paul O. Zelinsky, Dutton

1988   *Owl Moon* by Jane Yolen, illustrated by John Schoenherr, Philomel (Putnam)
Honor Books: *Mufaro's Beautiful Daughter* by John Steptoe, Lothrop

1989   *Song and Dance Man* by Karen Ackerman, illustrated by Stephen Gammell, Knopf
Honor Books: *Goldilocks* by James Marshall, Dial Press; *The Boy of the Three-Year Nap* by Dianne Snyder, illustrated by Allen Say; *Mirandy and Brother Wind* by Patricia McKissack, illustrated by Jerry Pinkney, Knopf; *Free Fall* by David Wiesner, Lothrop

1990   *Lon Po Po: A Red-Riding Hood Story from China* by Ed Young, Philomel (Putnam)
Honor Books: *Hershel and the Hanukkah Goblins* by Eric Kimmel, illustrated by Trina Schart Hyman, Holiday; *Color Zoo* by Lois Ehlert, Lippincott; *Bill Peet: An Autobiography* by Bill Peet, Houghton Mifflin; *The Talking Eggs* retold by Robert D. San Souci, illustrated by Jerry Pinkney, Dial

1991   *Black and White* by David Macaulay, Houghton Mifflin
Honor Books: *Puss'n Boots* by Charles Perrault, illustrated by Fred Marcellino, Farrar, Straus & Giroux; *"More, More, More," Said the Baby: 3 Love Stories* by Vera Williams, Greenwillow

1992   *Tuesday* by David Wiesner, Clarion
Honor Book: *Tar Beach* by Faith Ringgold, Crown

1993   *Mirette on the High Wire* by Emily Arnold McCully, Putnam
Honor Books: *Seven Blind Mice* by Ed Young, Philomel; *The Stinky Cheese Man and Other Fairly Stupid Tales* by Jon Scieszka, illustrated by Lane Smith, Viking; *Working Cotton* by Sherley Anne Williams, illustrated by Carole Byard, Harcourt Brace Jovanovich

1994   *Grandfather's Journey* by Allen Say, Houghton Mifflin
Honor Books: *Peppe the Lamplighter* by Elisa Bartone, illustrated by Ted Lewin, Lothrop; *In the Small, Small Pond* by Denise Fleming, Holt; *Owen* by Keven Henkes, Greenwillow; *Raven: A Trickster Tale from the Pacific Northwest* by Gerald McDermott, Harcourt; *Yo! Yes?* by Chris Raschka, Orchard

1995   *Smoky Night* by Eve Bunting, illustrated by David Diaz, Harcourt
Honor Books: *Swamp Angel* by Anne Isaacs, illustrated by Paul O. Zelinsky, Dutton; *John Henry* retold by Julius Lester, illustrated by Jerry Pinkney, Dial; *Time Flies* by Eric Rohmann, Crown

1996   *Officer Buckle and Gloria* by Peggy Rathmann, Putnam
Honor Books: *Alphabet City* by Stephen T. Johnson, Viking Penguin; *Zin! Zin! Zin! A Violin!* by Lloyd Moss, illustrated by Marjorie Priceman, Simon & Schuster; *The Faithful Friend* by Robert D. San Souci, illustrated by Brian Pinkney, Simon & Schuster; *Tops & Bottoms* by Janet Stevens, Harcourt Brace Jovanovich

1997   *Golem* by David Wisniewski, Clarion
Honor Books: *Hush! A Thai Lullaby* by Holly Meade, Orchard; *The Paperboy* by Dav Pilkey, Orchard; *Starry Messenger* by Peter Sis, Farrar, Straus & Giroux; *The Graphic Alphabet* by David Pelletier, Orchard

1998   *Rapunzel* by Paul O. Zelinsky, Dutton
        Honor Books: *The Gardener* by Sarah Stewart, illustrated by David Small, Farrar; *Harlem* by Walter Dean Myers, illustrated by Christopher Myers, Scholastic; *There Was an Old Woman Who Swallowed a Fly* by Simms Taback, Viking

1999   *Snowflake Bentley* by Jacquelline Briggs Martin, illustrated by Mary Azarian, Houghton Mifflin
        Honor Books: *Duke Ellington: The Piano Prince and His Orchestra* by Andrea Davis Pinkney, illustrated by Brian Pinkney, Simon & Schuster; *No, David!* by David Shannon, Scholastic; *Snow* by Uri Shulevitz, Farrar; *Tibet: Through the Red Box* by Peter Sis, Farrar, Straus & Giroux

2000   *Joseph Had a Little Overcoat* by Simms Taback, Viking
        Honor Books: *Sector 7* by David Weisner, Clarion; *The Ugly Duckling* by Jerry Pinkney, Morrow; *When Sophie Get Angry—Really, Really Angry . . .* by Molly Bang, Scholastic; *A Child's Calendar* by John Updike, illustrated by Trina Schart Hyman, Holiday

2001   *So You Want to Be President?* by Judith St. George, illus. by David Small, Philomel
        Honor Books: *Casey at the Bat* by Ernest Thayer, illus. Christopher Bing, Handprint; *Click, Clack, Moo: Cows That Type* by Doreen Cronin, illus. Betsy Lewin, Simon & Schuster; *Olivia* by Ian Falconer, Atheneum

2002   *The Three Pigs* by David Wiesner, Clarion/Houghton Mifflin
        Honor Books: *The Dinosaurs of Waterhouse Hawkins* by Barbara Kerley, illus. by Brian Selznick, Scholastic; *Martin's Big Words: The Life of Dr. Martin Luther King, Jr.* by Doreen Rappaport, illus. Bryan Collier, Hyperion; *The Stray Dog* by Marc Simont, HarperCollins

2003   *My Friend Rabbit* by Eric Rohmann, Roaring Brook
        Honor Books: *The Spider and the Fly* by Mary Howitt, illus. by Tony DiTerlizzi, Simon & Schuster; *Hondo and Fabian* by Peter McCarty, Holt; *Noah's Ark* by Jerry Pinkney, Seastar/North-South

2004   *The Man Who Walked Between the Towers* by Mordicai Gerstein, Roaring Brook Press
        Honor Books: *Ella Sarah Gets Dressed* by Margaret Chodos-Irvine, Harcourt; *What Do You Do with a Tail Like This?* by Steve Jenkins and Robin Page, Houghton Mifflin; *Don't Let the Pigeon Drive the Bus* by Mo Willems, Hyperion

Boston Globe–Horn Book Awards

Awarded annually since 1967 and sponsored jointly by *The Boston Globe* and *The Horn Book Magazine,* two prizes originally were given—one to recognize the outstanding text and one the outstanding illustration. Beginning in 1976, the categories were redefined: Outstanding Fiction or Poetry, Outstanding Nonfiction, and Outstanding Illustration.

1967   Text: *The Little Fishes* by Erik Haugaard, Houghton Mifflin
        Illustration: *London Bridge Is Falling Down* by Peter Spier, Doubleday

1968   Text: *The Spring Rider* by John Lawson, Crowell
        Illustration: *Tikki Tikki Tembo* by Arlene Mosel, illustrated by Blair Lent, Holt

1969   Text: *A Wizard of Earthsea* by Ursula K. Le Guin, Houghton Mifflin
        Illustration: *The Adventures of Paddy Pork* by John S. Goodall, Harcourt

1970   Text: *The Intruder* by John Rowe Townsend, Lippincott
        Illustration: *Hi, Cat!* by Ezra Jack Keats, Macmillan

1971   Text: *A Room Made of Windows* by Eleanor Cameron, Little, Brown
        Illustration: *If I Built a Village* by Kazue Mizumura, Crowell

1972   Text: *Tristan and Iseult* by Rosemary Sutcliff, Dutton
Illustration: *Mr. Gumpy's Outing* by John Burningham, Holt, Rinehart & Winston

1973   Text: *The Dark Is Rising* by Susan Cooper, McElderry/Atheneum
Illustration: *King Stork* by Trina Schart Hyman, Little, Brown

1974   Text: *M. C. Higgins, The Great* by Virginia Hamilton, Macmillan
Illustration: *Jambo Means Hello* by Muriel Feelings, illus. Tom Feelings, Dial

1975   Text: *Transport 7–41-R* by T. Degens, Viking
Illustration: *Anno's Alphabet* by Mitsumasa Anno, Crowell

1976   Fiction: *Unleaving* by Jill Paton Walsh, Farrar, Straus & Giroux
Nonfiction: *Voyaging to Cathay: Americans in the China Trade* by Alfred Tamarin and Shirley Glubok, Viking
Illustration: *Thirteen* by Remy Charlip and Jerry Joyner, Parents

1977   Fiction: *Child of the Owl* by Laurence Yep, Harper
Nonfiction: *Chance, Luck and Destiny* by Peter Dickinson, Little, Brown
Illustration: *Granfa' Grig Had a Pig and Other Rhymes* by Wallace Tripp, Little, Brown

1978   Fiction: *The Westing Game* by Ellen Raskin, Dutton
Nonfiction: *Mischling, Second Degree: My Childhood in Nazi Germany* by Ilse Koehn, Greenwillow
Illustration: *Anno's Journey* by Mitsumasa Anno, Philomel

1979   Fiction: *Humbug Mountain* by Sid Fleischman, Little, Brown
Nonfiction: *The Road From Home: The Story of an Armenian Girl* by David Kherdian, Greenwillow
Illustration: *The Snowman* by Raymond Briggs, Random House

1980   Fiction: *Conrad's War* by Andrew Davies, Crown
Nonfiction: Building: *The Fight Against Gravity* by Mario Salvadori, McElderry/Atheneum
Illustration: *The Garden of Abdul Gasazi* by Chris Van Allsburg, Houghton Mifflin

1981   Fiction: *The Leaving* by Lynn Hall, Scribner's
Nonfiction: *The Weaver's Gift* by Kathryn Lasky, Warne
Illustration: *Outside Over There* by Maurice Sendak, Harper

1982   Fiction: *Playing Beatie Bow* by Ruth Park, Atheneum
Nonfiction: *Upon the Head of the Goat: A Childhood in Hungary, 1939–1944* by Aranka Siegal, Farrar, Straus & Giroux
Illustration: *A Visit to William Blake's Inn: Poems for Innocent and Experienced Travelers* by Nancy Willard, illustrated by Alice and Martin Provensen

1983   Fiction: *Sweet Whispers, Brother Rush* by Virginia Hamilton, Philomel
Nonfiction: *Behind Barbed Wire: The Imprisonment of Japanese Americans During World War II* by Daniel S. David, Dutton
Illustration: *A Chair for My Mother* by Vera B. Williams, Greenwillow

1984   Fiction: *A Little Fear* by Patricia Wrightson, McElderry/Atheneum
Nonfiction: *The Double Life of Pocahontas* by Jean Fritz, Putnam
Illustration: *Jonah and the Great Fish* retold and illustrated by Warwick Hutton, McElderry/Atheneum

1985   Fiction: *The Moves Make the Man* by Bruce Brooks, Harper
Nonfiction: *Commodore Perry in the Land of the Shogun* by Rhoda Blumberg, Lothrop
Illustration: *Mama Don't Allow* by Thatcher Hurd, Harper

1986   Fiction: *In Summer Light* by Zibby Oneal, Viking/Kestrel
Nonfiction: *Auks, Rocks and the Odd Dinosaur* by Peggy Thompson, Crowell
Illustration: *The Paper Crane* by Molly Bang, Greenwillow

1987   Fiction: *Rabble Starkey* by Lois Lowry, Houghton Mifflin
Nonfiction: *Pilgrims of Plymouth* by Marcia Sewall, Atheneum
Illustration: *Mufaro's Beautiful Daughters* by John Steptoe, Lothrop

1988   Fiction: *The Friendship* by Mildred Taylor, Dial
Nonfiction: *Anthony Burns: The Defeat and Triumph of a Fugitive Slave* by Virginia Hamilton, Knopf
Illustration: *The Boy of the Three-Year Nap* by Diane Snyder, Houghton Mifflin

1989   Fiction: *The Village by the Sea* by Paula Fox, Franklin Watts
Nonfiction: *The Way Things Work* by David Macaulay, Houghton Mifflin
Illustration: *Shy Charles* by Rosemary Wells, Dial

1990   Fiction: *Maniac Magee* by Jerry Spinelli, Little, Brown
Nonfiction: *The Great Little Madison* by Jean Fritz, Putnam
Illustration: *Lon Po Po: A Red-Riding Hood Story from China* retold and illustrated by Ed Young, Philomel

1991   Fiction: *The True Confessions of Charlotte Doyle* by Avi, Orchard
Nonfiction: *Appalachia: The Voices of Sleeping Birds* by Cynthia Rylant, illustrated by Barry Moser, Harcourt
Illustration: *The Tale of the Mandarin Ducks* retold by Katherine Paterson, illustrated by Leo and Diane Dillon, Lodestar

1992   Fiction: *Missing May* by Cynthia Rylant, Orchard
Nonfiction: *Talking with Artists* by Pat Cummings, Bradbury
Illustration: *Seven Blind Mice* by Ed Young, Philomel

1993   Fiction: *Ajeemah and His Son* by James Berry, Harper
Nonfiction: *Sojourner Truth: Ain't I a Woman?* by Patricia C. and Fredrick McKissack, Scholastic
Illustration: *The Fortune-Tellers* by Lloyd Alexander, illustrated by Trina Schart Hyman, Dutton

1994   Fiction: *Scooter* by Vera B. Williams, Greenwillow
Nonfiction: *Eleanor Roosevelt: A Life of Discovery* by Russell Freedman, Clarion
Illustration: *Grandfather's Journey* by Allen Say, Houghton Mifflin

1995   Fiction: *Some of the Kinder Planets* by Tim Wynne-Jones, Kroupa/Orchard
Nonfiction: *Abigail Adams: Witness to a Revolution* by Natalie S. Bober, Atheneum
Illustration: *John Henry* retold by Julius Lester, illustrated by Jerry Pinkney, Dial

1996   Fiction and Poetry: *Poppy* by Avi, illustrated by Brian Floca, Orchard
Nonfiction: *Orphan Train Rider: One Boy's True Story* by Andrea Warren, Houghton
Picture Book: *In the Rain with Baby Duck* by Amy Hest, illustrated by Jill Barton, Candlewick

1997   Fiction and Poetry: *The Friends* by Kazumi Yumoto, Farrar
Nonfiction: *A Drop of Water: A Book of Science and Wonder* by Walter Wick, Scholastic
Picture Book: *The Adventures of Sparrowboy* by Brian Pinkney, Simon & Schuster

1998   Fiction and Poetry: *The Circuit: Stories from the Life of a Migrant Child* by Francisco Jiménez, University of New Mexico Press
Nonfiction: *Leon's Story* by Leon Walter Tijllage, illustrated by Susan L. Roth, Farrar, Straus & Giroux
Picture Book: *And If the Moon Could Talk* by Kate Banks, illustrated by Georg Hallensleben, Farrar, Straus & Giroux

1999   Fiction and Poetry: *Holes* by Louis Sachar, Farrar
Nonfiction: *The Top of the World: Climbing Mount Everest* by Steve Jenkins, Houghton Mifflin
Picture Book: *Red-Eyed Tree Frog* by Joy Cowley, illustrated by Nic Bishop, Scholastic

2000   Fiction and Poetry: *The Folk Keeper* by Franny Billingsley, Atheneum
Nonfiction: *Sir Walter Ralegh and the Quest for El Dorado* by Marc Aronson, Clarion
Picture Book: *Henry Hikes to Fitchburg* by D. B. Johnson, Houghton Mifflin

2001   Fiction and Poetry: *Carver: A Life in Poems* by Marilyn Nelson, Front Street
Nonfiction: *The Longitude Prize* by Joan Dash, illustrated by Susan Petricic, Farrar
Picture Book: *Cold Feet* by Cynthia De Felice, illustrated by Robert Andrew Parker, DK Ink

2002   Fiction and Poetry: *Lord of the Deep* by Graham Salisbury, Delacorte
Nonfiction: *This Land Was Made for You and Me: The Life and Songs of Woody Guthrie* by Elizabeth Partridge, Viking
Picture Book: *"Let's Get a Pup!" Said Kate* by Bob Graham, Candlewick

The Mildred L. Batchelder Award

Presented annually by the American Library Association, this award recognizes the most outstanding children's book originally translated from a language other than English. (Unless otherwise indicated, the author is also the translator.)

1968   *The Little Man* by Erich Kastner, translated by James Kirkup, illustrated by Rich Schreiter, Knopf, 1966

1969   *Don't Take Teddy* by Babbis Friis-Baastad, translated by Lise Somme McKinnon, Scribner, 1967

1970   *Wildcat under Glass* by Alki Zei, translated by Edward Fenton, Holt, Rinehart & Winston, 1968

1971   *In the Land of Ur: The Discovery of Ancient Mesopotamia* by Hans Baumann, translated by Stella Humphries, illustrated by Hans Peter Renner, Pantheon Books, 1969

1972   *Friedrich* by Hans Peter Richter, translated by Edite Kroll, Holt, Rinehart & Winston, 1970

1973   *Pulga* by Siny Rose Van Iterson, translated by Alexander and Alison Gode, Morrow, 1971

1974   *Petros' War* by Alki Zei, translated by Edward Fenton, Dutton, 1972

1975   *An Old Tale Carved Out of Stone* by Aleksandr M. Linevski, translated by Maria Polushkin, Crown, 1973

1976   *The Cat and Mouse Who Shared a House* by Ruth Hurlimann, translated by Anthea Bell, Walck, 1974

1977   *The Leopard* by Cecil Bodker, translated by Gunnar Poulsen, Atheneum, 1975

1978   No Award

1979   *Konrad* by Christine Nostlinger, translated by Anthea Bell, illustrated by Carol Nicklaus, Watts, 1977

Rabbit Island by Jorg Steiner, translated by Ann Conrad Lammers, illustrated by Jorg Muller, Harcourt Brace Jovanovich, 1978

1980   *The Sound of Dragon's Feet* by Alki Zei, translated by Edward Fenton, Dutton, 1979

1981   *The Winter When Time Was Frozen* by Els Pelgrom, translated by Raphael and Maryka Rudnik, Morrow, 1980

1982   *The Battle Horse* by Harry Kullman, translated by George Blecher and Lone Thygesen-Blecher, Bradbury, 1981

1983   *Hiroshima No Pika* by Toshi Maruki, Lothrop, 1982

1984   *Ronia, the Robber's Daughter* by Astrid Lindgren, translated by Patricia Crampton, Viking, 1983

1985   *The Island on Bird Street* by Uri Orlev, translated by Hillel Halkin, Houghton Mifflin, 1984

1986   *Rose Blanche* by Christophe Gallaz and Roberto Innocenti, translated by Martha Coventry and Richard Graglia, illustrated by Roberto Innocenti, Creative Education, 1985

1987   *No Hero for the Kaiser* by Rudolf Frank, translated by Patricia Crampton, illustrated by Klaus Steffans, Lothrop, 1986

1988   *If You Didn't Have Me* by Ulf Nilsson, illustrated by Eva Ericksson, translated by Lone Thygesen-Blecher and George Blecher, McElderry, 1987

1989   *Crutches* by Peter Hartling, Lothrop, 1988

1990   *Buster's World* by Bjarne Reuter, translated by Anthea Bell, Dutton, 1989

1991   *A Handful of Stars* by Rafik Schami, translated by Rika Lesser, Dutton, 1990

1992   *The Man from the Other Side* by Uri Orlev, translated by Hillel Halkin, Houghton Mifflin, 1991

1993   No Award

1994   *The Apprentice* by Pilar Molina Llorente, translated by Robin Longshaw, illustrated by Juan Ramón Alonso, Farrar, Straus & Giroux, 1993

1995   *The Boys from St. Petri* by Bjarne Reuter, translated by Anthea Bell, Dutton, 1994

1996   *The Lady with the Hat* by Uri Orlev, translated by Hillel Halkin, Houghton Mifflin, 1995

1997   *The Friends* by Kazumi Yumoto, translated by Cathy Hirano, Farrar, Straus & Giroux, 1996

1998   *The Robber and Me* by Josef Holub, edited by Marc Aronson, translated by Elizabeth D. Crawford, Holt, 1997

1999   *Thanks to My Mother* by Schoschana Rabinovici, edited by Cindy Kane, translated by James Skofield, Dial, 1998

2000   *The Baboon King* by Anton Quintana, translated by John Nieuwenhuizer, Walker

2001   *Samir and Yonaton* by Daniella Carmi, translated by Yael Lotan, Scholastic, 2000

2002   *How I Became an American* by Karin Gündisch, translated by James Scofield, Cricket/Carus, 2001

2003   *The Thief Lord* by Cornelia Funke, translated by Oliver Latsch, Scholastic, 2002

2004   *Run, Boy, Run* by Uri Orlev, translated by Hillel Halkin, Houghton Mifflin, 2003

The Laura Ingalls Wilder Award

Named in honor of the beloved author of the *Little House* books (who was also its first recipient), this award is presented by the Association of Library Service to Children of the American Library Association to the individual, either author or illustrator, whose work has over the years proved to be a significant contribution to children's literature. Originally awarded every five years, it was awarded every three years from 1980 to 2001. It is now awarded every two years.

1954	Laura Ingalls Wilder	1986	Jean Fritz
1960	Clara Ingram Judson	1989	Elizabeth George Speare
1965	Ruth Sawyer	1992	Marcia Brown

1970	E. B. White	1995	Virginia Hamilton
1975	Beverly Cleary	1998	Russell Freedman
1980	Theodore Geisel (Dr. Seuss)	2001	Milton Meltzer
1983	Maurice Sendak	2003	Eric Carle

The Coretta Scott King Award

Presented annually by the Social Responsibilities Round Table of the American Library Association, this award recognizes an African American author and illustrator (since 1974) who has made an outstanding contribution to literature for children in the preceding year. The award is named for the widow of civil rights leader and Nobel Peace Prize winner Dr. Martin Luther King, Jr., and it acknowledges the humanitarian work of both Dr. and Mrs. King.

1970   *Martin Luther King, Jr., Man of Peace* by Lillie Patterson, Garrard

1971   *Black Troubadour: Langston Hughes* by Charlemae Rollins, Rand

1972   *17 Black Artists* by Elton C. Fax, Dodd

1973   *I Never Had It Made* by Jackie Robinson (as told to Alfred Duckett), Putnam

1974   Author: *Ray Charles* by Sharon Bell Mathis, Crowell
        Illustrator: *Ray Charles* by Sharon Bell Mathis, illustrated by George Ford, Crowell

1975   Author: *The Legend of Africana* by Dorothy Robinson, Johnson
        Illustrator: *The Legend of Africana* by Dorothy Robinson, illustrated by Herbert Temple, Johnson

1976   Author: *Duey's Tale* by Pearl Bailey, Harcourt
        Illustrator: No Award

1977   Author: *The Story of Stevie Wonder* by James Haskins, Lothrop
        Illustrator: No Award

1978   Author: *Africa Dream* by Eloise Greenfield, Day/Crowell
        Illustrator: *Africa Dream* by Eloise Greenfield, illustrated by Carole Bayard, Day/Crowell

1979   Author: *Escape to Freedom* by Ossie Davis, Viking
        Illustrator: *Something on My Mind* by Nikki Grimes, illustrated by Tom Feelings, Dial

1980   Author: *The Young Landlords* by Walter Dean Myers, Viking
        Illustrator: *Cornrows* by Camille Yarbrough, illustrated by Carole Bayard, Coward

1981   Author: *This Life* by Sidney Poitier, Knopf
        Illustrator: *Beat the Story-Drum, Pum-Pum* by Ashley Bryan, Atheneum

1982   Author: *Let the Circle Be Unbroken* by Mildred Taylor, Dial
        Illustrator: *Mother Crocodile: An Uncle Amadou Tale from Senegal* adapted by Rosa Guy, illustrated by John Steptoe, Delacorte

1983   Author: *Sweet Whispers, Brother Rush* by Virginia Hamilton, Philomel
        Illustrator: *Black Child* by Peter Mugabane, Knopf

1984   Author: *Everett Anderson's Good-Bye* by Lucile Clifton, Holt
        Illustrator: *My Mama Needs Me* by Mildred Pitts Walter, illustrated by Pat Cummings, Lothrop

1985   Author: *Motown and Didi* by Walter Dean Myers, Viking
        Illustrator: No Award

1986   Author: *The People Could Fly: American Black Folktales* by Virginia Hamilton, Knopf
        Illustrator: *Patchwork Quilt* by Valerie Flournoy, illustrated by Jerry Pinkney, Dial

1987   Author: *Justin and the Best Biscuits in the World* by Mildred Pitts Walter, Lothrop
        Illustrator: *Half Moon and One Whole Star* by Crescent Dragonwagon, illustrated by Jerry Pinkney, Macmillan

1988   Author: *The Friendship* by Mildred D. Taylor, Dial
        Illustrator: *Mufaro's Beautiful Daughters: An African Tale* retold and illustrated by John Steptoe, Lothrop

1989   Author: *Fallen Angels* by Walter Dean Myers, Scholastic
        Illustrator: *Mirandy and Brother Wind* by Patricia McKissack, illustrated by Jerry Pinkney, Knopf

1990   Author: *A Long Hard Journey* by Patricia and Fredrick McKissack, Walker
        Illustrator: *Nathaniel Talking* by Eloise Greenfield, illustrated by Jan Spivey Gilchrist, Black Butterfly Press

1991   Author: *Road to Memphis* by Mildred D. Taylor, Dial
        Illustrator: *Aida* retold by Leontyne Price, illustrated by Leo and Diane Dillon, Harcourt

1992   Author: *Now Is Your Time! The African-American Struggle for Freedom* by Walter Dean Myers, HarperCollins
        Illustrator: *Tar Beach* by Faith Ringgold, Crown

1993   Author: *The Dark-Thirty: Southern Tales of the Supernatural* by Patricia McKissack, Knopf
        Illustrator: *Origins of Life on Earth: An African Creation Myth* by David A. Anderson, illustrated by Kathleen Atkins Smith, Sight Productions

1994   Author: *Toning the Sweep* by Angela Johnson, Orchard
        Illustrator: *Soul Looks Back in Wonder* compiled and illustrated by Tom Feelings, Dial

1995   Author: *Christmas in the Big House, Christmas in the Quarters* by Patricia and Fredrick McKissack, illustrated by John Thompson, Scholastic
        Illustrator: *The Creation* by James Weldon Johnson, illustrated by James E. Ransom, Holiday

1996   Author: *Her Stories* by Virginia Hamilton, illustrated by Leo and Diane Dillon, Scholastic
        Illustrator: *The Middle Passage: White Ships, Black Cargo* by Tom Feelings, Dial

1997   Author: *SLAM!* by Walter Dean Myers, Scholastic
        Illustrator: *Minty: A Story of Young Harriet Tubman* by Alan Schroeder, illustrated by Jerry Pinkney, Dial

1998   Author: *Forged by Fire* by Sharon M. Draper, Atheneum
        Illustrator: *In Daddy's Arms I Am Tall: African Americans Celebrating Fathers* by Javaka Steptoe, Lee & Low

1999   Author: *Heaven* by Angela Johnson, Simon & Schuster
        Illustrator: *I See The Rhythm* by Michele Wood, Children's Book Press

2000   *Bud, Not Buddy* by Christopher Paul Curtis, Delacorte
        Illustrator: *In the Time of the Drums* by Kim L. Siegelson, illustrated by Brian Pinkney, Hyperion

2001   Author: *Miracle's Boys* by Jacqueline Woodson, Putnam
        Illustrator: *Uptown* by Brian Collier, Holt

2002   Author: *Forged by Fire* by Sharon M. Draper, Atheneum
        Illustrator: *In Daddy's Arms I Am Tall: African Americans Celebrating Fathers* by Javaka Steptoe, Lee & Low

2003   Author: *Bronx Masquerade* by Nikki Grimes, Dial
        Illustrator: *Talkin' about Bessie* by E. B. Lewis, Scholastic

The Scott O'Dell Award for Historical Fiction

Established by the noted children's novelist Scott O'Dell and administered by the Advisory Committee of the Bulletin of the Center for Children's Books, this award is presented to the most distinguished work of historical fiction set in the New World and written by a citizen of the United States.

1984   *The Sign of the Beaver* by Elizabeth George Speare, Houghton Mifflin

1985   *The Fighting Ground* by Avi, Harper

1986   *Sarah, Plain and Tall* by Patricia MacLachlan, Harper

1987   *Streams to the River, River to the Sea: A Novel of Sacagawea* by Scott O'Dell, Houghton Mifflin

1988   *Charlie Skedaddle* by Patricia Beatty, Morrow

1989   *The Honorable Prison* by Lyll Becerra de Jenkins, Lodestar

1990   *Shades of Gray* by Carolyn Reeder, Macmillan

1991   *A Time of Troubles* by Pieter van Raven, Scribner's

1992   *Stepping on the Cracks* by Mary Downing Hahn, Clarion

1993   *Morning Girl* by Michael Dorris, Hyperion

1994   *Bull Run* by Paul Fleischman, Harper

1995   *Under the Blood-Red Sun* by Graham Salisbury, Delacorte

1996   *The Bomb* by Theodore Taylor, Flare

1997   *Jip: His Story* by Katherine Paterson, Lodestar

1998   *Forty Acres and Maybe a Mule* by Harriet Gillem Robinet, Atheneum

1999   *Out of the Dust* by Karen Hesse, Scholastic

2000   *Two Suns in the Sky* by Miriam Bat-Ami, Front Street

2001   *The Art of Keeping Cool* by Janet Taylor Lisle, Atheneum

2002   *The Land* by Mildred Taylor, Dial

2003   *Trouble Don't Last* by Shelley Pearsall, Knopf

National Council of Teachers of English Award for Excellence in Poetry for Children

This award is presented every three years (from 1977 through 1982 it was awarded annually) by the National Council of Teachers of English and was established to recognize a living poet's lifetime contribution to poetry for children.

1977	David McCord	1988	Arnold Adoff
1978	Aileen Fisher	1991	Valerie Worth
1979	Karia Kuskin	1994	Barbara Juster Esbensen
1980	Myra Cohn Livingston	1997	Eloise Greenfield
1981	Eve Merriam	2000	X. J. Kennedy
1982	John Ciardi	2003	Mary Ann Hoberman
1985	Lilian Moore		

The Phoenix Award

The Phoenix Award, first presented in 1985, is given annually by the International Children's Literature Association for a book published exactly twenty years earlier that did not, at the time, win a major award but has stood the test of time and merited recognition for its contribution to children's literature.

1985	*The Mark of the Horse Lord* by Rosemary Sutcliff, Oxford, 1965
1986	*Queenie Peavy* by Robert Burch, Viking, 1966
1987	*Smith* by Leon Garfield, Constable, 1967
1988	*The Rider and His Horse* by Erik Christian Haugaard, Houghton Mifflin, 1968
1989	*The Night Watchmen* by Helen Cresswell, Faber, 1969
1990	*Enchantress from the Stars* by Sylvia Louise Engdahl, Atheneum, 1970
1991	*A Long Way from Home* by Jane Gardam, Hamish Hamilton, 1971
1992	*A Sound of Chariots* by Mollie Hunter, Hamish Hamilton, 1972
1993	*Carrie's War* by Nina Bawden, Gollancz, 1973
1994	*Of Nightingales That Weep* by Katherine Paterson, Harper, 1974
1995	*Dragonwings* by Laurence Yep, Harper, 1975
1996	*The Stone Book* by Alan Garner, Collins, 1976
1997	*I Am the Cheese* by Robert Cormier, Pantheon, 1977
1998	*A Chance Child* by Jill Paton Walsh, Macmillan, 1978
1999	*Throwing Shadows* by E. I. Konigsburg, Atheneum, 1979
2000	*The Keeper of the Isis Light* by Monica Hughes, Atheneum, 1980
2001	*The Seventh Raven* by Peter Dickinson, Gollancz, 1981
2002	*A Formal Feeling* by Zibby Oneal, Viking, 1982
2003	*The Long Night Watch* by Ivan Southall, Methuen, 1984
2004	*White Peak Farm* by Berlie Doherty, Methuen, 1984

INTERNATIONAL AWARDS

The Hans Christian Andersen Award

This medal, named for the great Danish storyteller, is presented every two years by the International Board on Books for Young People to a living author and (since 1966) living illustrator whose works have made a significant, international contribution to children's literature.

1956	Eleanor Farjeon (Great Britain)
1958	Astrid Lindgren (Sweden)
1960	Erich Kastner (Germany)
1962	Meindert DeJong (United States)
1964	Rene Guillot (France)
1966	Author: Tove Jansson (Finland) Illustrator: Alois Carigiet (Switzerland)

1968   Authors: James Kruss (Germany) and Jose Maria Sanchez-Silva (Spain)
        Illustrator: Jiri Trnka (Czechoslovakia)

1970   Author: Gianni Rodari (Italy)
        Illustrator: Maurice Sendak (United States)

1972   Author: Scott O'Dell (United States)
        Illustrator: Ib Spang Olsen (Denmark)

1974   Author: Maria Gripe (Sweden)
        Illustrator: Farsid Mesghali (Iran)

1976   Author: Cecil Bodker (Denmark)
        Illustrator: Tatjana Mawrine (U.S.S.R.)

1978   Author: Paula Fox (United States)
        Illustrator: Otto S. Svend (Denmark)

1980   Author: Bohumil Riha (Czechoslovakia)
        Illustrator: Suekichi Akaba (Japan)

1982   Author: Lygia Gojunga Nunes (Brazil)
        Illustrator: Zbigniew Rychlicki (Poland)

1984   Author: Christine Nostlinger (Austria)
        Illustrator: Mitsumasa Anno (Japan)

1986   Author: Patricia Wrightson (Australia)
        Illustrator: Robert Ingpen (Australia)

1988   Author: Annie M. G. Schmidt (Netherlands)
        Illustrator: Dusan Kallay (Yugoslavia)

1990   Author: Tormod Haugen (Norway)
        Illustrator: Lisbeth Zwerger (Austria)

1992   Author: Virginia Hamilton (U.S.A.)
        Illustrator: Keveta Pacovská (Czechoslovakia)

1994   Author: Michio Mado (Japan)
        Illustrator: Jörg Müller (Switzerland)

1996   Author: Uri Orlev (Israel)
        Illustrator: Klaus Ensikat (Germany)

1998   Author: Katherine Paterson (U.S.A.)
        Illustrator: Tomi Ungerer (U.S.A.)

2000   Author: Ana Maria Machado (Brazil)
        Illustrator: Anthony Browne (Great Britain)

2002   Author: Aidan Chambers (Great Britain)
        Illustrator: Quentin Blake (Great Britain)

The Carnegie Medal

Awarded by the British Library Association to an outstanding book first published in the United Kingdom, this medal has been awarded annually since it was established in 1937 (the first award being presented to a book published in the preceding year). The date given is the date of publication.

1936   *Pigeon Post* by Arthur Ransome, Cape

1937   *The Family from One End Street* by Eve Garnett, Muller

1938   *The Circus Is Coming* by Noel Streatfield, Dent

1939   *Radium Woman* by Eleanor Doorly, Heinemann

1940   *Visitors from London* by Kitty Barne, Dent

1941   *We Couldn't Leave Dinah* by Mary Treadgold, Penguin

1942   *The Little Grey Men* by B. B., Eyre & Spottiswoode

1943   No Award

1944   *The Wind on the Moon* by Eric Linklater, Macmillan

1945   No Award

1946   *The Little White Horse* by Elizabeth Goudge, Brockhampton Press

1947   *Collected Stories for Children* by Walter de la Mare, Faber

1948   *Sea Change* by Richard Armstrong, Dent

1949   *The Story of Your Home* by Agnes Allen, Transatlantic

1950   *The Lark on the Wind* by Elfrida Vipont Foulds, Oxford

1951   *The Wool-Pack* by Cynthia Harnett, Methuen

1952   *The Borrowers* by Mary Norton, Dent

1953   *A Valley Grows Up* by Edward Osmond, Oxford

1954   *Knight Crusader* by Ronald Welch, Oxford

1955   *The Little Bookroom* by Eleanor Farjeon, Oxford

1956   *The Last Battle* by C. S. Lewis, Bodley Head

1957   *A Grass Rope* by William Mayne, Oxford

1958   *Tom's Midnight Garden* by Philippa Pearce, Oxford

1959   *The Lantern Bearers* by Rosemary Sutcliff, Oxford

1960   *The Making of Man* by I. W. Cornwall, Phoenix

1961   *A Stranger at Green Knowe* by Lucy Boston, Faber

1962   *The Twelve and the Genii* by Pauline Clarke, Faber

1963   *Time of Trial* by Hester Burton, Oxford

1964   *Nordy Banks* by Sheena Porter, Oxford

1965   *The Grange at High Force* by Philip Turner, Oxford

1966   No Award

1967   *The Owl Service* by Alan Garner, Collins

1968   *The Moon in the Cloud* by Rosemary Harris, Faber

1969   *The Edge of the Cloud* by K. M. Peyton, Oxford

1970   *The God Beneath the Sea* by Leon Garfield and Edward Blishen, Kestrel

1971   *Josh* by Ivan Southall, Angus & Robertson

1972   *Watership Down* by Richard Adams, Rex Collings

1973   *The Ghost of Thomas Kempe* by Penelope Lively, Heinemann

1974   *The Stronghold* by Mollie Hunter, Hamilton

1975   *The Machine-Gunners* by Robert Westall, Macmillan

1976   *Thunder and Lightnings* by Jan Mark, Kestrel

1977   *The Turbulent Term of Tyke Tiler* by Gene Kemp, Faber

1978   *The Exeter Blitz* by David Rees, Hamish Hamilton

1979   *Tulku* by Peter Dickinson, Dutton

1980   *City of Gold* by Peter Dickinson, Gollancz

1981   *The Scarecrows* by Robert Westall, Chatto & Windus

1982   *The Haunting* by Margaret Mahy, Dent

1983   *Handles* by Jan Mark, Kestrel

1984   *The Changeover* by Margaret Mahy, Dent

1985   *Storm* by Kevin Crossley-Holland, Heinemann

1986   *Granny Was a Buffer Girl* by Berlie Doherty, Methuen

1987   *The Ghost Drum* by Susan Price, Faber

1988   *Pack of Lies* by Geraldine McCaughrean, Oxford

1989   *My War with Goggle-Eyes* by Anne Fine, Joy Street

1990   *Wolf* by Gillian Cross, Oxford

1991   *Dear Nobody* by Berlie Doherty, Hamish Hamilton

1992   *Flour Babies* by Anne Fine, Hamish Hamilton

1993   *Stone Cold* by Robert Swindells, Hamish Hamilton

1994   *Whispers in the Graveyard* by Theresa Breslin, Methuen

1995   *Northern Lights* by Philip Pullman, Doubleday (U.S. title: *The Golden Compass*)

1996   *Junk* by Melvin Burgess, Andersen/Penguin

1997   *River Boy* by Tim Bowler, Oxford

1998   *Skellig* by David Almond, Hodder

1999   *Postcards from No Man's Land* by Aidan Chambers, Bodley Head

2000   *The Other Side of Truth* by Beverley Naidoo, Puffin

2001   *The Amazing Maurice and His Educated Rodents* by Terry Pratchett, Doubleday

2002   *Ruby Holler* by Sharon Creech, Bloomsbury

The Kate Greenaway Medal

Named for the celebrated nineteenth-century children's illustrator, this medal is awarded annually by the British Library Association to the most distinguished illustrated work for children first published in the United Kingdom during the preceding year. (Unless otherwise noted, the author is also the illustrator. The date given is the year of publication.)

1956   *Tim All Alone* by Edward Ardizzone, Oxford

1957   *Mrs. Easter and the Storks* by V. H. Drummond, Faber

1958   No Award

1959   *Kashtanka and a Bundle of Ballads* by William Stobbs, Oxford

1960   *Old Winkle and the Seagulls* by Elizabeth Rose, illustrated by Gerald Rose, Faber

1961   *Mrs. Cockle's Cat* by Philippa Pearce, illustrated by Anthony Maitland, Kestrel

1962   *Brian Wildsmith's ABC* by Brian Wildsmith, Oxford

1963   *Borka* by John Burningham, Jonathan Cape

1964   *Shakespeare's Theatre* by C. W. Hodges, Oxford

1965   *Three Poor Tailors* by Victor Ambrus, Hamilton

1966   *Mother Goose Treasury* by Raymond Briggs, Hamilton

1967   *Charlie, Charlotte & the Golden Canary* by Charles Keeping, Oxford

1968   *Dictionary of Chivalry* by Grant Uden, illustrated by Pauline Baynes, Kestrel

1969   *The Quangle-Wangle's Hat* by Edward Lear, illustrated by Helen Oxenbury, Heinemann
        Dragon of an Ordinary Family by Margaret May, illustrated by Helen Oxenbury, Heinemann

1970   *Mr. Gumpy's Outing* by John Burningham, Jonathan Cape

1971   *The Kingdom under the Sea* by Jan Pienkowski, Jonathan Cape

1972   *The Woodcutter's Duck* by Krystyna Turska, Hamilton

1973   *Father Christmas* by Raymond Briggs, Hamilton

1974   *The Wind Blew* by Pat Hutchins, Bodley Head

1975   *Horses in Battle* by Victor Ambrus, Oxford
        Mishka by Victor Ambrus, Oxford

1976   *The Post Office Cat* by Gall E. Haley, Bodley Head

1977   *Dogger* by Shirley Hughes, Bodley Head

1978   *Each Peach Pear Plum* by Janet and Allan Ahlberg, Kestrel

1979   *Haunted House* by Jan Pienkowski, Dutton

1980   *Mr. Magnolia* by Quentin Blake, Jonathan Cape

1981   *The Highwayman* by Alfred Noyes, illustrated by Charles Keeping, Oxford

1982   *Long Neck and Thunder Foot* by Michael Foreman, Kestrel
        Sleeping Beauty and Other Favorite Fairy Tales by Michael Foreman, Gollancz

1983   *Gorilla* by Anthony Browne, Julia McRae Books

1984   *Hiawatha's Childhood* by Errol LeCain, Faber

1985   *Sir Gawain and the Loathly Lady* by Selina Hastings, illustrated by Juan Wijngaard, Walker

1986   *Snow White in New York* by Fiona French, Oxford

1987   *Crafty Chameleon* by Adrienne Kennsway, Hodder & Stoughton

1988   *Can't You Sleep, Little Bear?* by Martin Waddell, illustrated by Adrienne Kennaway, Hodder & Stoughton

1989   *War Boy: A Country Childhood* by Michael Foreman, Arcade

1990   *The Whale's Song* by Dyan Sheldon, illustrated by Gary Blythe, Dial

1991   *The Jolly Christmas Postman* by Janet and Allan Ahlberg, Heinemann

1992   *Zoo* by Anthony Browne, Julie MacRae Books

1993   *Black Ships Before Troy* retold by Rosemary Sutcliff, illustrated by Alan Lee, Frances Lincoln

1994   *Way Home* by Libby Hawthorne, Anderson

1995   *The Christmas Miracle of Jonathan Toomey* by Susan Wojciechowski, illustrated by P. J. Lynch

1996   *The Baby Who Wouldn't Go to Bed* by Helen Cooper, Doubleday

1997   *When Jessie Came Across the Sea* by Amy Hest, illustrated by P. J. Lynch, Doubleday

1998   *Pumpkin Soup* by Helen Cooper, Doubleday

1999   *Alice's Adventures in Wonderland* illustrated by Helen Oxenbury, Walker

2000   *I Will Not Ever Eat a Tomato* by Lauren Child, Orchard

2001   *Pirate Diary* by Chris Riddell, Walker

2002   *Jethro Byrde-Fairy Child* by Bob Graham, Walker

Index